Marie-Antoinette

Praise for the works of Elena Maria Vidal:

"Poetic, lyrical passages….Readers [are] steeped in the culture, influences and motivations of a family unified by forces that invade their close-knit world and change the course of their lives." —D. Donovan of *The Midwest Book Review* on *The Paradise Tree*

"An imaginative, meticulously told history." —*Kirkus Reviews* on *The Paradise Tree*

"This is a stunningly lovely book, the perfect thing to get lost in for an afternoon." —*San Francisco Book Review* (starred review) on *The Paradise Tree*

"Meticulous research….lush provocative details." —*Portland Book Review* on *The Paradise Tree*

"Exhaustively researched and yet completely accessible for those who wish to understand the events from a very personal perspective." —Genevieve Kineke, *Canticle Magazine* on *Trianon*

"An unforgettable portrait of a royal life... *Madame Royale* is a fantastic tribute to one of Europe's most tragic, but courageous princesses." —Gareth Russell, author of *Popular* and *The Emperors* on *Madame Royale*

"A master of storytelling, the author makes you laugh and cry, right along with the characters. A true masterpiece, I rank this book along with the great Classics." —Wilsonville Public Library Blog on *Trianon*

Marie-Antoinette, Daughter of the Caesars

Maria Antonia Josepha Johanna of Habsburg-Lorraine, Archduchess of Austria, in April 1770.

Marie-Antoinette

DAUGHTER OF THE CAESARS:

REFLECTIONS ON HER LIFE, HER DEATH, HER LEGACY

BY ELENA MARIA VIDAL

MAYAPPLE Books

ST. MICHAELS, MARYLAND

Marie-Antoinette, Daughter of the Caesars

www.mayapplebooks.net

Cover image: Marie-Antoinette by Élisabeth Vigée Le Brun

All illustrations are in the public domain.

Copyright © 2016 by M. E. Russell
All Rights Reserved Worldwide. No part of this publication may be reproduced in any form without permission of the author except for review purposes.

ISBN-13: 978-1530934485
ISBN-10:1530934486

Marie-Antoinette, Daughter of the Caesars

DEDICATION

For my mother.

And with a special dedication to Sainte Jehanne d'Arc, the Maid of Lorraine, patroness of France.
"I was born for this."

Books by Elena Maria Vidal

Trianon: A Novel of Royal France

Madame Royale: A Novel

The Paradise Tree: A Novel

The Night's Dark Shade: A Novel of the Cathars

Please visit www.emvidal.com and the *Tea at Trianon Blog*, http://teaattrianon.blogspot.com.

Marie-Antoinette, Daughter of the Caesars

"It is now sixteen or seventeen years since I saw the queen of France, then dauphiness, at Versailles; and surely there never lighted on this orb, which she hardly seemed to touch, a more delightful vision. I saw her just above the horizon, decorating and cheering the elevated sphere she had just begun to move in, glittering like a morning star full of life and splendor and joy. Oh, what a revolution....Little did I dream that I should have lived to see such disasters fall upon her, in a nation of gallant men, in a nation of men of honor and of cavaliers! I thought ten thousand swords must have leaped from their scabbards, to avenge even a look which threatened her with insult. But the age of chivalry is gone; that of sophisters, economists, and calculators has succeeded..."—Edmund Burke, *Reflections on the Revolution in France*, 1790

"She was not a guilty woman, neither was she a saint; she was an upright, charming woman, a little frivolous, somewhat impulsive, but always pure; she was a queen, at times ardent in her fancies for her favourites and thoughtless in her policy, but proud and full of energy; a thorough woman in her winsome ways and tenderness of heart, until she became a martyr." —*The Life of Marie-Antoinette* by M. de la Rocheterie, 1893

Marie-Antoinette, Daughter of the Caesars

CONTENTS

	Acknowledgments	x
	Preface	xi
	Prologue	1
	Introduction	4
1	A Daughter of the Caesars	11
2	The Maid of Lorraine	35
3	The House of Bourbon	59
4	Scandal	90
5	The Temple of Love	97
6	Death and Coronation	110
7	Their Most Christian Majesties	126
8	Follies and Escapades	153
9	Marie-Antoinette and the Arts	163
10	Marie-Antoinette and Music	177
11	Marie-Antoinette and Fashion	187
12	Marie-Antoinette and Her Journey of Faith	197
13	Holidays at Versailles	206
14	The Children of Louis XVI and Marie-Antoinette	218

Marie-Antoinette, Daughter of the Caesars

15	Marie-Antoinette and Friendship	233
16	Gentlemen Friends	276
17	The Fersen Legend	291
18	Palaces, Châteaux, and Gardens	311
19	The Diamond Necklace	340
20	The Revolution	349
21	At the Tuileries	373
22	Les Adieux	411
23	The Agony	429
24	The Orphans	457
25	Legacy	477
	Notes	486
	Bibliography	522
	Index	539
	About the Author	549

List of Illustrations

Print of "Archduchess Maria Antonia"	ii
"La Reine" in Court Dress	viii
"Marie-Antoinette d'Autriche"	10
"Antoinette and Louis in their wedding clothes"	58

Marie-Antoinette, Daughter of the Caesars

"Birth of Louis XVI"	89
"Marie-Antoinette in peasant costume"	161
"At the Court Ball"	162
"Antoinette with a bust of Louis"	186
"Louis and Antoinette in a Eucharistic Procession"	196
"Marie-Antoinette prays before death"	196
"Dauphin Louis-Joseph"	229
"Madame Royale with her nurse"	230
"Marie-Antoinette at her churching"	230
"Dauphin Louis-Charles"	231
"Gabrielle de Polignac"	232
"Madame Élisabeth of France"	275
"Count Hans Axel von Fersen"	290
"Louis XVI and Marie-Antoinette in profile"	371
"Marie-Antoinette as Vesta" by Dumont	372
"Incarceration of the Royal family in the Temple"	409
"Murder of the Princesse de Lamballe"	410
"Louis XVI at his execution, Jenuary 21, 1793"	426
"Marie-Antoinette on trial"	427
"Marie-Antoinette and Madame Royale in prison"	428

Marie-Antoinette, Daughter of the Caesars

"Marie-Antoinette on her way to be executed"   455

"Madame Royale in the Temple prison"   456

"Duchesse d'Angoulême"   476

"Royalist print of Louis XVI received by St. Louis IX in Heaven"   485

ACKNOWLEDGMENTS

Marie-Antoinette: Daughter of the Caesars has been made possible due to the efforts and research of many scholars from across the globe. The internet has made accessible not only out-of-print memoirs, books of letters, and old histories but has made it easier to be in touch with historical experts. I would be nowhere without the expertise of Professor Maryse Demasy in Brussells, Belgium, who is perhaps one of the foremost specialists on Marie-Antoinette in the world. I wish also to thank author Catherine Delors, an expressive writer and meticulous in historical analysis. As of this writing, we await the publication of the biography of Princesse de Lamballe by author Geri Walton. Geri's articles have been helpful and I am grateful for her generosity in sharing her findings with me. My gratitude also extends to British historian and author Gareth Russell, whose research is always captivating. I would like to thank the members of the forum *Boudoir de Marie-Antoinette* whose expertise has been invaluable. Thanks to the writers on the various history blogs, including author Leah Marie Brown of *Titillating Tidbits*, Lauren on Marie-Antoinette's *Gossip Guide*, author Melanie Clegg of *Madame Guillotine*, Louise Boisen Schmidt at *This is Versailles*, Catherine Curzon of *A Covent Garden Gilflurt's Guide to Life*, "Tiny-Librarian" of *She who pwns people with history* and writer Anna Gibson of *Vive la Reine* and *Reading Treasure*. And I would be nowhere without my editor Robyn Mendelsohn, formerly of the BBC. I would also like to thank Egil Totland, Hillary Cotter, Lauren Boxhall, Genevieve Montgomery, Zsófia Hacsek, Meghan Ferrara, Felio Xilas Tsacrios, Christine Niles and Kaitlyn McCracken, who have been supportive over the years of my research.

PREFACE: WHAT THIS BOOK IS AND WHAT IT IS NOT....

Marie-Antoinette, Daughter of the Caesars is not meant to be a full biography of the Queen. The great biographies have all been written. Rather it is a collection of reflections about her life, her death and her legacy, based upon my research over the last thirty years. Whenever possible I have let the historical persons speak for themselves out of memoirs and letters. I try not repeat too many of the well-known anecdotes that are rehashed in other books but if I do, it is to look at the incident from a different angle. As far as biographies in English go, I cannot recommend highly enough the 1930's two volume work by Nesta Webster. If one can get around Nesta's extremist politics, her character studies of Louis XVI and Marie-Antoinette are astute and based upon original documents. Her research is exhaustive. I will cite other biographies as well throughout the course of the book. As for the subtitle, *Daughter of the Caesars*, I think it is important to see Marie-Antoinette in light of her Imperial heritage as a child of the Habsburg dynasty. The Habsburgs assumed the crown of the Holy Roman Empire in the 1400's, the crown which had originated with Charlemagne in the year 800, seen as the continuation of the Roman Empire of the West. The Habsburgs and their allies kept the Muslims from overrunning Europe at both the Battle of Lepanto in 1571 and at the battle of Vienna in 1683. Indeed, the four crowns which adorn the tombs of the Habsburgs in the Capuchin crypt in Vienna are the crowns of the Empire, of Hungary, of Bohemia, and of Jerusalem[1] the latter being a throwback to the days of the Crusaders. In those four crowns are symbolized much of the history of Christendom. The fall of Marie-Antoinette, as both Queen of France and the youngest daughter of the Imperial Family, is indicative of the end of Christian civilization and the birth of the secular state, which was the object of the French Revolution. Through her death, Marie-Antoinette has been dubbed "Martyred Queen of Christian Europe"[2] for in killing her the revolutionaries also symbolically killed all that she represented, the ancient heritage of Christendom.

Marie-Antoinette is often called the "last queen" of France. Indeed, she was the last consort of a reigning monarch to bear the title of *Reine de France et Navarre*. Those who followed lived in her shadow. Two of the women who replaced her as consorts of French rulers were of her blood. Marie-Louise of Austria, Empress of the French, was Marie-Antoinette's great niece; Marie-Amélie of Naples, styled "Queen of the French" was her niece. Her daughter, Marie-Thérèse-Charlotte, as first lady of the courts of Louis XVIII and Charles X, caused disappointment when she was not a carbon copy of her mother. As historian Chantal Thomas notes of Napoleon's betrothal to Marie-Louise:

> So that…the farce of legitimacy could be taken to the limit, the marriage contract sent to Vienna was an exact copy of Louis XVI and Marie-Antoinette's. And to celebrate the event, Gluck's *Iphigénie en Aulide* was performed at the Opera, in front of the Emperor of Germany, Franz II, and his entire court. Its first performance in Paris in 1774 had been a personal triumph for Marie-Antoinette. Seated next to her father, the future bride had listened to Agamemnon singing, on stage, of the pain of having to sacrifice his daughter….Napoleon awaited her at Compiègne, at the very spot where Louis XV and the dauphin had come to greet

Marie-Antoinette.[3]

Empress Joséphine and Empress Eugénie, both from non-royal backgrounds, reverenced Marie-Antoinette's memory and felt honored to live in the places where she had once dwelt. Joséphine imitated the Queen with her gardens and Eugénie had herself painted costumed as Marie-Antoinette at Petit Trianon. And so, although she was much-maligned, Marie-Antoinette has remained for her people the archetypal queen, to whom all queens who followed would be compared.

This book would have been impossible a decade ago, because the French language sources necessary for such a work were often difficult to acquire even on interlibrary loan. However, so much is now available on the internet and, to my joy, out-of-print books that I thought I would never find, I have discovered online, or tracked down in vintage book stores by googling. Rare books, such as the *Authentic Trial at Large of Marie-Antoinette*, which is the first English translation of the Queen's trial as originally printed in British newspapers in 1793, are now accessible online. Since I want this book to be a helpful tool for young scholars I have made sure there are lots of notes with further information. I expect this book to go through future editions since my own studies on the Queen never end; there is always more to learn.

Elena Maria Vidal

Solemnity of St. Joseph

March 19, 2016

St. Michaels, Maryland

Marie-Antoinette, Daughter of the Caesars

PROLOGUE: MARIE-ANTOINETTE AND ME

I began reading about Marie-Antoinette when I was nine. I was so moved by her story that I covered my school notebooks with drawings of her, and liked to coiffure my Barbie dolls in eighteenth century *poufs* with plumes which were duck feathers gathered in the park. I continued to read various books about Antoinette throughout the years. I first visited the Petit Trianon when I was seventeen years old. It was January, but the birds were singing in the gardens. There was a strong sense of timelessness that I experienced then and on successive trips. Others have confided to me a similar feeling of enchantment when wandering through the gardens of Trianon. The incident stayed with me for many years.

People frequently ask me why I write about Louis XVI and Marie-Antoinette. One of the reasons is that I keep encountering educated people who really think that Antoinette said "Let them eat cake." I continue to encounter Christians who think that Louis XVI and Marie-Antoinette were killed as punishment for some egregious wickedness or, at least, for unforgivable stupidity. Having read books about the royal couple since childhood, I knew they were misunderstood; it was only after a great deal more research that I came to see how completely false are the common beliefs about the King and Queen. But the demonization of Louis XVI and Marie-Antoinette in the popular mind is necessary in order to justify the excesses of the French Revolution. When people have a false and distorted view of history, then it is difficult for them to grasp the present, and almost impossible to meet the future with any kind of preparedness.

The French Revolution was not necessary, simply because it is never necessary to murder tens of thousands of people. Reform certainly was needed, but reform can happen without death. Louis XVI was an intrepid reformer. He was not afraid to break with the past and abolish outdated customs, while introducing new ways of doing things. Louis was not resistant to change, although that is how he is usually portrayed. The changes were slow but over time might have been effective, had the violent upheavals not swept everything away. Too often the violence is represented as a sad but unavoidable means of achieving freedom and democracy. For the French Revolution overturned not only the social order but it was ultimately an attack on the Catholic Church. Many Catholics were killed, especially those peasants who did not want their religion taken away.

Contemporary people love Marie-Antoinette for her glamor and style but mostly for her courage when the glamor disappeared. Hers is a tragedy akin to those of ancient Greece, yet without the element of total despair. For Antoinette remains a Christian heroine and her end is characterized by virtues which can be found in many an *acta sanctorum*. While we weep for her, we are simultaneously uplifted. Perhaps this quotation from Frances Hodgson Burnett's *A Little Princess* best expresses why Antoinette continues to inspire so many of us:

> It would be easy to be a princess if I were dressed in cloth of gold, but it is a great deal more of a triumph to be one all the time when no one knows it. There was Marie Antoinette when she was in prison and her throne was gone and she had only a black gown on, and her hair was white, and they

insulted her and called her Widow Capet. She was a great deal more like a queen then than when she was so gay and everything was so grand. I like her best then. Those howling mobs of people did not frighten her. She was stronger than they were, even when they cut her head off.
—*A Little Princess* by Frances Hodgson Burnett

INTRODUCTION: A REPUTATION IN SHREDS

She is the queen who danced while the people starved; who spent extravagantly on clothes and jewels without a thought for her subjects' plight. Such is the distorted but widespread view of Marie-Antoinette, Queen of France and Navarre (1755-1793), wife of King Louis XVI (1754-1793). Popular films have further damaged the image of the much-maligned Austrian archduchess, sent to France at age fourteen to marry the fifteen-year-old Dauphin. Sadly, the picture many people now have of Antoinette is of her running through Versailles with a glass of champagne in her hand, eating bonbons all day long, and rolling in the bushes with a lover. In reality, she was a teetotaler who ate frugally. She was notorious for her intense modesty. Even some prominent biographers, who have insisted upon the possibility of an affair with Swedish Count Axel von Fersen, have had to admit that there is no solid evidence. Yes, she had a gambling problem when young. She loved to entertain; her parties were legendary. She liked to dance, until dawn if she could, but settled down when she became a mother. She had a lively sense of humor. Her clothes, yes, were magnificent; volumes could and have been written about Marie-Antoinette's style. She did gradually introduce simpler fashions to France, however.

It is known that Queen Marie-Antoinette had high moral standards. She did not permit uncouth or off-color remarks in her presence. She exercised a special vigilance over anyone in her care, especially the young ladies of her household. As Madame Campan relates in her memoirs:

> All who were acquainted with the Queen's private qualities knew that she equally deserved attachment and esteem. Kind and patient to excess in her relations with her household, she indulgently considered all around her, and interested herself in their fortunes and in their pleasures. She had, among her women, young girls from the Maison de Saint Cyr, all well born; the Queen forbade them the play when the performances were not suitable; sometimes, when old plays were to be represented, if she found she could not with certainty trust to her memory, she would take the trouble to read them in the morning, to enable her to decide whether the girls should or should not go to see them, rightly considering herself bound to watch over their morals and conduct.[1]

In pre-revolutionary France it was for the King and the Queen to give an example of almsgiving. Louis XVI and Marie-Antoinette took this duty seriously and throughout their reign did what they could to help the needy. During the fireworks celebrating the marriage of the young prince and princess in May 1770, there was a stampede in which many people were killed. Louis and Marie-Antoinette gave all of their private spending money for a month to relieve the suffering of the victims and their families. They became very popular with the common people as a result, which was reflected in the adulation with which they were received when the Dauphin took his wife to Paris on her first "official" visit in June 1773. Marie-Antoinette's reputation for sweetness and mercy became even more entrenched in 1774, when as the new Queen she asked that the people be relieved of a tax called "the Queen's belt," customary at the beginning of each reign. "Belts are no longer worn," she quipped.[2] It was the onslaught of revolutionary propaganda that would eventually destroy her reputation.

The King and Queen were patrons of the Maison Philanthropique, a society founded by Louis XVI which helped the aged, blind and widows. The Queen taught her daughter Madame Royale to wait upon peasant children, to sacrifice her Christmas gifts so as to buy fuel and blankets for the destitute, and to bring baskets of food to the sick. Marie-Antoinette started a home for unwed mothers at the royal palace. She adopted three poor children to be reared with her own, as well overseeing the upbringing of several needy children, whose education she paid for, while caring for their families. She brought several peasant families to live on her farm at Trianon, building cottages for them. There was food for the hungry distributed every day at Versailles, at the King's command. During the famine of 1787-88, the royal family sold much of their flatware to buy grain for the people, eating the cheap barley bread in order to be able to give more to the hungry. The royal couple's almsgiving stopped only with their incarceration in the Temple in August 1792, for then they had nothing left to give but their lives.

Too often in the many articles about Marie-Antoinette that have surfaced over the years, Count Axel von Fersen is referred to as the "Queen's lover" or as her "probable lover." It is repeatedly disregarded that there is not a scrap of reliable historical evidence that Count Fersen and Marie-Antoinette were anything but friends, and that he was as much her husband's friend as he was hers. People are free to speak of Louis XV and Madame de Pompadour as "lovers" since they openly lived together for many years. But to speak that way of Marie-

Antoinette, who lost her life because she chose to stay at her husband's side, is the height of irresponsibility.

The Swedish nobleman was in the service of his sovereign King Gustavus III and Count Fersen's presence at the French court needs to be seen in the light of that capacity. The Swedish King was a devoted friend of Louis XVI and Marie-Antoinette and Gustavus, even more than the Queen's Austrian relatives, worked to aid the King and Queen of France in their time of trouble. Fersen was the go-between in the various secret plans to help Louis XVI regain control of his kingdom and escape from the clutches of his political enemies. The diplomatic intrigues that went on behind the scenes are more interesting than any imaginary romance. The Queen's relationship with her husband is more interesting as well. However, books and movies continue to add this sensationalism to Marie-Antoinette's life, as if anything could be more sensational than the reality. Serious modern and contemporary scholars, however, such as Frances Mossiker, Paul and Pierrette Girault de Coursac, Hilaire Belloc, Nesta Webster, Simone Bertière, Philippe Delorme, Jean Chalon, Chantal Thomas, Desmond Seward, Jean Petitfils and Simon Schama are unanimous in saying that there is no conclusive evidence to prove that Marie-Antoinette violated her marriage vows by dallying with Count Fersen.

As Jean Chalon points out in his biography *Chère Marie-Antoinette*, Fersen, who had many mistresses, saw the Queen as an angel, to whom he offered reverent and chaste homage. According to Chalon, Marie-Antoinette knew about sex only through conjugal love, where she found her "happiness," her *bonheur essentiel*, as she wrote to her mother. [3] If there had been any cause for concern about Count Fersen's presence at the French court as regards the Queen's reputation, the Austrian ambassador Count Mercy-Argenteau would surely have mentioned it in one of the reams of letters to Marie-Antoinette's mother Empress Maria Theresa, to whom he passed on every detail of the young Queen's life. Count Mercy had spies whom he paid well to gather information, but Fersen was not worth mentioning. Neither is he mentioned in a romantic way by other people close to Marie-Antoinette in their memoirs, such as her maid Madame Campan.

The accounts of those whose personal knowledge of the Queen, or deep study of her life, reveal her virtue, as well as her fidelity and devotion to her husband, are continually ignored. Montjoie in his *Histoire de Marie-Antoinette, Vol.1* (1797) quotes the words of her page, the Comte d'Hézècques:

> If one wishes to discover the prime cause of the misfortunes of this princess, we must seek them in the passions of which the court was the hotbed and in the corruption of her century. If I had seen otherwise I would say so with sincerity, but I affirm that after having seen everything, heard everything, and read everything, I am convinced that the morals of Marie Antoinette were as pure as those of her virtuous husband. [4]

But since so often the testimonials of French monarchists are seen as being an attempt to ingratiate themselves to the surviving Bourbons, here is what the Irish politician and author John Wilson Croker (1780-1857) wrote in his *Essays on the French Revolution*:

> We have followed the history of Marie Antoinette with the greatest diligence and scrupulosity. We have lived in those times. We have talked with some of her friends and some of her enemies; we

have read, certainly not all, but hundreds of the libels written against her; and we have, in short, examined her life with—if we may be allowed to say so of ourselves—something of the accuracy of contemporaries, the diligence of inquirers, and the impartiality of historians, all combined; and we feel it our duty to declare, in as a solemn a manner as literature admits of, our well-matured opinion that every reproach against the morals of the queen was a gross calumny—that she was, as we have said, one of the purest of human beings. [5]

It is an assessment with which I fully agree. I hope that in the future responsible scholarship about Queen Marie-Antoinette and her family comes to replace the lies which have fed the popular imagination for so long.

Marie-Antoinette, Daughter of the Caesars

MARIE-ANTOINETTE D'AUTRICHE.

1 A DAUGHTER OF THE CAESARS

"Who is she that cometh forth as the morning rising, fair as the moon, bright as the sun, as terrible as an army set in array?" —Canticle of Canticles 6:9

"And the virgin's name was Mary..." —St. Luke 1:27

On September 12, the fifth day within the octave of the Nativity of the Virgin, in 1683, the army of the Turkish Sultan, 300,000 strong, was miraculously defeated at the gates of Vienna after an attempt to sweep across Europe. The King of Poland, Jan Sobieski, had come to the aid of the Habsburg Emperor Leopold, and they attributed the victory to the intercession of the Black Madonna, borne by the Poles into battle. The triumph, won against overwhelming odds, saved Europe from becoming a Moslem colony, and September 12, already Feast of the Holy Name of Mary, was henceforth celebrated with great solemnity by the House of Austria. The name of "Maria" was given to every daughter of the family but all except the eldest were called by their second name. Hence, Marie-Antoinette during her lifetime was known by her two families as "Antoine" or "Antoinette."

I did not begin to understand Antoinette until I visited Vienna in 1995, the capital of Austria which, when Antoinette was born, the Imperial city of the Habsburg empire. I found it to be a city of order, cleanliness and beauty, with magnificent churches, palaces and gardens kept in their original splendor. The solemn alabaster Hofburg and the creamy yellow Schönbrunn, the two palaces in which the future Queen of France would spend her childhood, both project the aura of stateliness and majesty which was said to surround Antoinette herself. The Catholic statues and monuments express a joyful faith with an awareness of the soul's last end. Yet amid the grandeur and dignity of old Vienna there is always a touch of whimsy, with plenty of art, music and gardens. There were picture post cards of Antoinette in many shops, sold with the implicit understanding that she was their princess who had been sent to France to die. In Vienna, she was not the hated *l'Autrichienne* but a beloved Archduchess known for her generous heart, the youngest of many daughters of a beloved Empress-Queen.

There are numerous anecdotes about Antoinette and here is one of the first. In the early autumn of 1755, Empress Maria Theresa, expecting her fifteenth child, cheerfully made a wager with the Duke von Tarouka as to whether she would have a boy or a girl. The Duke thought it would be a boy. When he lost the bet, he sent the Empress her winnings, accompanied by the verse of Mestastio, who was to be the Italian tutor of the newborn archduchess:

> *Ho perduto: l'augusta figlia .*
> *A pagar m' ha, condamnato.*
> *Ma s'e vero ch'a voi simiglia*
> *Tutto l' mundo ha guadagnato.*[1]

Marie-Antoinette, Daughter of the Caesars

Thus from even before she was born, Antoinette was involved in gambling, a pastime from which she would glean a great deal of amusement as well as damage to her purse and her reputation. Was the little Archduchess like her mother as hoped? If one compares portraits, then yes, indeed she was in appearance. Hers was the same delicate beauty, pale flawless skin, pale blue eyes, and auburn-tinted blonde hair. Later, the Empress would write to Antoinette's future husband saying: "She will come to love you. I know, because I know her." [2] The Empress had insights into the heart of a daughter who in many ways was so like herself: passionate, strong-willed, motherly, and indomitable, especially when in a corner. But that was all to come later.

Antoinette celebrated her birthday on November 1, the Feast of All Saints, although the actual date of birth was the Feast of All Souls, November 2, considered a day of prayer and penance on behalf of the faithful departed, to be accompanied by meditations on death and judgment. On November 2, 1755, an earthquake of apocalyptic proportions struck Portugal, the home of Antoinette's godparents the King and Queen of Portugal. It was one of the worst earthquakes in recorded history. King Joseph and Queen Mariana Victoria were spared simply because they had left Lisbon for the country on a sudden whim the day before. Because it was All Souls Day a great number of people in Lisbon were in churches to gain the special indulgence, which may have led to more victims. Around 40,000 people were killed by the falling buildings and the resulting tsunami. Europeans would see the event as a portent of doom. While Antoinette shunned superstition, the catastrophe which coincided with her entry into the world made an impression upon her mind, at least according to Madame Campan, who with hindsight was perturbed by the cataclysm and the connection it had with her Queen. [3] The Empress was not superstitious either. However, on at least two occasions that we know of, Maria Theresa took her youngest daughter to persons with mystical gifts to be assured that the future would not be too dark. But the truth was never fully imparted to her. If the Empress had known all that would happen to her child she would have died of sorrow on the spot.

On Novenber 3, 1755, Maria Antonia Josefa Johanna of Lorrraine-Austria was baptized in the anticamera of the Hofburg Palace. She was christened by the Archbishop of Vienna, Cardinal von Trautson. The Empress preferred to have her children baptized by the Papal Nuncio, however the new nuncio, Cardinal Visconti, had not yet been formally presented at Court and was therefore ineligible to perform the ceremony. The child's brother Joseph and sister Maria Anna stood in for her godparents the King and Queen of Portugal; ironically they bore the identical names as the King and Queen. Another irony was that the Portuguese queen, Mariana Victoria, a Spanish princess, had once been betrothed to Louis XV as a child and had lived at Versailles as the Infanta-Queen. She had been sent home when it was decided that Louis XV was to marry the Polish princess Marie Leszczyńska.

The baby was christened "Maria" for the Blessed Virgin Mary, to whom the Habsburg lands had been dedicated by Ferdinand III in the following words, carved on a column in the heart of the capital:

> To God, infinite in goodness and power, King of heaven and earth, by whom kings reign; to the Virgin Mother of God, conceived without sin, by whom princes command, whom Austria, devoutly loving, holds as her Queen and Patron; Ferdinand III, Emperor, confides, gives, consecrates himself,

children, people, armies, provinces, and all that is his, and erects in accomplishment of a vow this statue, as a perpetual memorial.[4]

The child was called "Antonia" in honor of St. Anthony of Padua the Wonder-worker, who was not only the patron saint of Portugal, the home of her godparents, but also revered in the House of Austria. In 1620, Emperor Ferdinand II overcame the Protestant forces at the Battle of the White Mountain, making Bohemia Catholic once again. The Emperor had great devotion to St. Anthony, also known as "Hammer of Heretics," who shared with him the baptismal name of "Ferdinand." [5] At the same battle, St. Teresa of Avila, the Carmelite mystic who had recently been canonized, allegedly appeared to the Catholic soldiers, encouraging them on to victory. The name "Teresa," already popular in Spain, thus spread to the Habsburg lands in the east and into the Imperial Family. In thanksgiving for winning the Battle of the White Mountain, the Emperor dedicated a church in Prague to both Our Lady Victorious and St. Anthony of Padua. The church was given to the Carmelite Fathers who housed therein a miraculous statue of the Infant Jesus. Several of Maria Theresa and Francis Stephen's daughters bore the name "Antonia" for St. Anthony.

St. Joseph, the husband of the Virgin Mary and the Foster Father of the Christ Child, had gained great popularity in Italy and Spain in the fifteenth and sixteenth centuries due to the writings of the Franciscan St. Bernardine of Siena and the Carmelite St. Teresa of Avila. As devotion to Saint Teresa spread from the Spanish Habsburgs to the Austrian Habsburgs and into France, devotion to St. Joseph accompanied it. The names "Joseph" and "Josepha" began to appear in the Imperial Family; it was Antoinette's third name, followed by her fourth name "Joanna." St. John the Evangelist had long been a favorite among rich and poor, peasants and nobles, as the youngest Apostle who reclined upon the Heart of the Savior, who later faithfully stood at the foot of the Cross with the Blessed Mother. He was also the saint of the visions of the Apocalypse. And we must not forget St. John the Baptist, the cousin and herald of Jesus and long a well-beloved saint in Christendom. Another maiden of Lorraine called Jeanne Darc, who had been sent to save France, had been named for St. John long ago.

In November of 1755, the Archduchess Antonia was in swaddling clothes, and placed in the care of a wet nurse, Frau Weber, whom she would always regard as her foster-mother. Maria Constantia Weber, the wife of the Viennese magistrate Georg Weber, was distinguished for her beauty and virtue but most of all for her ability in caring for infants. As wet-nurse of the new imperial baby, she moved into the Hofburg Palace with her own little boy. Frau Weber's son Joseph Weber was three months older than the Archduchess and would later, with Monsieur de Lally-Tollendal of the Irish-French Jacobite family as a ghost writer, author one of the first biographies of Antoinette in the form of his memoirs. Here is a passage from the *Memoirs of Maria-Antoinetta* by Joseph Weber, whom the future Queen of France would always refer to as her "foster brother" or *frère de lait*:

> Maria Theresa was a good mother as well as a great Queen. Her tenderness seemed as soft as her courage appeared majestic and sublime. No sooner had she entrusted her child to my mother than she adopted us all. She rewarded the long services of my father with a considerable pension, and a grant of apartments in the Hotel de la Chancellerie. A pension was settled on my

mother, and one also on each of her children. As for me, whose lot it was to be nourished with the same milk that Maria-Antoinetta was, Her Imperial Majesty desired my mother, while I was a child, to take me with her whenever she went to pay her respects to the young Princess whom she had suckled.

The daughter of the Caesars then made me join in the sports of her infancy, in which the Empress herself took a part; and, as at that age no thing had yet made me sensible of the immense distance between myself and her with whom I played, the august and good Maria-Theresa, fearing to give me pain if she bestowed her caresses partially, often took me on one of her knees when she held her daughter on the other, and honoured me with embraces similar to those she lavished upon her.[6]

What strikes me about this charming story from Weber's memoir is that even as an infant, Antoinette never had her mother to herself. She did not display resentment of Weber but was generous to him all of her life. Yet perhaps it explains the tenacity with which she held onto to her female friendships.

Antoinette was the fifteenth child in a family of sixteen. Her parents were the Holy Roman Emperor and Empress but they were very informal as royals go. "The Imperial family," said Goethe, as quoted by Maxime de la Rocheterie, "is nothing more than a large German bourgeoisie." Rocheterie, in his classic biography of Antoinette, describes the household in which the future Queen was reared:

> Etiquette was unknown. The emperor and empress liked to live in the midst of their subjects kind and friendly toward all but restraining familiarity by respect. Unfortunately they were so absorbed by the

care of the policy and administration of their vast empire that they had little leisure to superintend the education of their numerous children. They confided them to tutors and governesses whom they chose with care and to whom it appears they gave their instructions without, however, seeing that they were carried out. [7]

It is, of course, notorious how her own family's casualness about etiquette would make living at Versailles quite a challenge for the teenaged Antoinette. In such a loving if rather haphazard environment, the little Archduchess, called "Antoine," blossomed into a lively and attractive child. While she was not outstandingly pious or studious, she learned her prayers and was carefully catechized. She very much enjoyed her musical instructions—Gluck was her teacher— her dancing lessons, and anything to do with pets, especially dogs and horses. She was taught to draw and sketched a likeness of her deceased father in red chalk when she was ten.[8] She did well at languages, including Latin and Italian, and showed an interest in history. As Vincent Cronin says: "She learned Austrian history and the Austrian version of French history, notably different from the French version, for it failed to mention that France was God's gift to the planet Earth...."[9] Theater was her passion, especially comedy. When preparing to go to France to be married, two actors helped to improve her French diction, which Louis XV thought to be inappropriate when he heard of it. The French king sent the priest Abbé Vermond to take over the future queen's studies; he became her confessor as well. There was some concern over her health, since from the age of eight she had experienced nervous spasms when upset. "Antoine has convulsions," her mother wrote. "She loses consciousness for an hour."[10] Nevertheless, the princess learned to speak, walk and move with beauty and grace, as if on stage.

Although her portraits show her neatly coifed, in reality the small Archduchess had a wild mop of curly red-gold hair which her governess kept out of her face with a black woolen band. Over time the hairband tore the hair out at the roots. When it came time to prepare the child for her future in France, the French hairdresser who was brought to Austria had to be very creative in order to make her presentable, using a carefully managed *coif à la française*, which became an immediate sensation at the Imperial Court. She also had her teeth straightened with gold braces. What the portraits never show is that Antoinette had faint pock marks on one side of her mouth, the only flaw in her creamily translucent skin. The Empress insisted that her daughters dress modestly and in the traditional "Spanish" mode of the Habsburgs, which meant that while their clothes were beautiful they were never in the height of fashion. Antoine therefore was never interested in fashion or encouraged to be so until after she arrived in France.[11]

Antoine's mother taught her to play cards.[12] Knowing of the French court, Empress Maria Theresa probably feared that if her daughter did not learn how to win certain games of chance, she would lose all her money. Gambling was rife at all the courts of Europe; the Viennese actually played for much higher stakes than the French, which did not help Antoinette when she started having all night card parties as a twenty-year old Queen of France. However, her mother also instilled in her a great concern for the poor and a sense of duty towards all who were unfortunate; there are many accounts of the young archduchess' charity.[13]

Due to her delayed and imperfect education, which did not really begin until age thirteen when Abbé Vermond took charge, Antoine had a Manichean view of the world, everything was black or white and all the people were good or bad. Anyone against the Austrian alliance was bad. Plus her mother had inculcated in her that the court of France was a cesspool of vice and that she was to be constantly vigilant for the protection of her soul. It only served to give the teenager a morally superior attitude towards those with whom she was to dwell.

The word most often used to describe the youthful Antoinette by those in charge of her was "dissipation." Now in French, *dissipation* has a slightly different meaning from our English version of the word. As Nesta Webster explains in *Louis XVI and Marie-Antoinette Before the Revolution*:

> The gravest reproach brought against [Marie-Antoinette]...is her tendency to 'dissipation,' a word which must not...be translated by the English word dissipation signifying wild gaiety, even dissoluteness, but simply a love of distraction and a disinclination to give fixed attention to any subject."[14]

I wonder if today she would have been diagnosed as genuinely having an attention deficit disorder. Sadly, the wandering mind of a young girl would cause her to be forever labeled as "dissipated" by those who misunderstood or mistranslated the original meaning.

Before sending Antoine to France, Maria Theresa took her daughter to a convent in Vienna to see a nun with visionary gifts. The mother was worried that Antoine's budding piety would be harmed at the corrupt Court of France. The nun earnestly studied the glowing young face for a long time. Then she said: "She will have reverses, but will turn to religion at the last." Maria Theresa burst into tears.[15] It is also reported that the Empress consulted Fr. Gassner the "thaumaturgus" in regard to the girl's future. Fr. Gassner regarded the princess with a serious expression before replying: "There are crosses for all shoulders." [16][17]

The **Empress Maria Theresa** (1717-1780), Antoinette's mother, can be counted among the greatest of Christian monarchs. She was born an Archduchess of Austria and became Queen of Hungary and Queen of Bohemia when her Habsburg father died, but held the title of Holy Roman Empress because her husband, Francis Stephen of Lorraine, had been elected Emperor. The marriage was a love match, although not without problems, and produced sixteen children. [18] People have accused Maria Theresa of betraying her motherhood by marrying her children all over Europe in order to forge alliances, but she was not doing anything different from other royal parents. Furthermore, she was the mother of her people as well, and allying the empire with foreign nations was a way to promote peace. [19] Especially it was important to cement an alliance with France, the traditional enemy of Austria. Antoinette was the sacrificial lamb for that project, but that is what it was to be a princess of Hungary and Bohemia, an Archduchess of Austria.

One noblewoman described being presented to Empress Maria Theresa:

Her Majesty entered followed by the three princesses. My husband and myself each sank upon the left knee and kissed the noblest, the most beautiful hand that has ever wielded a scepter. The Empress gently bade us rise. Her face and her gracious manner banished all the timidity and embarrassment we naturally felt in the presence of so exalted and beautiful a figure as hers. Our fear was changed to love and confidence. [20]

The Emperor and Empress made pilgrimages to the

Marian shrine of Mariazell "Mary's Throne" in the Styrian Alps, accompanied by their numerous offspring. They once left two gold hearts, symbolic of the hearts of Maria Theresa and Francis Stephen, at the feet of the miraculous statue of the Virgin. Antoinette was a bit of a wayward child, extremely charming and affable, devoted without being outstandingly religious. Yet she, the future *reine-martyre*, often knelt before the ancient statue of the Virgin with her family.

Unlike many other rulers, including her own son, Empress Maria Theresa, although she was a patroness of the arts and sciences, was not enamored with the philosophies made fashionable by the Enlightenment. In her youth she had loved dancing and riding, but in widowhood she grew more reclusive and strict, always garbed in black. When Francis died in 1765, Maria Theresa was inconsolable, but she kept herself busy governing the Empire and writing letters to all of her daughters, telling them what to do. She was always especially worried about Antoine; even when she was dying she wept as she mentioned her youngest daughter's name. Maria Theresa passed away on November 29, 1780 at the age of 63. Her nemesis, Frederick the Great of Prussia, who had given her no end of trouble, upon hearing of her death, said: "She has done honor to the throne and to her sex; I have warred with her but I have never been her enemy." [21]

Maria Theresa is buried in the Capuchin crypt in Vienna, the traditional burial place of the Habsburgs. I visited the crypt in 1995 and was able to pray at her tomb. My heart was touched in a way which is difficult to describe. It was shortly after my return from Austria that I found in the cellar the beginning of a novel about Marie-Antoinette that I had begun writing about a decade earlier. I decided to finish the book and called it *Trianon*.

Through his mother, an Orléans princess, **Francis Stephen of Lorraine**, Antoinette's father, was a descendent of Henri IV and the Bourbons, as well as Mary Queen of Scots and the Stuarts. Through his father, he was the grandson of Charles of Lorraine and Eleanor of Austria. Duke Charles of Lorraine helped his brother-in-law, the Holy Roman Emperor Leopold I, withstand the Turks at the siege of Vienna in 1683. Francis Stephen was later sent from Lorraine to Vienna to be brought up at the court of Leopold's son, Emperor Charles VI, where he developed a deep affection for his cousin, Charles VI's eldest daughter and heir, Maria Theresa, and his feelings were passionately reciprocated. It was arranged that the two should marry and they did so in 1736. According to the Pragmatic Sanction of 1713, females could inherit the Habsburg lands. Nevertheless, the war of the Austrian Succession was fought before Maria Theresa's inheritance was recognized by all of Europe in 1748. France objected to the husband of Maria Theresa being Duke of Lorraine, since it gave Austria a foothold in France. So Francis Stephen renounced his inheritance of the Duchy of Lorraine and became Grand Duke of Tuscany instead. In 1745, he was elected Holy Roman Emperor, after much diplomatic wrangling by his wife. Although Maria Theresa handled the politics and matters of state, Francis handled the money, investing wisely so that the Habsburg-Lorraine dynasty and the Empire went from near financial collapse to great prosperity. In the meantime, Francis Stephen sired a family of sixteen children with Maria Theresa. Although he adored his wife and children, he philandered with other women, inspiring Maria Theresa to start a Chastity Commission to hunt out unfaithful husbands and their mistresses. Francis Stephen became a Freemason in 1731, which also displeased his wife.

Francis Stephen was especially fond of his youngest daughter Antoine. On his way to Innsbruck for the marriage of his son Leopold to the Spanish Infanta in August of 1765, he suddenly ordered the coach to be stopped. Although he had already kissed his children good-bye, he sent back to Schönbrunn for the Archduchess Antonia, saying "I must see her again." The nine year old was brought at once; the father embraced her, gazing at his child's face with a look of such great love that she was never to forget it. [22] Sadly, Francis became ill during the course of the wedding festivities and died at Innsbruck. He left the following words for his children:

> Never be indifferent before what appears to you to be evil, nor attempt to find it innocent... We are not put into this world merely to amuse ourselves... What kind of people we should frequent is also a delicate matter, for they may often lead us into many things against our will... Friendship is one of the pleasures of life, but one should be careful to whom one entrusts this friendship and not be too prodigal of it... This is why I advise you, my dear children, never to be in a hurry to place your friendship and trust in someone of whom you are not quite sure. [23]

As has been noted, Antoinette was the fifteenth child in a family of sixteen, and the youngest daughter of eleven girls. Several children died in infancy or toddlerhood, long before Antoine was born. Here we will describe only those whom she knew so the reader may gather more of a sense of her childhood, which ended at age fourteen when she married. The eldest surviving sister was **Archduchess Maria Anna** (1738-1789), or "La Marianne" as Empress Maria Theresa referred to her in her letters to Antoinette. [24] Maria Anna had numerous physical handicaps, including a crooked back and weak lungs. It was early on decided that she was unmarriageable and so she was encouraged to become a nun. She eventually became the Abbess at Klagenfurt monastery in the Austrian Alps; it may be through her influence that Antoinette acquired some of her liturgical books, such as *The Little Office of The Blessed Virgin Mary: According to the Usage of the Cistercian Order*. The Abbess, who eschewed society as much as it eschewed her, was a patroness of the arts and sciences like her father the Emperor, and was perhaps one of the most intellectual of the sisters. She died at the age of 51.

When traveling in Austria in 1995 I visited a former Carthusian monastery at Gaming. Like many monastic communities in what was once the Holy Roman Empire, the monastery in Gaming was closed down in the late 1700's by the orders of **Emperor Joseph II**, who did not tolerate any contemplative orders, those who were not doing "practical" work. Joseph (1741-1790) was Antoinette's bossy oldest brother, as different from her as night from day, although he claimed to be fond of his little sister. Joseph was an "enlightened despot." He had two disastrous marriages to wives who both died young, leaving him a widower with a little girl, who also died. Joseph's first marriage was to Isabella of Parma (1741-1763), daughter of Élisabeth of France and granddaughter of Louis XV. The princess appears to have been a happy little girl but she fell into depression when her mother died in 1759. In spite of Joseph's being passionately in love with the exquisite Isabella, she did not return his feelings, and although she gave him a daughter, she became more listless and unhappy. Isabella latched onto Joseph's sister Maria Christina (Mimi), and the two were inseparable friends. Isabella's letters to Mimi are often gushing and tender; people often misinterpret them as being the proof of a lesbian liaison, not realizing that it was the very innocence of such a friendship that made the loving words possible between such carefully brought up, devout Catholic ladies. Nevertheless, Isabella's letters also showed a tendency to obsession, particularly with death. Weakened by miscarriages, Isabella died of a stillbirth complicated by smallpox.

Two years after Isabella's death, Joseph became Emperor and married Maria Josepha of Bavaria (1739-1767), to whom he was not in the least attracted and whom he treated with coldness. Being still in love with Isabella, he did not want to marry again but did so for political reasons and to beget an heir. Maria Josepha, friendless and alone, wasted away at the Habsburg court and died of smallpox after two heartbreaking years of marriage. She was buried in the Capuchin crypt and was later blamed for passing on smallpox to Joseph's sister from her tomb.

Joseph was a liberal, and like many liberals he could be quite tyrannical when it came to imposing his ideas of freedom upon everyone else. He tried to secularize his country by making the Church subservient to the state, influenced as he was by new ideas of the Enlightenment. Strange that he had the same goal as many of the revolutionaries in France, although he was intent upon keeping the imperial power. His sister Antoinette did not approve of his so-called reforms,[25] which involved the closing of monasteries, which was being done by the revolutionaries in France as well. Some people speculate that if Joseph had lived longer he may have done more to help his sister the Queen of France in her hour of need than either his brother Leopold or his nephew Francis did as emperors. But that is speculation. No matter how much he loved his sister, he was an emperor first, and would have done what he thought was best for Austria.

However, because he died young, we will never really know.

Archduchess Maria Christina (1742-1798), known in the family as "Mimi," was said to be the Empress' favorite daughter, although her siblings regarded her as a manipulative tattle-tale. Mimi, who was not only clever and talented but a beauty, was the only daughter allowed to marry for love. In 1766 she took advantage of her mother's new widowhood to talk her into letting her marry her cousin, Prince Albert of Saxony, Duke of Teschen. The couple ruled in Hungary before settling into being Governors of the Austrian Netherlands. Mimi later had a great deal of trouble implementing Joseph's so-called reforms which were hated in the Netherlands, and disapproved of by Mimi herself. She visited Antoinette at Versailles in 1786, and the sisters often exchanged loving letters. As biographer Melanie Clegg writes in *Marie-Antoinette: An Intimate Biography*:

> Maria Antonia, who was thirteen years Mimi's junior, came to loathe her [elder] sister whose bossy, high-handed ways and intellectual snobbishness left her with a permanent suspicious dread of what would later be termed 'bluestocking'. For the rest of her life, Maria Antonia would eschew the company of intellectually sophisticated women, such as the cultivated and delightfully louche *salonnières* of Paris, in favor of what she regarded as more straightforward and much less challenging companions, who shared her own interests....[26]

Mimi and Albert were eventually driven out of the Netherlands by Napoleon, managing to salvage their remarkable art collection. Sadly, Mimi lost her only child to death. With her husband and child, she was buried in the Capuchin crypt in Vienna with the rest of the Habsburgs.

Archduchess Maria Elisabeth (1743-1808), called "Liesl," was lovely but like Mimi also had a sharp tongue. She was supposed to have gone to France to marry Louis XV but was prevented not only by Louis' mistress Madame du Barry but by an attack of smallpox, which disfigured her. This was tragic on more than one level. How helpful it would have been for Antoine to have an older sister at Versailles who was already Queen of France! Instead, Antoine had to face the French court practically alone and without her family. Meanwhile, Liesl became fat and crabby; Joseph eventually expelled her from the Imperial court, as he did all his sisters. She went to live with La Marianne and discovered a religious vocation, becoming an Abbess.

Archduke Charles Joseph (1745-1761) was a clever, handsome boy who knew just how clever and handsome he was. His parents adored him. He was determined to oust his elder brother Joseph from the succession and become Holy Roman Emperor himself someday. It never happened for he died from smallpox when not quite sixteen. He is reported to have said to his weeping mother: "You should not weep for me, dear mother, for had I lived, I would have brought you many more tears!" [27] His words, no doubt, were true.

Archduchess Maria Amalia (1746-1804) had a stubborn disposition and was the only daughter who refused to even pretend to follow her mother's advice after she was married. She was therefore shunned by the Empress, although her younger sisters were quite fond of her. Considered one of the prettiest sisters in a family of beauties, she had been determined to marry the man she loved the way Mimi had. Maria Theresa, having recovered her strength of mind, would not hear of it. Instead Amalia had to marry Ferdinand of Parma, another grandson of Louis XV. They had several children although they both cheated on each other, and Amalia later behaved so badly people thought she was mad. Maria Theresa worried that the rumors about Amalia would make it to France and soil Antoine's reputation; indeed it may have contributed to the French people's readiness to believe anything unsavory about their Queen. As a widow, Amalia was driven out of Parma by Napoleon's army and sought refuge in Bohemia, where she died in Prague in 1804.

Leopold II (1747-1792), called "Poldy," is often overlooked because his reign lasted only two years. Nevertheless, he had the most children of any of his siblings—sixteen, just like his parents—with the exception of Maria Carolina, who had eighteen. He stood in as proxy bridegroom at some of his sisters' weddings. Although his demeanor is described as being cold and intellectual, he was by far the handsomest of his surviving brothers and quite the ladies' man. His parents had intended for him to become a priest but as he approached manhood it became clear that he did not have a vocation. He eventually married Maria Luisa of Spain, the sweet pious mother of his sixteen children, the oldest of whom, Francis II, was to be the last Holy Roman Emperor. While Leopold displayed concern in his letters to Antoinette for her safety and that of her family, as the violence of the French Revolution escalated, he was not displeased to see the French monarchy destabilized. His son and heir would be much less concerned. It was only when the revolutionary government showed itself to be belligerent that Francis II realized that a Pandora's Box had been opened and the Habsburg Empire was threatened. Leopold's sudden and unexpected death in 1792 at age 45 stirred up rumors of poison. Antoinette felt his loss greatly.

The children considered part of the younger set of Habsburg siblings begins after Leopold, and includes

Maria Johanna, Maria Josepha, Maria Carolina, Ferdinand Charles, Maria Antonia and Maximilian Francis. By the time the six last children came along, Empress Maria Theresa and Emperor Francis Stephen were no longer as vigilant in making certain that their orders were followed and that their offspring were receiving the education and discipline they needed. There was no trouble, however, with **Archduchess Maria Johanna** (1750-1762) and **Archduchess Maria Josepha** (1751-1767), sweet and docile girls who were being brought up together. Then Johanna contracted a virulent case of smallpox after receiving an inoculation, which was known to occur. She died at age twelve, much to her family's horror, especially Josepha's. But soon Josepha was being groomed to marry Ferdinand of Naples and being painted in honor of the occasion, for she would become a queen. There is at least one portrait of Josepha in blue which is often mistaken for Antoinette; they both possessed the same delicate winsomeness so it is an easy mistake to make. Before Josepha embarked for Naples, she followed the custom of Habsburg brides and went with her mother to pray in the family vault in the Capuchin crypt. She fell ill with smallpox shortly thereafter; the Empress was convinced that it was because the tomb of Joseph's second wife, Josepha of Bavaria, who had recently died of the same dread disease, had not been sealed properly. This is probably not the case, since Josepha's rash appeared a mere two days after her visit to the crypt, and the incubation period for smallpox is usually about a week.[28] Josepha died on the day she was supposed to have left to be married, and her younger sister Maria Carolina was chosen to go in her place.

Archduke Ferdinand (1754-1806) took over the job of being the bridegroom at his sisters' proxy marriages after Leopold married and moved away. He himself was betrothed at age nine to Maria Beatrice d'Este, the only child and heir of the Duke of Modena. The couple was married in 1771 and thus Ferdinand became the founder of the House of Austria-Este. He and Maria Beatrice had ten children. He was granted the rule of Lombardy and they moved to Milan where they lived until Napoleon invaded. Ferdinand died in 1806; he never ruled in Modena but his oldest son did after the defeat of Napoleon.

Archduchess Maria Carolina (1752-1814), known as "Charlotte" in her family, was the sister closest to Antoine due to the fact that they were reared together by Countess Lerchenfeld and later by Countess Brandeis. Charlotte was the least pretty of the girls but the most like her mother in intelligence, temperament and political acumen. Even as Johanna and Josepha were well-behaved, Charlotte and Antoine were a pair of disobedient scamps, with Charlotte leading Antoine into all kinds of mischief and unruly behavior. Their antics came to an end in 1767, when it was decided to divide the two, as their mimicry and giggling were causing a stir at court. [29] Furthermore, Charlotte had to prepare to take Josepha's place as the bride of Ferdinand of Naples. She had originally been told she was to marry the Dauphin but now it was urgent that an Archduchess be sent to fill Josepha's place in Naples. The sisters, who never saw each other again after Charlotte left for Naples as Queen Maria Carolina, were heartbroken to be separated. It was particularly traumatic for Antoine, to whom Charlotte had been like a second little mother, and ever after she tried to recapture the relationship with her women friends. After Charlotte arrived in her new kingdom she wrote home about her dreadful wedding night and how being intimate with her new husband was a martyrdom.[30] Her experiences may have influenced Antoine to have a fearful view of marital relations. The marriage produced eighteen children and Maria Carolina eventually gained the upper hand with her husband. The sisters corresponded in Italian until Marie-Antoinette was imprisoned in the Temple, and even then Lady Hamilton, a close friend of the Queen of Naples, was able to bring messages back and forth between them.

Although Maria Carolina's life was not as tragic as her younger sister's, it was equally tumultuous. Like Antoinette, she was unpopular with her people. She dabbled in freemasonry and liberalism, turning against them when she heard of the violence of the French Revolution. From the surviving Mesdames de France, who came to see her after their escape, she heard details about some of Antoinette's ordeals. She did everything she could to withstand Napoleon and the Revolution, but ended her days in exile in Vienna, the last of Maria Theresa's children to die, in 1814. Three women in Maria Carolina's family were to marry into France. Her favorite granddaughter Marie-Louise of Austria became Empress of the French, and another granddaughter, her namesake Caroline of Naples, married the Duc de Berry. Her daughter Marie-Amélie married Louis-Philippe d'Orléans and became Queen of the French in 1830.

Our heroine, the **Archduchess Maria Antonia** (1755-1793), our Antoine, was not a great beauty like some of her older sisters but she was one of the girls most like the Empress. Her loveliness was in her graceful movements and in the charm of her personality. There had been no particular plans for Antoine's marriage—she was seen as an extra daughter—until Josepha died. Since Charlotte had to go Naples in Josepha's place, Antoine would have to go to France in Charlotte's place. When the Empress discovered that her youngest daughter was half-literate at age thirteen, it created a major crisis, and a bevy of tutors and beauty professionals rushed to the Hofburg to make the wild little Archduchess into a Dauphine. If she had married a prince of the empire and died quietly in her bed, then she would not be any better known than her sisters are. But because she married the Dauphin of France, with whom she was to share "the most beautiful crown in the world" [31] she became the most famous, or infamous, of them all.

As mentioned earlier, Antoinette was more like her mother than most people realize. They both loved dancing, riding, interior decorating, sleigh-riding and the simple joys of family life. Antoinette imitated her mother's refusal to drink alcohol. They both loved fresh air: in Vienna, the courtiers froze from the palace windows being opened in the dead of winter, which Maria Theresa insisted would prevent consumption. It seems the Empress did all the things she would later scold her daughter for, including mitigating etiquette, and ignoring convention. Maria Theresa used her frequent pregnancies as an excuse to modify the rules or escape them completely. Her close friends were exempt from etiquette and she made exceptions for people she liked: she had her old governess buried in the Capuchin crypt with the Habsburgs. She made herself accessible to her subjects, calling them "her children" and going among them incognito. How Antoinette would be scolded for doing the same things she had learned from watching her mother.

Archduke Francis Maximilian (1756-1801) was destined for the Church. He became the Archbishop and Elector of Cologne and Grand Master of the Teutonic Knights, among other titles. "Max," as he was called, was an early patron and benefactor of the young Beethoven. He visited his sister Antoinette at Versailles in the 1770's and was the occasion for diplomatic drama when the Princes of the Blood made a fuss about calling upon him. In the 1790's he was deputized by the Pope to officiate at Imperial coronations in Frankfurt, crowning his brother Leopold II and later his nephew Francis II. Max faced ill-health and political upheavals at the turn of the century which led to his death at age 45.

Perhaps the story of the childhood meeting of Mozart with Antoine and her family is partly apocryphal, but it has some elements worth reflecting upon. In one picture, the little Archduchess Antoine is shown leaning against her mother Empress Maria Theresa as the young prodigy is introduced. It is said that Mozart slipped and fell at one point; when Antoine ran forward to help him get up, he asked her to marry him. Mozart then ensconced himself upon the Empress' lap, and Maria Theresa kissed him. According to Mozart biographer Otto Jahn: "He was particularly proud of the Empress's notice. When they were encouraging him to play at a small German court, where there were to be some persons of high rank, he answered that he had played before the Empress, and was not at all afraid." [32] Later, when the boy Mozart was taken to Versailles, he tried to kiss Madame de Pompadour, the mistress of Louis XV, but La Pompadour pushed him away. He asked, "Who is this that does not want to kiss me?—the Empress kissed me."[33]

The French royal family was much more welcoming than the courtesan, however. Queen Marie fed Mozart with her own hands, speaking to him in German, while her daughters kissed him and visited with his family in the royal apartments.[34] He was obviously a very engaging little boy, to everyone but Madame de Pompadour, that is.[35]

2 THE MAID OF LORRAINE

"The Voice said to me: 'Go into France!' I could stay no longer." —St. Joan of Arc

Historian Chantal Thomas in her book *The Wicked Queen* discusses how royal princesses sent to marry in a foreign country for the sake of an alliance were no better than hostages. To quote:

> While still an adolescent, the fiancée was torn from her family, her country, her mother tongue. She found herself on enemy ground, delivered as the hostage in a pact concluded between her father and the father of her future lord and master. This traffic in foreign girls, who arrived decked out like icons and to whom all possible homages were made, was conducted with indifference and cynicism, motivated by purely political calculation. The girls were the guarantee of alliances whose stakes they did not understand. All they knew when they left their

childhood homes was that they would never return...Is it possible to imagine anyone more defenseless than these young exiles, confronted by a court protocol which in itself comprised a whole new language to learn on top of French? Their *faux pas* were mocked, their mistakes in French and their confusion over titles mimicked...Hostage princesses slept with one eye open. At court, that bastion of honors and flattery, scene of the latest dances, a state of war was forever brewing, and they risked being its first victims at any given moment.[1]

On the 21st of January, 1770, the betrothal ring arrived from France. How strange that on the same day twenty-three years later, Louis XVI would perish on the guillotine in the sight of all the people. The French ambassador the Marquis de Durfort arrived on April 16, 1770 with the official request for the hand of the Archduchess Maria Antonia from His Most Christian Majesty Louis XV. The next day, Antoine had to solemnly renounce all rights to the Austrian succession. On April 19, dressed in cloth of silver, her mother took her by hand and escorted her to the high altar of the Augustinian Church, a few steps away from the Hofburg in Vienna, to be married by proxy to the Dauphin. Her brother Archduke Ferdinand stood in for the far away Louis-Auguste. Afterwards the registry was signed; it is reported that the Empress Maria Theresa's hand trembled as she put her signature as a seal upon her daughter's nuptials. There is a holy card of St. John the Baptist, one of Antoinette's patron saints, which she gave to her main *femme de chambre*, Thérèse Durieux and her sister Barbe Durieux, as a token of farewell. The sisters were members of the Archduchess Antoine's entourage, who are mentioned in the letters of the Empress Maria Theresa to the Marquise d'Hennezel. She was to leave the maids behind in Austria. The card was given to them on the occasion of Antoine's marriage-by-proxy in April 1770 in Vienna in which she became the Dauphine of France. Her words to her maids are, in Latin and incorrect French:

Auspice Deo / Soyez persuadée chere Durieu que je penserai toujours a vous et que ne n'oubliere jamais les peines que vous avez eu avec moi c'est dont vous assure / votre tres fidele / Antoine Archiduchesse

Auspice Deo literally translates "Under the auspices of God" which means not only having faith in God but to trustingly place one's destiny in the hands of God. A rough translation of the rest of the message reads: "Be persuaded, dear Durieu, that I will think always of you and the pains you have taken with me, may this assure you. Your very faithful, Archduchess Antoine." One can only imagine the trouble the handmaid went through with her turbulent adolescent charge while preparing Antoine to leave her home forever and become a future Queen of France. [2]

After the sumptuous festivities, the Archduchess-Dauphine went on a monastic retreat for prayer and meditation, in which she also confessed and received Holy Communion. The retreat ended with a visit to her father's tomb in the crypt of the Capuchin monastery in Vienna. Yes, it was the same crypt where her sister Josepha allegedly contracted smallpox. On April 21, 1770, the youngest Archduchess left her family home forever. The moment came when she was to bid farewell to her mother. They had become particularly close in the last few months because the Empress had decided to keep Antoine constantly at her side, day and night, in order not to lose the opportunity to instruct the little bride in the duties of her new state in life. There was profuse weeping, not only on the part of the mother and her child, but the members of the imperial household, both servants and courtiers mourned the loss of their Archduchess, as did the citizens of Vienna.[3] She knelt for her mother's blessing. In the future she would see her sister Mimi and her brothers Joseph and Max; she would never see her mother or her other siblings again. Although this is what usually happened to princesses, Antoine had been ill-prepared, and found being torn from her family and homeland particularly traumatic. In some ways, she stopped maturing inside and remained psychologically at the age of fourteen, at least until she was forced to mature during the Revolution.

The Empress Maria Theresa wrote the following letter to the Dauphin Louis-Auguste after bidding a tearful farewell to her wayward Antoine on April 21, 1770.

Your bride, my dear Dauphin, has just left me. I do hope that she will cause your happiness. I have brought her up with the design that she should do so, because I have for some time foreseen that she would share your destiny. I have inspired her with an eager desire to do her duty to you, with a tender attachment to your person, with a resolution to be attentive to think and do everything which may please you. I have also been most careful to enjoin in her a tender devotion towards the Master of all Sovereigns, being thoroughly persuaded that we are but badly providing for the welfare of the nations which are entrusted to us, when we fail in our duty to Him who breaks sceptres and overthrows thrones according to his pleasure.

I say then to you, my dear Dauphin, as I say to my daughter: 'Cultivate your duties towards God. Seek to cause the happiness of the people over whom you will reign (it will be too soon, come when it may). Love the king, your grandfather; be humane like him; be always accessible to the unfortunate. If you behave in this manner, it is impossible that happiness can fail to be your lot.' My daughter will love you, I am certain, because I know her. But the more that I answer to you for her affection, and for her anxiety to please you, the more earnestly do I entreat you to vow to her the most sincere attachment.

Farewell, my dear Dauphin. May you be happy. I am bathed in tears. [4]

The following is an excerpt of the letter the Empress composed for her daughter on the same day. The letter has often been criticized as an example of Maria Theresa's controlling personality, but it is important to remember that she was not only a mother sending an immature fourteen-year-old into a den of iniquity but also a Sovereign who must answer for the peace of her empire if the treaty fell through due to Antoine's lack of upbringing. The advice she gives contains everything for a solid spiritual life in the world as well as what it means to be a Catholic princess.

RULES TO BE READ EVERY MONTH

When you waken, on rising, immediately go down on your knees and say your morning prayers. Then do a little religious reading, even if only for ten minutes or so without being distracted by anything or having spoken to anyone. Everything depends on a good beginning to the day and on the intention with which you begin. This can transform even indifferent actions into good and worthy ones. This is a point you must be quite firm about; its execution depends only on you, and it can influence your spiritual and temporal happiness. It is the same with evening prayers and examining your conscience; but I repeat, your morning prayers and a little religious reading are the most important matters to remember.

Always tell me what books you are reading. Pray as often as you can during the day, especially at Holy Mass. I hope that you will listen to it and learn from it every day, and go twice on Sundays and feast days, if that is the custom at your court. However much I would like you to occupy yourself in praying and with good reading, I would not however wish you to think of introducing something which is not customary in France: you must not claim that something is exceptional, nor cite what is customary here, nor ask for it to be imitated; on the contrary you must conform totally to what is the custom at your court.

Go after dinner if possible and especially on Sunday, to Vespers. Pray in the evening and when you pass in front of a church or a cross, but behave normally while doing so, as this does not prevent your heart concentrating on inner prayers, the presence of God being all that is necessary for this whatever the occasion; your incomparable father had that quality to perfection.

On entering a church, allow yourself to feel only great respect and do not let your curiosity run away with you, as this will lead to distractions. All eyes will be fixed on you; therefore do not give rise to talk. In France people behave in a very respectable way while in church and also while in public; you do not find, as you do here, oratories which are too comfortable, and which often give rise to carelessness in people's bearing and talk, which scandalizes many in France. Remain on your knees for as long as possible, that is the best way to give an example. Do not allow yourself to assume overly serious expressions as they can seem hypocritical; in that country especially, you must avoid that reproach.

Do not read any book, however indifferent it may be, without your confessor's approval: this is even more necessary in France than elsewhere; because there are always books being published there which seem pleasant and erudite, but behind this respectable façade they are pernicious with regard to religion and morals. I therefore beg you my daughter not to read any book, not even a pamphlet, without your confessor's permission; I expect you, my dear daughter to behave thus as a very real proof of love for your good mother, and respect for my advice, as I wish only for your salvation and happiness. Never forget the anniversary of your late dear father's death and mine when the time comes: until then you can pray for me on my birthday.[5]

The letter also urges the recitation of the Angelus, Holy Communion on feasts of the Mother of God, and forbearance in speaking of the Jesuits, who had recently been abolished from France.[6]

The trip to France continued as it began, with tears and farewells. Antoine stopped to see La Marianne at the Abbey of Klagenfurt in the Carinthian Alps and bade good-bye to her brother Joseph at Melk with its fabulous library. After journeying through the German lands, the former Antoine, now styled "Marie-Antoinette, Dauphine of France" arrived at the French border for the ordeal of the *remise* or handing over of the hostage/princess to her new countrymen. Contrary to popular belief, the Dauphine was not stripped naked in public but was privately dressed in French attire by her new ladies.[7] The ordeal was in bidding farewell to her Austrian retinue, some of whom had been close friends since childhood. She wept, knowing that there was no going back and that she would never see her mother again. Perhaps the most hair-raising part of the *remise* were the gruesome tapestries depicting the Greek myth of the calamitous and bloody marriage of Jason and Medea, a bizarre choice of decoration for welcoming a bridal party. One of the tapestries portrayed Jason's second wife being burned alive by her clothes. The teenager gasped and wondered aloud if it was an omen.[8] Baroness Oberkirch, a young lady from an Alsatian noble family, who would encounter Antoinette on and off over the years, was present at the handing over at the border and later at the formal entry into Strasbourg. The great Goethe was also present; both baroness and writer were appalled by the tapestries. However, the surroundings did not diminish the beauty of the Dauphine, who emerged from the pavilion arrayed in cloth of gold like the goddess of the dawn; the Baroness said that Antoinette looked "a thousand times more charming" in her new French clothes, describing her as having a lily and rose complexion and the Habsburg lip which gave her mouth an air of slight disdain, as well as being slender, graceful and stately in spite of her extreme youth.[9]

Following the consternation of having Medea inflicted upon her, Antoinette was rapturously received in Strasbourg by her new subjects, with a blaze of illuminations so that the entire city seemed to be aglow. Little boys dressed as Swiss guards escorted her into the city and little girls in traditional Alsatian costumes strewed flower petals before her. She spent the night in the episcopal palace as the guest of the Bishop-Cardinal Prince de Rohan. In the morning at the Cathedral she met the Bishop-Cardinal's nephew, the Prince-Bishop Louis de Rohan, who would himself become a Cardinal and would be persuaded to arrange the purchase of a certain necklace. It was Antoinette's first experience with the imperious Rohans, who were the premier family of France after the Bourbons. No doubt on that bright day in May the Cardinal and his nephew the Bishop were charm and chivalry incarnate. The scene at the Cathedral is poignantly described in Frances Mossiker's book *The Queen's Necklace*:

> Prince-Bishop Louis led her to the high altar. She knelt on the red velvet prie-dieu at the altar's base. Prince Louis lifted the monstrance for the benediction. While silvery notes of harp strings tinkled down from the lofty choir, these two were joined in sacred and intimate communion. His fine hand, with its jeweled bishop's ring, upraised to bestow God's blessing, her head bowed to receive it, they shared the sacrament of benediction—these two who were to destroy each other. [10]

However, at the moment the future appeared to be radiant. Strasbourg was a triumph for the fourteen year old Dauphine. The same enthusiastic welcome was repeated in every town the princess entered along the way to Paris, and the joy appeared to be genuine. In the meantime, an apprehensive Dauphin Louis-Auguste at Versailles was following his bride's progress via his maps, hoping that the ordeal of the wedding festivities would soon come and go. [11]

A day before meeting her husband, the princess bride stopped at Châlons where she was treated to a play. Although she followed along with the script in front of her, the child was obviously uneasy. To quote a letter to the Empress from Count Starhemburg, who was accompanying the new Dauphine: "All the while she made faces, bit her lips, held her fingers and her handkerchief in her nose, scratched her head constantly, leaned back on her chair, in sum, did not conduct herself as fittingly as I would have desired." [12] She grew more nervous as they approached their destination. The last stop was Soissons, and it was a Sunday so they rested.

There were many disgruntled people in France at that time; Louis XV, once called the Well-Beloved, was no longer popular due to being ruled by his courtesans, the latest of whom, according to gossip, had been a *bona fide* prostitute. All the kingdom's woes were blamed on the late Madame de Pompadour and the current Madame du Barry. Because of Madame de Pompadour, France had been dragged into the Seven Years War, which ended in a humiliating defeat by England and the loss of territories, including Canada. The French economy had never recovered from the loss. As it stood at the time, Madame du Barry had added to the tarnishing of the royal dignity, since she was the illegitimate daughter of a friar and a seamstress who, after a polished convent education, had worked briefly in a brothel. Never had a genuine prostitute been the king's *maitresse en titre*, and the entire court felt degraded, most especially the children and grandchildren of His Majesty. It brought to mind the prophecy that had heralded the coming of Jeanne d'Arc, the prophecy that said even as France had been lost by a woman, it would be saved by a virgin from Lorraine.[13] Thus a popular ditty spread through the land:

France,
It seems to be your destiny
To be subjugated to Woman
Your salvation came from the Maiden
Your death will come from the Whore. [14]

Thus the youngest daughter of Francis of Lorraine entered France bathed in the legend and mystique of

Jeanne d'Arc, the Maid of Lorraine, and like Jeanne great things were expected of her. From the beginning she was set up to be the virgin opposing the whore, but woe to her should she ever be perceived as a whore herself. Later, Antoinette would even don male attire, heightening the connection between herself and the Maid, *La Pucelle*, sent to save France. [15] In 1770, France did not need to be saved from the English but from economic ruin and moral decline. Like Jeanne d'Arc, Antoinette had the challenge of winning over the Dauphin, who in Antoinette's case was her fifteen year old bridegroom. Unlike the Maid of Lorraine, the Dauphine did not have heavenly voices to guide her, only her mother, writing from afar, her mother's ambassador Comte de Mery-Argenteau, and the tutor Abbé Vermond.

Furthermore, she had the additional problem of having a husband who had been strongly against marrying her. Louis-Auguste's late parents and his aunts, that is, the people whom he most respected, had been against the Austrian alliance, seeing it as the work of Madame de Pompadour and the godless Choiseul, who referred to young Louis and his brothers and sisters as the "Dresden knick-knacks."[16] By 1770 La Pompadour was dead, and in her place was Madame du Barry, who belonged to the anti-Austrian clique. Young Dauphin Louis-Auguste's aunt and godmother, the feisty old maid Madame Adélaïde, daughter of Louis XV, never let her godson forget that his bride was not only an enemy of France, but that she had been brought over by a middle class courtesan, La Pompadour, who also had reddish hair and was named "Antoinette."

The title "Dauphin" literally meant "dolphin" and its origins have become lost, although it had nothing to do with dolphins and is thought by some to date back to a Celtic phrase for "chief of a territory." [17] It was used to designate the rulers of various territories, none of which were near the ocean and most of which were mountainous. In 1343, the Dauphin of Viennois ceded his lands to the French crown, lands which eventually became known as the Dauphiné. Charles VI (1368-1422) was the first to grant the province Viennois and title of Dauphin to his eldest son and heir to the throne, although before it had belonged to various members of the French royal family. One of the first royal French heirs known as the Dauphin was the future Charles VII (1403-1461) who was aided by Joan of Arc. The official title was *Premier fils de France et Dauphin du Viennois* (First son of France and Dauphin of Viennois). When the heir was not the king's son or grandson he was not known as Dauphin, but as "Monsieur."

It had long been the custom at the French court to ride out to meet the bride. On May 14, 1770, Louis and Antoinette saw each other for the first time in the forest of Compiègne, just a few miles from the spot where Jeanne d'Arc had been captured by the Burgundians at the gates of the town of Compiègne. In the town was a Carmelite monastery, patronized by the late Queen Marie Leszczyńska and the princesses. The Polish Queen, her daughters, and her daughter-in-law Marie-Josèphe de Saxe, would visit the nuns in the cloister, bringing their sewing. Once when the Queen's feet were cold she asked the nuns to join her in a dance, and they did so. [18] In the future the new Dauphine would provide a dowry for a poor girl called Mademoiselle Lidoine who, as Mother Thérèse de Saint-Augustin, would lead the nuns to martyrdom during the Terror of 1794. But as Louis-Auguste and Antoinette bashfully peered at each other during those intial awkward moments, it was spring and the sun was shining. Louis-Auguste had been warned by his tutor the Duc de La Vauguyon to beware of the wiles of the female sex, so he remained aloof. He did not want to be ruled by a woman the way his grandfather was. Plus, his bride was little more than a child. Thus Antoinette had the easy task of winning over Louis XV, who immediately found her enchanting, as well as the monumental challenge of seducing his grandson, her own betrothed husband, who was determined not to become entrapped by her. All the while, she had hostile forces awaiting her first mistake.

At this point a few words are needed to describe the *château* which became Antoinette's home from May 1770 until October 1789. It is generally referred to by the French as a *château*, not as a "palace" or *palais*, because a *château* is by definition a country dwelling. After several harrowing childhood experiences in the Louvre-Tuileries' antique galleries and dark passageways, young Louis XIV wanted light, color, fresh air, gardens, fountains, lakes, forests, pageantry, hunting, and dancing. He chose his father Louis XIII's cherished hunting lodge at a tiny hamlet called Versailles and built around it like an oyster shell around a pearl. The rose-gold edifice which emerged over the years had the enchantment of an abode upon which a traveler in a Perrault fairy-tale might stumble by accident. Each gallery and each chamber was more exquisite than the next, peopled by courtiers and damsels in glittering array, all adhering to a complex code of etiquette like the steps of a ballet. Louis XIV liked order as well as beauty and he possessed the charisma and strength of personality to see that his wishes were carried out. Along with his personal qualities he also had money, hoarded for him in his youth by the ambitious Fouquet and later by the brilliant Colbert. After the court began to be established there in the late 1670's, Colbert made certain that Versailles was a showcase of French craftsmanship, with the finest of furniture, architecture, porcelain, silks, and fashions being on display to the diplomats and travelers who visited from all over Europe.

Versailles was open to French subjects as well, as long as they were decently attired, although beggars always managed to get inside, too. Merchants and craftsmen had their stalls for selling their goods, and visitors could do their shopping as if at the most glamorous mall in the world. They could also watch the royal family dine and wander into the state rooms and go just about anywhere except the Queen's room when she was bathing or dressing. They could watch the Queen and princesses in childbirth, though. The King and Queen and members of the royal family went about the crowds of Versailles with little practical protection, although all the gentlemen were armed with swords; only once in a century and a half did a madman try to assassinate the monarch, Louis XIV's great grandson Louis XV. It seems the Kings and Queens of France never felt they had to be protected from their own people. How everything was to change....

Towards the beginning of the eighteenth century, the Sun King was running out of money, not because of Versailles, or even because of his many mistresses and their children, but because of the series of ruinous wars which sapped the country of its man power and resources. Furthermore he had revoked the Edict of Nantes, which had granted protection to the Huguenots, those French Protestants who made up the bulk of the middle class, forcing most of them to emigrate. The economy was thus weakened on several fronts. Louis XIV was therefore one of the worst of kings as well as one of the greatest. He was great because he made France the strongest, most influential country in Europe. His failure was that in achieving the heights of glory he was simultaneously sowing the seeds of disaster, an economic and political disaster of epic proportions which would, generations later, be left to two teenagers to try to manage. For by the time Antoinette arrived at Versailles, the plumbing was antiquated, and extensive renovations were required in order to make the *château* more habitable. The outlying village of Trianon had been cleared away and was part of the park of Versailles, with two small villas with exquisite gardens, called Grand Trianon and Petit Trianon. Many of the trees of the park had become overgrown, and would receive extensive pruning and chopping down under Louis XVI. And under Antoinette, there would once more be a village at Trianon.

A word should also be said about the formidable etiquette which Antoinette would have to learn. The word "etiquette" literally meant "ticket" because of the slip of paper required in order to enter certain parts of the *château* in order to view the royals doing whatever they happened to be doing. The rituals and ceremonies of etiquette were part of the pageantry surrounding the monarch and every member of his family. Court etiquette originated as an extension of the liturgical rituals of the Catholic Church, particularly from the great monasteries which in the first centuries of the French kingdom and throughout the Middle Ages were instrumental in spreading learning and culture as well as peace and prosperity. Etiquette had become a means of maintaining the respect and the aura of majesty around the person of the monarch and took on a life of its own. As those who have watched the British production of *Downton Abbey* will recognize a few of the traditions as being endemic not only to Versailles but to stately private homes as well. For that matter, every monastery and religious house had its own customs and rituals which guided everyday behavior. At Versailles, members of the Royal Family were not allowed to pour a glass of water or reach for food. Meals, drinks, and garments had to be handed or served to them, usually on silver trays. Ladies at Versailles walked in a distinctive manner; they never lifted their feet so as not to step on the train of the woman in front of them. Antoinette excelled at what is called the "Versailles glide." A lady never held hands or linked arms with a gentleman, which was practically impossible anyway because of the wide skirts. Instead, a lady was to place her hand on top of the gentleman's bent arm as they strolled along. A lady and a gentleman were only allowed to touch each other's fingertips when promenading together in public.

The King and Queen always had a *fauteuil* (armchair) to sit on. In their presence, no one else was allowed an armchair, unless they were also a monarch. A chair with a back but no arms was allowed for those closest in rank to the king, such as his brother or children. The *tabouret*, a padded stool was awarded to those holding the rank of duke or duchess. Lesser ranking nobility would be expected to stand. A lady never sat with her back touching the back of the chair. People who wanted to speak to the King could not knock on his door. Knocking on doors was forbidden; since 1694, people scratched on doors with their little fingers, which caused many people to grow the nail on the pinky finger longer than the others. Only pages were allowed to open doors. If anyone desired to leave a room, they had to wait for the page to open the door. People entered a room according to rank, princes first, then officers of the court, and finally courtiers. The page opened both halves of the tall double door for a prince, but for lower ranked dignitaries, only one side would open. A young lady, even if married, always kept the door open if conversing with a gentleman not her husband or a member of her family. The Queen never sat at the same table with men not part of the Royal Family and she never walked about the palace alone, but always accompanied by two ladies-in-waiting. Such rules Antoinette would try to change or totally ignore when she became Queen.

On May 16, 1770 the Dauphin Louis-Auguste of France married Marie-Antoinette Archduchess of Austria. She spent the previous night at the *château* of La Muette. The Dauphin was already at Versailles because according to etiquette the bride and groom were not to sleep under the same roof until after the ceremony. There was a family supper with the King, his daughters, and her new ladies-in-waiting; she was also introduced to her new brothers-in-law, the Comtes de Provence and Artois, ages fourteen and twelve. Much to the disgust of Mesdames Tantes, Madame du Barry had been included by Louis XV, which confused and embarrassed the innocent bride. In the morning, the Dauphine left for Versailles at nine. When she arrived at the *château*, Louis XV received her on the ground-floor in the apartments of his late daughter-in-law, Marie-Josèphe de Saxe; they conversed for awhile. She also met her new sisters-in-law, Madame Clothilde, age eleven and Madame Élisabeth, who was six years old. She was presented with the jewels which by right belonged to every Dauphine. The bride was dressed in cloth of silver and white brocade, covered with diamonds and pearls, with wide hoops which overwhelmed her slender frame.[19] The gown has also been shown in pictures as lavender and other colors, from which one can guess it must have shimmered in the various lights. Unfortunately, the bodice did not fit properly, which may have been due to the natural growth of the bride as well as to the fact that Antoinette's back was slightly crooked so that one shoulder was higher than another. [20] Her later gowns had one shoulder padded. [21] Although every court dress had an open back, with the chemise showing through the lacings, the opening in Antoinette's gown was wider than etiquette allowed but there was little anyone could do at the last moment. The gown was later made into mass vestments which were lost in the Revolution.

The wedding party then convened in the apartments of the king where the procession was formed. The groom and his bride, their fingertips touching, processed to the Royal Chapel and to the high altar, followed by the Louis XV. They knelt together on a cushion placed on the steps of the sanctuary. The Archbishop of Rheims, Monseigneur de la Roche-Aymon, Grand Almoner, blessed them with holy water, and then blessed the thirteen pieces of gold and the wedding rings as well. Then the Dauphin took the ring and placed it on the fourth finger of the Dauphine, invoking the Three Persons of the Blessed Trinity. She gave him his ring in the same manner. The archbishop pronounced the nuptial benediction, and Mass began, with the choir chanting the motets of Ganzargue. At the *Our Father* a canopy of silver brocade was held over their heads and remained throughout the Communion and final blessing. As mass was concluded, the parish registry was presented to Louis XV at his *prie-dieu* for the King to sign. After the ceremony, a lightening storm struck. To quote Rocheterie:

> ….But despite the splendour of the celebrations and the promising aspect of the future at that moment, certain obstinate pessimists could not help regarding the rumbling of the storm as a menace from Heaven ; and the superstitious recalled that the young wife, in signing the marriage register, had let fall a blot of ink which had effaced half her name. [22]

It should be kept in mind that the new Dauphine was not used to signing her name "Marie-Antoinette." She was used to writing plain "Antoine" and must have hesitated before writing the rest of her new name just long enough to make the inkblot. Madame Campan, who was at the time the Reader to the Mesdames Tantes with the name of Mademoiselle Genet, recorded the impression the new Dauphine made on the French Royal Family in her memoirs:

The Dauphiness, then fifteen years of age, beaming with freshness, appeared to all eyes more than beautiful. Her walk partook at once of the dignity of the Princesses of her house, and of the grace of the French; her eyes were mild, her smile amiable. When she went to chapel, as soon as she had taken the first few steps in the long gallery, she discerned, all the way to its extremity, those persons whom she ought to salute with the consideration due to their rank; those on whom she should bestow an inclination of the head; and lastly, those who were to be satisfied with a smile, calculated to console them for not being entitled to greater honours.

Louis XV was enchanted with the young Dauphiness; all his conversation was about her graces, her vivacity, and the aptness of her repartees. She was yet more successful with the royal family when they beheld her shorn of the splendour of the diamonds with which she had been adorned during the first days of her marriage. When clothed in a light dress of gauze or taffety she was compared to the Venus dei Medici, and the Atalanta of the Marly Gardens. Poets sang her charms; painters attempted to copy her features. One artist's fancy led him to place the portrait of Marie Antoinette in the heart of a full-blown rose. His ingenious idea was rewarded by Louis XV. [23]

As Antonia Fraser notes in her biography of

Antoinette, the wedding of the Dauphin Louis-Auguste and "the Daughter of the Caesars" was the "finest royal wedding that anyone had ever seen; indeed, the King thought so himself."[24] Expectations for the young couple were higher than ever. The event was not only opulent but enchanting, with the palace illuminated by lanterns and shining from afar. All the court was assembled in finest array, and the climax of the festivities was a ball, to be held in the new Versailles opera house, built for the occasion, despite the specter of bankruptcy that yawned in the shadows like a bottomless abyss. The wedding dinner took place there on May 16, the day itself, as the new Dauphine had one of her first experiences of the *grand couvert*, that is, dining in public. As at every wedding, mishaps occurred, although in the case of Antoinette's wedding, as in just about everything in her life, the mishaps turned out to be cataclysmic. Thunder, rain and lightning on the night of the wedding postponed the fireworks display at Versailles. In Paris a fireworks display was held on May 30 in which an accident caused a stampede and hundreds of people were killed. Horrified, Louis and Antoinette gave their spending money for a month to relieve the injured and the survivors of those killed; the Dauphine visited as many of the afflicted in their homes as she could. [25]

Yet another, subtler disaster for Antoinette occurred at the grand ball on the night of May 19. Even at a ball, or I should say, especially at a ball, etiquette reigned. The dancers danced the minuet according to precedence: the royal family first, then the Princes of the Blood, followed by the dukes, the counts, and on down the ranks of the nobility. The minuet was a dance of complicated movements which had to be learned and practiced from childhood in order to master it; it was one of the last outward signs of nobility which separated the upper class from the rising *bourgeoisie*. Madame de

Brionne, a former mistress of Choiseul and his fellow Lorrainer, connived with Comte Mercy the Austrian ambassador to honor the Dauphine by allowing Madame de Brionne's daughter to dance immediately after the Princes of the Blood. Now Madame de Brionne had married a distant Lorraine relative of Antoinette's father, which made her daughter, the fifteen year old Anne-Charlotte de Lorraine de Brionne, Antoinette's cousin. Louis XV consented to the dance only to be faced with nearly two hundred courtiers threatening to boycott the ball, as word circulated that an obscure Lorraine relation was to take precedence over the great houses of the French nobility. Although the full boycott did not materialize, the ladies having spent too much on their gowns to forgo such an occasion, many refused to dance and others left early. The Dauphin's youngest brother, the twelve-year-old Comte d'Artois, danced the minuet twice, before and after Mademoiselle de Brionne, in an effort to cushion the perceived insult to the nobility of France, but the harm was done. It was seen as an effort of Antoinette to put her own relations ahead of the French people. This was ridiculous, since Antoinette had little to do with Madame de Brionne's project, through which that lady hoped to gain in social standing. However, in a letter to her mother, the Dauphine showed that she innocently approved of Mademoiselle de Brionne's dance, and thought of it as honoring her dead father, Francis of Lorraine.

However, as pointed out by Thomas E. Kaiser in his article "Ambiguous Identities,"[26]Antoinette mistakenly continued to support and advance the Brionne family in other affairs, ahead of those who saw themselves as more worthy of her interest due to rank. In doing so she was also favoring Choiseul, whom she credited with the happiness of being Dauphine, and later Queen, of France. To favor Choiseul in itself displeased both Louis

XV and Louis XVI, since the former minister had been dismissed by Louis XV, and Louis XVI saw the *choiseulistes* as his enemies. At any rate, she alienated potential allies due to her favors for the Lorraine-Brionne family, who only repaid her by shameful behavior. The Brionne son and heir, the dreadful Prince de Lambesc, whom Antoinette had showered with favors, in 1780 rode his carriage through a Eucharistic procession, injuring a priest and several other people. In 1785, Madame de Brionne herself betrayed the Queen by supporting Cardinal de Rohan during the Diamond Necklace fiasco. At Antoinette's trial, the Brionne family continued to haunt her, for she was asked if she planned to annex Lorraine to Austria, her favor for Lorrainers being well-known.

People often forget that in spite of France being an absolute monarchy there was much over which the sovereign had no control. For instance, when choosing members of the nobility for various court offices, the King or Queen traditionally could not choose whomever they wanted but had to make the appointment according to heredity and prestige. When fourteen-year-old Antoinette arrived in France the lady singled out to be her guide was not a warm, motherly person but the one who was next in line for such an exalted office. It was Anne-Claude-Louise d'Arpajon, Vicomtesse de Noailles, who had been the first lady-in-waiting to the late Queen Marie Leszczyńska and was therefore a stickler for etiquette. The Polish Queen had been strict about etiquette since she was the daughter of a dethroned king and later a neglected wife so she enforced the rules in order to maintain respect. Madame de Noailles tried to maintain the same standards in the household of the young Dauphine but to no avail. As Madame Campan shrewdly describes in her memoirs:

Marie-Antoinette, Daughter of the Caesars

While doing justice to the virtues of the Comtesse de Noailles, those sincerely attached to the Queen have always considered it as one of her earliest misfortunes not to have found, in the person of her adviser, a woman indulgent, enlightened, and administering good advice with that amiability which disposes young persons to follow it. The Comtesse de Noailles had nothing agreeable in her appearance; her demeanour was stiff and her mien severe. She was perfect mistress of etiquette; but she wearied the young Princess with it, without making her sensible of its importance. It would have been sufficient to represent to the Dauphiness that in France her dignity depended much upon customs not necessary at Vienna to secure the respect and love of the good and submissive Austrians for the imperial family; but the Dauphiness was perpetually tormented by the remonstrances of the Comtesse de Noailles, and at the same time was led by the Abbé de Vermond to ridicule both the lessons of etiquette and her who gave them. She preferred raillery to argument, and nicknamed the Comtesse de Noailles *Madame l'Etiquette*.[27]

Antoinette rebelled against the stringency of the etiquette, which she did not think was necessary, and as Queen she changed some of the rules. She also chose people for offices not from the usual noble families but based upon her liking of them and whether she thought them capable. It would amaze us how much resentment she caused among the nobles, resentment which her enemies put to work against her. Nevertheless, Madame de Noailles and her husband were loyal monarchists and died on the guillotine during the Revolution.

The wedding ring placed upon Antoinette's finger by Louis-Auguste came to have a strange history. In 1771, while washing her hands, the ring came off and disappeared. Shortly after the birth of her first child in 1778, a small package was sent to Antoinette by the Curé of the church of the Madeleine in Paris, containing her ring and a message, saying: "I have received under the seal of confession the ring which I send to your Majesty; with an avowal that it was stolen from you in 1771, in order to be used in sorceries, to prevent your having any children." Antoinette never sought to discover the identity of the pathetic person who had tried to use witchcraft to render her infertile.[28]

"Antoinette and Louis in their wedding clothes."

3 THE HOUSE OF BOURBON

"I am convinced that if I had to choose a husband from the three brothers, I would still prefer the one heaven gave me: his character is steadfast and although he is awkward, he is as attentive and as kind as possible to me."—Marie-Antoinette to Maria Theresa, 15 December 1775

In her letters to her mother, Antoinette writes fondly of her "two families," meaning the Habsburgs and the Bourbons[1] In spite of the warm way she describes Louis' family to her mother, referring to the Mesdames as "my aunts" and Louis' siblings as "my brothers and sisters," in keeping with the manner of the times, the Bourbons were a peculiar lot to her. The King's overt womanizing had triggered a backlash in his devout family and among many of the courtiers, so that they tended to retreat into Jansenist prudery and preoccupations with death. The expulsion of the Jesuit order and the rise of enlightenment freethinking, encouraged by the late Madame de Pompadour, caused many of the more conservative courtiers to mistrust the Austrian alliance and the Archduchess whom La Pompadour had plotted to bring to France. For her part, Antoinette regarded with suspicion and scorn anyone who was against the Austrian Alliance, while she respected and promoted those such as Choiseul, who had brought about the Alliance, in spite of his freethinking tendencies. In taking this course of action, she often found herself at odds with her husband, who detested Choiseul. It was no more than a child's way of seeing everything in black and white, and an attempt to promote Austrian interests as she had been bidden to do by her family. Along with politics, there were a thousand petty intrigues, jealousies and internecine rivalries within the Royal Family itself; although on a certain level they loved each other. The rivalry between Louis and his brothers was especially intense, as Antoinette would come to discover. On more than one occasion, Antoinette was known to have given thanks to God that she had married Louis and not Provence or Artois, who both were known to have tempers, although they were considered better looking than Louis, especially Artois, and a great deal more charming. But looks and charm are not everything. She obviously valued Louis' character, which contradicts the rumor that Antoinette was shallow.

A word must be said about the baptismal customs of the French Royal Family, particularly under the Bourbons. While most of the children were baptized privately the day of their birth, their formal christening ceremony was often postponed until they could walk and talk. During the reign of Henri IV, three of his children, including the future Louis XIII and the future Queen of Spain, were christened in an elaborate public ceremony, at which there were three fonts, several bishops, and numerous wax tapers, tapestries and silver tissue.[2] At private royal baptisms, the princes received their title, which represented the apanage or the lands and territories they would someday govern, with the exception of a child who was born a Dauphin. For the first few years of his life, Louis XVI was called nothing but "Berry", the Duc de Berry being the title he received on the day of his birth. At his christening a few years later, which he shared with his brothers and sisters, he formally received his Christian name of "Louis-Auguste."[3] The princesses would initially be called Madame la Première, or Petite Madame or Madame Royale, etc. until they in turn received their Christian names at their christening. This was to change under Louis XVI and Antoinette, whose children were born, baptized with water and christened with the holy oils all on the same day, receiving their Christian names and titles, too.[4] The custom of being formally and officially baptized within hours and days of birth, dressed in pure white, spread throughout France and all ranks of society.

Louis XV (1710-1774) was the grandfather of Antoinette's husband the Dauphin. A shy man with multiple insecurities, Louis XV adored his family, which did not prevent him from scandalizing them repeatedly by his lifestyle. Part of the old King's problem was that he had been an orphan, the only surviving son of the golden couple of Versailles, the young Duc and Duchesse de Bourgogne. His mother was the high-sprited and unruly Marie-Adélaïde de Savoy who, in spite of being spoiled by Louis XIV, grew up to be a charming consort of the future heir to the throne. Louis XV probably did not remember his mother, for she died of measles when he was two. He nearly died himself, for after his heartbroken father followed his mother to the grave, both Louis, then called the Duc d'Anjou and his older surviving brother, the Duc de Bretagne, fell ill. Louis' brother the Duc de Bretagne was killed by the doctors' overzealous bleeding. However, Madame de Ventadour, the royal governess, locked the toddler Louis away from the doctors and cared for him herself, saving his life. He emerged from his sickroom as the only surviving heir to the throne. When his great grandfather Louis XIV died on September 1, 1715, Louis XV began his reign at age five.

It is always hard being an orphan; it is particularly hard when the orphan is the titular head of the most powerful kingdom in Europe, without parents or even grandparents to watch over his best interests. Louis XV was placed in the care of the Regent, his cousin the Duc d'Orléans. As was the custom, when still a small boy, he was taken away from Madame de Ventadour and given over to the care of male tutors. He was physically well-cared for and received a fine education but it is said that the lack of feminine nurturing was something for which he later overcompensated. In the meantime, he was betrothed to the Infanta Mariana Victoria, his three-year-old Spanish cousin, who came to live at Versailles when Louis XV was eleven. The marriage never came to be, since when Louis was fifteen it was considered important for him to have a wife old enough to beget children. Not only were children a matter of import, but it was seen as crucial to find the teenager a wife before he fell under the spell of a mistress. A Polish princess, Marie Leszczyńska, was chosen. She was several years older than Louis but at the time it did not matter. Louis XV and his Queen were happy together for many years and ten children were born to them.

Much to his wife's heartbreak, Louis strayed, and strayed and strayed. In 1744, he repented while in the throes of a near fatal illness; his confessor insisted that he issue a public confession as well. The people of France, who had prayed for his healing, began to call him the "Well-Beloved." The King had also promised God during his illness that if he recovered he would rebuild the ruined church of St. Geneviève, dedicated to the patroness of Paris. Over the next several decades, a magnificent neo-classical church was built to house the relics of the shepherdess saint; sadly, during the Revolution, it was desecrated and turned into a mausoleum called the Panthéon.

At any rate, long before the church was even begun, Louis had fallen back into his old ways. In 1745, Jeanne-Antoinette Poisson, after first being tutored in etiquette, became his official mistress with the title of Madame la Marquise de Pompadour. The court was scandalized, not that the King had another mistress but that Madame de Pompadour was from a *bourgeois* family. It was one thing for the King to sin with an aristocrat; to sin with a commoner showed a complete lack of respect for his family, for his court and most of all, for his crown. In fact, the entire kingdom was degraded, in the eyes of many, especially in the eyes of the King's growing son and daughters. To her credit, the Marquise tried to get along with everybody, even the Queen. The prince and princesses despised her, calling her "Pom-Pom" and *Maman Putain* which means "Mama Whore." Louis XV ignored them; he found La Pompadour immensely entertaining for her wit, charm, and cultured mind. She became his best friend and most trusted advisor.

In matters of intimacy, the Marquise was said to have a cold temperament; after five years they gave up their sexual relationship although she continued to bear the name of *maitresse en titre*. To the disgust of many in the court, the King's valets began to procure young maidens for him.[5] A house called the Parc aux Cerfs was established in the town of Versailles for the girls to stay. It was on the site of what had been a "park of the stags" in Louis XIII's time. The King wanted young, innocent girls because it decreased the chances of contracting syphilis. Madame de Pompadour felt herself safe as the Parc aux Cerfs protected her from having potential rivals at Court. The King never went there but the girls were brought to him in the palace. After their time with the King they would be given a dowry and helped to marry well. The expense of such a harem did not help the depleted coffers of the state, and made the people lose respect for the crown.[6]

Such was Madame de Pompadour's influence in diplomatic matters that she was blamed for France's disgrace in the Seven Years War, and the loss of Canada to England. The Marquise patronized the arts and was known for her exquisite taste as well as her huge expenditures. She sponsored Voltaire, Diderot and other scions of the Enlightenment, much to the horror of the devout Royal Family. She engineered the expulsion of the Jesuits from France and rejoiced when the entire Order was banned by the Pope. Madame de Pompadour wielded more power than many a queen, but it all came to an end when she died of tuberculosis in 1764 at the age of forty-two. But before she died, she had maneuvered the King into the Austrian Alliance.

Four years later, Queen Marie died; Louis thought briefly of marrying again, and negotiations were made with Empress Maria Theresa for the hand of her daughter Archduchess Maria Elisabeth. But then he met Jeanne Bécu, the illegitimate daughter of a friar and a seamstress. Many whispered Jeanne had been a prostitute; the King went to extraordinary lengths to enoble her, including a mock marriage to the Comte du Barry. By this time, Louis XV's children were grown; his grandchildren, growing up. The Dauphin Louis-Ferdinand died in 1765, followed by his Dauphine, leaving behind a family of orphans, with an awkward young boy as heir to the throne of France.

Marie Leszczyńska (1703-1768) was the Queen of Louis XV. She was the last Queen of France before Antoinette. Marie tightened up the rigorous court etiquette that Antoinette later relaxed because it was so suffocating. The daughter of a dethroned monarch and wife of a blatantly unfaithful husband needed the highly ritualized pomp to maintain her rank more than did the "daughter of the Caesars." [7] Marie Leszczyńska's father was the ex-king of Poland and her early life was complicated by upheaval and exile. Yet for this very reason, she was chosen to be the bride of the teenaged Louis XV, because she had no political entanglements. Her father Stanislaus Leszczyński was delighted when a messenger from Versailles arrived to ask for his daughter's hand. At age twenty-two Marie married the sixteen-year-old King. She was pretty, devout, and had received an excellent education. They were happy and lived amicably together for about a decade; the Queen gave birth to ten children. Later, she was blamed for throwing Louis XV out of bed on certain holy days, but that may be only gossip. Perhaps she had a health issue; after giving birth to so many children it was not unlikely. At any rate, Louis began a career as a womanizer, his most famous mistress being, of course, Madame de Pompadour, who ruled France at his side.

Queen Marie quietly devoted herself to her faith and her family. Courtiers mocked her Polish ways and called her *La Polonaise* even as later they would call Antoinette *L'Autrichienne*. All of Marie's children were as religious as she was; her youngest daughter Madame Louise became a Carmelite nun and a Blessed of the Church. Some of her grandchildren were quite pious as well, especially Louis XVI, Madame Clothilde, and Madame Élisabeth. Clothilde was declared a Venerable and Louis XVI and Madame Élisabeth have been regarded as martyrs by many. When Marie died in 1768, two years before Antoinette's arrival in France, Louis XV sincerely mourned the mother of his children, and we hope he regretted causing her such pain with his infidelities.

Louis the Dauphin (1729-1765), christened Louis-Ferdinand, was the only surviving son of Louis XV and the father of three kings of France, including Louis XVI. The opposite of his father, he preferred books and music to hunting and dancing. He had a brother one year younger, Philippe, Duc d'Anjou, a beautiful boy who was painted by Barrière blowing bubbles. When he was sick his nurses put the dirt from the grave of Saint Médard in his food, in the hopes of curing him. In their misguided zeal they put in so much dirt the child experienced organ failure and died at age two in 1733. It was probably stories of such horrendous mishaps that made Antoinette determined to personally supervise the care of her children. As a teenager, Louis-Ferdinand had a brief marriage to the Spanish Infanta, Marie-Thérèse-Raphaëlle, with whom he was desperately in love, and she with him. Her death in childbirth drove him nearly out of his mind and it was with many tears that he consented to marry again. A dedicated Catholic and the leader of the Devout party at court, he encouraged the cult of the Sacred Heart of Jesus, in spite of ridicule from the sophisticated element. He did everything in his power to keep the Jesuits from being expelled from France, knowing that they were the best hope against the anti-Christian tendencies of the *philosophes* because of their emphasis on learning and the excellent schools which they ran. He and his second wife Marie-Josèphe de Saxe were deeply committed to each other and to the proper education and upbringing of their children. Louis-Ferdinand would take his children to view the local parish register, to see their names inscribed along with the names of the lowliest peasant children, to show them that all distinctions of rank vanish in the eyes of God.[8] He would also take them to see the peasant huts, so they could see how most of the French people lived. Louis-Ferdinand was only thirty-six years old when he passed away from tuberculosis, leaving a heartbroken wife Marie-Josèphe, who died not long afterwards, and five young children.

Louis-Ferdinand left his papers with his sister Madame Adélaïde, to be passed on to Louis-Auguste when he came of age or ascended the throne. It is strange how the oldest son of every generation of the Bourbon family died in youth or infancy before inheriting the crown, almost recalling the tenth plague of Egypt. Some claim it is because of Louis XIV's refusal to consecrate France to the Sacred Heart; it is beyond me to analyze the ways of the Almighty. Although Louis-Ferdinand had been dead for several years when Antoinette arrived, his was still a strong presence in the family, especially where his sisters and his eldest surviving son were concerned. Young Louis-Auguste did all he could to honor his father, receiving Holy Communion on the anniversary of his death, and trying to have the same political views, for he saw the late Dauphin as the model of the perfect Christian prince.

At a time when the French court was ruled by Madame de Pompadour and influenced by the *philosophes*, there came into the midst of such a loose and free-thinking environment a devout Catholic princess. Daughter of the Elector of Saxony, **Marie-Josèphe** (1731-1767) was destined to become the mother of three Kings of France. All in all, she bore thirteen children, losing several babies and children to early deaths, including the beloved Louis-Joseph, Duc de Burgogne, whose death from tuberculosis of the bone was to haunt Louis XVI, as well as possibly infecting him with the same disease.

Marie-Josèphe faced enormous challenges. In addition to a husband who was still in love with his first wife, the Dauphine had to contend with the anti-religious element at Versailles, which prevailed in spite of the pious queen and princesses. Little by little Marie-Josèphe won the love and respect of her husband as they worked together to educate their surviving children, focusing on a solid religious formation, while striving to maintain the Catholic faith at the court in spite of the blatant immorality of Louis XV. She made a point of visiting the Carmelite nuns of Compiègne with her mother-in-law Queen Marie; as they sewed clothes for the poor, the rough cloth used by the nuns often made Marie-Josèphe's fingers bleed. [9] With her restrained yet kindly and dignified manner, the Dauphine became greatly loved; it is said she even got on well with Madame de Pompadour. She helped to patch up disagreements between her husband and his father. Her nickname was "Pépa."

However, one thing that Marie-Josèphe took a stand against, other than the expulsion of the Jesuits, was the marriage of her son Louis-Auguste to one of daughters of Empress Maria Theresa of Austria. This is because Marie-Josèphe's mother was a Habsburg Archduchess, the daughter of Emperor Joseph I, Empress Maria Theresa's uncle, and Marie-Josèphe had always been told that Maria Theresa had stolen the throne from her mother. According to the Pragmatic Sanction of 1713, women could inherit the Habsburg lands, but Charles VI planned for the inheritance to go to his own daughter, Maria Theresa, not his older brother's daughters, who were consequently left out of the succession. As a result, Marie-Josèphe was suspicious of the Austrian alliance, not trusting her Habsburg relatives.

Marie-Josèphe cared for her husband Louis-Ferdinand in his fatal illness and followed him to the grave two years later in 1767. It was a great tragedy for her five remaining children, for whom the influence of such a strong mother was irreplaceable. Although Marie-Josèphe was against the Austrian alliance, her death before the arrival of Antoinette of Austria was unfortunate, since she of all people would have been most fitted to give loving guidance to her vivacious daughter-in-law, adrift in a foreign court. It was later said, however, that Antoinette's second son Louis-Charles bore a strong resemblance to his paternal grandmother, Marie-Josèphe de Saxe.[10]

The **Daughters of Louis XV**, later called "the Aunts" or "Mesdames Tantes" of Louis XVI, played a key part in the life of the court of France when Antoinette arrived, even those who were dead or gone away still made their presences felt. There is, alas, a tendency to lump them together, as eccentric elderly ladies surrounded by spoiled lap dogs. While the lap dogs were omnipresent, the Mesdames themselves each had unique qualities. Nattier painted them all at least once, but since the artist tended to make all women look similar it is sometimes difficult to get a sense of their individual personalities. The oldest and only married daughter of Louis XV and Queen Marie Leszczyńska was **Madame Louise-Élisabeth of France** (1727-1759), called Madame Royale and later the Duchess of Parma by marriage. She and her twin sister Madame Henriette, born on the Vigil of the Assumption, grew up during the happiest time of their parent's marriage. Élisabeth, known for her intelligence and confidence, was not a beauty but had her father's piercing dark eyes. To quote author Catherine Delors:

> On August 14, 1727, Queen Marie Leszczyńska gave birth to twin girls, the first born being Marie-Louise-Élisabeth, known as Madame Élisabeth, or simply, as the King's eldest daughter, Madame. Louis XV, who was only seventeen, had of course been hoping for a male heir, but he was nonetheless delighted by the birth of the girls. 'People said I could not have

children,' he went around repeating, 'and see, I made two!'

Élisabeth is his darling, his Babette. She has never been considered pretty, but she is bright, vivacious, willful. Yet dynastic politics lead Louis XV to arrange her marriage to her cousin, Philippe de Bourbon, younger son of the King of Spain. It is considered a mediocre match for a Fille de France ('Daughter of France') to marry a foreign prince unlikely to succeed to any throne, but Louis XV wants to reinforce the family ties with the Spanish Bourbons.

The bride is only twelve, and she is heartbroken when she must leave Versailles and her twin, Madame Henriette. 'Tis forever, my God, tis forever,' she sobs in the arms of her sister. Indeed it was often true at the time: as a rule a princess, once married abroad, never set foot again in her native country. That is, for instance, what happened to Marie-Antoinette. But, as we shall see, Madame Élisabeth will never allow herself to be bound by rules applicable to ordinary princesses.[11]

Élisabeth returned to France for visits, staying a year each time, so she became familiar with her sister-in-law the Dauphine and her nieces and nephews. To the disgust of her siblings, she befriended La Pompadour. Her husband Philippe inherited the Duchy of Parma from his mother and so he and Élisabeth went to live there, thus founding the House of Bourbon-Parma. Their oldest daughter Isabelle married Marie-Antoinette's brother Joseph and their only son and heir Ferdinand married Antoinette's sister Maria Amalia. On her final trip to Versailles, Élisabeth died of smallpox in 1759 and was buried in the royal crypt at Saint Denis next to her twin sister.

Madame Anne-Henriette (1727-1752) was the fraternal twin of Madame Élisabeth. Her short life left an indelible mark on the court for her quiet and reserved but strong personality. Devoted to music, she was a gifted cellist; Nattier painted her playing her favorite instrument. With an exquisite appearance and the gift of conversation, she was quite close to her father the King, presiding at her father's small suppers and *soirées*. Her life, however, was marked by disappointments. After suffering the separation from her twin, she fell in love with her second cousin Louis-Philippe, Duc de Chartres, heir to the dukedom of Orléans. The future father of Philippe Egalité returned her love, but Louis XV himself would not countenance the match, as he was reluctant to strengthen the claim that the Orléans family had to the throne by giving them one of his daughters. He also feared offending the Spanish Bourbons, who also were in line to inherit the French crown. The lovers were parted. Henriette rejoiced when her sister Madame Élisabeth returned to France for visits, but the friendship of Élisabeth with La Pompadour caused a rift between the twins. It was Madame Henriette along with the Dauphin and Madame Adélaïde who called the mistress *Maman Putain* or "Mama Whore" and they saw Élisabeth's partiality as an offense to their already outraged mother the Queen. Henriette died of smallpox at the age of twenty-four; the tomb she was to share with her twin at the Basilica of Saint Denis was desecrated during the Revolution.

In the late 1730's, Louis XV's finance minister Cardinal Fleury convinced him that the cost of rearing all of his daughters at court was growing too expensive. It was decided therefore to send the five youngest children, including the baby Madame Louise, to the Benedictine Abbey of Fontevraud in Normandy to be brought up. As Adélaïde, Victoire, Sophie, Thérèse, and

Louise were being made ready to travel, six year old Adélaïde began to have a tantrum, begging not to be sent away. Her parents relented and so **Madame Adélaïde** (1732-1800) grew up at Versailles. Of the daughters of Louis XV, she was one of the most comely and ambitious. After her sister Henriette's death, Adélaïde became the sister with whom her father rode and talked. It caused the evil-minded to spread a rumor that the King had an incestuous relationship with his own daughter and that she was the mother of his illegitimate son the Comte de Narbonne. No serious historian has ever given credence to the story. But it shows that Antoinette was not alone in being targeted with grotesque libels.

Adélaïde became a generous benefactress of many charities for the poor and a patroness of the arts, particularly of women artists. She never married because there was at the time no prince of high enough rank for a Daughter of France. Louis XV enjoyed bestowing funny nicknames on his children and for some inexpicable reason Adélaïde was dubbed *Loque* ("Rags.") Madame Campan notes in her memoirs that the Princess had an abrupt, domineering manner and a choleric temper, as well as "a most insatiable desire to learn: she was taught to play on all the instruments, from the French horn…to the Jew's harp."[12] In addition to music, Madame Adélaïde occupied herself with the study of Italian, English, calculus, painting, the potter's wheel and watchmaking. Working with her brother the Dauphin, she was head of the Devout Party and was strongly against La Pompadour and all her works, including the Austrian Alliance. When her brother and his wife died, she tried to mother his orphaned children. The young Duc de Berry (Louis XVI) was very much under her spell. Worried that Berry was too quiet, Madame Adélaïde once told him to run, shout, and break anything he wanted in her apartments.[13]

After the death of her mother the Queen, Adélaïde was the highest ranking lady at the French court, and remained so until the arrival of Antoinette. It has been claimed that she coined the phrase *L'Auchrichienne* to describe her nephew's foreign wife. Her relationship with Antoinette was always a complex one. On the surface Adélaïde displayed loving concern for Antoinette, giving her the key to the apartments of the Mesdames, and being a font of motherly advice. In her role of aunt she was probably sincere. In her role of princess and politician she was threatened and worried by the effervescent and effortlessly beguiling teenager, who in her view imperiled not only the equilibrium of the Dauphin but might possibly acquire influence with the King himself. Ironically, Madame du Barry was likewise menaced by the pretty new Dauphine, who showed by her pert answers that she was quite capable of quashing any rivals to her position as First Lady of France. The fact that Madame Adélaïde adroitly tried to use Antoinette to humiliate La Barry by encouraging the princess to snub the concubine, thereby driving a wedge between Antoinette and Louis XV, shows that Adélaïde was cunning and determined when it came to games of power. She also built a rampart between Antoinette and her husband by keeping young Louis from even trying to consummate the marriage for years, thus isolating the Austrian girl and neutralizing any influence she might have had. All of this was to backfire, of course, and become part of the tragedy of the fall of the monarchy. Adélaïde herself was to die in exile in a faraway land, the last of the children of Louis XV amd Marie Leszczyńska.

Madame Victoire (1733-1799) was five when she was sent from home to live at the medieval Abbey of Fontevraud with her three little sisters. The Abbey was famous for being the burial place of the first Plantagenet king of England, Henry II and his Queen, Eleanor of Aquitaine, as well as their son Richard I. Although French princesses had been educated there for centuries, it is still odd that such small girls were sent so far from home when the excellent school of Saint Cyr, founded by the second wife of Louis XIV for the sole purpose of educating aristocratic young ladies, was practically on the grounds of Versailles. We can only guess that the drafty Norman monastery offered a less expensive tuition than the stylish girls' school. The princesses were nevertheless accompanied by an extensive entourage, including a steward, ten maids, twelve bodyguards, a policeman, a dancing master and a music master. They had several carriages, coachmen, postilions, grooms, outriders, thirty-two horses and four donkeys. The Abbess herself served them at table, having been elevated to the rank of Duchess so as to be in accord with etiquette. They had, however, no doctor, which was to have tragic repercussions. In 1744, Madame Thérèse, eight years old, contracted smallpox; there was no one to give her medical care but the local barber. [14] The little girl died and was buried with the Plantagenets. Whenever she transgressed the rules of the Abbey, Madame Victoire was sent to pray among the tombs as a penance, which for the rest of her life caused her to struggle with "paroxysms of terror"[15] which in modern times we might interpret as panic attacks.

When her education was completed, Victoire returned to Versailles at age fifteen to take up her role as a Daughter of France. For Victoire, this meant being ruled by Adélaïde, and together they acted as patronesses of the arts and sponsored many charities. Victoire was particularly generous with all that she had. Of nervous temperament, she found solace in her food, and struggled during Lent when it came to giving up her favorite dishes. This may explain the nickname her father gave her: *Coche* or "Old Sow." Madame Campan tells the story of how a visiting bishop soothed Madame Victoire's scruples by telling her she was not required to abstain from her beloved waterfowl, as it was considered more fish than fowl.[16] She grew plump; her dark beauty, inherited from her father as seen in the Nattier portraits, became a memory. Victoire was devastated when her youngest sister Louise became a nun. In the end, she was one of the last of her sisters to die, witnessing all the disasters which were to overtake her House, scattering and killing most of her family.

One of the many advantages of having the younger princesses brought up in a monastery is that for ever after any eccentricities they displayed could be blamed upon their early existence as convent boarders. Thus when **Madame Sophie** of France (1734-1782) displayed bashfulness by not looking people in the eye, it is forgotten that her father Louis XV also struggled with shyness, and was attributed solely to her years of monastic seclusion. Like Victoire, who also survived Fontevraud, Sophie returned to court at age fifteen. Madame Campan, who was Reader to the Mesdames, has harsh words for Madame Sophie in her memoirs, depicting her as "ugly" and generally bizarre beyond words, scurrying from place to place with sideway glances like a rabbit.[17] However, as Madame Delors points out, Madame Campan's portrayal of Sophie should be taken with circumscription. To quote:

> Madame Campan herself gives us the key to her animosity towards Sophie: the princess 'read alone.' That is, she didn't need Madame Campan's services as a Reader. Imagine if every princess had shown similar insolence! Madame Campan, heaven forbid, would have become obsolete. She took her revenge, a petty one, by leaving us this venomous portrait of the

princess.[18]

For reasons perhaps known only to himself, Louis XV called her *Graille* or "Scrap." She especially dreaded thunderstorms. For many years, a portrait of Madame Sophie by Lié-Louis Périn-Salbreux was considered to be of Antoinette, but it was finally recognized by the unique parquet design on the floor from Madame Sophie's apartments. The gown, too, is not fashionable and would never have been worn by the style-conscious twenty-one year old Queen. The dark eyes are certainly not those of Antoinette.[19] Louis XVI held all of his aunts in high regard, and after Sophie died of dropsy in 1782 while still in her forties, the King and Queen named their youngest daughter after her. There is speculation based upon her behaviors that Sophie may have had a mild form of Asperger's syndrome, which some think her nephew Louis XVI also had. In that case, the behaviors had nothing to do with growing up in a monastery but were purely neurological.

Madame Louise-Marie of France (1737-1787), also known as Blessed Thérèse de Saint-Augustin, was the youngest daughter of King Louis XV and Queen Marie Leszczynska. The descendant of Saint Louis, she was later to become the spiritual daughter of Saint Teresa of Avila. Like her sisters she was reared by the Benedictines. She managed to glean the best from both monastic life and from court life: a disciplined but warm personality, radiant with the love of God, as well as a strong sense of *noblesse-oblige* towards the disadvantaged. Only a babe-in-arms when she was sent to Fontevraud, her nature was bolder than her sisters, as exemplified by the manner in which she determinedly tried to climb out of her crib as a toddler, only to fall on the stone floor and be found unconscious by the nurse.[20] The same surgeon-barber who later presided over the death of Madame Thérèse was summoned and in spite of his insistence that the princess was uninjured, as she learned to walk it became clear that her body leaned to the left and her back was slightly hunched as if with scoliosis.[21] None of the physical damage hindered the expansion of her kindly disposition; as her mother the Queen wrote of her: "I have never seen so sweet, so touching a face as the little one's, though it is pinched with sadness. There is something moving, gentle, and spiritual about her."[23]

Returning to Versailles as a young teenager, her father gave her the nickname of *Chiffe* or "bad silk." Louise visited the Carmelites with her mother and longed to become a nun. There was a plan to marry her off to Bonnie Prince Charlie, but it came to nothing. Before entering the cloister, she tried to assist the Jesuits who had been abolished from France. Knowing she would have limited access to books once she was in the monastery, she had Madame Campan read for five hours a day works of history, an indulgence for whch she later apologized to the Reader.[24] She was asked by Archbishop Beaumont to postpone her entry into Carmel for several years, due to the many deaths in her family; the prelate knowing that the loss of Madame Louise to the cloister would be more than her surviving sisters could bear.[25]

In 1770, at age thirty-three, Louise chose the poorest and most rigorous Carmelite monastery in France, that of Saint Denis, very close to the Basilica where the Princess' mother Queen Marie was buried. There she begged to be treated the same as the rest of the nuns. Although she had prepared herself for the hardships of monastic life, what she found most difficult was using a certain narrow and steep staircase. The princess was used to being escorted up and down the wide, shallow stairs of the palace.[26] In spite of the steep stairs, and the mockery of persons such as Voltaire, Louise persevered in her calling. After six months, she was given the veil by the papal nuncio, assisted by the young Dauphine Antoinette, her nephew's bride, who was deeply moved by the clothing ceremony and was close to sobbing aloud. The mantle used at the clothing had belonged to the great Holy Mother St. Teresa herself, lent to the Carmel of St. Denis by the Carmel of the Rue de Saint-Jacques in Paris. Louise was thenceforth called Soeur Thérèse de Saint-Augustin. A year later, on September 12, the Feast of the Holy Name of Mary, the novice pronounced her vows.[27] The bells of the monastery began to peal, and then those of the Basilica and parish churches and soon the bells all over France were ringing for joy that Louis XV's daughter had made an oblation of her life to God. Her mission was to pray for the salvation of France and of France's King.

After her arrival at Compiègne, Antoinette had asked to be taken to meet Madame Louise at the Carmel of Saint Denis on May 15, 1770, the eve of her wedding. The Dauphine threw herself into the arms of her new aunt, saying: "I feel that I have an infinite need of your prayers. I shall come again soon."[28] It was the beginning of a close relationship, in which Antoinette would often visit the Carmel, sometimes alone and sometimes with her husband, to seek the prayers of Madame Louise. In her turn, Madame Louise would tell Antoinette about any persons who needed assistance. She often petitioned Antoinette for dowries for impoverished young ladies who wanted to become nuns. One young girl, Mademoiselle Lidoine, to whom the Dauphine gave a dowry at Madame Louise's plea, became the prioress who led the Blessed Martyrs of Compiègne to the scaffold on July 17, 1794. When she became a mother at last, Antoinette brought her children to meet the nun, and her daughter she prepared by giving the child a doll dressed in the Carmelite habit. A phrase in Madame Campan's anecdotes, which did not appear in the original memoirs, quotes Antoinette calling Madame Louise "the most intriguing little Carmelite in the kingdom." Since the quote was not part of the original work, perhaps it was added by editors of later editions. At any rate, it seems unlikely that Antoinette would accuse her husband's venerable aunt of being an "intriguer."[29] Madame Louise, Blessed Thérèse, died on December 23, 1787, after having inhaled a strange powder that was most likely poisoned. The powder arrived at the Carmel in an anonymous package with some feathers and a note with the words "the relics of the Eternal Father." Who would want to kill Madame Louise? It seems she had many enemies among those who plotted the Revolution. Her last words were: "Full gallop, into heaven!" Louis XVI and Antoinette must have felt her loss keenly, for hers was a wise voice among many foolish ones.

The **Dauphin Louis-Auguste, Duc de Berry**, the future Louis XVI, was born on August 23, 1754. According to the custom in the House of Bourbon, he was baptized at birth but not christened with the holy oils until a later formal ceremony. Like all the boys in the Bourbon family, "Louis" was one of his names. "Auguste" was the second name of St. Louis IX of France and so Berry was doubly named for the sainted crusader-king.[30] August 25, the feast of St. Louis, was his name-day, and kept with special festivity when he became King. Louis-Auguste and his brothers and sisters were the last generation of French royals to grow up at Versailles. There were several siblings who did not survive childhood, including the delightful Marie-Zéphyrine, who died in 1755 at age five, and Louis-Joseph-Xavier, the Duc de Bourgogne, who passed away after an agonizing struggle with tuberculosis of the bone at age nine in 1761. Burgogne, as he was called, had been considered the hope of the dynasty and of France, since he was fearless and clever, energetic and daring, another Louis XIV it seemed. However, he fell from a toy horse and shortly afterwards began to limp; it was found he had a tumor in his thigh. An operation ensued but the boy could no longer walk; consumption had set in. Utterly beloved by his parents and grandparents, the very thought of Bourgogne's death was met with total horror, and every medical option was taken in order to spare his life. His younger brother, the bashful, near-sighted Louis-Auguste, Duc de Berry, had been seen as the unhealthy, extra son. The doctors thought that Berry's presence might cheer his dying older brother in the sick room. Berry was removed from the nusery and his governess Madame "Maman" Marsan at age five. He was put through the breeching ceremony in which he was dressed in pants for the first time and handed over to the men to bring up. His governor, the Duc de la Vauguyon, dubbed Bourgogne *le Fin* (the Clever) and Berry *le Faible* (the Weak). Berry was made to sit with his dying brother. Death from tuberculosis is not pretty to watch; it was surely a tortuous experience for a small boy, especially since he himself contracted tuberculosis and began to cough up blood. But Berry was regarded as not likely to live to adulthood and so worth the sacrifice if it helped Bourgogne. Bourgogne died anyway; the parents were overwhelmed by grief. Berry managed to survive with the proper care. Nevertheless, tuberculosis is a disease which can remain inactive for many years but can later recur. It can have many side effects, including depression, as well as stimulating a voracious appetite; both Louis and his brother Provence struggled with obesity which may have been induced by a tubucular condition.[31] The tuberculosis would come back to haunt him, infecting at least two of his children, including the son he would name Louis-Joseph-Xavier after his older brother.

At the death of his father in 1765, Berry became Dauphin. By the standards of the era, Louis-Auguste could be considered handsome. He had thick dark eyebrows, an aquiline Bourbon nose, deep set, large blue-grey eyes, and a full sensual mouth. The Duchess of Northumberland, a friend of Choiseul's, was at Versailles for Louis and Antoinette's wedding; she said: "The Dauphin disappointed me much. I expected him to be horrid but I really liked his aspect. He is tall and slender with a *très intéressant* figure and he seems witty. He has a quite pale complexion and eyes. He has a mass of fair hair very well planted."[32] As a teenager, Louis-Auguste was tall and thin, soon to be the tallest man at Court, and enjoyed intense physical exercise, such as hunting and hammering at his forge. His physical strength became legendary; he could lift a shovel to shoulder height with a young boy standing on the end of it. Possessing a hardy appetite, he developed a paunch as he approached his thirties. He was often clumsy and diffident in his manner although not without dignity in his bearing. The efforts of his detractors to make him unattractive and therefore unlovable serve the purpose of giving his wife an "excuse" for chronic infidelity, another highly-popularized myth.

There can occasionally be seen casual speculation on the internet as to whether Louis-Auguste had what we now call Asperger's syndrome. It is virtually impossible to accurately diagnose a dead person. In Louis-Auguste's case it is important to recognize that in the face of the loss of his parents and the seeming rejection by his grandfather, he became emotionally closed-off, as well as secretive. As a teenager, much of his boorish behavior was probably deliberate and the only way he had to rebel against what he saw as the artificial and hypocritical behavior of his elders. From what we know about Asperger's, however, including the tendency to poor social skills, and the resultant social isolation and frustration, as well as the intense absorption in hobbies; the symptoms can certainly be applied to the adolescent Louis-Auguste. Persons with Asperger's are also often characterized by wearing shabby clothes, because they choose comfort over appearances. There is the love of structure, rules and lists, accompanied by heightened intellectual capacities, all of which are characteristic of Louis-Auguste. Most of all, the tendency to stand out as an ungraceful genius, or "geek" as we would call it, and have sudden bursts of rough behavior, describe the husband of Antoinette.[33]

Louis-Auguste was notoriously involved with hunting and lock-smithing. He was painfully shy and awkward, but he could also display a ferocious temper.[34] He and his brothers sometimes fought, using coarse language. During the Revolution, the American diplomat and statesman Gouveneur Morris recorded in his private diary a morbid rumor told to him by his friend, Madame de Flahaut, that

> ...The King [Louis XVI] is by Nature cruel and base. An Instance of his Cruelty among others is that he used to spit and roast live Cats. In riding with my friend I tell her that I cannot believe such Things. She tells me that when young he was guilty of such Things. That he is very brutal and nasty, which she attributes principally to a bad Education. His brutality once led him so far while Dauphin as to beat his Wife, for which he was exiled four Days by his Grandfather Louis XV. Untill very lately he always used to [spit] in his hand as being more convenient. It is no Wonder that such a Beast should be dethroned.[35]

Perhaps it should be kept in mind that Madame de Flahaut was at the time the mistress of the Bishop of Autun, better known as the infamous and shady revolutionary Charles-Maurice de Talleyrand-Perigord. Mr. Morris, when not enjoying the company of his own mistress, was hobnobbing with aristocratic revolutionary agitators, such as the Lafayettes; from such people he could hardly hear anything good about either Louis XVI or Antoinette. Although there were times when Mr. Morris did reach out in genuine compassion to the King in his troubles, the circles he frequented were not immune to the gossip sown by Louis-Auguste's brother, the Comte de Provence. The roasted cat story and the wife-beating story sound like the kind of calumnies Provence and his wife, known as Monsieur and Madame, would spread, even printing pamphlets on their private press. The idea of Louis beating Antoinette is ludicrous and has not been given credence by most serious biographers. To strike a woman was against Louis' code of chivalry, which he would observe in a crisis by refusing to allow his guards to fire on a crowd where there were women.

Louis-Auguste has been described as being dirty and malodorous; granted that he was an active young man, not a powdered and pampered courtier, and working with metal was not clean work; neither were his daily riding and hunting. Under Antoinette's influence he began bathing every day, as she did. Among his collection of eccentricities was his passion for building and construction, including masonry and carpentry. Not only would he be constantly remodeling his private apartments but he would stop and help the workmen around the palace with their mortar and lifting heavy stones, boards and tiles.[36] He was informal and blunt. He annoyed his first cousin Ferdinand of Parma for writing in a familiar way without first asking to write without etiquette.[37] When he spoke, he mumbled in two registers, uncontrollably shifting between a grating falsetto and a rough base. He sang dreadfully out of tune and had no sense of music in general. Later, he trained himself to speak in public effectively. He had a loud discordant laugh which was known to frighten newcomers to Versailles. When engaged in conversation, he had a bad habit, probably caused by his nearsightedness, of standing too close to people, so that they had to back away to keep him from stepping on their feet.[38] He obviously did not always pick up on social cues. His governor Monsieur de la Vauguyon was widely blamed for neglecting his training, especially by the *choiseulistes*; Antoinette herself blamed Vauguyon for all of Louis-Auguste's problems. She later took total credit for his improved behaviors.[39] He caused consternation by hunting the wild cats on the roof at night when their yowling kept him awake.[40] He was profoundly modest and self-effacing about his own talents and his own worth. In spite of it all he grew into a "brave and righteous man." [41]

All one has to do is read anything he wrote to see that Louis XVI was an intelligent young man. He could read and speak several foreign languages, knew Latin as well as his native tongue, was a skilled amateur cartographer, and enjoyed the tragedies of Shakespeare as well as of the great French dramatists Corneille and Racine. He kept a painting of Erasmus in his private apartments. He was fascinated with scientific inventions, which as King he did a great deal to promote. As a teenager he wrote and published a book of maxims for rulers, setting the type himself on his Tante Adélaïde's printing press. He presented a beautifully bound copy to Louis XV, his *Papa-roi*. The King, however, saw it as a reproach to himself and ordered the type broken up.[42]

Most of all, Louis was a dedicated Roman Catholic, keeping track of his Confession and Communion days in his journal. He was made Grand Master of the Military Order of St. Lazarus and Our Lady of Mount Carmel as a boy, taking seriously his obligations as a lay military Carmelite, daily praying the Divine Office and attending regular meetings.[43] He was dedicated to seeing that his father's wishes for France were carried out, and interiorly rebelled against being forced into a marriage that his father would not have approved of.[44]

Louis-Stanislas-Xavier (1755-1824), the **Comte de Provence,** was a younger brother of Louis-Auguste, and often his nemesis. A handsome young man, his eyes radiated intelligence. His appearance was gradually marred by his excessive weight as well as a skin disease, which caused hair loss and was unpleasant to look upon.[45] Called by Monsieur de la Vauguyon *le Faux* (the False) Provence was better able to shine than Louis-Auguste, convincing everyone of his cleverness. He knew several languages well and his Latin was so good he could have been a Latin professor. Possessing a quick mind, he was often frustrated by his older brother's slowness and clumsiness. In one incident, Louis-Auguste broke a porcelain knick-knack that belonged to Provence, who was so angry he struck him, and Antoinette had to intervene to stop a fight. A congenital malformation of the hips made it impossible for him to ride and he had to follow the hunts in a cabriolet. In spite of his inability to sit a horse, his stables were full of exquisite mounts. In 1775, he invested in the manufacture of Cligancourt porcelain by Deruelle and it became known as the "Porcelain of Monsieur"— "Monsieur" being his title after Louis XVI began his reign. Later he had a problem with gout, but then he was a *gourmande*, relishing the delights of the table. His chef at Versailles was equal to none. Provence was a consummate plotter. His printing press at Versailles produced pamphlets against Louis XVI and Antoinette. Provence and his wife, Marie-Joséphine de Savoie, were certainly responsible for circulating the gossip about Antoinette. Provence spent his life jockeying for power by trying to undermine his brother. He especially intrigued against Louis XVI during the Revolution, corresponding with revolutionaries. How much his plotting contributed to the fall of the monarchy is explored in the novel *Madame Royale*.

Charles-Philippe (1757-1836), the **Comte d'Artois**, called *le Franc* (the Candid) by Monsieur de la Vauguyon, inherited his grandfather's good looks and careless charm with the ladies. A superb dancer, he was often asked by Louis to dance with Antoinette at balls. Gossip would make him her lover, but the two had nothing but a brotherly and sisterly relationship, sharing many interests such as gardening, gambling, acting and horse-racing. He later became part of her coterie. Artois married Marie-Thérèse de Savoie in 1773, the younger sister of Provence's wife. They had four children in all, two girls and two boys. Both girls died as infants. The boys were Louis-Antoine, the Duc d'Angoulême and Charles-Ferdinand, the Duc de Berry. The birth of Louis-Antoine in 1775 caused great distress and embarrassment for Antoinette since she did not yet have children. In the meantime, Artois chased Madame de Polastron, one of Antoinette's ladies, which will be discussed in detail later. Artois was blatantly unfaithful to his wife, who eventually turned to religion as the years went on. Artois became more politically active, and represented the royalist resistance to the changes agitated by the revolutionaries, forcing him to flee with his family after Bastille Day in July of 1789.

Marie-Clothilde of France (1759-1802), Queen of Sardinia, was the eldest surviving daughter of Louis,

Dauphin of France and Marie-Josèphe de Saxe. Orphaned as a small girl, Clothilde, like her sister Madame Élisabeth, received a pious upbringing at the hands of their governesses Madame de Marsan and Madame de Mackau. Clothilde, who always had a weight problem, was nicknamed *Gros-Madame* as a young girl. At sixteen, she was married by proxy to the heir of the Sardinian throne, Charles Emmanuel. Charles Emmanuel's sisters were already married to Louis XVI's brothers, becoming Antoinette's difficult sisters-in-law, the Comtesses de Provence and d'Artois. The Comte and Comtesse de Provence escorted Clothilde to Savoy where she married Charles Emmanuel on September 6, 1775. The young couple found they had much in common, especially their deep devotion to their Catholic faith, and so the arranged marriage became a love match. Charles-Emmanuel was not discouraged by Clothilde's weight but said that it gave him more of her to love. Sadly, after seven years of trying to have children, they remained infertile, and chose to live in continence as brother and sister.

The French monarchy has become infamous to posterity for stories of dangerous liaisons. Louis XIV and his ladies, Louis XV and his Parc aux Cerfs, the Fersen legend, etc. are the standard fare served to the public for generations. Not only does scandal sell books and movies but it reinforces the modern conviction that all royals were decadent and corrupt. The Bourbon dynasty, nevertheless, was remarkable not only for the amorous escapades of some of the kings, but for souls of fortitude and devotion, especially among the ladies. Queens Marie-Thérèse d'Espagne d'Autriche and Marie Leszczyńska endured their husbands' infidelities with fortitude, while giving an example of virtue and devoted motherhood to the kingdom. The daughters of Louis XV, in spite of their eccentricities, were known to be pious souls, charitable towards the poor and the religious houses. The youngest sister of Louis XVI, however, outshines them all. She possessed the benevolence and common touch which distinguished the descendants of Henri IV.

Madame Élisabeth (1764- 1794) became an orphan at the age of three and was reared by her governesses. She was a stubborn child but eventually conquered her willfulness so that gentleness and kindness became her most outstanding character traits. She was also quite playful and mischievous. Once at a party at the *château* of Meudon, when Élisabeth was only three, she amused herself by clinging to Louis-Auguste's coattails, following him from room to room, refusing to let go. The courtiers noticed, and crowded around to see the sight, but pressed in on the children so tightly that Élisabeth's safety was threatened. Louis picked her up, hoisting her on his shoulder, saying: "Gentlemen, take care you do not crush my little sister, or she will not come to see you again." [46] To quote from a biography of the princess:

> Madame de Marsan asked the king to appoint Madame de Mackau, who was living in retirement in Alsace, as sub-governess. This choice proved to have all the elements required to work a happy change in the nature of a self-willed and haughty child. Madame de Mackau possessed a firmness to which resistance yielded, and an affectionate kindness which enticed attachment. Armed with almost maternal power, she brought up the Children of France as she would have trained her own children; overlooking no fault; knowing, if need were, how to make herself feared; all the while leading them to like virtue. To a superior mind she added a dignity of tone and manners which inspired respect. When her pupil

gave way to the fits of haughty temper to which she was subject, Madame de Mackau showed on her countenance a displeased gravity, as if to remind her that princes, like other persons, could not be liked except for their virtues and good qualities.[47]

Madame Élisabeth and Antoinette became fast friends, with the new Dauphine often sending for the little sister to play hide-and-go-seek and other games. They became as close as blood sisters and in the dark days that would come they became spiritual sisters as well.

"Birth of Louis XVI"

4 SCANDAL

Il y a bien du monde à Versailles aujourdhui.
—Marie-Antoinette to Madame du Barry

Once I ran across an article entitled "Top 5 Marie-Antoinette Scandals" which was an incredibly misleading portrayal of the Queen and had little bearing on reality. Antoinette, in spite of being from a generation known for its fast pace of living, did not conduct herself in a manner which gave public scandal. There is no evidence for an affair with Count Fersen. As for Diamond Necklace fiasco, she was the innocent victim, not the cause. However, Antoinette did not live as sedately as former Queens of France had done. Her excesses as a twenty-year-old, including her flamboyant attire, her late night card parties, and some of her escapades, such as walking incognito with her sister-in-law and ladies on the palace terrace in the moonlight, were considered inappropriate behaviors for female members of the Royal Family. This was why her mother,

Empress Maria Theresa, rebuked her so strongly in her letters for even slight infractions. As Lady Antonia Fraser notes in her biography of Antoinette: "Sins that would be venial in any other girl were far more consequential in the future Queen of France." [1]

The scandals which perhaps most affected Antoinette's life were situations which had been going on long before she set foot in France. The fact that the most powerful woman at the court of Louis XV was not his pious wife or daughters but his mistress set the stage for Antoinette's tragedy. For one thing, her marriage was arranged by a courtesan, Madame de Pompadour. As a child bride, Antoinette was quick to notice that the person with the most influence over her husband's grandfather the King was Madame du Barry, of whom the young Dauphine innocently exclaimed, "I shall be her rival!" [2]

As mentioned previously, Jeanne Bécu, Comtesse du Barry, was the successor of Madame de Pompadour in Louis XV's affections. At the court of Versailles she had her own clique, the *barryistes*, who opposed the *choiseulistes* which had arranged the marriage of the Dauphin Louis-Auguste to Antoinette of Lorraine-Austria. Madame du Barry and her *barryistes* were allied with the Dauphin and the Mesdames, who belonged to the Devout party or *dévots*, in being against the Austrian alliance. Needless to say, the daughters of Louis XV, although Madame du Barry was more or less on their side, would have disliked anyone who illicitly shared their father's bed, on moral grounds. Led by Madame Adélaïde, they encouraged the teenaged Antoinette not to speak to Madame du Barry. The young princess shunned the courtesan, causing a diplomatic crisis. Madame Adélaïde was therefore able to humiliate Madame du Barry as well as create a rift between Antoinette and Louis XV, in addition to making the entire *barryiste* cabal an enemy of the young Dauphine. It caused uncomfortable incidents such as dirty water being poured onto Antoinette as she and her sister-in-law the Comtesse de Provence were walking beneath the windows of Louis XV's apartments. Antoinette had the wit to turn it into a joke, running upstairs to the King and saying playfully: "Why, Papa, just look at my dress! You must keep your household in better order."[3] Louis XV was too obsessed with La Barry's charms to risk offending the mistress. Antoinette did not understand that in her vulnerable position as bride of an unconsummated marriage she could not afford to make enemies. I think that Madame Adélaïde ultimately had good intentions, thinking it was for the good of France to weaken any influence of the Austrian bride. Ultimately, through pettiness and indiscretion, Mesdames Tantes damaged the reputation of their nephew's wife and therefore caused damage to the crown.

Most of all, Antoinette saw her mother, who never gave in to anybody, give in to Madame du Barry. It occurred, of course, when the Empress pleaded with her daughter to stop shunning the royal mistress, who had complained to Louis XV that the Dauphine was snubbing her. On one level, of course, Antoinette was being manipulated by the Aunts to shun the mistress, for their own purposes. However, there are other reasons she did not want to speak to Madame du Barry, who had been insolent to her from the day she arrived at Versailles. As Antoinette wrote to Empress Maria Theresa on October 13, 1771: "...If you could see, as I do, everything that happens here, you would realize that that woman and her clique would never be satisfied with just a word, and that I would have to do it again and again. You may be sure that I need to be led by no one when it comes to politeness."[4] Antoinette not only wanted to keep the mistress in her place, that is, in what

Antoinette thought her place should be, but she wanted to uphold morals and decency by not giving public approval to a sinful relationship. Upholding morality was something which her mother had impressed upon her as the duty of a Catholic princess. The excuse the Empress gave as the reason why Antoinette should be friendly to Madame du Barry was because Louis XV demanded it, and he was to be obeyed. As she wrote her daughter on September 30, 1771: "You have one goal only – it is to please the king, and obey him."[5] In the eyes of her elders a fifteen year old girl was bound to obey those in authority over her, but Antoinette thought the case demanded a different approach.

To put the entire intrigue in perspective, it was the kind of power play that happened every day in courts all over Europe. I sometimes wonder that if Antoinette had lived to be an old lady and had died peacefully in her bed, if anyone in posterity would have given the incident between her and Madame du Barry a second thought. Because Antoinette died stripped of all human dignity, after being destroyed in practically every way a woman can be destroyed, with her reputation in shreds, people are always looking for reasons that led to such a dreadful fate. Hence the focus on the early rift with La Barry, which but for the debacles that followed, would have been forgotten.

In the end, although Antoinette eventually obeyed the king and her mother and spoke to the mistress, the fact that she had made an issue of it made her someone whom Madame du Barry came to respect. On New Year's Day, 1772, Antoinette passed La Barry and looking at her said the words which soon became known in all the courts of Europe: "There are many people at Versailles today."[6] Ultimately, it was not Antoinette who gave scandal; it was she who had to resist being scandalized. It was she who had to take a stand, which she would continue to do when as Queen she sought to reform the morals of the court. Madame du Barry tried to send her diamonds to smooth things over, but Antoinette could not be bought.[7] Maxime de la Rocheterie has the following reflections on the matter:

> This was the end and proper solution...of that long and scandalous wrangle which, in contempt of all order, natural and divine, a mistress, dragged from the mud, had held at bay a princess of the royal blood, the wife to the heir to the crown of France....For those who reason coldly, with that haughty indifference to the moral aspect of a question, and regard for material interest alone, which is one of the traditions of modern diplomacy, it is easy to understand the disquietude of the empress, her incessant recommendations...but it is more easy to comprehend—we would willingly say, to share—the virginal repugnance of Marie-Antoinette. Perhaps the motives of the empress were more prudent; but those of the dauphiness were incontestably finer....If politics condemn her, public honor absolves her.[8]

Most people are not aware that Madame du Barry was raised in a convent and, in spite of her lifestyle, always considered herself to be a Catholic. This is not to mitigate the very real scandal that the King gave to his people by taking a mistress. In Madame du Barry's case, however, at least she was not actively working against the Church like Madame de Pompadour. It was Madame du Barry who built the chapel at Petit Trianon. She never tried to pretend to be anything other than a fallen woman and did not try to bend or break the laws of the Church in regard to reception of Holy Communion, as other people have done in her situation. Also, when Louis XV was dying, Madame du Barry left the King's side so he could be reconciled with his Savior. She retired to the Abbey du Pont-aux-Dames near Meaux-en-Brie, where the reports of her conduct are mixed; she unfortunately but not surprisingly misbehaved by parading around in all of her dresses and, bizarrely, tearing apart birds' nests, perhaps giving vent to grief and frustration. [9]

However, Antoinette's situation in those years before she became a mother was tenuous, especially from a political point of view. Her marriage was not consummated and the potential of an annulment was hanging over her. Even when she became Queen, Louis XVI deliberately kept her out of political matters in the beginning of his reign, encouraging her to divert herself at Petit Trianon. Let us recall that he thought that Madame Pompadour had ruined France and so was suspicious of women meddling in political affairs.

Since as a child-bride Antoinette noticed that it was Madame du Barry who ruled, it became important for her to give the impression that she was her husband's mistress as well as his wife. She wanted to appear to be the one who influenced his decisions, even though she did not, as the matter of Bavaria proved in 1778, and the American Revolution as well. Her brother frequently pressured her to use her role as consort for Austrian interests. Louis XVI, to Joseph's frustration, continued to do what he thought was best for France, not what was best for Austria. Placed in a very awkward situation, Antoinette would use clothing to establish herself, dressing in the height of fashion like a courtesan, quite a contrast to the late Queen Marie. Early in their reign, the King and Queen held a costume ball where everyone came in dress from the era of *le bon roi Henri*, with Antoinette herself garbed as Henri IV's beloved mistress, Gabrielle d'Estrées. It was part of Antoinette's attempt to show that she was loved by her husband, and that she was his *maitresse en titre* as well as his Queen.

She wanted to be perceived as the person most influential with Louis XVI. Unfortunately, in an attempt to assert herself at a hostile court, she made it easier for her enemies to portray her as a loose woman. In the minds of many her expensive and fashionable dress was a sign of decadence and careless morals. [10]

Here is one more story featuring the Maid from Lorraine versus the Concubine. Antoinette had only been married for a few weeks when one of her maids, Madame Thibault, fell upon her knees, begging the Dauphine to intervene with Louis XV for Madame Thibault's son, who was condemned for killing an officer of the King's guard in a duel. Antoinette went to the King and procured a pardon for the young man. Later Antoinette was told that Madame Thibault had also thrown herself at the feet of Madame du Barry, who had obtained a pardon for the youth as well. Antoinette sweetly replied: "That confirms the opinion I always had of Madame Thibault, she is a noble woman, and a brave mother who would stop at nothing to save her child's life; in her place I would have knelt to Zamore if he could have helped me."[11] Zamore was Madame du Barry's African page, who later betrayed La Barry during the Revolution. Both Antoinette and Madame du Barry would meet their end on the scaffold, Antoinette calmly and Madame du Barry in a fit of terror.

5 THE TEMPLE OF LOVE

"Her virtue is intact, she is even austere by nature rather than by reason." —Joseph II to Archduke Leopold about Marie-Antoinette, 1778

The Temple of Love is one of the most unforgettable places in the gardens of the Petit Trianon, on a little island directly behind the house. Queen Marie-Antoinette commissioned the architect Mique to design and build the neo-classical structure in 1778. The Temple of Love was not built to celebrate the Queen's mythical love for Count Fersen, as some authors have hinted; Fersen was a mere acquaintance at the time. Lady Antonia Fraser maintains that it was built to celebrate the love of the King and the Queen for each other and the consummation of their marriage, delayed for many years.[1]

The consummation took so long because Antoinette was a mere child when she was married; she was fourteen but looked as if she were twelve, and Louis was not eager to deflower a little girl. He waited for her to mature. He also approached his bride in a restrained manner because his tutor Vauguyon had inculcated in him the dangers for France when a king became enthralled by a woman, as had happened to his grandfather Louis XV. Louis could probably see himself becoming quite easily enthralled with Antoinette, and so he held himself back until he could be certain of her. Where, then, did the phimosis theory come from, and the gossip about Louis being impotent, etc? If there was a problem, it was not Louis' but Antoinette's. Where do these rumors come from, that end up in books and movies?

Of the marriage of Louis and Antoinette much has been written. Just as the bed linens would be scrutinized after their nights together by Comte Mercy's and Comte Aranda's spies,[2] so has every word they uttered or wrote, or what was uttered or written about them, been dissected and analyzed and interpreted in various ways. While such scrutiny has mostly happened in regard to their physical relations as husband and wife, people have also been trying to figure out their feelings for each other. Did they really love each other? Was Louis really an ungracious, impotent dolt, incapable of being a true husband? Was he himself completely unlovable as he has often been described? Did sexual frustration drive Antoinette to spend money, typical of the Freudian interpretation?

As I wrote in the preface of the novel *Trianon*, the story of Louis and Antoinette is not a typical love story. Indeed, it is more than a love story. Why? Because of the fortitude and courage they displayed at the gates of hell. Louis and Antoinette, through the trials of their marriage and of their time, fulfilled for each other one of the goals of the sacrament of matrimony, to help each other reach Heaven. That is because, as Philippe Delorme writes in his excellent biography of the Queen, as troubles grew around them, the more Louis and Antoinette turned to each other for support, and the more they were forged into one.[3] Although they endured many ups and downs throughout the course of their union, perhaps more than ordinary couples do because of the rarefied atmosphere of the Court, one can trace a pattern of growing affection between them, even from the first difficult years.

In the beginning we find them two complete strangers, not only from foreign countries and cultures but from families that had recently been enemies. Although they were related by blood and shared the same faith, they both had been brought up in different atmospheres. Antoinette grew up in a loving, casual but highly moral environment; Louis in regimented surroundings where scandal and corruption lurked around every corner. Even their approaches to religion diverged; for Antoinette there had been more of an emphasis of warmth, confidence and trust in God whereas at Versailles there were always the vestiges of Jansenistic prudery to counterbalance the parade of loose morals. In their personalities they appeared to have nothing in common. According to biographer Vincent Cronin:

> In obvious ways they were strikingly different: Louis beginning to put on weight, Antoinette slim; he steady, she quick; he reserved, she open; he with few close friends, she with many; he awkward, she majestic; he seeing the dark side, she the bright; he a keen reader, she bored by books; he unmusical, she happy with harp and clavichord.[4]

To Antoinette, Louis must have seemed to be the oddest boy she had ever met, especially when in her experience she had no one to compare him to but her brothers. Likewise, Louis knew only his Aunts and his little sisters compared to whom Antoinette must have seemed like a force of nature descending upon the decorous halls of Versailles.

Furthermore, they had to contend with the constant scrutiny from their elders, as well as the gossip which filtered into the court from whatever Antoinette confided to the Mesdames. The public atmosphere at the court caused their most private business to be discussed and lampooned. It was the beginning of the obsession with Antoinette's body which would lead to the pornographic pamphlets designed to destroy her reputation. In the meantime, Antoinette was also being spied upon by Ambassador Mercy, who was reporting to her mother. Mercy had one of Antoinette's maids and two of her maidservants to report to him every detail of the young girl's life.[5] Louis-Auguste found out that much of what Mercy was passing on to the Empress about himself was not true.[6] Mercy, eager to remain at Versailles, wanted to convince the Empress that he was indispensable to her and to the alliance. His reports were calculated to make Louis look bad.[7]

Comte Florimund de Mercy-Argenteau (1727-1794), the Austrian ambassador to the court of His Most Christian Majesty the King of France and Navarre, was a career diplomat, and when Antoinette arrived in France, he was next in line to becoming Imperial Chancellor, an office he did not desire. He was comfortable at Versailles and enjoyed his life in Paris, where he kept his mistress at the Petit Luxembourg with 15.000 bottles of wine. In order to remain in France he had to calmly present Antoinette to her mother as being in a continual state of crisis which only an experienced diplomat like himself, trusted by both the Empress and her daughter, could handle. Mercy made all the problems of the marriage sound as if they were Louis' fault. Ironically, if it had not been for Mercy, I think that the problems between Louis and Antoinette would have worked themselves out sooner. But perhaps not. At any rate, his weekly reports to the Empress contained details of Antoinette's doings; she later could not figure out how her mother knew about them. It never occurred to her that Mercy was spying on her.

Mathieu-Jacques de Vermond, known as the Abbé Vermond (1735-1806), was the French priest sent by Louis XV to Austria to help Antoinette learn French. He followed her to France, at his own expense, where he remained Antoinette's tutor while she was Dauphine, teaching her religion, history and French literature.[8] He devised a clever way of teaching which engaged the easily distracted Dauphine, although she did her best to change the topic at hand to one more entertaining. Under his tutelage she read several serious works of history including David Hume's *History of England*, which was one of Louis' favorite books as well. Antoinette liked it, too, although Hume was "a Protestant" she lamented.[9] She also truly enjoyed *Memoires de l'Estoile* about Charles IX, Henri III, and Henri IV.[10] Antoinette came to respect and admire Henri IV and Louis XIV, because "One was good and the other was great."[11] When she became Queen, the Abbé served as her Reader and secretary. A homely man, the Abbé was a worthy priest of solid doctrine who advised Antoinette spiritually and at times served as her confessor. He was genuinely devoted to her well-being and she trusted him with her life. However, he tended to view the customs of Versailles as absurd which only encouraged Antoinette to view them the same way.[12] He was not liked by Louis-Auguste or the Mesdames because he was known to be passing on information to Mercy. His brother was the physician who would deliver Antoinette's first child. Antoinette usually ended her letters to her mother by saying "the Abbé places himself at your feet."[13] It was the Abbé whom, in late 1780's, Louis XVI would send to bring Antoinette the news of her mother's death.

Although Antoinette was separated from her mother at a young age, and even before that did not see her on a daily basis, her mother remained a strong presence in her life. From afar, the Empress Maria Theresa gave detailed advice about religious practice, love-making, court etiquette, politics, health, and children. It was incredibly annoying to Antoinette at times but in the long run she emerged with a strong inner sense of her religious and marital commitments. When Antoinette received the first letter from her mother at Versailles in the spring of 1770, the fourteen-year-old lapsed into her native German and exclaimed: "*Gott sei Dank!*" or "Thanks be to God!"[14] For ten years, between 1770 and 1780, Antoinette's life was shaped by the correspondence with her mother which she anticipated with a mixture of joy and trepidation. The letters are replete with loving words; Antoinette's are especially full of cheer, liveliness and devotion. She always ended her letters saying things like: "I love and embrace you with all my soul"[15] and "Will my dear Mama permit me to embrace her tenderly?"[16] Her struggles with homesickness were intense. "I can swear to you that I have not received one of your dear letters without having the tears come to my eyes because I am separated from so kind and loving a mother; and although I am well situated here, I still ardently wish I could see ... my very dear family for a moment at least...."[17] While the Empress is affectionate as well, she frequently scolds her child, as would any normal mother. However, what was the worst thing for Antoinette's relationship with Louis was that her mother was using her as a political tool. In her letters the Empress often tries to get Antoinette to use her influence at the French court to benefit Austria.

Unfortunately, as long as Antoinette was under the thumbs of Mercy and the Empress, Louis-Auguste could not completely trust her with political matters. As King, he overturned Heaven and earth to keep his bride away from politics by encouraging her to be focused on her projects at Trianon and on her friends. He engineered the friendship with Madame de Polignac to pull her away from Mercy's influence. As Louis XVI he gave into her on any number of small matters that conferred upon her an illusion of power when actually he was keeping her at arm's length from serious affairs of state. It was not out of weakness or guilt on Louis' part but deliberately done by him. Louis and Antoinette did not really become close until after the Empress died and Mercy lost his influence.

The main problem is that they were both too young and psychologically immature to be married. Although many royals married young to perfect strangers, both Louis and Antoinette were more child-like emotionally than many others of the same age. They had both lost fathers to whom they were each devoted. They had both lost their mothers as well, even though Antoinette could still write to hers. If they had each been given a few more years to grow up, the union would have had a happier beginning. But the ambitions of their elders forced upon them a marriage which became a matter of failure and humiliation at a vulnerable age. It is a miracle that they were ever able to have normal marital relations. It was good, as Vincent Cronin points out, that they found at last that they shared much:

> At a deeper level they possessed traits in common. Both had a lot of heart: they felt for those less fortunate than themselves, they loved their children and were happiest when with them. Both had a sense of duty and wanted above everything to do their job

well.[18]

The first decades of the twentieth century saw the rising popularity of the theories of Sigmund Freud. Freud believed that sexual drives are the basis of all human behavior. While many of Freud's original disciples diverged from him in various ways, there is no underestimating the widespread influence Freud has had upon modern life and the current attitudes towards the human person. Among Freud's close friends was the popular Austrian novelist and playwright Stefan Zweig, who in spite of his enormous literary success ended his life in suicide.

Among Stefan Zweig's most famous works is his biography *Marie-Antoinette: the Portrait of an Average Woman* which views the Queen's life in Freudian terms, especially when it comes to the first seven years of her marriage. Louis XVI is portrayed as a repressed, impotent, dull-witted, indifferent husband, who drove his wife to gambling, dancing and spending exorbitant amounts of money as an outlet for her thwarted impulses. Zweig was the first to impart to the public the image of the sexually frustrated teenaged princess, which successive authors and filmmakers continue to promote to this day. The drawback of the Freudian theory is that it does not explain why others at the French court, who were enjoying unmitigated pleasures of the flesh, were spending much more money than was the adolescent Antoinette.

In 1937, Nesta Webster debunked the Freudian analysis in her two volume study of Louis and Antoinette. In discussing the yet unconsummated marriage of the King and Queen, Webster says the following of Antoinette's sorrow:

It is...unnecessary in her case to resort to Freudian

methods of psychoanalysis in order to understand her state of mind. Her feelings were really quite simple. For however much the unnatural conditions of her marriage may, and indeed must, have reacted on her nervous system, the dominating thought that emerges from her letters from those of Mercy to Maria Theresa is her great longing for children....On Sundays, when the garden of Petit Trianon was thrown open to the public, the Queen would go among the family parties collected there and call for the children to be brought up and presented to her, then she would ask their names, and shower on them bonbons and kisses....But beyond this natural trouble of a woman was the sorrow of a Queen who had given no heir to the throne. The letters of Maria Theresa, urging on her the necessity for fulfilling her destiny as mother of a Dauphin, must have felt like turning a knife in the wound, for the Empress showed little human sympathy or understanding for her daughter's unhappy position....[19]

The despair of not giving birth to an heir, as well as the unfulfilled natural longing for a child, combined with the exuberant high spirits of a girl who loved parties and dancing, created for Antoinette an image of frantic giddiness, soiling her reputation for all time, and leading to rumors of wanton behavior. It is ironic because her brother Joseph described the Queen as having *aucun tempérament*, that is, she had little or no temperament or inclination for sensuality.[20] According to Louis' biographer Petitfils, Antoinette used entertainments to escape unpleasant marital duties, which were painful and awkward, due to her own physical problems. Her fear of pregnancy caused nervous instability, which is not the same as sexual frustration. She longed for a child but had anxieties. The entire scenario made Louis-Auguste a person of ridicule. He suffered, humiliated.[21] Of Louis XVI, Webster writes:

> To trace the King's inferiority complex solely to this cause [the unconsummated marriage] after the Freudian manner is...contrary to all evidence, since this complex existed long before his marriage and continued after [the union was consummated]. Never did Louis XVI display more self-confidence than during the Guerre des Farines while his marriage still remained unconsummated, never less than during the Revolution when he had become the father of a family.[22]

On July 22, 1773, Louis told his grandfather that Antoinette was truly his wife. "*C'est ma femme!*" he exclaimed, and the King embraced them both.[23] According to the letters written by the Queen to her mother the Empress Maria Theresa, the young couple had indeed begun to attempt to consummate the marriage as early as 1773. On August 13, 1773, Antoinette wrote that she and Louis were in perfect union and had experienced "*beaucoup de joie*," a "great deal of joy," which makes one guess that the experience was pleasurable.[24] Antoinette was seventeen and Louis eighteen. In their ignorance, they thought they had already succeeded but soon discovered that they had not.[25] Dr. Lasonne had already confirmed there was no physical obstacle to the consummation of the marriage.[26] La Martinière, physician of Louis XV, examined the Dauphin to make sure there was not a reason for lack of consummation. The Dauphin was found to be in perfect health, however, the Dauphine was too young for sex. Author Simone Bertière, in her biography *L'Insoumise*, maintains that Antoinette had a "narrowness of passage" which made consummating the marriage difficult for both spouses.[27] To quote:

> Marie-Antoinette suffered from a condition known in the court as '*l'étroitesse du chemin*', [a narrowness of passage], that made her frigid. The research by Simone Bertière, a specialist in the lives of France's seventeenth and eighteenth-century queens, shatters the myth of a semi-impotent, foppish king, and a sluttish queen, favourite targets of scurrilous pamphlets that inflamed the mobs of 1789. It also undermines the most influential biography of Marie-Antoinette, written by Stefan Zweig in Vienna in 1932 after he discovered uncensored correspondence between the queen and her domineering mother, the Empress Maria Theresa.
>
> 'Since then, the presumed impotence of Louis and his cowardice in refusing an operation to correct a small physical malformation have been accepted as a matter of fact, sufficient to explain the queen's neurotic instability,' Bertière said, commenting on her 700-page biography, *Marie-Antoinette, l'Insoumise* (the Rebel). 'But Zweig did not compare these letters with those sent by the Hapsburg ambassador to the empress which leave no doubt at all that Louis XVI did not suffer from malformation.' It was not until seven years after marrying the Dauphin that Marie-Antoinette, 'a little girl paralysed by terror', lost her virginity. From the first fruitless night the physiological realities which, according to Bertière, nineteenth and twentieth-century historians glossed over, were the object of intense court records, letters and diplomatic exchanges that described their sexual characteristics in detail. [28]

Zweig is responsible for spreading the phimosis theory, a theory that keeps appearing in contemporary books and on the internet, although authors such as Webster, Bertière, Cronin, and Fraser have done their best to show it to be erroneous. The phimosis theory insists that Louis had to undergo a circumcision. However, he went riding every day during the time period of the supposed surgery, when surgery in that delicate area would have rendered riding impossible. Simone Bertière repeatedly quotes the various doctors' reports of examinations of Louis which say there was no physical reason why he could not consummate the marriage, i.e., no phimosis. Both Nesta Webster and Antonia Fraser deny the mythical surgery as well. According to Webster: "...Joseph II was able to give the right advice which eventually led to the consummation so devoutly hoped for without recourse being made to the much talked of operation."[29] As for Fraser, she writes: "In the end it was not a case of phimosis, the overtight foreskin mocked by *Les Nouvelles de la Cour*....In January 1776, Moreau, a surgeon of the Hôtel-Dieu hospital, was pronouncing the operation [on Louis XVI] unnecessary and a few months later Marie-Antoinette was increasingly sure the surgeon was right....So there was never an operation."[30]

In the summer of 1777, Louis XVI and Antoinette fully consummated their marriage at last. On August 30, 1777, Marie-Antoinette wrote her mother: *Je suis dans le bonheur le plus essential pour toute ma vie.* "I am in the most essential happiness of my entire life."[31] Mercy's letter to the Empress confirmed the joyful event. On August 19 at 10 in the morning, while Antoinette was leaving her bath, Louis came in and stayed with her for an hour and fifteen minutes.[32] The doctor Lassone had instructed Louis and later assured him the marriage was completely consummated. They were aged twenty-two and twenty-one years respectively. The bride had physically matured and was emotionally ready for the duties of being a wife and mother. Her readiness can be attributed in part to her friendship with Madame de Polignac, who helped Antoinette overcome any fears about sex and pregnancy that she had absorbed from her sister Maria Carolina's letters and perhaps also from watching her sister-in-law Isabella die after great sufferings in childbirth. As for Louis he told Madame Adélaïde that he had such pleasure in his relations with his wife that he wished it had happened sooner.[33] In the future he would usually make his romantic visits to her in the mornings, slipping into her room quietly, even when she would stay at Petit Trianon.[34] The Empress found it appalling that they did not sleep together the entire night; Antoinette had to explain that it was not the French custom. To celebrate their matrimonial success, in 1778 Antoinette commissioned the architect Mique to design and build the neo-classical structure called the Temple of Love. It became a marriage which all the forces of hell could not sunder.

6 DEATH AND CORONATION

"He told me the pitiful state of the Kingdom of France. And he told me that I must succour the King of France." —Saint Jeanne d'Arc

On June 8, 1773, Louis-Auguste accompanied Antoinette on her official entry into Paris. It had been three years since her arrival in France but she had never formally been introduced to the people of Paris. Louis-Auguste and his brothers had taken her to the masked opera ball in Paris during the previous Carnival, but they had all gone incognito. The Dauphin and Dauphine were cheered all the way into town. Their reputation for virtuous living had preceded them. The people had heard of Antoinette's beauty and generosity. For instance, she wrote to her mother of the devastating fire at the Hôtel-Dieu:

> ... All the gazettes will be talking about the cruel fire at the Hôtel-Dieu; they have had to move the sick

into the [cathedral of Notre Dame] and the Archbishop's palace. There are usually five or six thousand sick in the hospital; in spite of the care that was taken, it was impossible to prevent a part of the building from burning...The Archbishop published a letter ordering a charity drive; I sent a thousand *écus*. I never mentioned it; I am being given embarrassing compliments, but they say it must be so as it gives a good example....[1]

Louis' plain, blunt manner appealed to one and all. Stories of his magnanimity were repeated everywhere. They drove through the streets of Paris to the welcoming blare of trumpets and thunder of cannon. After Mass at Notre Dame, they went to the church of Sainte-Geneviève, where they prayed at the tomb of the shepherdess who protected the city. They dined at the Tuileries palace. On the balcony of the palace, they showed themselves ten times to a mixture of silent awe and ovations of delight. Afterwards, they walked arm-in-arm in the open gardens, the crowds thronging around them, but Louis ordered the guards not to push the people back. The Dauphin answered all of the speeches in a calm, polite and gracious manner, which touched many hearts. Antoinette was so moved by the acclaim that tears rolled down her cheeks. It was on the balcony that the old Duc de Brissac, governor of Paris, commented to Antoinette: "Madame, two hundred thousand people have fallen in love with you."[2] That glorious moment of popular acclaim would later stand out in tragic contrast to the hatred that would follow. Antoinette was to painfully learn the fickleness of human praise.

Later that year, on October 16, 1773, Mercy had reason to record another of the Dauphine's good deeds. There may have been others but she tried to be discreet and was embarrassed when her charities were made public. To quote Mercy:

> On October 16th, Mme la Dauphine was following the King at the hunt in an open carriage when there occurred a very untoward event. The stag, closely pursued by the dogs, jumped into an enclosed garden which its owner was then working. The animal, who could see no exit, became enraged ... and gored [the man] twice, once in the thigh, the other in the body, leaving him mortally wounded.
>
> The wretched man's wife ... seized with despair, ran toward a group of hunters she could see in the distance. It was the King and his suite. She shouted for help, announcing her husband's accident and, at that moment, fell down in a faint. The King ordered that she be taken care of and, having given marks of compassion and kindness, rode on...
>
> Mme la Dauphine, who had returned, got out of her carriage, ran toward the woman, and held out some perfume to her nose, which made her come out of her faint. Mme la Dauphine gave her all the money she had with her, but what was even more admirable was the kind and consoling way in which HRH talked to the poor woman. Finally, Mme l'Archiduchesse, who was touched, shed tears and, at that moment, caused more than a hundred spectators to do the same...
>
> Then, having called for her carriage, Mme la Dauphine gave orders that the peasant woman be taken in it back to her cottage which was in a neighboring hamlet. Her Royal Highness waited right there for her carriage to return; she asked about the care of the wounded man...I cannot describe to Your Majesty the greatness or intensity of the sensation caused by the event, not only among the courtiers,

but even more among the people of Fontainebleau....

The public in Paris [seems very moved;] whenever Mme la Dauphine's name comes up, it evokes a universal cry of joy and admiration.[3]

On Holy Thursday, March 21, 1774, Monsieur de Beauvais, the Bishop of Sénez, was summoned to preach before the King in the chapel of Versailles. He preached on the verse Jonah 3:4: "Forty more days and Nineveh shall be destroyed," exhorting the King and his court to conversion. Within a fortnight, Louis XV came down with smallpox, while residing with Madame du Barry at Petit Trianon. The King's doctors insisted upon him being carried back to the main palace, against the inclinations of Madame du Barry and her circle, who wished to keep the King away from his family.[4] The Court avoided him for fear of contagion. The Dauphin and Dauphine were sent away. The King's daughters, Madame Adélaïde, Madame Victoire, and Madame Sophie braved the sick room to care for their father. Every two hours they would send messengers to their Carmelite sister at her monastery to let her know how the patient was doing. Madame Louise, in her turm, sent her profession crucifix to her dying parent. In the meantime, the Duc de Richelieu threatened to throw the Curé of Versailles out the window if he mentioned the Sacraments to the King. Madame Louise prayed at her monastery, prostrate in front of the Blessed Sacrament, for her father to be reconciled with God. On May 4, the King was visited by Monsieur de Beaumont, the Archbishop of Paris, and by Cardinal de la Roche-Aymon, the Grand Almoner of Versailles, who spoke with him for a long time. Afterwards, he sent for Madame du Barry and bade her farewell. She left the *château* the next day; in a fury, it is reported, but at least she obeyed her King's final command. After much ado about nothing, accompanied by hemming and hawing, a confessor was finally sent for. Many of the more progressive members of the Court seemed determined that the King should die outside the Church, but their objections were overcome. A blind and holy priest, the Abbé Maudoux, came to hear the confession of Louis XV, and the next day he received his Viaticum from the Cardinal Grand Almoner, with the princesses kneeling nearby. As the ciborium containing the Blessed Sacrament came into the sick room, the King tried to rise from his bed so he too could kneel. The Cardinal asked that the King issue a public statement of his repentance for the benefit of his people, and he did so most willingly. Afterwards he died peacefully, on May 10, 1774, at age 64. As Louis XVI wrote to his aunt Madame Louise: "The graces God bestowed on him were very consoling. He died holding the crucifix and reciting the prayers himself."[5] It was three o'clock in the afternoon.

The moment the King died, a burning candle in the window was snuffed out, and a mob of courtiers rushed to where Louis and Antoinette were standing anxiously together in her apartments. The young couple fell to their knees and prayed together: "May God guide us and protect us! We are too young to reign!"[6] In light of everything that would follow, it is heartbreakingly poignant that the reign of Louis XVI began with a prayer. Not every prayer of the new King and Queen was to be answered as they hoped, but there can be no doubt that they would be given the strength to bear the great trials asked of them.

When the Last Will and Testament of Louis XV was opened, it bore witness to the late King's genuine repentance:

In the name of the Father, of the Son and of the Holy

Ghost. What follows are my last wishes. I give back my soul to God, my Creator, and conjure Him to have pity on a great sinner entirely submissive to His holy will and to the decisions of His Holy, Catholic, and Apostolic Church. I pray the Blessed Virgin, and all the saints, particularly my patron St. Louis, to intercede for me with Jesus Christ, my Divine Redeemer and Savior, that He may obtain for me pardon of my sins, who have so often offended and so ill served him I ask pardon of all those I may have offended or scandalized, and beg them to forgive me and pray for my soul.[7]

The corpse of Louis XV was literally rushed off to be buried at Saint Denis, for fear of contagion. In the meantime, the entire royal family were swiftly packed up and taken to the *château* of Choisy where they stayed for nine days until the danger passed. The Mesdame Tantes in particular were quarantined, since all three princesses contracted smallpox from their father. The grotesque death of Louis XV from smallpox encouraged Louis XVI and other members of the family, who had never had the disease, to be inoculated. Inoculation would usually cause a fever and a milder outbreak of pustules, although it could at times be fatal. Louis XVI, his brothers and the Comtesse d'Artois were inoculated. According to the British ambassador to France Lord Stormont, the King "gave orders no one was to attend him who had not had smallpox and has had the humanity to extend this order to his lowest servants." Antoinette, who watched over her husband, wrote to her mother that he "has not many spots but he has spectacular ones on his nose, wrist, and chest which begin to whiten."[8]

At Choisy, the new King said: "I feel that the universe is going to fall on me."[9] His first act as sovereign was to state that he would no longer be styled as "Louis-Auguste" but as "Louis." He summoned the Comte de Maurepas to be his advisor. Maurepas was recommended by Louis' father, his late tutor Vauguyon and by his Tante Adélaïde, as an able minister. Maurepas had been exiled from court by Louis XV for writing verses about Madame de Pompadour, and thus was inimical to the *choiseulistes*. Antoinette wanted Louis to have Choiseul as his advisor but in the matter of ministers as in other political matters he did what he thought best for France. He also sought to find ways to distract Antoinette from meddling in affairs of state.

As for the new Queen, she gave a good example of dignified piety during the period of mourning, according to what Mercy wrote to the Empress.[10] The Empress rejoiced that Antoinette was behaving so well and that the King had given her Petit Trianon as her own, since it had always belonged to "favorites" of the King. Louis and Antoinette decided from the beginning that they would give a good example of married life. By giving Antoinette the estate of Trianon, the King showed that Antoinette was his mistress as well as his wife. He also gave it to her to shield her from the intrigues of the court, against which she would be helpless, and to keep her from trying to exert Austrian policy in affairs of state. In their innocence Louis and Antoinette never imagined that living in a house last inhabited by Madame du Barry and built for Madame de Pompadour would reflect badly on the vivacious young Queen. For the moment, the Empress was overjoyed and wrote to her daughter on June 16, 1774: "Religion and morals...have not been forgotten....All the universe is in ecstacy."[11] She also praised Antoinette for refusing *la ceinture de la reine* or "the Queen's belt" which was a tax levied at the beginning of every reign. Antoinette's quip "Belts are no longer worn"[12] saved the people from the tax and endeared her to them. On the feast of Corpus

Christi, Louis and Antoinette and other members of the Royal Family joined a Eucharistic procession at Chaillot, mingling with the crowd of worshippers.[13] The common people were happy to have a devout King and Queen.

On September 1, 1774, Louis and Antoinette, who had spent the summer at various smaller *châteaux*, were reinstated at Versailles, with Louis moving into the King's suite and Antoinette into the Queen's nearby. Later, Louis would build a private passage connecting his bed chamber with Antoinette's, so that their intimate moments could be more secluded from the court. Louis also convened his new cabinet of ministers, having fired most of his grandfather's regime. To many this action in itself showed the young King's independent thinking and strength of mind, contrary to popular legend.[14] At his first cabinet meeting Louis set the tone he desired for his reign by saying: "I wish to acquire a thorough knowledge of all that concerns the prosperity of my kingdom. Above all, gentlemen, do not forget St. Louis' maxim: 'Everything unjust is impossible.'"[15] To the official in charge of planning *Menus-Plaisirs* that is "Lesser Pleasures" or entertainments for the King, Louis said: "My *Menus-Plaisirs* are to walk about in the park."[16] He made sure his servants were paid on a regular basis. Under his grandfather, his tutors would go for years without being paid, such was the financial straits of the Court of Louis XV. His biggest challenge, other than the enormous national deficit, was what to do about the *parlements*, which had troubled his grandfather's reign. The *parlements* were the highest law courts run by magistrates and lawyers who had bought their positions. They were part of the *noblesse de robe*, the nobles of wealth, as opposed to the hereditary nobility, the *noblesse d' épée*, the nobles of the sword. There were thirteen *parlements* throughout the country but the most important was the *parlement* of Paris, known as the *Parlement*, which traditionally registered the edicts of the King, especially as pertains to taxation. If the Paris *Parlement* refused to register an edict, the King could go before the magistrates in royal state under a dias, called a *lis de justice* or "bed of justice" and compel *Parlement* to register the edict. Louis XV had had so many clashes with *Parlement* over taxation that he had suspended its sessions. However, at Maurepas' urging, Louis recalled *Parlement* in November 1774, and went before them in his velvet and ermine robes at the Palais de Justice where he sat enthroned. All the lawyers knelt until told to rise. Speaking firmly and strongly, he asked them to register his edicts and then said:

> The King my grandfather, challenged by your resistance to his orders, took what measures were necessary to maintain his authority and administer justice. Today I am calling you back to the functions which you should never have laid aside. This is a favor I am doing you; never forget it.[17]

Thus in the first year of his reign Louis XVI showed that he was going to be his own man and rule in the way he deemed best for his people.

However, already in the first year of his reign there were shadows of things to come. In August of 1774 Louis had also appointed Anne Robert de Turgot as his finance minister. The finances of the kingdom had been in a shambles since the disastrous Seven Years War with England. The deficit was 22 million *livres* with a projected 78 million to come. People who later blamed Antoinette for the deficit seemed to forget that Louis XVI inherited it. Through a series of edicts, Turgot attempted to reform the tax code by reducing the privileges of the nobility. He also wanted to establish a free market in grain. But the bad harvest of 1774 compounded with the shaky new regulations to create the "Flour Wars" with a scarcity of bread in some places leading to riots and social unrest.[18] Turgot repressed the riots and restored controls over the grain market. And so the problem of the national debt remained unsolved.

In spite of the Flour Wars, Louis' early actions and words as King combined to make him extremely popular with his subjects, and Antoinette as well, in a way that verged on idolatry. It was scary, for it set the people up for great disappointments if any flaws were detected or if anything went wrong, which is, of course, what happened. Louis was to maintain his popularity with the common people until September, 1789. Antoinette, however, since she was her husband's mistress as well as his wife, would fill the role of scapegoat for the ills of the nation, as mistresses had in the past. Being a foreigner made her even more suspect. But that was all to come. For Louis XVI and Antoinette the spring and summer of the coronation was a happy season in their lives, full of hope and popularity.

As an example, there was a popular print called "The Happy Day of France" portraying an allegorical representation of Louis XVI and Antoinette in honor of the coronation. The print shows Louis and Antoinette riding in a chariot pulled by a lion and a lamb, with fat, healthy children playing before them, and classical gods, goddesses, nymphs and fawns standing in the sidelines, surrounded by festoons of roses. Above the royal couple, angels are blowing trumpets, heralding what was expected to be a golden age, and not just a golden age but an apocalyptic age. The picture was vaguely reminiscent of the verse from Isaiah about the lamb and the lion, ending with the words: "and a little child shall lead them." (Isaias 11:6) It seemed that a new era of innocence, joy, prosperity and happiness for France was being born.[19]

On June 11, 1775, Trinity Sunday, Louis XVI was crowned at the Cathedral of Rheims, the sacred center of the realm. The festivities went on for days before and after the coronation itself, with both solemn religious ceremonies and lively festivals in the streets. Antoinette went everywhere with Louis, sometimes incognito, and she was usually accompanied by Louis' little sisters, the exuberant Madame Élisabeth and the plump Madame Clothilde. Although some ministers had tried to persuade Louis to have a simple civil ceremony to save money, Louis insisted on the traditional nine hour religious ceremony, to be followed by the King giving the blessing to the sick: "The King touches you, God heals you."[20] The *sacré* or coronation rite could be traced back to the baptism of the Frankish chieftain Clovis on Christmas Day in 496, at the hands of Saint Remigius, for whom Rheims was named. It also marked the foundation of the Christian kingdom of France, called by subsequent popes "the Eldest Daughter of the Church."[21] According to the traditional story:

> 'Bow thy head, O Sicambrian', said St. Remigius to the royal convert 'Adore what thou hast burned and burn what thou hast adored.' According to a ninth-century legend found in the life of St. Remigius, written by the celebrated Hincmar himself Archbishop of Reims, the chrism for the baptismal ceremony was missing and was brought from heaven in a vase (ampulla) borne by a dove. This is what is known as the Sainte Ampoule of Reims, preserved in the treasury of the cathedral of that city and used for the coronation of the kings of France from Philip Augustus down to Charles X.[22]

The baptism of Clovis was followed by the gradual

conversion and baptism of the Frankish nation, and thus the rite of the *sacré* represented the recommitment of the entire French people to the vocation of their baptism. The balm from the Holy Ampulla was mixed with sacred chrism and the king was anointed in a similar way as a priest at an ordination, on the head, chest, back and on the palms of the hands. The royal robes were based upon priestly garments: there were the tunic, the dalmatic and the royal mantle, all of azure blue velvet and sprinkled with *fleurs-de-lys* of gold. The garments represented the orders of subdeacon, deacon, and priest.Thus the King shared in both the Kingship and the Priesthood of Christ. Among laymen, the King of France could partake of both species at Holy Communion. He received the charismatic gift of healing as well; after his coronation he touched those afflicted with scrofula. [23] The sword of Charlemagne, *Joyeuse*, was also included in the rite. Charlemagne or Charles the Great, King of the Franks, was crowned Emperor of the Roman by Pope Leo III at St. Peter's Basilica on Christmas day in the year 800. It was at that time that Christmas began to be celebrated with greater festivities, although Epiphany continued to have higher liturgical rank. To the French the triumphant cry of *Noël*, originating either from the Latin word for birthday (*natalis*) or the French word for news (*nouvelles*), became the word for Christmas.[24]

By the late tenth century, the line of Charlemagne, called the Carolingians, had weakened and Hugh Capet, a relative of another house, was elected to be King of France. Hugh Capet was anointed and crowned in 987; his name was associated with the *cappa* or cape of Saint Martin of Tours which his family had in their possession.[25] The Capet family would rule until 1270 when their Valois cousins succeeded to the crown, to be followed by the Bourbons in 1589. Louis XVI was a descendant of Hugh Capet, of Charlemagne, of Clovis and in his person he embodied a long tradition of both religious faith and political authority. The name of Capet was not his but would surface during the Revolution as a form of mockery for the kingship as a medieval institution.

The coronation was to take place at Rheims, where Jeanne d'Arc had once come to crown Charles VII. Many Americans seem to be convinced that monarchy is an intrinsically evil institution. They are not able to see beyond their own time and their own political process. People do not have trouble accepting the fact that St. Joan of Arc donned male apparel and led armies to victory. What seems to disturb many people, however, is that she gave her help to a king, and worse yet, to a King of France. I once read a comment in which someone said that Saint Louis of France was a saint "in spite of being a king." We can with certainty guess that Saint Louis saw his kingship as a vocation in which he served God and man. What is more, he saw it as a calling to share in the Kingship of Christ, from Whom he held his authority and to Whom he had to render an account. Saint Joan, in her simple piety, viewed kingship in a similar manner. She honored her King Charles VII, although he was far from being a saint, because in doing so she gave honor to Christ the King. The office was deserving of respect, even if the man was not. On her banner she bore an image of Christ the King surrounded by the *fleur de lys*, the lilies of royal France. Saint Joan frequently made explicit reference to the fact that she was called to serve God by assisting the French monarch. At her trial she announced:

> As for the good work I have done...I must needs leave that with the King of Heaven, who sent me to Charles, son of Charles King of France, who shall be King. And you shall see that the French will very

soon achieve a great task which God will send to the French, and such that almost the whole Kingdom of France will tremble. And I say it, so that when it comes to pass it will be remembered that I said it.[26]

The Maid believed her country had a mission from God, a task to fulfill. No doubt Louis XVI saw it in the same way.

The coronation of Louis XVI was as magnificent as finances permitted, with an almost theatrical aura, as the exquisite Gothic sanctuary and apse were covered by neo-classical columns and drapery. The music was by the court composer François Giroust, which has been preserved. Antoinette was not crowned; it was Louis' decision that she should not share his coronation in order to save expenses and besides, queens were usually crowned only after they showed themselves to be fertile.[27] There was also a political motive. As a Habsburg, an Austrian and a Daughter of the Caesars, it was not politic for Antoinette, the child of a foreign enemy power, to be crowned. Although other Queens of France had been crowned and even had their own coronations, Antoinette was to sit in the gallery as a spectator. It seems, however, that as a very active spectator she immensely enjoyed the pageantry and ritual, being intensely moved. In a letter to her mother, Antoinette later declared it a day she would never forget, even if she lived to be a hundred, telling how she wept profusely throughout the *sacré*.[28] Simone Bertière insists that her tears were merely a childish knee-jerk reaction; that the religious significance of the ceremony totally escaped her and she was only awed by the people's cheers.[29] While her untrained mind was flighty and immature, I do not think we can doubt that she was truly touched at the center of her being. "We are obliged to work for the people's happiness. The king appeared to me to be penetrated by this truth," she explained to the Empress.[30] In his letters to Maria Theresa:

> [Mercy] mentions the emotion of the Queen at the moment of the Coronation; her tears flowed so fast that she was obliged to leave her seat and retire to regain her composure; she returned amid shouts and applause that echoed through the cathedral, while all the world wept in sympathy; and the King raised his head and looked at her with an adoration that he could not conceal. His Majesty had been greatly affected by her emotion, had spoken incessantly of her tears; and had shown feelings never before stirred in him. He mentions the little walk of the King and Queen arm-in-arm, in simple dress, at seven o'clock in the evening, through the long gallery crowded with visitors, *'de monde, même de peuple'* their Majesties without guards or escort, in the midst of their subjects; and that the people, drunk with joy, greeted them with indescribable warmth.[31]

According to the *Gazette de France*:

> On June 14th, the King rode in a cavalcade to the Saint-Remi Abbey. His Majesty was accompanied by the Count of Provence, the Count of Artois, the Duke of Orléans, the Duke of Chartres, the Prince of Condé, the Duke of Bourbon and by many other Lords and great officers. He attended Mass in the Abbey and performed his Devotions through the Cardinal of la Roche-Aymon's hands. Then, in the Park of the Abbey, he touched 2,400 people who had the disease of scrofula and distributed charity to them. In the afternoon, the King took a walk in the park and from there went to the camp of the French and Swiss Guard units. The People, who were

following His Majesty, showed their Master how delighted they were because of his presence.

The day of Corpus Christ, the King accompanied by the Count of Provence, the Count of Artois, and Princes of Royal Blood, followed the procession and attended the Great Mass...in the Metropolitan Church. The Queen, Madame, Madame Clotilde, Madame Elizabeth, the Duchess of Bourbon, and many Court Lords and Ladies were also present.[32]

Even amid the hatred of the Revolution, Louis would never quite lose the aura of his *sacré*. Several times during the Revolution he was able to calm angry mobs and thus buy time for himself and his family. Even at the scaffold his presence elicited awe. To quote from *History Today*:

The personal popularity of Louis XVI, *libelles* notwithstanding, lasted until at least September 1789. Most of what went wrong until then was blamed upon his wicked, despotic, deceiving ministers – or, later, upon his Austrian wife. Indeed, as his blood streamed through the floorboards of the scaffold on 21 January 1793 people rushed forward to dip their handkerchiefs in the mystical fluid while others reproached them for sacrilege. Clearly, Louis XVI still had the capacity to inspire a reverence that was at least semi-religious, right to the end.[33]

7 THEIR MOST CHRISTIAN MAJESTIES

"The Queen looked upon the destiny of her sisters as far beneath her own." —Madame Campan

Louis XVI was perhaps one of the best educated men to ever sit upon the throne of France. Nevertheless, Antoinette often lamented that his education had been deficient, although scholastically his was much superior to her own. He especially admired the classic literature of his own country and was thoroughly acquainted with it. As Madame Campan penned many years later:

> The Abbé de Radonvilliers, his preceptor, one of the Forty of the French Academy, a learned and amiable man, had given him and Monsieur a taste for study. The King had continued to instruct himself; he knew the English language perfectly; I have often heard him translate some of the most difficult passages in Milton's poems. He was a skillful geographer, and

was fond of drawing and coloring maps; he was well versed in history, but had not perhaps sufficiently studied the spirit of it. He appreciated dramatic beauties, and judged them accurately. At Choisy, one day, several ladies expressed their dissatisfaction because the French actors were going to perform one of Molière's pieces. The King inquired why they disapproved of the choice. One of them answered that everybody must admit that Molière had very bad taste; the King replied that many things might be found in Molière contrary to fashion, but that it appeared to him difficult to point out any in bad taste?[1]

Antoinette genuinely thought that where social graces were concerned, Louis' tutelage had been shamefully neglected by his governor the Duc de la Vauguyon, whom she already disliked for being against the Austrian alliance. She was correct in that Louis' education had been focused on the high ideals of being the heir of St. Louis without enough practical experience in government or military matters, or even the rudimentary skills of a courtier, such as dancing and small talk. She received a scolding from her mother and brother Joseph for daring to label Louis XVI as "poor man" in a letter to the Austrian minister Count Rosenburg.[2] Mercy tried to defend Antoinette by telling the Empress that *pauvre homme* was an endearment like *bon homme* but Maria Theresa would have none of it, and thought that Antoinette's respect for her husband and her King was sorely lacking.[3] Perhaps the Empress understood more than Antoinette did the perilous political and economic situation which was at stake. Then as now, Louis XVI is renowned for his alleged personal shortcomings yet few people understand the gravity of the situation with which he was faced upon his accession. As Nesta Webster expresses it in her study *Louis XVI and Marie-Antoinette before the Revolution*:

> Everyone agrees in calling him weak, but who has tried to put himself in his place and consider the problems that confronted him? To settle the grievances of each class, without irritating the other classes, to relieve the sufferings of the peasants, without antagonizing the nobles, to give greater liberty to the Protestants, without alienating the Church, to reform government, without shaking the foundations of the State, to revive the spirit of the army, without plunging the country into war, to reduce taxation, and at the same time restore the ruined finances. to regenerate morals, to purify the court, and last but not least reconcile the factions within the royal family itself....These were the problems the boy of nineteen was called upon to face, and that he has been described as weak and imbecile for failing to solve.[4]

As previously discussed, Louis may have had Asperger's Syndrome, which of course, no one understood at the time. In spite of his awkward social skills, he had a wide array of interests of both the indoor and outdoor variety. He was fascinated with scientific inventions, which he encouraged, and with geography, outfitting a sea voyage of discovery in the Pacific Ocean. He would read his mail as his ministers delivered their reports, without missing a word of what his ministers said. He subscribed to several international newspapers, as a means of keeping informed of events and of the opinions of others. Louis XVI is always portrayed as politically inept and indifferent, and yet he built up the French navy and army so that Great Britain was defeated in the war for American independence. The ships and soldiers outfitted by King Louis were later used by Napoleon Bonaparte to conquer Europe. During the Revolution, he tried to avoid bloodshed at all costs and would not leave the country because he did not want to abandon his people to the fanatical minority which had seized power. His calm in the face of the calamities is usually interpreted as phlegmatic indifference, but by remaining composed, he was often able to regain control of violent situations. Louis XVI was more and more conflicted between his duties as father of his people and father of his family. He tried early in the Revolution to try to persuade the Queen to escape with their children, but she refused to leave his side.

Louis was sincerely devout, following the Ten Commandments and precepts of the Church to the best of his ability. According to Madame Campan:

> ...Austere and rigid with regard to himself alone, the King observed the laws of the Church with scrupulous exactness. He fasted and abstained throughout the whole of Lent. He thought it right that the queen should not observe these customs with the same strictness. Though sincerely pious, the spirit of the age had disposed his mind to toleration. Turgot, Malesherbes, and Necker judged that this Prince, modest and simple in his habits, would willingly sacrifice the royal prerogative to the solid greatness of his people.[5]

One of the problems Louis had to deal with in his reign was Gallicanism. Gallicanism is defined as:

> ...A restraint of the pope's authority in the Church in favour of that of the bishops and the temporal ruler. It is important, however, to remark at the outset that the warmest and most accredited partisans of

Gallican ideas by no means contested the pope's primacy in the Church, and never claimed for their ideas the force of articles of faith.[6]

Gallicanism stood against Ultramontanism, which emphasizes the prerogatives and powers of the Pope, in temporal as well as spiritual matters. In the kingdom of France, Gallicanism meant that the king would appoint bishops and send their names to the pope to be ratified. The negative side of Gallicanism meant that, because the Church in France had a great deal of wealth and political power, the persons recommended to the king for bishoprics were usually wordly men, sons of great families, who used the Church to further family or personal ambitions. This led to a decline of religious faith in France, and the growth of cynicism and atheism which the *philosophes* promoted. Among other ecclesiastical powers held by the king of France, but never recognized by the Vatican, included the right of kings of France to assemble church councils in their dominions; to make laws and regulations touching ecclesiastical matters. The king's permission was needed for papal legates to enter France and exercise their authority there. The bishops could not obey a papal summons without the king's permission. Royal officers could not be excommunicated for any deed committed in the exercise of their royal duties. Papal bulls could only be approved by the king before they took effect in France.[7] The interference of French royal authority in church matters can in no way be compared to the Henrician schism in England. However, it paved the way for the Revolutionary government to seize complete control of the Church and all ecclesiastical property. After the French revolutionary government seized control of the Church, Louis XVI, after receiving guidance from the Pope, refused to receive Communion from a priest not in union with Rome. He also vetoed the law forcing priests to be deported for not denying the papal supremacy, even though it brought the angry populace upon the palace in June 1792. [8]

Accompanying Gallicanism was the neo-Gallican rite. In the early centuries of Christianity in France the rite common in those territories directly ruled by the King was called the "Gallican" rite, which resembled in many ways the Byzantine rites of Eastern Christianity.[9] While the old Gallican rite was replaced by the Latin rite in the Middle Ages, there lingered a neo-Gallican rite in which some prayers and ceremonies differed slightly from the Roman missal, with lots of accomodations for the various dioceses. In Paris before the Revolution there was a unique missal and breviary for the Archdiocese of Paris which emphasized local saints and saints admired by the French, including persons not regarded as particularly saintly today, such as Charlemagne. When Louis and Antoinette lived at Versailles, they observed the "rite of Versailles" which included special prayers for everyone in the royal family, and prayers for every undertaking of the king. In fact, prayers for the king replaced prayers for the Pope.[10] Those rites, which are occasionally revived by traditionalist groups, disappeared from regular usage during the Revolution.

People who came to Versailles to see the King and Queen were usually able to do so at the daily procession to noon Mass in the Royal Chapel. Drums announced his coming as he entered the chapel, usually with the Queen at his side, except when she was staying at Trianon, where she had her own chapel. One observation that many travelers to Versailles had, particularly British visitors, was the fact that the Mass was exceedingly short, even on Sundays, and that courtiers talked throughout the service. No one seemed to be paying attention to the priest on the altar. The choir was more a focus of the congregation than the sacred mysteries; they focused on the King most of all. It seems the royal behavior left much to be desired. One Richard Garmston was shocked to see the King and his brothers talking during Mass, while Sir Simon Romilly claimed to see Louis XVI laughing while smiling at the heavily rouged court ladies in the galleries.[11] Whether such stories are true in every detail is questionable; however, it can be safely deduced that religious practice in France had genuinely fallen into decline on every level of society. It would take the blood of the martyrs of the Revolution to restore the Catholic Church in France.

On a personal level, Louis XVI struggled with "melancholy" at various times throughout his life, perhaps due to the childhood infection with tuberculosis. His doctors recommended outdoor exertion for his health, which of course, included hunting. With a regimen of exercise as part of his strict routine he was able to keep the depression at bay. He was also encouraged to hunt by his confessor, Abbé Soldini, who also saw it as a way the teenaged Louis could build a relationship with his grandfather Louis XV. He regularly ate at the hunt suppers with his grandfather at the invitation of Madame du Barry. In practically every book, article or blog post about Louis XVI, it is usually pointed out that hunting was his passion. However, a love of the chase was not something unique to Louis. Hunting is what the nobility did, all nobles, unless some kind of physical handicap prevented them.[12] It had, of course, originated as a way of procuring food to feed large households and families. Even in the most decadent of times before the Revolution of 1789, the game was killed not for mere sport, but to be eaten. That the Bourbon kings of France would devote themselves to such sport should not come as a great surprise, since Versailles was originally built to be a hunting lodge.

From the days of Louis XIII hunting was almost a daily activity. The post of Grand Huntsman was among the highest in the realm. Some of the other royal residences, Rambouillet, Compiègne, Fontainebleau, and La Muette were hunting lodges as well. According to David Grubin:

> All of Versailles was initially an immense hunting area, with the original *château* grounds being ten times larger than they are today. In the area now called the Grand Park, the royal family and the court continued this hunting tradition, both on horseback and on foot....Hunting on horseback was an activity reserved to the nobility in prerevolutionary France, truly the sport of kings. Gifts of fresh game were one way in which nobles showed their generosity to those who did not share their privileges. Such gifts reminded the recipient of his lower place in the social order while demonstrating the nobility of the giver. For the king and his retinue, the Royal Hunt was a noble pursuit. Invitations to the Royal Hunt were greatly coveted, and the king used these invitations to show favor and gain support. Hunts were generally followed by elaborate dinners, sometimes with guest lists in the hundreds....[13]

It was at a hunt that an English lady named Mrs. Thrale observed the young Antoinette on horseback, saying:

> 20 Octr 1775 begins. This Morning we drove into the Forest as they call it to see the Queen ride on Horseback. We were early enough to see her mount, which was not done as in England by a Man's hand, but the right foot is fixed in the Stirrup first & then drawn out again when the Lady is on her Saddle. The

Horse on which the Queen rode was neither handsome nor gentle, he was however confined with Martingales &c. & richly caparison'd with blue Velvet & Silver Embroidery: the Saddle was ill contrived—sloping off behind—& a Pommel so awkward that no Joyner could have executed it worse,—there was a Handle by the Side I saw. While we were examining the Furniture and Formation of the Horse, the Queen came to ride him, attended by the Duchess de Luignes, who wore Boots & Breeches like a Man with a single Petticoat over them, her Hair tyed & her Hat cocked exactly like those of a Man, Her Majesty's Habit was Puce Colour as they call it her Hat filled with Feathers and her Figure perfectly pleasing. She offered her Arm to the King's Aunts who followed her to the Rendezvous in a Coach, as they were getting out, but they respectfully refus'd her Assistance.[14]

Antoinette was said to be a fine and fearless rider, often donning male apparel.[15] She won much public acclaim for taking care not to destroy the gardens and crops of the peasants when hunting, forbidding her attendants to do the same even if it meant losing track of the hunt. Such common courtesy was rare. Madame Campan records another incident of Antoinette's compassion for the poor, as follows:

A circumstance which happened in hunting, near the village of Achères, in the forest of Fontainebleau, afforded the young Princess an opportunity of displaying her respect for old age, and her compassion for misfortune. An aged peasant was wounded by the stag; the Dauphiness jumped out of her calash, placed the peasant, with his wife and children, in it, had the family taken back to their cottage, and bestowed upon them every attention and every necessary assistance. Her heart was always open to the feelings of compassion, and the recollection of her rank never restrained her sensibility. Several persons in her service entered her room one evening, expecting to find nobody there but the officer in waiting; they perceived the young Princess seated by the side of this man, who was advanced in years; she had placed near him a bowl full of water, was stanching the blood which issued from a wound he had received in his hand with her handkerchief, which she had torn up to bind it, and was fulfilling towards him all the duties of a pious sister of charity.[16]

Antoinette's courtesy extended to those of her household. Antoinette once stopped hunting for two weeks because the wife of her head groom was expecting a child at any moment and she did not wish to part the husband from the wife at such a moment. On another occasion, an attendant's horse kicked her, bruising her foot, but Antoinette made no mention of the injury until the hunt was over so as to not humiliate the culprit. As a young princess, Antoinette had been banned by her mother from joining the hunt on horseback. The Empress feared that she would have a miscarriage, or at least ruin her complexion. The Dauphine, being married and technically no longer subject to her mother, eventually insisted on riding with her husband, finding it a way to capture his attention. Gaining Louis' regard was, of course, vital for conceiving a child. According to Yonge:

> The latter part of the year 1771 was marked by no very striking occurrences. Marie Antoinette had carried her point, and had begun to ride on horseback

without either her figure or her complexion suffering from the exercise. On the contrary, she was admitted to have improved in beauty. She sent her measure to Vienna, to show Maria Teresa how much she had grown, adding that her husband had grown as much, and had become stronger and more healthy-looking, and that she had made use of her saddle-horses to accompany him in his hunting and shooting excursions. Like a true wife, she boasted to her mother of his skill as a shot: the very day that she wrote he had killed forty head of game. (She did not mention that a French sportsman's bag was not confined to the larger game, but that thrushes, blackbirds, and even, red-breasts, were admitted to swell the list.) And the increased facilities for companionship with him that her riding afforded increased his tenderness for her, so that she was happier than ever. Except that as yet she saw no prospect of presenting the empress with a grandchild, she had hardly a wish ungratified.[17]

It was at the hunting lodge of La Muette that in 1774 the young Louis XVI and Antoinette broke with protocol by strolling arm in arm, like "man and wife," before crowds of people who cheered them deliriously. It was considered contrary to etiquette for royal spouses to display affection in public. The new King and Queen wanted to break with such stiff and antiquated customs. By the way, when Louis XVI recorded "nothing" in his journal on July 14, 1789 when the Bastille was stormd by the mob, it meant that he had caught nothing while hunting. It did not mean that he was indifferent or oblivious to the violence in Paris, since it is obvious from his actions that he was quite concerned. It is just one more ridiculous canard which even educated people continually spout about Louis XVI.[18] Sadly, when the various hunting laws protecting the game were overturned by the Revolution, there were orgies of peasants killing animals in various parts of France, both large and small game, not to eat but out of rage, leaving the woods and fields full of corpses.

The following is a portrait in words of Antoinette by Sainte-Beuve based upon the account of the Comte de La Marck:

> The queen's beauty in her youth has been enthusiastically praised. She was not a beauty, if we take her features in detail: the eyes, although expressive, were not very fine, her aquiline nose seemed too pronounced. 'I am not quite sure that her nose belonged to her face,' said a clever observer. Her lower lip was more prominent and thick than one expects in a pretty woman; her figure also was a little full; but the general effect was of a noble manner and sovereign dignity. Even in *negligé* hers was the beauty of a queen, rather than of a woman of fashion.
>
> 'No woman,' said M. de Meilhan, 'ever carried her head better, and it was so set upon her shoulders that every movement she made was instinct with grace and nobility. Her gait was stately, yet light, and recalled Virgil's phrase, *incessu patuit dea* ["she was in truth a goddess"]. And there was in her person a still rarer quality,—the union of grace and of the most imposing dignity.'
>
> Add a dazzlingly fresh complexion, beautiful arms and hands, a charming smile, and tactful speech which found its inspiration less in the mind than in the heart, in the desire to be kind and to please. [19]

It is sometimes said of Antoinette that she hated France and the French, and most of all hated being the Queen. None of this is true. Antoinette saw being Queen of France, in spite of the many inconveniences and burdens attached to the role, as being the apex of earthly existence. She preferred for her daughter Madame Royale to remain in France as a princess of France, married to a French-born prince, rather than arrange a marriage for her with a king of another country. Also, Antoinette did not want to be separated from her daughter as she herself had been divided from her family at such a tender age. Madame Campan attests to these facts in her memoirs, while relating some events that occurred in 1787. To quote:

> I had an opportunity on this occasion, as indeed on many others, of judging to what extent the Queen valued and loved France and the dignity of our Court. She then told me that Madame, in marrying her cousin, the Duc d'Angoulême, would not lose her rank as daughter of the Queen; and that her situation would be far preferable to that of queen of any other country; and that there was nothing in Europe to be compared to the Court of France; and that it would be necessary, in order to avoid exposing a French Princess to feelings of deep regret, in case she should be married to a foreign prince, to take her from the palace of Versailles at seven years of age, and send her immediately to the Court in which she was to dwell; and that at twelve would be too late; for recollections and comparisons would ruin the happiness of all the rest of her life. The Queen looked upon the destiny of her sisters as far beneath her own....[20]

The following is an excerpt of a letter from Antoinette to her mother Empress Maria Theresa, written on February 17, 1777. Antoinette was twenty-one years old and had been Queen of France for almost three years. It demonstrates that in spite of the popular perception of being brainless, the young Queen had an awareness of the political situation in Europe. At the time the letter was written, Antoinette was at the height of the partying phase of her life, and not actively engaged in political affairs; Louis XVI encouraged her not to become involved. That she had a basic sense of what was going on, long before the Revolution when she played a larger role in the political scene, shows that she had inherited some of her mother's astuteness. When she says that "it would be the greatest good fortune if these two sovereigns [her husband and her brother Joseph]...could trust each other" she is referring primarily to the fact that Louis did not trust the Emperor and would not go along with his plans. She was also acutely aware of the intrigues of the court and accurately predicted that the appointment of Cardinal Prince Louis de Rohan as Grand Almoner would bring "many intrigues;" it certainly brought about the Diamond Necklace fiasco.

> Although I have very little experience of politics, I cannot help being worried about what is happening everywhere in Europe. It would be very terrible if the Turks and the Russians went back to war. At least here I am very sure they want to keep the peace. If my brother had come, I think, like my dear Mama, that his acquaintance with the King would have been very useful for the general good and quiet. It would be the greatest good fortune if these two sovereigns, who are so close to me, could trust each other, they could settle many things together and would be protected from the lack of skill and the personal interests of their ministers.
>
> The Grand Almoner is at death's door; Prince Louis [de Rohan] will replace him in that office. I am

really annoyed by this, and it will be much against his own inclination that the King will appoint him; but two years ago he allowed himself to be surprised by M. de Soubise and Mme. de Marsan into a half promise, which they converted into a full one by thanking him, and which they have just now used to the full. If he [Rohan] behaves as he always did, we will have many intrigues. [21]

One of the principle myths about Antoinette is that she manipulated Louis and out of guilt for his shortcomings, he did everything she asked him to do. To her frustration, and that of her Austrian relatives, Louis had a mind of his own and stubbornly held to the course of action he thought best for France. At the beginning of Louis' reign, Antoinette connived to reinstate Choiseul as Foreign Minister. Choiseul had been dismissed by Louis XV right after her arrival in France in 1770, and Antoinette never gave up trying to restore him to power. However, her husband did not like or trust Choiseul and would have none of it. In 1777, Antoinette found herself once again at odds with Louis over the Bavarian matter. Her brother Emperor Joseph sought to invade and dismember Bavaria as an attempt to absorb it into the Habsburg territories. Louis refused to back him and without French support, Joseph's plans came to nothing. Antoinette begged Louis in tears to help the Emperor and the King refused, quite firmly.[22] Antoinette also did not think it prudent for Louis to help the Americans in their fight for independence against Great Britain, but nothing could change his mind. It was not until after the Empress Maria Theresa died and Antoinette became the mother of Louis' children that she began to have any influence in political matters. Even so, Louis still preferred her to keep busy with her projects at Trianon.

Contrary to myths of Versailles being an orgy of

immorality when she was Queen, Antoinette tried from the beginning of her husband's reign to reform the morals of the court, which did not always endear her to the nobles. Under Louis XV and his mistresses, too often licentious behavior had been a path to popularity and successs. Antoinette made a rule that she would not receive any lady who was separated from her husband. She also abolished a regulation that prohibited the Queen from sitting at table with any men but members of the royal family. Henceforth, her ladies could dine with her accompanied by their own husbands at the King's table. To quote from Yonge:

> Such an exclusion from the king's table of those who were its most natural and becoming ornaments had notoriously facilitated and augmented the disorders of the last reign; and it was obvious that its maintenance must at least have a tendency to lead to a repetition of the old irregularities. Fortunately, the king was as little inclined to approve of it as the queen. All his tastes were domestic, and he gladly assented to her proposal to abolish the custom. Throughout the reign, at all ordinary meals, at his suppers when he came in late from hunting, when he had perhaps invited some of his fellow-sportsmen to share his repast, and at State banquets, Marie Antoinette took her seat at his side, not only adding grace and liveliness to the entertainment, but effectually preventing license, and even the suspicion of scandal; and, as she desired that her household as well as her family should set an example of regularity and propriety to the nation, she exercised a careful superintendence over the behavior of those who had hitherto been among the least-considered members of the royal establishment. Even the king's confessor had thought the morals of the royal pages either

beneath his notice or beyond his control; but Marie Antoinette took a higher view of her duties. [23]

Antoinette took the court pages under her charge as well; since they were mostly young boys away from their parents, she behaved as a mother, gently correcting their misbehavior and praising their achievements and successes.

The Royal Family of France was seen as belonging to the people. The *château* of Versailles was open to the public; anyone could enter as long as they were appropriately attired. For gentlemen this meant wearing a sword; swords could be rented at the gates. As for ladies, they had to have a hooped petticoat. The tradition of freedom and openness meant that the royal family often dined surrounded by crowds of people; the princesses were required to give birth in public. Merchants set up stalls in the grand salons, selling ribbons and snuff; beggars roamed the corridors. Security did not seem to be an issue. Unfortunately, such liberty led to Antoinette being stalked by a mental patient, but she refused to have the culprit arrested, and begged him to be allowed his liberty, since he was not dangerous. Madame Campan relates the situation as follows:

> Among the characteristics which denoted the goodness of the Queen, her respect for personal liberty should have a place. I have seen her put up with the most troublesome importunities from people whose minds were deranged rather than have them arrested. Her patient kindness was put to a very disagreeable trial by an ex-councillor of the Bordeaux Parliament, named Castelnaux; this man declared himself the lover of the Queen, and was generally known by that appellation. For ten successive years

did he follow the Court in all its excursions. Pale and wan, as people who are out of their senses usually are, his sinister appearance occasioned the most uncomfortable sensations. During the two hours that the Queen's public card parties lasted, he would remain opposite her Majesty. He placed himself in the same manner before her at chapel, and never failed to be at the King's dinner or the dinner in public. At the theatre he invariably seated himself as near the Queen's box as possible. He always set off for Fontainebleau or St. Cloud the day before the Court, and when her Majesty arrived at her various residences, the first person she met on getting out of her carriage was this melancholy madman, who never spoke to any one. [24]

There was another case in which Antoinette interceded for Messieurs de Bellagarde and de Moustiers, whose families had petitioned her. It seems that the gentlemen were being persecuted unjustly; the Queen obtained a new hearing for them, and they were released. "As a token of gratitude, Madame de Bellegarde had a picture painted in which she was represented with her husband kneeling before the queen … the queen was greatly touched, and placed the picture in her apartment."[25]

Chateaubriand, who saw the Queen at Versailles in his youth, described Antoinette as being "enchanted with life."[26] She was indeed a lady of immense charm, possessing those subtle qualities which win hearts. There is much talk about how and why Antoinette was hated by the French people, but it is forgotten that she was also greatly loved by many, especially after they came face-to-face with her. Men were ready to die in order to save her. Another reason for the Fersen legend is that people assume that since Count Fersen risked his life and made many sacrifices for Antoinette and her family it must have been because she was sleeping with him. Yet she had the identical effect on other men as well, men who were not even part of her circle of friends, and with whom she was not romantically linked in the rumor mill. Mirabeau and Barnave, two dedicated revolutionaries, were won over by the Queen after meeting her, and afterwards did everything they could to save her. Barnave was quite taken with the entire royal family, especially after spending hours in the coach with them after the capture at Varennes in June 1791. "The Queen treated him with affectionate politeness which had led to her being given the title of 'Mary full of grace (*Marie pleine de graces*).'"[27] Later, in the Temple prison, the guard Toulan, a zealous revolutionary, was completely smitten by the Queen, and risked his life to retrieve Louis XVI's wedding ring for her. He tried to help her escape, and the Chevalier Jarjayes as well, but the Queen would not leave her children.

Nesta Webster, in *Louis XVI and Marie-Antoinette before the Revolution* draws an intriguing comparison between Antoinette and her devout sister-in-law:

> Madame Élisabeth was undoubtedly a saint, and her unblemished reputation, which no one dared assail, has been contrasted with the character for frivolity attributed to Marie-Antoinette. But if Marie-Antoinette had displayed throughout the piety of Madame Élisabeth, if she had never indulged in those four years of "dissipation," never gambled, never exceeded her dress allowance, never figured on the stage at Trianon, would she have escaped calumny? When one considers the forces ranged against her one is inclined to answer "no." It must be remembered that Madame Élisabeth gave no cause for envy, she had obstructed no one's path to the throne, and she

had none of the personal charm and elegance that distinguished Marie-Antoinette. A woman who goes like wine to the heads of men is naturally more vulnerable to the tongue of calumny than one whom no one would associate with romance....Marie-Antoinette had the power of inspiring passionate and almost uncontrollable adoration. [28]

Antoinette is not the only one in the history of queens, great ladies, and women in general, who had the ability to inspire chivalrous devotion in men. Certainly, Mary Queen of Scots likewise possessed a similar personal charisma. The speech of Elizabeth Tudor to her troops as the Spanish armada approached is another example. Queen Marie of Romania also had the gift of inspiring heroism in her supporters. So did Marie-Antoinette's mother, the Empress Maria Theresa, especially when she presented herself before the Hungarian nobles, an occasion Antoinette looked to in her own troubles. Such ladies had the gift of inspiring valiance in men.

Dining in public was a custom which Antoinette found intolerable and she did her best to limit it after she became Queen. She did not realize that by changing centuries old customs, she was initiating the upheavals of the Revolution. Madame Campan describes how she found the custom of dining in public a mortification:

> One of the customs most disagreeable to the Queen was that of dining every day in public. Maria Leczinska had always submitted to this wearisome practice; Marie Antoinette followed it as long as she was Dauphiness. The Dauphin dined with her, and each branch of the family had its public dinner daily. The ushers suffered all decently dressed people to enter; the sight was the delight of persons from the

country. At the dinner-hour there were none to be met upon the stairs but honest folks, who, after having seen the Dauphiness take her soup, went to see the Princes eat their *bouilli*, and then ran themselves out of breath to behold Mesdames at their dessert....She also freed herself from the necessity of being followed in the Palace of Versailles by two of her women in Court dresses, during those hours of the day when the ladies-in-waiting were not with her. From that time she was accompanied only by a single *valet de chambre* and two footmen. All the changes made by Marie Antoinette were of the same description; a disposition gradually to substitute the simple customs of Vienna for those of Versailles was more injurious to her than she could possibly have imagined.[29]

By discarding and disregarding old customs, Antoinette introduced triple rupture at court, young versus old, *petite noblesse* against ancient nobility, intimate life versus public life. It was an inversion of the order imposed by the Sun King. Both Louis and Antoinette were enemies of etiquette and *representation*, the latter meaning that royalty was continually on-stage. Such chipping away was seen by some as sowing the seeds of revolt, as well as substituting Austrian manners for French traditions.[30]

Since the state rooms at Versailles were open to the public, even the Queen's bedroom, it was necessary to have a place to go for minimal privacy. The *petit appartement de la reine* was a suite of rooms at Versailles used by the Queens of France in their private hours. In Antoinette's time the *petit appartement de la reine* consisted of two libraries, a bathroom, *le salon doré* and the boudoir, called *la méridienne*. In 1781 Louis XVI ordered the architect Mique to design the small octagonal chamber for Antoinette in honor of birth of their first son the Dauphin Louis-Joseph. It was a place for the Queen to rest in the afternoons after dinner and before the festivities of the evening. It was also the place where she received her dressmaker and decided which clothes she was going to wear to certain events. *La méridienne* was decorated in grenadine blue silk and in spite of the destruction of revolutions and centuries has been skillfully recreated by French craftsmen. The *salon doré* on the other hand, was where the Queen would recieve guests and those who sought her patronage or benefaction.

In the meantime, Louis XVI, from the moment he ascended the throne was active in making reforms; he was considered a liberal-minded monarch. Anyone who thinks Louis XVI was a lazy, sluggish, do-nothing king need only examine the six volumes of laws passed during his reign. He wanted to reform the feudal tax system, which is why he called the Estates-General in 1789. If all the nobles and wealthy clergy had been minimally taxed, there would have been no deficit. In 1774 Louis XVI placed Turgot in charge of finances and introduced free circulation of grain. He also founded the School of Medicine in Paris. In 1775 the *droits d'octroi* (excise duties) were reduced, prison reform begun, and the death penalty for deserters was abolished. In 1776 Louis XVI signed the six edicts of Turgot comprising the abolition of the *corvée*. The *corvée* was an old law which forced the peasantry to maintain the roads. The *parlements* resisted the edicts, preventing them from becoming law. In the same year he reduced his household. In 1778 more taxes were reduced. In 1779 the king abolished servitude and other reforms were made. In 1780, further reductions in the royal household were made, hospital reform was begun, prison reform continued, most torture was abolished. In 1784 relief from oppressive laws was given to Jews. In 1786 Louis enacted more hospital reform, as well as aid to the deaf, and provisions made for lost children. Then, in 1787, steps were taken towards the total abolition of the *corvée*, in addition to more reductions in the royal household, and full civil rights accorded to Jews and Protestants. In 1788, the year before the Revolution began, all forms of torture were abolished, greater freedom given to press, steps towards abolition of *lettres de cachet* which was a warrant that, when signed by the monarch, could mean imprisonment without trial. In 1789 came Louis' boldest move: he summoned the Estates-General in an attempt to reform the tax sytem.[31]

It is fairly well-known that without the military and financial aid given by Louis XVI to the American colonists in their struggle for independence from Great Britain, our nation may never have arisen. The King of France was reluctant to go to war, recoiling from both the expense and the shedding of blood; he did so only when convinced that it would benefit France in the long run. Antoinette was initially against assisting the Americans; she thought it set a dangerous precedent to help the colonists rebel against their king. Nevertheless, once war was declared, she did not hesitate to embrace the joint cause of France and America. According to Lafayette she once greeted him by saying: "Give me news of our good Americans, of our dear Republicans!"[32] Lafayette may have colored her words with his own enthusiasm for the cause. However, the general repartee in the French court over the American revolt is rather humorous, or at least it would be, had the consequences for France not been so tragic. When Antoinette's brother, Emperor Joseph II, was visiting Versailles, some pro-American French lady kept badgering him about the colonists' revolt. Finally, the Holy Roman Emperor curtly replied: "Madame, I am a royalist by profession."[33] When Lafayette joined the followers of Mesmer, Louis XVI asked him, ironically: "What will Washington think when he hears that you have become the first apothecary of Mesmer?" [34]

The King and Queen graciously received Benjamin Franklin, Thomas Jefferson, John Adams, Gouveneur Morris and other Americans at Versailles. Louis XVI was depicted in art with Benjamin Franklin and George Washington. Louis showed mercy to the enemy as well, by insisting that the sick and wounded British soldiers be treated as his own subjects. He also gave the order that the French navy was not to harm the English fishermen.[35] In the HBO production of *John Adams*, Louis XVI was portrayed as being a foppish popinjay. In real life, the King did not laugh at Adams at their first meeting, although he mumbled "*Pas un mot!*" "Not a word!" out of surprise that Mr. Adams did not yet speak French, the language of diplomacy.[36] Adams did learn French and he and King Louis came to have respect for each other; Adams described the young King as having "goodness and innocence" in his face.[37] As for Louis XVI's opinion of Adams, McCullough writes: "Vergennes, speaking for the King, offered praise [to Adams] for 'the wise conduct that you have held throughout the tenure of your commission,' as well as 'the zeal with which you have furthered the cause of your nation, while strengthening the alliance that ties it to His Majesty.'"[38] John Adams described Antoinette thus:

> She was an object too sublime and beautiful for my dull pen to describe...Her dress was everything that art and wealth could make it....She had a fine complexion indicating her perfect health, and was a handsome woman in her face and figure....not a feature of her face, nor a motion of any part of her person, especially her arm and her hand, could be

criticized as being out of order.[39]

All in all, John Adams loved the France of Louis XVI and Antoinette, in spite of his homesickness. To quote from McCullough's biography:

As ardently as he longed for home, he hated to leave Paris, hated to leave France, and expected he would never return. 'The climate is more favorable to my constitution than ours,' he acknowledged to Abigail. He loved the food, the civility of everyday life. The French were 'the happiest people in the world...and have the best disposition to make others so. There is such a choice of elegant entertainments in the theatric way, of good company and excellent books that nothing would be wanting for me in this country but my family and peace to my country to make me one of the happiest of men.'[40]

Unfortunately, the bankruptcy France incurred by the war caused the political crisis in France to escalate, leading to the bloody Revolution of 1789 and to the deaths of Louis and Antoinette. But Louis XVI did indeed show foresight in his decision to help the colonies. Twice the new nation would come to the aid of France when France was in dire need. I always have thought that in addition to saying "Lafayette, we are here," General Pershing should have said "Louis XVI, we are here" since without the King's help America may never have become a nation.

The reign of Louis XVI in the years before the French Revolution has been reassessed by historians in the 20th and 21st centuries. Louis had many great accomplishments as a political leader and was widely admired by the other sovereigns of Europe while still in his twenties. Louis' victory over England threatened to upset the hegemony of the British Empire, especially since the French were beginning to make headway in the Far East. Louis tried to reverse previous losses and see the growing British dominance in India come to an end. He allied with the Maratha Empire and took the side of the Sultan of Mysore in the Second Anglo-Mysore War in the hope of breaking the dominance of the British East India Company, curtailing British influence in India and increasing French influence. He welcomed the envoys of Tipoo Sahib, the Sultan of Mysore, to Versailles. Antoinette was so fascinated by their exotic attire she summoned Madame Tussaud to recreate them in wax.[41] It was under King Louis XVI that France first took a serious interest in Vietnam and, indirectly, helped bring about the victory of the last great imperial dynasty of Vietnamese history. Perhaps this is one of the reasons so many pamphlets, both political and pornographic, were sent into France by the British government in an attempt to foment discord and destroy the French monarchy.

In 1785 Louis XVI commissioned the naval hero La Pérouse to outfit two ships for an expedition to explore the unknown regions of the Pacific Ocean. Louis and Antoinette were fascinated with Oceania, having each heard of the discoveries of Captain James Cook. Captain Cook was the first European to circumnavigate New Zealand. His explorations were acclaimed all over Europe; it is said that when news of his death came to Versailles in 1779, the Queen burst into tears. Later, in her cell in the Conciergerie, one of the few books provided for Antoinette *was The Voyages of Captain Cook*, which was said to have been her favorite. Louis did not want the British to outstrip the French in nautical explorations; along with La Pérouse he engaged an astronomer, a physician, three biologists, a mathematician and three draftsmen. The Catholic chaplains who were to accompany the yoyage were trained as scientists as well. The King, who was a skilled amateur cartographer and geographer, painstakingly mapped out the voyage which lasted for three years. The adventurers pinpointed the exact location of previously unknown Pacific Islands. In 1788, however, La Pérouse and his men encountered cannibals and the crews of both frigates perished miserably. One man escaped with maps and charts so that the voyage was not in vain. The tragedy destroyed the theory of the *philosophes* that man in his primitive state was benign and peaceful. It is interesting that even amid their misfortunes, the thoughts of the King and the Queen went to the mysterious lands on the other side of the world. Antoinette, other than journeying from Austria to France in 1770, never traveled—it would have cost too much money—and she never saw the ocean. Louis saw the Atlantic Ocean once at Cherbourg in 1785, but never crossed it; as a geographer he probably longed to explore the ends of the earth had it been compatible with his duties as King. His vicarious explorations of Oceania by means of La Pérouse meant a great deal to him. As mentioned above, it is telling that on the morning of his death he asked: "Is there any news of Monsieur de La Pérouse?"[42]

8 FOLLIES AND ESCAPADES

"We adored her without thinking of loving her."
—the Prince de Ligne

There was so much sadness in her life that we forget that Antoinette possessed a genuinely happy disposition as well as the gift of seeing the droll side of every situation. She loved living and had the ability to laugh at herself. As a young Queen she enjoyed driving around the grounds of Versailles by herself in a cabriolet, something no queen had ever done before. Once the eighteen-year-old Antoinette dressed as a Grey Nun in order to see her busy young husband in his study, quite diligent and intent upon being a good king. Louis did not recognize the "good sister" at first and when he saw her convulsed with laughter, he thought she was ill. It was several minutes before he realized the nun was really his wife. Another time, at a state banquet, she made pellets out of bread and threw them at Louis across the table. People were shocked, but much more so when she cheered very loud at the horse races on the Bois de Boulogne. Louis had to keep telling her to be quiet. On the way to a *soirée* in Paris, Antoinette's coach broke down so she hired a taxi to get to the party on time. "I came in a *fiacre*!" she gleefully told everyone, but the Parisians did not view the event with humor. It is the mistake of a sheltered young girl, who did not realize the dangers.

It is unfortunate that such instances of youthful high spirits were twisted into something vicious by people who did not understand humor that was not obscene, or a sense of adventure that was not connected with dangerous intrigues. Few were indifferent to Antoinette, however. She was either loved with a reverence akin to piety, or hated with a fury. One of her first escapades occurred early in her husband's reign. Antoinette had been reading a history book about the Incas and conceived the idea of going outside at dawn to see the sun rise. Louis gave his consent to the adventure, as long as he did not have to come along, and as long as Antoinette was properly escorted. Accompanied by Madame de Noailles and several of her ladies, as well as bodyguards, Antoinette fulfilled her dream of experiencing the sights and sounds of early morning, and the colors of a glorious sunrise. "How beautiful it is!" she exclaimed, and she said she understood why the Incas worshipped the sun. Unfortunately, like almost everything else in her life, it was turned into something evil by the gossips. Soon after the first pornographic pamphlet about her appeared in Paris and at Versailles, called *Le Lever d'Aurore*, which transformed the innocent adventure into an orgy. Louis was furious; he had police find the culprit, who was a priest, and had him thrown in jail. It was only the beginning of the pamphlet industry which would flourish at Antoinette's expense.[1] Her brother-in-law Artois was usually portrayed as her lover, although other pamphlets showed her participating in mass orgies with both sexes.

The escapades of sleigh-riding, going incognito to the opera ball, hunting and watching the horse races in the Bois de Boulogne, were harmless past-times for a twenty-year-old queen. Gambling, however, became a serious addiction. It must be kept in mind, however, that Antoinette was not the only one. Gambling was an entrenched part of court life from the days of Louis XIV. As scholar Ross Hamilton describes it:

> Gambling obsessed all levels of French society during the Enlightenment. Louis XIV held *appartements du roi* given over to gambling three times a week at Versailles, the queen hosted a nightly game, and courtiers scheduled additional occasions for play. Hosts so frequently acted as bankers for games to entertain their guests that satirists, chroniclers, and moralists complained that compulsive gambling had destroyed other forms of social entertainment. In Paris ten authorized *maisons de jeux* operated games involving some degree of skill (*jeux de commerce*) but essentially they served as fronts for more lucrative chance-driven games (*jeux de hasard*). Gambling also took place at the two great Paris fairs during almost four months of the year, all year long at foreign embassies, and eventually at gambling houses at the Hotel de Gesvres and later at the Hotel de Soissons. In addition to these legal venues, the large number of clandestine Parisian gaming rooms, lighted by tripots, made one visitor comment that 'flaming pots set Paris ablaze,' and gambling was by no means restricted to Paris. The 'Age des Lumieres' was lighted by gambling. Although official prohibitions referred to both religious and sociological dangers

from gambling, within the context of the period, risking large sums at play became an analogy for risking one's life in battle. Having the courage to risk and winning or losing with equal equanimity demonstrated indifference to material gain and thus served as a means of displaying hereditary status.[2]

In the Old Regime, gambling was one of the only "honorable" ways in which the often cash-strapped aristocrats, who were forbidden to engage in trade, could make money. It also replaced the thrill of war. It required a certain amount of discipline to gamble well; one had to have mastery over facial expressions so as not to reveal one's thoughts about winning or losing, or one's strategy. A noble had to be able to lose with grace and promptly pay debts. Antoinette had been taught as a child by her own mother to gamble, because the Empress knew that a princess who could not play well would soon be separated from her money. Futhermore, the stakes at the court of Austria were much higher than at the court of France, which made Antoinette an intrepid player. As a teenager, she became inordinately attached to the practice. As she began to have gambling debts, Louis XVI, who was trying to save the government finances and give an example of thrift, forbade her to play any more games of chance, except for lotto and *cavagnole* which were played for low stakes. The Queen, however, preferred games with high stakes, such as lansquenet and faro. While at Fontainebleau, she begged her husband to let her have one last game in honor of her twenty-first birthday. He gave permission and, sending for the "gambling bankers" from Paris, Antoinette made sure the game went on for three days. Louis told her that she and her friends were "a worthless lot."

Gambling in France did not disappear with the fall of

the monarchy. The revolutionaries who replaced Louis and Antoinette had their own share of gambling debts. According to historian Russell T. Barnhart:

> The mania for gambling had been transferred from defunct, monarchical Versailles to the thriving, bourgeois Palais Royal, where the five main gaming clubs throbbed from noon till midnight. During the Revolution, Prince Talleyrand won 30,000 francs at one club, and after Waterloo in 1815, Marshal Blucher lost 1,500,000 francs in one night at another. To bring the situation under control and raise taxes for the state, in 1806 Napoleon legalized the main clubs, which from 1819 to 1837 grossed an enormous 137 million francs.[3]

In addition to losing money gambling, Antoinette also spent more money on jewels than she should have. Early in her husband's reign, the jeweler Boehmer approached her with some spectacular diamond earrings. She already had more than enough jewels; along with the crown jewels she had a private collection that had been part of her dowry, in addition to the jewels Louis often gave her as gifts. However she wanted the girandole earrings badly, and was able to bring the enormous price down by having some of her own diamonds used in the jeweler's design. Having saved a little money, she then fell prey to a pair of diamond bracelets which she bought on an impulse, after likewise bringing the price down. But the Queen had overspent her allowance and had to go to the King for more money. Louis did not scold her but quietly remarked that it was no wonder she had no money, since she was so fond of diamonds. The story of her extravagance spread far and wide across France and even to Vienna, via Mercy, although Maria Theresa acted like she had merely read about it in the newspapers. She scolded her daughter but since Antoinette had already been scolded many times for other lesser matters, she did not take her mother's words to heart.[4] Unfortunately, those purchases from Boehmer would lead everyone to later believe that she was guilty of swindling Cardinal de Rohan in the Diamond Necklace scandal.

Antoinette also enjoyed betting on horses. Louis' cousin, the Duc de Chartres, who loved English customs, had introduced horse-racing to France in the mid-70's. He and Louis' youngest brother the Comte d'Artois, as well as the Duc de Lauzun, a dashing courtier with a bad reputation, began to have horse races regularly, usually at the Bois de Boulogne. Antoinette found the sport to be the height of excitement, and forgot all decorum required for a Queen by cheering for her favorite mounts. Caught up in the moment, her usual candor became more pronounced when speaking to gentlemen; when people saw her speaking freely to a man like Lauzun, eyebrows were raised. The horse-racing and gambling took up only a short period of Antoinette's life, and yet it is something for which she is remembered, even before her numerous charities. In order for the excesses of the Revolution to be justified, the failings of a teenage queen are held up for posterity.

Another pastime of Antoinette's which caused no end of gossip was the delight she took in sleigh rides, no doubt as a reminder of her childhood in Austria. Why this innocent winter recreation was considered the height of decadence tells us how the French were used to viewing their queens: as living secluded at Versailles. The sleigh rides occurred during the harsh winter of 1775-76, when Antoinette's sister-in-law the Comtesse d'Artois was waiting to give birth. No doubt, Antoinette was depressed and had to be away from Versailles and in the fresh air. The parties were described as a delight for the eye by Madame Campan, with the jingle bells and plumed horses.[5] It was while sleigh riding that Antoinette befriended the Princesse de Lamballe, whom she made the Superintendent of her household, much to the universal disapproval of the court.

It was during those first three years of her husband's reign, before becoming a mother, that Antoinette's reputation was destroyed by those who gave an evil interpretation to her light-hearted distractions. As her biographer Rocheterie affirms:

An extraordinary thing was that this passion for pleasure did not sensibly alter the basis of piety which the queen owed to the principles of her mother and to the instruction of her father; and despite all the errors which the ambassador did not cease to point out to the empress, often with exaggeration, Marie Antoinette continued to give to the court an example of regularity in her religious practices; and she often called a halt in the whirl of frivolity which we have just described, but of which we must not exaggerate the character.

Some historians have tried to make use of certain imprudences to asperse the young woman, and, above all, of the so-called revelations due to the fatuity of certain men admitted to her intimacy; people have talked of the loves of Marie Antoinette. True history has done justice to these calumnies. During this period of dissipation, from the point of view of morals she committed no error. 'In all that concerns morality, there has never been in the conduct of the queen the slightest act which has not borne the imprint of a soul virtuous, upright, inflexible in all the principles which make for honesty of character.... No one is more entirely convinced of this fact than the king.' Such is the testimony which Mercy gives in the beginning of the reign of Louis XVI, and which all his later correspondence confirmed; and such is the opinion expressed later by a brother, Joseph II, who was severe and ill-disposed toward the queen….After having studied these reports, there is no impartial historian who will not agree with the words of Mercy and Joseph II., and who…will not subscribe to these lines of one of the men who knew Marie Antoinette best: 'Her so-called gallantry was never more than a sentiment of profound friendship, perhaps somewhat marked, for one or two persons, and a general coquetry natural to a woman and to a queen desirous of pleasing every one. At the very time when her youth and lack of experience might have led us to take certain liberties with her, there was never one of us who had the happiness of seeing her every day who dared to be guilty of the smallest indecorum: she acted the queen without being conscious of it, we adored her without thinking of loving her.'[6]

"Marie-Antoinette *à la paysanne*- in peasant costume"

Marie-Antoinette, Daughter of the Caesars

"Artois and Antoinette followed by the Comte and Comtesse de Provence, at one of the last court balls, held in 1785. The costumes were designed by Boquet of the Opera."

9 MARIE-ANTOINETTE AND THE ARTS

"But the most remarkable thing about her face was her brilliant complexion. I have never seen any so dazzling." —Madame Élisabeth Vigée-Lebrun on Marie-Antoinette

The reign of Louis XVI is famous for the decorative arts it produced, particularly furniture in *le style Louis XVI*, or neo-classical style, which perhaps should be called *le style Marie-Antoinette*, since the Queen encouraged it as a replacement for rococo. Inspired by the excavations at Pompei, the Louis XVI style is still cherished for its sturdy simplicity, made glamorous with gold leaf, silk or velvet. Antoinette patronized the finest cabinetmakers or *ébénistes*, such as the German immigrant Jean-Henri Riesener, who by 1774 had been given the title *ébéniste du roi*. Riesener, known for his meticulous and ingenious designs, placed the royal insignia of

Antoinette's initials in bronze gilt on the pieces he made for her. During the Revolution, he managed to retrieve many of the pieces at public auction, taking off the Queen's initials in order to resell her furniture. To his dismay, he had trouble selling them, because without her insignia the value was decreased, and thus he died in relative poverty in 1806. The Queen also employed several *menuisiers* or chairmakers, such as Jean-Baptiste-Claude Sené, who in 1788 made a suite of chairs for the *château* of Saint Cloud, as well as gilders like Louis-François Chatard, who gilded and painted the furniture. She also favored Georges Jacob, who constructed for her the *fauteuil de toilette*, or dressing chair, capable of swiveling 360 degrees. The chair, delivered in 1787, could be found in Antoinette's bedchamber at Petit Trianon. She also enjoyed wall sconces, candlesticks and andirons based upon nature or myth, so Parisian bronzer Claude-Jean Pitoin created many such items in the shape of bouquets of flowers, grape vines, animals, mythological beasts, tree branches, leaves, fruits, ribbons, torches and many other whimsical forms, all gilded.

The masterpieces celebrating the styles of classical antiquity through Antoinette's inspiration include the mother-of pearl boudoir at the *château* of Fontainebleau. Called the *boudoir de la Reine* or silver bedroom, it was built at the order of Louis XVI as a retiring room for the Queen in 1786. Fontainebleau, built by the Valois kings but used by the Bourbons as a hunting lodge, was primarily visited by the royal couple in the autumn, as a place where they could experience more privacy and less formality. The silver boudoir linked the King's room with the Queen's; it is small and intimate with paneling painted in opalescent silver, colorfully decorated with intricate mythological characters and delicate floral wreaths. The furniture is inlaid with mother-of-pearl, including the Queen's famous mother-of-pearl *secrétaire* built by Riesener.

Antoinette loved the exotic, being interested in ancient as well as distant cultures. Along with encouraging furniture design based upon Greek and Roman antiquity, she cultivated the Egyptian style. Twenty years or so before Napoleon Bonaparte would bring scholars to study Egypt during his campaign there, triggering a world-wide fascination with the land of the pharaohs, Antoinette had her craftsmen imitate the artistry of that most ancient and mysterious of kingdoms. In the gold-leafed stucco moulding in the ceiling of her state bedroom at Versailles, she had a winged sphinx added next to double-headed Habsburg eagle, as well as golden sphinx andirons in the fireplace. She definitely favored the sphinx motif, which also had deep roots in Greek mythology; there are several sphinxes on guard outside the Belvedere at Trianon; in the gilt paneling of her *salon doré*, also at Versailles; the arms of the chairs of the silver bedroom at Fontainebleau have sphinx heads, and they are found in the paneling as well. The sphinx was a symbol used by the Freemasons at the time but, in Antoinette's case, she probably thought them curious and cryptic and therefore romantic. In many ways the Queen's tastes paved the way for the great Romantic movement of the next century.

Among Antoinette's early fascinations was the Near East, synonymous with the Ottoman Empire, long an enemy of Austria but often an ally of France. It was the beginning of the Orientalism which would spill over into the literature, art and fashion of nineteenth century romanticism. Already, ladies of the court wore plumed turbans, tassels and embroidered slippers. In 1774, at the start of his reign, Louis ordered a *boudoir turc* for Antoinette at Fontainebleau, completed in 1777. Censers, pearls, crescents, turbans and wheat were featured in gold-leaf on the paneling and in the vivid patterns of the lush Turkish carpet. The furniture was comfortable with many cushions; the bed, festooned with gold silk drapes, was flush against a large looking-glass. The Turkish boudoir was immediately above the state bedroom and was a place the Queen could retire to rest during the day.

The imitation of Chinese motifs in French art, furniture, and architecture, called *chinoiserie*, blossomed in France under Madame de Pompadour. Antoinette embraced it as well, hiring the artist Jean-Baptiste Pillement to help her create a Chinese *fantaisie* at Petit Trianon. Although it no longer exists, Pillement built a Chinese pavilion in the gardens of Trianon, with a carousel on which the riders sat astride carved dragons and peacocks, while guests played billiards, cards and croquet. There was also a small Chinese tea house. As well as having several pieces of Sèvres porcelain decorated in the Chinese mode, Antoinette also had marvelous knick-knacks directly from China itself, incluing vases, perfume bottles, statues of various birds and animals, many carved from semi-precious stones such as jade and lapis lazuli. Today they appear in museums throughout the world; a few have found their way home to Versailles and Petit Trianon.

Too often the popular image of Antoinette over the years has been that of a woman of few accomplishments, interested in nothing but clothes and jewelry. Such an image does a great disservice to a lady who among her many interests acquired a mastery of the art of needlework in her short life. Like all girls of aristocratic birth, Antoinette was taught sewing and embroidery as a child. One pastel sketch by Liotard of the young Archduchess Antoine shows her "knotting," a form of tatting in which a shuttle was used. Ladies often carried a knotting shuttle around with them just as they would carry a fan.

Later, when Antoinette was sent to France to marry the Dauphin Louis-Auguste, she continued to have lessons in embroidery along with lessons in dancing and music. When being read to or even when conversing with friends and family, her hands were not idle, but busy with handiwork.[1] In July of 1770, the teenager wrote the following words to her mother Empress Maria Theresa: "I read, write, or work since I am embroidering a waistcoat for the King which has not progressed much, but I hope that with God's grace, it will be finished in a few years."[2]

While Antoinette's progress as an adolescent may have been slow, over the years she became quite adept, embroidering upholstery for chairs and cushions, as well as church vestments. She was skilled with petit point and tapestry, creating her own designs. This is known especially because of the artifacts which remain from her days in prison, such as the silk purse she crafted and embroidered with tiny rosebuds for her children's governess Madame de Tourzel. Antoinette's daughter reports how in the Temple prison the Queen "worked a good deal of tapestry."[3] While awaiting death in the Conciergerie the Queen steadied her nerves by embroidering a cherub on a piece of tapestry. The work was never completed.

There were several women artists who rose to prominence during the reign of Louis XVI, and four, including Élisabeth Vigée-Lebrun, were admitted to the *Académie Royale de Peinture et de Sculpture* on May 31, 1783. The other three were Anne Vallayer-Coster (1744-1818), Adélaïde Labille-Guiard (1749-1803) and Marie-Gabrielle Capet (1861-1818). Madame Vallyer-Coster, from a family of artists and craftsmen, enjoyed royal patronage, painting the Queen as well as the Mesdames Tantes, who were great patronesses of the arts. She excelled at still life as well as portraiture, although the former did not pay as well as the latter. However, Antoinette encouraged her in the art of still life, especially her paintings of flowers. The Queen was later present at Vallyer-Coster's wedding to a prominent attorney, a high honor indeed. Vallyer-Coster survived the Revolution and was patronized by the Empress Joséphine, although she was never as successful as in the Old Regime. She lived to see the Bourbon Restoration, making a gift of one of her still lifes to Louis XVIII. Her works are known world-wide and many can still be seen in the Louvre.

Madame Labille-Guiard, the daughter of a haberdasher, was not as close to the Queen as the others; her personal life was quite stormy. As a young girl she worked in the same milliner shop as the future Madame du Barry. Taught to paint miniatures by a family friend François-Elie Vincent, whose son she later married, she eventually moved on to full-sized portraits. She won the patronage of Madame Adélaïde of France and painted several members of the Royal Family, including Louis' sister Madame Élisabeth, as well as politicians and prominent aristocrats. During the French Revolution she was forced to renounce her royal patronage by burning an unfinished painting of the King's brother the Comte de Provence, later Louis XVIII. In her lifetime, Labille-Guiard's portraits were considered inferior to those of Madame Lebrun, although modern art critics have come to acknowledge that Labille-Guiard's technique is superior.

A native of Lyon, Mademoiselle Capet came under the tutelage of Madame Labille-Guiard. Her skill in portraiture won her the patronage of the Mesdames and other royals and persons of influence. She lived under the protection of Madame Labille-Guiard first at the Louvre, and later with her and her second husband,

Monsieur Vincent. Since Mademoiselle Capet did not always sign her work, many paintings became lost or misidentified and she fell into obscurity.

Madame Élisabeth Vigée-Lebrun (1755-1842) was the official court portrait painter at Versailles during the reign of Louis XVI. Finding an artist able to create a likeness of Antoinette that pleased her mother the Empress was a lengthy process, but in 1778 a portrait by Madame Lebrun did just that, showing the Queen in court dress but with her hair unpowdered.[4] She painted Antoinette many times, capturing the Queen's personality while simultaneously perfecting her own art. In her memoirs, she describes Antoinette thus:

> Her arms were superb, her hands small and perfectly formed, and her feet charming. She had the best walk of any woman in France, carrying her head erect and with a dignity that stamped her queen in the midst of her whole court; and yet this majestic mien in no wise diminished the sweetness and gentleness of her expression. Her features were not regular; she had inherited the long and narrow oval peculiar to the Austrian race—her eyes, almost blue in color, were rather small—her nose was delicate and pretty, and her mouth not too large, although her lips were somewhat thick. But the most remarkable thing about her face was her brilliant complexion. I have never seen any so dazzling.[5]

One of my favorite works of Madame Lebrun is a sketch the artist did of Antoinette after her death, showing her going to heaven, where Louis and the two children who died are awaiting her. Her hair is trailing down and she carries the palm of martyrdom. The artist, who was a friend of the Queen's, was too overcome with grief to finish the picture.

As readers of *Trianon* may recall, the novel opens with a scene of Madame Élisabeth Vigée-Lebrun painting what became the portrait of Antoinette and her children. In the famous ensemble painting by Madame Lebrun, the Queen is shown wearing only a few pearls, while sitting near the jewel cabinet. The symbolism of this was to emphasize that for Antoinette her children were her true jewels. When the painting was begun in 1786, the Queen was expecting baby Sophie; the gown she is wearing is a maternity gown, as can be seen by the open and adjustable front. The emphasis of the painting was supposed to be the other children getting the cradle ready for the new baby. However, by the time the picture was completed in 1788, little Sophie had been born and had died. Hence, the cradle is shrouded in mourning cloth. After the death of her oldest son Louis-Joseph, Antoinette had the image hidden away; she could not bear the sight of it. Nevertheless, it was considered a highly accurate likeness of her. Louis XVI declared to the artist when first gazing at the portrait of his wife and children: "I do not understand much about painting, but you make me love it."[6]

Author Catherine Delors relates how other than the forementioned Vigée-Lebrun, one of the most accurate portrayals of the Queen is a 1788 portrait by Wertmüller. To quote Madame Delors:

> This portrait shows Marie-Antoinette in 1788, when she was 33. It was painted by Adolf Ulrik Wertmüller, a Swede who was a member of the Royal Academy in Paris. Indeed, according to Madame Campan's *Memoirs*, this is, along with the more famous portrait of the Queen with her children by Madame Vigee-Lebrun, the best likeness of Marie-Antoinette. Madame Campan, as the Queen's

> *Première Femme de Chambre*, or First Chambermaid, saw Marie-Antoinette on a daily basis. I trust her judgment on the matter of the likeness. You can see a shift in the manner in which Marie-Antoinette chose to be depicted, one short year before the Revolution. For one thing, the emphasis is no longer on ornate dresses, giant paniers or shimmering fabrics. Neither is the Queen dressed '*en gaulle*,' in a simple white linen gown. That portrait, beautiful as it is, was the subject of much derision. People remarked jokingly that the Queen had been painted in her chemise. Here Marie-Antoinette seems to be wearing a simple riding habit. No accusations of immodesty can be made because her kerchief comes up to her chin. The sobriety and dark colors of the clothing shift the attention to the Queen's face. The features are also different from earlier images. The nose is less small and straight, the lips are thicker, the eyes more prominent than in Madame Lebrun's idealized portraits. But I read a lot of energy and determination in these eyes, no longer dreamy, in the manner in which the head is proudly held backwards. This is the Queen who will assume a foremost political role during the Revolution. I believe that Madame Campan is right. Here at last we get a glimpse of the real Marie-Antoinette.[7]

As much as I love the work of Madame Lebrun, it is true that in many of her portraits of Antoinette she was aiming for the misty, dreamy look, rather than an accurate likeness. While the *en gaulle* portrait is definitely an idealized representation, it embodies the life of simplicity and innocence which the Queen tried to create at Petit Trianon.

From the time I first started to write about Antoinette,

Marie-Antoinette, Daughter of the Caesars

I have received comments from devout people about the low-cut gowns that she wore. Let me explain once again that, in the decadent old world, it was etiquette in most of the courts of Europe for ladies' formal attire to include a plunging *décolletage*. It was considered perfectly correct as long as the proper corset was worn. The gown which evoked some disapproval for Marie-Antoinette was not one of the low-cut court gowns but the simple white linen dress which she favored for her leisure time at Petit Trianon. The portrait in which she is shown thus had to be withdrawn from the public gaze because people took offense at seeing their Queen painted in casual attire. Now to us, the white dress is perfectly modest, but to people of the eighteenth century, it looked as if she were in her chemise, without the stiff *grand corps* corset prescribed for ladies of the royal family. Furthermore, it was interpreted as being a pro-Austrian picture, since linen came from Flanders, one of the Habsburg territories, and the rose the Queen held was seen as a symbol of the House of Austria. In order to quell the outrage, Madame Vigée-Lebrun had to quickly come up with another painting. In 1783 the artist completed the portrait called "Marie-Antoinette *à la rose*" showing the Queen appropriately garbed in a silk court gown and headdress, trimmed with lace, ribbons and plumes. She is wearing pearls, as befits a queen, with hair powdered and face rouged, in accord with court etiquette. She looks as if she has just stepped into her garden on a summer evening, bathed in moonlight. The nocturnal quality of the portrait softens the formality of her attire, alluding to Antoinette's love of nature, and the fact that she was much more at ease in her gardens than she was in the Hall of Mirrors.

Antoinette was often painted as various characters from Greek and Roman mythology, as was the custom of the time. It was thought to be the Queen in a certain miniature at a special exhibition at the Philip Mould Gallery in London in 2012. Dated 1781, Antoinette is shown as some kind of a classical deity, holding coral and rushes, crowned in pearls, with a dolphin at her side.[8] I am wondering if Antoinette is supposed to represent Venus, the goddess of love and beauty who, according to the myth, rose out of the foam of the sea. Furthermore, coral, symbolizing joy and happiness, has a classical association with that goddess. Venus was the wife of Vulcan, god of the forge. Perhaps the portrait was a gift for Louis XVI, whom she once likened to Vulcan because of his dedication to his locksmith work. A dolphin was on the coat-of-arms of the Dauphin. I think this miniature was intended as an intimate gift from the Queen to the King to celebrate the birth of their son and heir in 1781. Also, since the lady in the painting is immersed in water, it may be reminiscent of the happy occasion when Louis XVI interrupted Antoinette as she was finishing her bath and finally and fully consummated their marriage on August 30, 1777.[9]

During the Revolution, Antoinette was painted mostly by the Polish potraitist Kucharski and the French portraitist Dumont. Madame Élisabeth Vigée-Lebrun had fled France along with many other of Antoinette's friends. Kucharski painted the beautiful unfinished pastel portrait of the Queen in 1792, intended as a gift for her children's governess, Madame de Tourzel. The painting survived the Revolution, including the storming of the Tuileries. Kucharski also painted the Princesse de Lamballe, Madame Élisabeth de France and the Comte d'Artois. Dumont, who was imprisoned by the Revolutionary tribunal and barely escaped the guillotine, was known for his strong royalist sympathies. He mostly painted miniatures. In 1789, however, he painted a delightful portrait of Antoinette playing with her two surviving children, Madame Royale and the Dauphin

Louis-Charles, in the gardens of Trianon. Later, around 1791, he painted Antoinette as a vestal virgin, standing beside an altar while holding a vase of lilies with a profile of Louis XVI on it. Louis XVI kept the picture on his desk in the Tuileries; the original has since been lost and only an engraving remains. The fact that Antoinette is depicted as dedicated to the goddess of the hearth, speaks of her devotion to family life, especially to her husband and children.

The subject of many portraits during her lifetime, the Queen of France was sketched during her last moments by Jacques-Louis David. He sketched her from a window as she was riding by in a cart on the way to the guillotine. Some say the sketch is more of a caricature than an accurate depiction, in that David might have made the Queen appear worse in order to mock her. Ironically, David, the hardened Revolutionary and friend of Robespierre's, would later paint Napoleon and Joséphine being crowned at Notre Dame.

In our discussion of Antoinette and the arts, a word must be said about the magnificence of Sèvres porcelain. Before their untimely deaths, Louis XVI and Antoinette patronized the national porcelain, as was their duty. They usually had simple taste compared to the revolutionaries who took over the government. The *laiterie* (dairy) at Rambouillet, which Louis created as a gift to Antoinette, featured the famous "breast cup" and other vessels. The dairy and its porcelain vessels were supposed to celebrate all that was wholesome and natural, from breast-feeding, which most noblewomen shunned, to the manual labor that went into running a dairy. The aristocracy had traditionally looked down upon manual labor and peasant life. Louis XVI and Antoinette wanted to show that it was good and beautiful and life-giving. The royal dairy was a sort of monument to the way that staples such as cheese and milk were produced. At times, Louis' taste could often be more elaborate then his wife's. Between 1778 and 1782, Sèvres manufactured for Louis XVI a series of vases with handles shaped as busts of infants, young women, and old men, hence the name *vases des âges*. They bore an additional decoration of "jewels" composed of enamel drops over gold foil. The vases were designed by Jacques-François Deparis and can be found at the Walters Art gallery in Baltimore, Maryland. Sèvres survived the Revolution, and had a gaudy resurgence during the reign of Napoleon, who also patronized the opulent porcelain, just like the kings and queens whom he had replaced.

Not only did Antoinette patronize talented women artists, helping them achieve official posts in the royal court and but she also assisted women writers. According to an article by Mary D. Sheriff:

> In 1774...the *Journal des dames* reappeared under Marie-Antoinette's protection after a five-year suspension. Madame de Montaclos dedicated the new publication to Marie-Antoinette, who had lent her support in late 1773, when she was still a dauphine. Although Marie-Antoinette may not have advocated many of the political and moral stances taken by the *Journal des dames*, she maintained her patronage of the publication....Finally, today the *Bibliotheque Nationale de France* also houses many novels from the eighteenth century bound with the arms of Marie-Antoinette. It is not so important for the Queen actually to have read the books: it was enough that she owned them to enhance a writer's reputation.[10]

She patronized lady novelists by permitting her personal coat-of-arms to be on their books.[11] Writing novels was one of the few respectable ways that gentlewomen had of making a living. Although she was not the reader that Louis was, Antoinette did enjoy novels as well as dramas. It is interesting that the Queen read the novel *Les Liaisons Dangereuses* by Chodleros de Laclos; like the plays of Beaumarchais, it exposed the vices of the nobility, which Marie-Antoinette had tried to reform at the Royal Court. She named her adopted daughter Ernestine after an opera for which Laclos wrote the libretto. The opera was based upon a favorite novel of the Queen's by Madame Riccoboni called *Ernestine*.[12] As with the works of Beaumarchais, Antoinette kept a false cover on *Les Liaisons Dangereuse*, since her husband had banned it for popular consumption and she did not wish to give scandal. Of course, she had many books in her library which would give nothing but edification. Here is a sample of books from her private library at Versailles. There was a small library at Petit Trianon as well. The Latin and French books are bound in citron Moroccan leather and have triple gilt fillet borders.[13] The covers are stamped with Antoinette's coat of arms. The titles are: *Collection de Moralistes Anciene, L'Office de la semaine sainte, à l'usage de la maison du roi* by the Abbot of Bellegarde, *Les Plaideurs* by Jean Baptiste Racine, *Officium parvum B. Mariæ Virginis, ad usum ordinis Cisterciensis, Histoire des Celtes, nouvelle édition* by Simon Pelloutier. To translate, the books are *Collections of Ancient Moralists, The Office of Holy Week, The Litigants* by Jean Baptiste Racine, *The Little Office of The Blessed Virgin Mary: According to the Usage of the Cistercian Order*, and *History of the Celts* by Simon Pelloutier.[14] It should be remembered that Antoinette had two sisters who were nuns and a brother who was a bishop, and history was one of her favorite subjects.

10 MARIE-ANTOINETTE AND MUSIC

Chantons, célébrons notre reine!
Chantons, célébrons notre reine.
L'Hymen qui sous ses loix t'enchaîne,
Va nous rendre à jamais heureux.
—Gluck's *Iphigénie en Aulide*

In 1782, the Paris Opera burned down, killing ten people, which did not stop a couturier from coming up with a new shade called *opéra brûlé*, which is one reason why Antoinette stayed away from the color orange. Louis ordered that a new Opera be built, designed by Lenoir, on the Porte Saint-Martin. It was completed in record time, due to monetary incentives from Antoinette, who dearly loved the entire opera experience, taking great care over the design and décor of her new box. Her presence at the Opera on any given evening assured the monetary success of the performance, since people bought tickets as soon as they heard she would be attending.[1] From childhood,

Antoinette had loved music, and as an adult composed her own songs. Singing soprano, she performed in operettas in her prvate theater at Petit Trianon. Some of the musical comedies she enjoyed took a swipe at the nobility, such as Pierre-Alexandre Monsigny's opera *Le Roi et le Fermier* ("The King and the Farmer") in 1780. As a young girl, she studied under the famous composer Christoph Willibald Gluck whom she later brought to France when she was Queen. Among his most famous operas is *Orpheus and Eurydice*, which originally debuted in Vienna in 1762. It is based upon the myth of Orpheus, who tried to release his beloved wife from the underworld. Unlike the myth, the opera of Gluck has a happy ending. One of the loveliest pieces from *Orpheus and Eurydice* is the "Dance of the Blessed Spirits." It is interesting that the Queen so loved this opera; to listen to it is to have a glimpse into her soul. In another opera by Gluck, *Iphigénie en Aulide*, the chorus of "Sing, let us celebrate our queen" immediately became Antoinette's anthem, as it was sung to praise her at the Paris debut of the opera in 1774. "Let us sing, celebrate our Queen! / Hymen, who binds you in his laws/ Will make us happy forever." As the Queen's maid, Madame Campan, describes it:

> Paris did not cease, during the first years of the reign, to give proofs of pleasure whenever the Queen appeared at any of the plays of the capital. At the representation of 'Iphigenia in Aulis,' the actor who sang the words, 'Let us sing, let us celebrate our Queen!' which were repeated by the chorus, directed by a respectful movement the eyes of the whole assembly upon her Majesty. Reiterated cries of '*Bis!*' and clapping of hands, were followed by such a burst of enthusiasm that many of the audience added their voices to those of the actors in

order to celebrate, it might too truly be said, another Iphigenia. The Queen, deeply affected, covered her eyes with her handkerchief; and this proof of sensibility raised the public enthusiasm to a still higher pitch.[2]

The opera *Iphigénie* was a political and moral triumph for the young Queen. The road to production had been a bumpy one. The composer also had to contend with Madame du Barry, who favored the Italian Piccini over Gluck. Even before Gluck arrived in Paris, Louis XV's mistress tried to undermine him, and many silly lies were spread about his character and abilities. All falsehoods were put to flight when Gluck appeared and conquered Paris with his *Iphigénie*. Professor Amy Wygant of the University of Glasgow describes in her article entitled "Fire, Sacrifice, Iphigénie" how the sacrifice of Iphigenia in Gluck's opera foreshadowed that of Antoinette herself:

> And it seems that, in the midst of the public mania occasioned by the opera, [Marie-Antoinette's] identity had somehow merged with that of the erstwhile sacrificial victim. We know...that on the night of 10 January, when the new queen was in the audience, Le Gros, singing the part of Achille, modified the second act chorus, *'Chantez, célébrez votre reine'*, sung as he introduces Iphigénie to his countrymen. On this occasion, Le Gros turned to the queen and sang, *'Chantons, célébrons notre Reine,/Et l'hymen qui sous ses lois l'enchaîne/Va nous rendre à jamais heureux!'* The queen reportedly wept tears of joy....In about twenty years, in 1793, this crowd would see to her execution, and this returns us to the odd ability of music to prefigure the political. Marie-Antoinette

had literally patronized a revolution in music, and allowed herself from its beginning to be collapsed upon its most fragile figure. Both of them, Iphigénie and the young queen, in these early days, frustrated the structure of sacrifice.[3]

The anthem *"Chantons, célébrons notre reine!"* would be sung again for Antoinette's niece Marie-Louise, as well as for Antoinette's own daughter Marie-Thérèse when she returned to France in 1814 after twenty years of exile. The triumph of Iphigénie was followed by the successes of the operas *Armide* and *Iphigénie en Tauride*. Gluck arranged his music to suit Antoinette's tastes and he proclaimed that being in France had rejuvenated his creativity.

Louis had his own anthem, too. The royalist anthem *"Vive Henri IV"* was from Collé's 1770 opera *La partie de chasse d'Henri IV*. In 1774 it was often sung to honor Louis XVI, became popular again during the Restoration in 1814. Here are the lyrics which celebrate the monarch who was seen by the French people as the epitome of justice, kindness, and virility.

Vive Henri IV
Vive ce roi vaillant !
Vive Henri IV
Vive ce roi vaillant !
Ce diable à quatre
A le triple talent
De boire de battre
Et d'être un vers galant.

A translation would be: "Long live Henri IV! /Long live this valiant king! / That devil with/A triple talent/ Drinking, fighting/And being gallant." It was an attempt to identify the Bourbon dynasty with the popular first

Bourbon monarch, Henri IV, who was also the last monarch to summon the Estates-General. Louis XVI had also been seen as sharing with the King from Navarre an easy manner with the common folk, a rough, friendly manner, a love of the chase, as well as a strong sense of justice. Early in their reign, the King and Queen held a costume ball where everyone came in dress from the era of *le bon roi Henri*, with Antoinette herself garbed as Henri's beloved mistress, Gabrielle d'Estrées.[4] It was part of the Queen's attempt to show that she was loved by her husband, and that she was his mistress as well as his wife. During the Restoration, members of the Bourbon family, especially the daughter of Louis XVI, the Duchesse d'Angoulême, were frequently welcomed with the anthem.[5] After the fall of the Bourbons in 1830, the anthem was no longer played, and soon became a relic of the past.

Another of Antoinette's favorite composers was André Grétry (1741-1813). Grétry was a staunch supporter of the throne and the Queen was godmother of his daughter, Antoinette. One of his most popular operas was *Richard Coeur-de-Lion*, which debuted at the Comédie-Italienne in 1784. Blondel's aria "*Ô Richard! Ô mon roi,*" sung in honor of the imprisoned English crusader king, became the royalist anthem during the French Revolution. It is often forgotten that numerous French people continued to honor and love the sovereigns in spite of the troubles and the tidal wave of revolutionary propaganda. The knowledge that they had some loyal subjects encouraged Louis XVI and Antoinette to stay in the country in 1789 when they probably should have departed. Here are the words of first stanza of the aria, in French and English:

Ô Richard! Ô mon roi!
L'univers t'abandonne;

Sur la terre il n'est donc que moi
Qui m'intéresse à ta personne!
Moi seul dans l'univers,
Voudrais briser tes fers,
Et tout le reste t'abandonne!

O Richard! O my king!
The Universe abandons you!
On earth, it is only me
Who is interested in you!
Alone in the universe
I would break the chains
When everyone else deserted you!

"*Ô Richard! Ô mon roi!*" was sung by the Flanders regiment and the Royal Bodyguards at a banquet at the Versailles opera house on October 1, 1789. The Bodyguards were holding the banquet to honor the regiment which had been brought to Versailles to protect the Royal Family due to the recent disturbances. The Royal Family appeared to overwhelming cheers; the little Dauphin Louis-Charles walked the length of the banquet table without upsetting a single glass. As the Queen had feared, the appearance of the Royal Family at the dinner was distorted by the gazettes, and was seen as being an attack on the National Assembly. On October 5 the *château* was invaded by rioters, and Louis XVI, Antoinette, Madame Élisabeth and the children were taken to live at the Tuileries in Paris. In four years the King and Queen would both be dead, with Madame Elisabeth soon to follow, and the children left to languish in prison. "*Ô Richard! Ô mon roi*" continued to be sung by royalists; the words were sometimes changed to "*Ô Louis, Ô mon roi.*" As for Monsieur Grétry, although he lost all of his property during the Revolution he did not lose his life, and continued to be honored for his music.

Musicians from various nations and backgrounds were welcomed at Versailles by Louis XVI. Joseph Boulogne (1745-1799), the Chevalier de Saint-Georges, known as *le Mozart noir* or "the black Mozart," was one of the most enigmatic gentlemen at Versailles in the years immediately preceding the French Revolution. The son of a Caribbean slave woman, the Chevalier's presence in the highest circles of society contradicts the view many people have of royal France being a place of restriction. On the contrary, the reign of Louis XVI was a truly open and diverse era, in which talent was rewarded and the gifted could go far. Antoinette called the Chevalier "my favorite American" and asked that the gifted violinist and composer give her musical instruction; the King nominated Saint-Georges director of the Royal Opera House in Paris. Unfortunately, the nomination was sabotaged by three women who sang and danced in the Paris Opera. They petitioned the Queen, saying the delicacy of their consciences would not permit them to take orders from "a mulatto." In order to save the Queen from embarrassment, Joseph withdrew his name. The Queen responded by inviting him to play duets with her at musicales at Versailles. A crack shot and master horseman, Joseph was known as a ladies' man. A skilled athlete and swordsman, the Chevalier also frequented the Palais Royal in Paris and was part of the coterie of the Duc d'Orléans. With such company, it is not surprising that he became the first African French freemason and eventually fought for the revolutionary government. Nevertheless, he had so many aristocratic connections that his art was not as appreciated by the new regime as it had been by Louis and Antoinette. Joseph died of a bladder disease four years after the King and Queen were killed, in 1799.

There came for Antionette a last night at the Opera.

Scottish aristocrat Grace Elliot was a warm-hearted, rather scandalous lady. She had great sympathy for the plight of the French Royal Family during the Revolution, in spite of her intimacy with the Duc d'Orléans. Mrs. Elliot recorded her impressions of the last public appearance of Antoinette at a theater, as follows:

> After the 20th of June, the people who wished well to the King and Queen were desirous that her Majesty should sometimes appear in public, accompanied by the Dauphin, a most interesting, beautiful child, and her charming daughter, Madame Royale. In consequence of this she went to the Comédie Italienne with her children, Madame Élisabeth, the King's sister, and Madame Tourzelle, governess to the royal children. This was the very last time on which her Majesty appeared in public. I was there in my own box, nearly opposite the Queen's; and as she was so much more interesting than the play, I never took my eyes off her and her family. The opera which was given was *Les Evénemens Imprévus*, and Madame Dugazon played the *soubrette* [female servant]. Her Majesty, from her first entering the house, seemed distressed. She was overcome even by the applause, and I saw her several times wipe the tears from her eyes.
>
> The little Dauphin, who sat on her knee the whole night, seemed anxious to know the cause of his unfortunate mother's tears. She seemed to soothe him, and the audience appeared well disposed, and to feel for the cruel situation of their beautiful Queen. In one of the acts a duet is sung by the *soubrette* and the valet, where Madame Dugazon says: *Ah! Comme j'aime ma maîtresse* [Ah! How I love my mistress]. As she looked

particularly at the Queen at the moment she said this, some Jacobins, who had come into the playhouse, leapt upon the stage, and if the actors had not hid Madame Dugazon, they would have murdered her. They hurried the poor Queen and family out of the house, and it was all the Guards could do to get them safe into their carriages.[6]

Marie-Antoinette, Daughter of the Caesars

"Antoinette with bust of Louis XVI"

11 MARIE-ANTOINETTE AND FASHION

"A dress of white percale, a gauze *fichu*, a straw hat—such was the toilet at Trianon, a fresh and charming toilet which set off the supple figure and brilliant complexion of the goddess of place but whose extreme simplicity enraged the sellers of silk at Lyons...."—M. de la Rocheterie

As a young Dauphine, Antoinette was criticized for her shabby clothes and undignified manner. She was encouraged to show more interest in fashion by Louis XV and the Mesdames Tantes.[1] Slowly, she began to take an interest in clothes. She tended to get ideas from Madame du Barry rather than from the Mesdames Tantes, however, and as Queen she hired the most creative *couturière* in Paris, Rose Bertin. Since then, Antoinette has been the symbol of extravagance and decadence of the *ancien-régime*. It is overlooked that from the moment of their succession in 1774, she joined her husband in desiring to cut back on the enormous expenses of the court. She refused to collect the customary *droit de ceinture* tax levied on behalf of the queen at the beginning of every reign. Moreover, her charities were quite extensive. The Queen's spending on hairstyles and gowns was nothing compared to the extravagance of the mistresses Madame du Barry and Madame de Pompadour in the previous reign. Antonia Fraser in her biography of Antoinette says that when the eighteen-year-old queen adopted the elaborate *poufs*, it actually caused a lucrative trade in feathers to spring up in Paris. Patronizing French luxury goods was a duty of the crown. According to Lady Fraser:

> ...Paris was a city dependent on the financial support of the noble and rich to maintain its industries, which were in the main to do with luxury and semi-luxury goods. For foreigners, fashion was part of the point of being in Paris....As the Baronne d'Oberkirch remarked on her first visit to the French capital, the city would be sunk without its luxurious commerce....Against the spectacle of an exquisitely dressed Queen, her appearance a work of art in itself—French art— must be put in the balance of the dress bills that mounted, and the dress allowance that was never enough.[2]

Within a very few years, as she matured, the Queen herself had introduced much simpler fashions and hairstyles. Her simple white dresses were not well-received, and were seen as an attempt to patronize the Flemish weavers of the Habsburg Empire over the French silk merchants. How ironic that Antoinette was given the nickname of *Madame Déficit* by her enemies in the 1780's at a time when she was trying to be cut expenses in her household and in her wardrobe, which included having old gowns refurbished so that they could be worn again.

There is no doubt that she went over her budget, especially as a young Queen, on clothes, jewelry, gambling and gardening. Nesta Webster, in *Louis XVI and Marie-Antoinette before the Revolution*, breaks down the Queen's expenditures. It should be noted that in 1774 when Louis XVI became King, Antoinette was put on pretty much the same budget as the staid Queen Marie in 1727. However, the *livre* had decreased in value, while costs had risen due to inflation. Interestingly, even Queen Marie had exceeded the limits of her privy purse and had to ask for extra money, three times. To quote Webster:

> Under the old régime, the expenses of the Queens of France were paid out of at least three different funds. These were:-
> 1. The sum for the maintenance of the Queen's household, which for centuries had stood at 600,000 *livres*....This sum had long proved inadequate and had to be supplemented by what was called the *dépenses extraordinaires*, which by July 1774...had mounted up to two million *livres*....The Queen had no control over these *dépenses extraordinaires*, which led to great abuses.
> 2. The *cassette de la Reine* (or privy purse) for alms, presents, pensions, and other acts of generosity...but not for anything in the way of dress. For this, Marie Antoinette received the same as Marie Leszcinska, that is 96,000 *livres* a year, and out of it she continued to pay pensions accorded by the late Queen....
> 3. The Wardrobe, for which 120,000 livres was allowed yearly, a fund which was administered entirely by the *dame d'autours* (lady of the bedchamber)....[3]

Because Antoinette insisted upon paying, out of the *cassette de la reine*, the pensions of the old servants of the late Queen, although Comte de Mercy begged her to drop them, she went over the budget of her privy purse. In addition, she paid pensions for her own retired servants. She refused to petition her husband for more money; it was Comte de Mercy, the Austrian ambassador, who intervened for her allowance to be increased.[4]

The Queen's ladies were given commissions from various merchants for buying their wares for the royal wardrobe; likewise, the ladies were permitted to sell the gowns after the Queen was finished with them, and pocket the money. Such confusion and potential for abuse contributed to the Queen's expenses going beyond the budget, along with the high prices of her dressmaker, Rose Bertin.

Caroline Weber in *Queen of Fashion* discusses how Antoinette used fashion as previously only royal mistresses had used it, as a means of strengthening her position in a hostile court, where she was a foreigner. Former queens had been less stylish; her clothes, therefore, caused quite a stir.[5] Antoinette's situation in those years before she became a mother was tenuous, especially from a political point of view. Her brother frequently pressured her to use her role as consort for Austrian interests. Placed in a very awkward situation, Antoinette used clothes to establish herself; her interest in fashion was not mere hedonism. Once Antoinette became the mother of a Dauphin, of course, her position changed dramatically, and her influence on the King became genuine. She no longer needed the flamboyance, and dressed with greater moderation. She had become, however, like the mistresses of old, a convenient scapegoat for all the problems of the nation. As the determined and energetic mother of the next king, she was perceived as a threat to the adversaries of the crown. The pornographic pamphlets, the epithets such as *Madame Déficit*, were only the beginning of the attempts to weaken the esteem of the people for the Queen.

In spite of Antoinette's preference for simple attire, a court gown was required on all formal occasions at Versailles for the Queen, the princesses, and all ladies who had been formally presented to the Queen. To be presented, a lady had to be from a family that had been noble before the year 1400 and had to be sponsored by another lady who had already been presented. Also, Antoinette had made it clear that she would not receive ladies who lived apart from their husbands. At the presentation the lady would enter the Salon of Nobles at Versailles and curtsey deeply three times before the Queen, who sat enthroned. Then removing her right glove, she would bow to the ground and kiss the hem of the Queen's gown, then rise and withdraw, walking backwards. A court gown was comprised of narrow bodice, and skirt wide enough to fit over the side baskets called panniers, and a lengthy train. The back of the bodice never closed all the way so that the sheer chemise showed through the lacings. The fact that the bodice was always low cut, revealing most of the bosom and shoulders must have made many women feel quite exposed when garbed in court dress for the first time. The only excuse not to wear court dress was if a lady were great with child, as Antoinette was once when receiving the Venetian ambassador. She apologized to him for her attire, or else there might have been a diplomatic incident.[6] A *grand corps* corset had to be worn with a court gown; only the highest princesses in the land, including the Queen, had the "privilege" of wearing it, and only on formal occasions. It was stiffer than a regular corset and, made with whale bone stays, covered more of the torso while unnaturally pushing up the bosom. As a young Dauphine, Antoinette refused to wear the *grand corps* at first but eventually gave in due to pressure from the family.

Court apparel was required for gentlemen as well, involving breeches, waistcoat and coat, of the finest fabrics and elaborately embroidered with silk and gold and silver threads as well as studded with precious gems. Even hunting clothes were richly embroidered. Men wore jewelry as well, including jeweled shoe buckles, buttons, clips, pins, rings, and scabbards. Some gentlemen, such as Count Axel von Fersen, wore earrings. Men regularly wore high heeled shoes, hair powder and lip rouge. Appearing at court could be ruinous for a nobleman of limited finances. Louis XVI started his own revolution by walking about Versailles in a plain brown suit with his diamond-studded Order of the Saint-Esprit as the sole adornment.

Antoinette had a wardrobe book for every new season with swatches of her garments and she would use a pin to choose what she was going to wear on any given day. Ladies changed several time a day, wearing different outfits to correspond to the different hours. Every great lady had such a book, not just the Queen. The Queen's *Wardrobe Book of 1782* survives; it was in the care of the Comtesse d'Ossun. It is notable for the many swatches of simple, casual attire. The Queen seemed to prefer various shades of blue, from navy to turquoise to robin's egg to cornflower. She particularly favored cornflower, which was popular at court at as "the color of the King's eyes." The court of Louis XVI was known for names which honored the Royal Family when it came to the colors of cloth, with a blondish colour called *cheveux de la reine*, being the same shade as Antoinette's hair.[7]

In the early 1780's, Antoinette abandoned the ostentatious styles which characterized her first few years as Queen, substituting them with simple attire. Especially at Petit Trianon, the gowns of lawn or muslin were worn not only by the Queen but by all the ladies present. As described in Rocheterie's biography:

> At Trianon there was no ceremony, no etiquette, no household, only friends. When the queen entered the salon the ladies did not quit their work nor the men interrupt their game of billiards or of trictrac. It was the life of the chateau with all its agreeable liberty, such as Marie Antoinette had always dreamed, such as was practised in that patriarchal family of the Hapsburgs, which was as Goethe has said, 'Only the first bourgeoise family of the empire.' They all met together for breakfast which took the place of dinner; afterwards they played cards chatted or walked and assembled again for supper which was served early. No fine dressing no complicated head dresses whose exaggerated height had forced the architect to enlarge the dimensions of the doors and provoked the reprimands of Maria Theresa. A dress of white percale, a gauze *fichu*, a straw hat—such was the toilet at Trianon, a fresh and charming toilet which set off the supple figure and brilliant complexion of the goddess of place but whose extreme simplicity enraged the sellers of silk at Lyons....[8]

Indeed, Antoinette's simple tastes drew even more criticism than her former opulence. With her unpowdered hair and linen and cotton dresses, she was accused not only of trying to put the French silk merchants out of business in favor of her brother's Flemish weavers, but she was blamed for lowering the prestige of the monarchy by being too casual. According to an article on the Queen's hairstyles by scholar

Desmond Hosford:

> Marie-Antoinette's excesses during the 1770s had been criticized, but when the queen curtailed such luxury she was again found to be at fault. In 1778, Marie-Antoinette gave birth to a daughter, which did not solidify her political situation, but the birth of a dauphin in 1781 meant that she had finally fulfilled her duty to France. Unfortunately, according to Léonard, 'At the end of the year 1781, that is to say, when the queen had given to France the first Dauphin, who died in 1789 . ... Her Majesty was in danger of losing the charming locks whose suave color had passed into fashion under the name *cheveux de la reine*.'
>
> Léonard's solution to the queen's predicament was no less than to cut her hair and to abandon the imposing coiffures that he had created. Instead, he invented the *coiffure à l'enfant*, a simple *style frisé* with curls in the back, which characterized the second half of the reign. This simplification of the queen's hairstyle was also effected in her attire as she entered the age of maturity. However, the queen's new simplicity was as unpopular as her former extravagance. One fashion that Marie-Antoinette adopted, a loose-fitting simple gown of muslin, became known as the *chemise à la reine*. In 1783, Vigée-Lebrun painted the queen in such a gown, and the work was so severely criticized when it was exhibited at the *Salon of the Académie royale de peinture et de sculpture* that year that the painting had to be withdrawn.[9]

No matter what she did, there were those who would complain. Some criticism is par for the course when one is a public figure. In Antoinette's case, her Austrian birth made her an object of suspicion from the moment she stepped onto French soil, even among the royal family. For those who sought political power by undermining the royal regime, the Queen of Louis XVI, with her beauty and youthful imprudences, was the perfect target.

Many people ask what became of Antoinette's clothes and jewels after the fall of the monarchy. People particularly want to know what became of her wedding gown. Like many of the Queen's gowns which were designed for special occasions, the wedding gown was made into a set of vestments and donated to the Church. As for her other gowns, the Queen would usually have them refurbished so that they could continue to be worn. Antoinette tended not to be wasteful but displayed thrift when it came to recycling old clothes and shoes. Those gowns and cloaks that were not eventually made into vestments were given to the lady-in-waiting in charge of the wardrobe, who could then sell them or keep them as souvenirs.[10] As for the jewels, a few pieces were smuggled out of the country before the fall of the monarchy and eventually came to the Queen's daughter Madame Royale. Most of the royal jewels fell into the hands of the revolutionaries in August 1792 and scattered to the four winds. Napoleon managed to gain possession of some of the crown jewels. Over the next several generations, jewels that had belonged to Antoinette would turn up in various places, such as with the Youssopov family in Russia. To trace the fate of all the jewels extensive detective work is required and the findings would certainly fill a tome. The best lesson from it all is *Sic transit gloria mundi*.

Marie-Antoinette, Daughter of the Caesars

"Louis XVI and Marie-Antoinette in the Eucharistic procession on May 4, 1789."

"Marie-Antoinette prays before death."

12 MARIE-ANTOINETTE AND HER JOURNEY OF FAITH

Je meurs dans la religion catholique, apostolique et romaine, dans celle de mes pères, dans celle où j'ai été élevée et que j'ai toujours professée.

"I die in the Catholic, Apostolic and Roman religion, that of my fathers, that in which I was brought up, and which I have always professed." — Last Letter of Marie-Antoinette

In her last letter the Queen said that the Catholic religion is the one which she had always believed and practiced, but like many people she had a faith journey in which her soul grew and matured. Although faith is a private matter there is much to learn about how Antoinette's belief system strengthened her in difficult times. Many are not aware of Antoinette's affiliation with the Carmelite Order, a contemplative order which was introduced to France in the thirteenth century under royal patronage. When the Discalced Carmelite Reform came to France from Spain in the early seventeenth century, the Royal Family assisted the nuns. The French court was shaken in 1674 when Louise de la Vallière, the former mistress of Louis XIV, publicly begged Queen Marie-Thérèse for forgiveness and entered a Carmelite monastery. There were many connections of the later Bourbons with Carmel, particularly the patronage of Queen Marie Leszczyńska and her daughter Madame Louise. When Louise herself chose to become a Carmelite nun in 1770, it cemented the spiritual ties between those in the worldliness of Versailles and those in the austerity of the cloister. Antoinette continued the traditional connection between the Carmelite Order and the Royal House of France. Antoinette married the Dauphin in the same year that Madame Louise entered the monastery. The young princess offered to represent Louis XV at the ceremony at which his daughter Louise received the habit of Carmel, since it was too painful for the King and the rest of his family to be present. So it was the teenaged Antoinette who veiled the new "Soeur Thérèse de Saint-Augustin." The ceremony made a huge impression on her and it is said that she wept copious tears, as girls her age tend to do when overwrought. However, in the years that followed, Antoinette would visit her husband's aunt three times year at the Carmel of Saint Denis, of which she was a benefactress. It was later claimed by the nuns that Antoinette visited Madame Louise at the Carmel more than anyone else in the Royal Family.[1] When Antoinette's daughter Madame Royale was old enough to visit, Antoinette had a doll dressed as a nun so that the little girl would not be afraid when she saw her great aunt. According to Madame Campan, Madame Louise as a nun was deeply involved in church affairs; she was always petitioning her nephew's wife, so that Antoinette allegedly called her: "the most intriguing little Carmelite in the kingdom."[2] It is doubtful that the Queen really said such a thing about a woman whom she so highly respected. It was at the request of Madame

Louise that Antoinette granted a dowry to a poor, pious girl named Mademoiselle Lidoine, so that she could enter the Carmel of Compiègne. Mademoiselle Lidoine became the Mother Prioress of the heroic Martyrs of Compiègne, who like Antoinette, died on the guillotine during the French Revolution.

Antoinette spent the first fourteen years of her life in Austria, worshiping in rococo churches and listening to the music of Haydn and the Italian composers. Architecture and music in that time and place celebrated the glory of God in the beauty of His creation. As Queen, her desire to promote beauty around her, especially in the lives of those whom she loved, was an outgrowth of the culture in which she was reared. She loved theater, acting, opera, ballet, painting, gardens and everything that enhanced the loveliness of the natural order. Hers was a piety that was loving, gentle and courteous, but real and unflinching nevertheless. Antoinette's approach to faith was joyful and non-judgmental, free from the rigorist approach of Jansenism that so tainted a great deal of French piety in the years preceding the Revolution. Perhaps that is another reason why she did not want to be seen as a *dévote*.[3] Nevertheless, even as a young bride, she had the moral courage to defy the King in regard to Madame du Barry.

It is known that the young Archduchess Antonia was not an outstandingly pious child, but she was carefully taught her faith. Her mother, Empress Maria Theresa of Austria was a deeply observant Roman Catholic, who prayed novenas with her children and took them on pilgrimages to places such as Mariazell. Mariazell or "Mary's Throne" is a shrine to Our Lady high in the mountains. Antoinette made her First Holy Communion there in 1769.[4] The Empress and the Emperor her husband traveled there with all of their children and left two gold hearts symbolic of their united love for the

Mother of Jesus at the foot of her ancient and miraculous statue. She instilled in her daughters the importance of being faithful wives and staying with their husbands, no matter what.

As Queen, Antoinette's faith was practical and manifested itself in her extensive charities, including a home for unwed mothers called the Maternity Society. She encouraged her children to make sacrifices on behalf of the poor. She assisted at daily Mass, confessing and receiving Holy Communion on a regular basis, and lived, to all appearances, as a Roman Catholic in good standing. Her regular confessor as a young Queen was a blind priest of renowned holiness, Abbé Maudoux, who heard the last confession of Louis XV. She kept chapels at all of her residences, and made vestments and altar cloths. At the chapel at Petit Trianon over the altar there was a painting of Louis IX and his Queen, Marguerite of Provence going to St. Thibaud of Marly to ask his prayers for offspring. The painting must have had great meaning for Antoinette as she prayed. Antoinette demonstrated her devotion to the Mother of God by offering white silk garments for the statues of the Blessed Virgin and the Child Jesus at the shrine of Notre Dame de Montflière. Since the year was 1778 we can assume that the offering was connected with the birth of the Queen's first child, Madame Royale. She built a chapel at Saint-Cloud, which the King bought for her as a place to take her tubercular son.

After the death of her mother and loss of two of her children in the 1780's, Antoinette became more noticeably devout, growing closer to her pious sister-in-law, Madame Élisabeth. While under house arrest at the Tuileries palace, Antoinette and Élisabeth connived at getting non-juring priests, i.e., those who were faithful to the Pope, into the palace for secret Masses and confessions. It is supposedly the time when a few historians claim she had a romantic *rendez-vous* with Count Axel von Fersen. However, the atmosphere at the Tuileries was more like the catacombs than *Dangerous Liaisons*.

Before her death, when her children had been taken from her, her little son abused and her husband executed, the Queen again sought prayer and the sacraments, affirming in writing her loyalty to the Catholic Church. The priest Abbé Magnin who received her last confession in the Conciergerie later publicly affirmed those facts. Lenôtre's *The Last Days of Marie Antoinette* includes some revealing first hand accounts, including the testimony of the priest who, in spite of the great risks, was able to say Mass for the Queen before her death. Mademoiselle Fouché was a lady who often saw to the needs of prisoners and it was she who acquired all that was needed for the Mass to be said. Abbé Magnin stated the following:

> The day of the sacred ceremony being agreed upon, the gaoler came to meet us during the night at a particular spot, and took us into the prison. I heard the Queen's confession. Mademoiselle Fouché was prepared to receive her Saviour and the two gendarmes assured me that they also were ready, and earnestly desired to communicate in these fortunate and unexpected circumstances.
>
> I celebrated Holy Mass and gave the Communion to the Queen, who, as she fortified herself with the Eucharistic bread, received from God the courage to bear uncomplainingly all the torture that awaited her. Mademoiselle Fouché and the two gendarmes were at the same time admitted to the divine banquet. Having undertaken to tell my story in few words, I cannot possibly dwell upon the emotion to which so touching a scene must give rise....[5]

In pre-revolutionary France it was for the King and the Queen to give an example in performing charitable works. Louis XVI and Antoinette took this duty seriously and throughout their reign did what they could to help the needy. Louis XVI often visited the poor in their homes and villages, distributing alms from his own purse. During the difficult winter of 1776, the King oversaw the distribution of firewood among the peasants. As mentioned previously, Louis was responsible for many humanitarian reforms. He went incognito to hospitals, prisons, and factories so as to gain first-hand knowledge of the conditions in which his people lived and worked. In harsh winter of 1783-84 he gave three million *livres* to the poor and other winters as well.[6] The King and Queen were patrons of the *Maison Philanthropique*, a society founded by Louis XVI which helped the aged, blind and widows. The Queen taught her daughter Madame Royale to wait upon peasant children, to sacrifice her Christmas gifts so as to buy fuel and blankets for the destitute, and to bring baskets of food to the sick. Antoinette took her children with her on her charitable visits to foundling hospitals.[7] According to Maxime de la Rocheterie:

> Sometimes they went to the Gobelins; and the president of the district coming on one occasion to compliment her, she said, 'Monsieur you have many destitute but the moments which we spend in relieving them are very precious to us.' Sometimes she went to the free Maternity Society which she had founded, where she had authorized the Sisters to distribute sixteen hundred *livres* for food and fuel every month and twelve hundred for blankets and clothing, without counting the baby outfits which were given to three hundred mothers. At other times she went to the School of Design also founded by

her to which she sent one day twelve hundred *livres* saved with great effort that the rewards might not be diminished nor the dear scholars suffer through her own distress. Again she placed in the house of Mademoiselle O'Kennedy four daughters of disabled soldiers, orphans, for whom she said, 'I made the endowment.'[8]

The Queen adopted three poor children to be raised with her own, as well overseeing the upbringing of several needy children, whose education she paid for, while caring for their families. She brought several peasant families to live on her farm at Trianon, building cottages for them. There was food for the hungry distributed every day at Versailles, at the King's command. During the famine of 1787-88, the royal family sold much of their flatware to buy grain for the people, while they ate the cheap barley bread in order to be able to give more to the hungry. Madame de la Tour du Pin, a lady-in-waiting of Antoinette's, recorded in her spirited memoirs the daily activities at Versailles, including the rumors and the gossip. Her pen does not spare Louis XVI and Antoinette, which is why the following account is of interest. Every Sunday, Antoinette would personally take up a collection for the poor, which the courtiers resented since they preferred to have the money on hand for gambling. The Queen supported several impoverished families from her own purse. As Madame de la Tour du Pin describes:

> We had to be there before seven, for the Queen entered before the chiming of the clock. Beside her door would be one of the two Curés of Versailles. He would hand her a purse and she would go around to everyone, taking up a collection and saying: 'For the poor, if you please.' Each lady had

her '*écu*' of six francs ready in her hand and the men had their '*louis.*' The Curé would follow the Queen as she collected this small tax for her poor people, a levy which often totaled as much as much as one hundred '*louis*' and never less than fifty. I often heard some of the younger people, including the most spendthrift, complaining inordinately of this almsgiving being forced upon them, yet they would not have thought twice of hazarding a sum one hundred times as large in a game of chance, a sum much larger than that levied by the Queen.[9]

Louis and Antoinette contributed a great deal throughout their reign especially to the care of orphans and foundlings. There is a picture of an occasion in February, 1790, after their removal to Paris, when the King, the Queen and their children toured such a facility, where the nuns cared for abandoned babies and little children. As is reported by Maxime de la Rocheterie, the young Dauphin, soon to be an orphan himself was particularly drawn to the foundlings and gave all of his small savings to aid them.[10] The King and Queen did not see helping the poor as anything extraordinary, but as part of being a Christian. The royal couple's almsgiving stopped only with their incarceration in the Temple in August 1792, for then they had nothing left to give but their lives.

The hallmark of a Christian is charity which involves the ability to forgive. Whatever faults and flaws Louis and Antoinette may have had, there can be no doubt that they bore wrongs patiently and tried to forgive their enemies. As Louis XVI stated in his Last Will and Testament, written on Christmas Day, 1792, less than a month before he was killed: "I pardon with all my heart those who made themselves my enemies, without my having given them any cause, and I pray God to pardon them, as well as those who, through false or misunderstood zeal, did me much harm."[11] The King did not want to be avenged. "I exhort my son, should he have the misfortune of becoming king, to remember he owes himself wholly to the happiness of his fellow citizens; that he should forget all hates and all grudges, particularly those connected with the misfortunes and sorrows which I am experiencing...."[12]

Antoinette's forgiveness has an especially supernatural aura. When the Queen wrote her last letter to her sister-in-law, she was hours away from death. She had been put through the ordeal of a humiliating trial, designed to break her will. Her little son had been dragged from her arms and tormented into accusing his own mother of unnatural crimes. That Antoinette made an effort to forgive those who had tried to destroy her by corrupting her little boy surely was a result of grace. Here are her words: "I beg pardon of all whom I know, and especially of you, my sister, for all the vexations which, without intending it, I may have caused you. I pardon all my enemies the evils that they have done me."[13] Not only does the Queen forgive but she asks forgiveness. Humility and compunction drown any bitterness or recriminations, although certainly in her agony she experienced the full range of emotions. Only a person of sincere and profound faith could make that leap from agony to the heights of martyrdom.

13 HOLIDAYS AT VERSAILLES

"Thank God the endless Carnival is over!" — Empress Maria Theresa

As previously mentioned, Charlemagne or Charles the Great, King of the Franks, was crowned Emperor of the Romans by Pope Leo III at St. Peter's Basilica on Christmas Day in the year 800. It was at that time that Christmas began to be celebrated with greater festivity in Europe, although Epiphany continued to have higher liturgical rank. To the French the triumphant cry of *Noël*, originating either from the Latin word for birthday (*natalis*) or the French word for news (*nouvelles*), became the word for Christmas. Advent is the four week preparation for Christmas, which in earlier times had been longer and as rigorous as Lent. In the eighteenth century, Advent was still a time of fasting and days of abstinence from meat in Catholic countries, although it was punctuated by feast days such as St. Nicholas Day on December 6, the Immaculate Conception on December 8 and other saints' days depending on the diocese. For Antoinette, it was a time of increasing her charitable works. The Queen made the needs of the indigent a priority, especially in the cold of winter. Antoinette is all too commonly characterized as someone who ignored the plight of the poor. In reality, her charities were quite extensive. She also took great care to instill a love of the needy in her children. At Christmastime, during a particularly brutal winter, the Queen had them renounce their Christmas gifts in order to buy food and blankets for the destitute. As Maxime de La Rocheterie relates:

> One year, on the approach of the 1st of January, she had the most beautiful playthings brought from Paris to Versailles; she showed them to her children, and when they had looked at them and admired them, said to them that they were without doubt very beautiful, but that it was still more beautiful to distribute alms; and the price of these presents was sent to the poor.[1]

The Queen's generosity was well-known by her contemporaries, in spite of her efforts to be discreet, and the efforts of her enemies to portray her as a decadent spendthrift. In the difficult winter of 1788-89, the Seine froze over; the wolves were able to cross into the suberbs of Paris. Food was scarce and people were starving to death. Louis and Antoinette devoted themselves to aiding those in in need. When the Queen heard of special cases of suffering she sent a trusted servant to investigate or went herself, often to the cottages near Versailles, to discover how she could best be of assistance. What good she did, she tried to do in secret. Necker, upon discovering one of her benefactions, begged the Queen to be allowed to make it public. "Be sure, on the contrary," she replied, "that you never mention it. What good could it do? They would not believe you."[2] However, enough people heard of her charities so that in Paris they spontaneously built monuments of snow in her honor. One bore the profiles of Louis and Antoinette, with verses praising the royal generosity in the time of crisis.

Reine, dont la beauté surpasse les appas
Près d'un roi bienfaisant occupé ici la place.
Si ce monument frêle est de neige et de glace,
Nos coeurs pour toi ne le sont pas.

De ce monument sans exemple,
Couple auguste, l'aspect bien doux pur votre coeur
Sans doute vous plaira plus qu'un palais, qu'un temple
Que vous élèverait un peuple adulateur.[3]

On Christmas Day at Versailles, after confessing and receiving Holy Communion, the King would touch the sick, even as on the day of his coronation. It was an ancient tradition which fell into disuse during the early part of the reign of Louis XIV because, due to the King's refusal to forsake his immoral lifestyle, he could not receive Holy Communion. His later years saw his reformation and the renewal of the ceremony on Christmas day and other high holy days. Unfortunately, after the initial pious years of Louis XV's reign, the tradition ceased for decades, due to the rule of many mistresses. Louis XVI restored the healing ceremony, and on every Christmas day until his imprisonment he could be found praying over his sick subjects, after receiving the Eucharist.[4]

On the twelfth day of Christmas came Epiphany or *la Fête des Rois*, celebrating the visit of the Magi to the Infant Jesus. Every French family, including the Royal Family, celebrated with a *galette des rois*, or King Cake. The cake was a puff pastry filled with marzipan, and hidden inside was a *fève*, which meant fava bean, although often it was a small charm of some kind. The member of the family who received the piece of cake with the *fève* became King or Queen for the day.[5] Epiphany also marked the beginning of Carnival, the celebratory season before the penitential season of Lent.

As a young girl, Antoinette embraced the festivities of Carnival with alacrity, especially the masked balls. Since members of the royal family were constantly surrounded by semi-liturgical ceremonies, at the masked ball the princes and princesses could engage in something vaguely resembling normal human interaction. The wearing of a mask, although it did not always endow total anonymity, lightened the tight protocol so that royals could mingle and converse with others in society. In February of 1773, Antoinette wrote to her mother Empress Maria Theresa, relating how she went with her husband the Dauphin Louis to the Opera ball in Paris:

> We went—M. le Dauphin, the comte, and comtesse de Provence and I—last Thursday to the Opera Ball in Paris; we kept the utmost secret. We were all masked; still, we were recognized after half an hour. The duc de Chartres and the duc de Bourbon, who were dancing at the Palais Royal right next door came to meet us and asked us pressingly to go and dance at Madame de Chartres'; but I excused myself from it as I had the King's permission for the Opera only. We returned here at seven and heard Mass before going to bed. Everybody is delighted with M. le Dauphin's willingness to have this outing since he was believed to be averse to it.[6]

In January of 1774, Louis and Antoinette once again ventured incognito into Paris to the Opera ball, accompanied by Louis' two brothers and their wives.

Here is Comte de Mercy's description of the event in a letter to Empress Maria Theresa:

> The three Princes and Princesses came on the 30th of January to the masked ball at the Opera; measures had been so well taken that they remained a long while without being recognized by anyone. M. le Dauphin [Louis] behaved splendidly; he went about the ball talking indiscriminately to all those he met on his path, in a very gay and decorous manner introducing the kind of jests suited to the occasion. The public was enchanted with this conduct on the part of M. le Dauphin, it made a great sensation in Paris and they did not fail, as always happens in these cases, to attribute to Madame la Dauphine the improvement they noticed in her consort's way of showing himself....
>
> The Princes and Princesses came back a second time to the Opera ball on Sunday, the 6th of this month [February]; but this time their presence was less well concealed and consequently there was a greater influx of people to the theater. However, nothing improper or embarrassing resulted, and Madame la Dauphine, who did not unmask, drew on herself all the applause and admiration with which all the public always hastens to do homage to her, both owing to the people to whom she spoke and the things she said to them.[7]

It was at the Opera ball on January 30 that Antoinette first met Count Axel von Fersen, chatting with him behind her mask, in the presence of her husband and in-laws, but no eyebrows were raised by this playful incident. The Empress Maria Theresa was more concerned with her daughter getting sick from exhaustion, and at the end of the 1773 Carnival wrote:

"Thank God it is all over...."[8] Later, she expressed reservations about the young Queen's taste in fashion. On March 5, 1775, after Louis XVI had ascended the throne of France, the Empress penned:

> Thank God the endless Carnival is over! That exclamation will make me look very old, but I must admit that all those late evenings were too tiring; I feared for the Court's health and for the order of it's usual habits, which is an essential point....In the same way I can't prevent myself raising a point which many gazettes repeat all too often; it is the coiffure you use; they say that from the forehead it is thirty-six inches high, and with so many feathers and ribbons to adorn it![9]

Antoinette responded by saying:

> Although Carnival did amuse me a great deal, I agree that it was time it was ended. We are now back to our usual routine....It is true that I take some care of the way I dress; and, as for feathers, everyone wears them, and it would be extraordinary not to wear them. Their height has been much curtailed since the end of the balls....[10]

After Antoinette became a mother in December of 1778, her participation in Carnival was greatly mitigated, since she preferred not be too far away from her babies at night. It is sad that the enjoyment of the masquerade balls during her teenage years would later lead to many false rumors about her lifestyle.

Versailles is not usually associated with Lenten penance, but fasting and abstinence, as well as some mortification, were observed there by many during the Old Regime. For one thing, there would be no plays or operas performed; all the public theaters were closed in France during Lent. The daughters of Louis XV were known for their scrupulous observance of fasting and abstinence, although Madame Victoire found such penance especially trying. According to Madame Campan:

> Without quitting Versailles, without sacrificing her easy chair, she [Madame Victoire] fulfilled the duties of religion with punctuality, gave to the poor all she possessed, and strictly observed Lent and the fasts. The table of Mesdames acquired a reputation for dishes of abstinence....Madame Victoire was not indifferent to good living, but she had the most religious scruples respecting dishes of which it was allowable to partake at penitential times....The abstinence which so much occupied the attention of Madame Victoire was so disagreeable to her, that she listened with impatience for the midnight hour of Holy Saturday; and then she was immediately supplied with a good dish of fowl and rice, and sundry other succulent viands.[11]

Their nephew Louis XVI was also known for his fastidious observance of Lent, as recorded once again by the faithful Madame Campan:

> Austere and rigid with regard to himself alone, the King observed the laws of the Church with scrupulous exactness. He fasted and abstained throughout the whole of Lent. He thought it right that the queen should not observe these customs with the same strictness. Though sincerely pious, the spirit of the age had disposed his mind to toleration.[12]

Some of the King's tolerant behavior included the permitting of certain games at court during Lent. During the Lent of 1780, the Austrian ambassador Comte de Mercy was shocked to discover Louis XVI playing blind man's bluff with Antoinette and some members of the Court. Count Mercy described the scandalous scene to the Empress Maria Theresa:

> Amusements have been introduced of such noisy and puerile character that they are little suited to Lenten meditations, and still less to the dignity of the august personages who take part in them. They are games resembling blind man's bluff, that first lead to the giving of forfeits, and then to their redemption by some bizarre penance; the commotion is kept up sometimes until late into the night. The number of persons who take part in these games, both of the Court and the town, makes them still more unsuitable; everyone is surprised to see that the King plays them with great zest, and that he can give himself up wholly to such frivolities in such a serious condition of State affairs as obtains at present.[13]

Given the long hours that Louis XVI devoted to affairs of state and the fact that people often complained that he was too serious and reserved, it seems that Mercy should have been pleased to see the King come out of his shell a little and take some recreation. But then, Mercy often tried to cast Louis in an unfavorable light. As far as the Empress was concerned, however, Lent was not the time for any games. Louis' devotion was sincere all the same; he was constant in his routine of prayer and good works, observing the fasts of the Church for Lent and the Ember days even throughout his imprisonment.[14]

The King's sister, Madame Élisabeth, also steadfastly kept the discipline of Lent in both good times and bad. In the Temple prison, the jailers mocked the princess' attempts to keep Lent as best she could. Louis XVI and Antoinette's daughter, Madame Royale, who shared her aunt's imprisonment, recorded it thus:

> Having no fish, she asked for eggs or other dishes on fast-days. They refused them, saying that in equality there was no difference of days; there were no weeks, only decades. They brought us a new almanac, but we did not look at it. Another time, when my aunt again asked for fast-day food they answered: 'Why, *citoyenne*, don't you know what has taken place? None but fools believe all that.' She made no further requests.[15]

As for Antoinette herself, she did not fast and abstain throughout every day of Lent as Louis did; her health did not permit it. However, after baby Madame Sophie died in 1787, it was noted that the Queen became more fervent in her devotions, especially during Lent. Jean Chalon in *Chère Marie-Antoinette* notes that in 1788 she gave orders that her table strictly comply with all the regulations of the Church.[16] Even the Swedish ambassador remarked: "The queen seems to have turned devout."[17]

In France, as in other Christian nations, decorated eggs were given as gifts at Easter. The custom began in the fourth century when eating eggs were banned by the Church during the Lenten fast. On Easter Sunday, it was the tradition at Versailles from the days of Louis XIV for the King to be given the largest egg laid during Holy Week. The eggs of Versailles would be decorated with colors and gold leaf and be blessed on Easter Sunday, then distributed by the King to his courtiers and servants.

There were usually many eggs that needed to be eaten, due to the long fast, and so omelettes were generally part of the feasting on Easter Sunday. During Eastertide, it was also the time for anyone who wished to be considered a practicing Catholic to make their "Easter Duty" which meant receiving Holy Communion at least once between the first Sunday of Lent and Trinity Sunday. It also meant that if the individual was conscious of grave sin they had to go to confession, because it is forbidden to receive the Eucharist if one has committed a serious or mortal sin. Those who refused to confess and receive Communion were usually a source of scandal to the faithful. Both Louis XIV and Louis XV went for many years without making their Easter duty. However, to Louis XVI and Antoinette, the Easter duty was a matter of importance and they each went to great lengths during the Revolution to perform their Easter duties.

Pentecost occurs on the fiftieth day after Easter and commemorates the descent of the Holy Spirit upon the Apostles of Jesus Christ, and thus is the birthday of the Church. In royal France it was a day kept with great festivity, with solemn high masses and sermons. Many people came to Versailles to watch the "Procession of the Blue Ribbons" which was a procession of the members of the Order of the Holy Spirit, with their blue sashes and diamond stars. Pentecost Sunday, and the following Monday, were kept as national holidays until the Revolution abolished it in 1795.

La Fête Dieu or Corpus Christi marked the transition from spring to summer. It celebrated the Catholic teaching on the Holy Eucharist with great solemnity. The King, Queen and court would process around the town of Versailles with the Blessed Sacrament under a canopy. Tapestries from the reign of Louis XIV were used to make the altars of reposition throughout the town, and the entire court would stop at each place for Benediction. On the feast of Corpus Christi, following his succession to the kingship, Louis and Antoinette and other members of the Royal family mingled with the citizens of Chaillot in a Eucharistic procession, the first of many Eucharistic processions of their reign. A year later, after his coronation, Louis and Antoinette led a *Fête Dieu* procession in the city of Rheims. Their last Eucharistic procession at Versailles occurred on May 4, 1789, on the occasion of the opening the Estates-General.

August 15 was the feast of the Assumption of the Blessed Virgin Mary, the patronal feast day of the Kingdon of France, since France had been dedicated by Louis XIII to the Mother of Jesus in 1637. Along with the dedication went the Vow of Louis XIII for every parish to have a procession in honor of the Mother of God on Assumption Day. Louis XIII had made the vow as a prayer to God for an heir, and the future Louis XIV was born to him and his Queen, Anne of Austria, on September 5, 1638 after twenty-three years of marriage. The Assumption was also the official *fête* for the Queens of France, since most, if not all, bore the name "Marie" somewhere in their name. A solemn Mass would be offered in the royal chapel; the King and Queen would process with their entire households to the chapel. They processed to Mass everyday but the procession on the Assumption included the entire Royal Family and all their attendants. Everyone was dressed in their finest array; it was a glorious sight for which many people came from far away to watch. On August 15, 1785, as the procession was lining up to begin, Louis and Antoinette discovered the criminal charade of the Diamond Necklace, never imagining it would precipitate the greatest upheaval in the history of France.

November 1 was All Saints Day or La Toussaint,

followed by All Souls Day on November 2, which happened to be Antoinette's birthday. La Toussaint was a holiday: all businesses were closed, and French families would visit the graves of departed loved ones with large bouquets of chrysanthemums. At Versailles, La Toussaint was another traditional day for the King to touch the sick, who would be allowed into the *château* to kneel in the gallery as the King came in procession after receiving Holy Communion.[18] It was customary in France to set a place at the table in honor of those relatives who had gone before, as well as lighting candles for them in church, and most of all, enrolling their names in Masses for the faithful departed. Because All Souls was kept in a solemn, subdued manner, Antoinette's birthday was usually celebrated on November 1. In 1776, All Saints Day was the occasion of the three day card party in honor of Antoinette's birthday, held in Princesse de Lamballes's quarters. Unfortunately, it opened her up to a great deal of gossip, and made many people question her respectability. On All Souls Day, people went to church and to cemeteries and crypts to pray for the dead and gain the All Souls indulgence for those in purgatory. Thus the liturgical year ended on a serious note which looked towards the last things.

14 THE CHILDREN OF LOUIS XVI AND MARIE-ANTOINETTE

Marlbrouk s'en va-t-en guerre,
Mironton, mironton, mirontaine,
Marlbrough s'en va-t-en guerre,
Ne sait quand reviendra.
Ne sait quand reviendra.
— "Marlbrouk s'en va-t-en guerre"

Antoinette had a great love for children. As a young girl, she asked her ladies and servants to bring their children with them when in attendance upon her; hence the scene in her apartments was a bit chaotic with all the little ones running about, not to mention all the dogs. Even as King and Queen, both Louis and Antoinette were often accompanied by a train of assorted youngsters as they went about their day at Versailles; the kindness they each showed to the children who lived at Versailles was reciprocated with love. Before her children were born, Antoinette adopted an orphaned peasant child, named François Michel Gagné, but he was called "Jacques" by his grandmother and several brothers and sisters. The Queen called him "Armand" and she reared Armand as her own son, providing for his entire family, including music lessons for one of his brothers. It was difficult for Armand when the Queen had her own children, as well as adopting others, since he was no longer the center of all her attention. As a teenager, he rebelled, joined the Revolution and was killed in the wars. Meanwhile, around 1787, Antoinette adopted the daughter of servants named Marie-Philippine Lambriquet, whom she called "Ernestine," to be a companion for her daughter Madame Royale. She dressed her as a princess and gave her all the same toys as her own daughter. Ernestine was referred to as "the girl who is always with Madame Royale" and Antoinette said during the Revolution: "What will become of us is uncertain...but never forget that Ernestine is my daughter." She added that she and Ernestine would "love each other for eternity."[1] Even the governess Madame de Polignac treated her as if she were another royal child.[2] It gave rise to the rumor that Ernestine was really a bastard daughter of Louis XVI by a serving maid, but most biographers of Louis completely discount it. Around 1790, when they were under house arrest at the Tuileries in Paris, Antoinette adopted three orphan girls whose parents, who had been servants in the King's household, died within months of each other. The two oldest were sent to a Visitation convent to be educated but the youngest, Jeanne Louise Victoire, called "Zoé," who was the same age as the little Dauphin Louis-Charles, lived in the royal apartments at the Tuileries. Antoinette would have adopted many more children had she been able. Those whom she could not actually bring to live in the palace, she provided for generously.

At the time of the Royal Family's disastrous flight to Montmédy in June 1791, Antoinette sent Ernestine and Zoé to safety. Ernestine was entrusted to her birth father. Zoé joined her blood sisters at the Visitation Monastery, where she eventually became a nun and died in 1814 at the beginning of the Restoration. During the violence of the Terror, Antoinette, in the Temple prison, was anxious for news about her adopted children and tried to discover where they were. She managed to find out that Zoé and her two sisters had been taken to their relatives in the country. Of Ernestine, she could discover nothing, except that her father had been guillotined. Ernestine had actually been whisked out of France by an *emigré* family and died in exile.

Most people are unaware that the Queen adopted a young African boy and had him brought up at Versailles. In 1787, the famous traveler Chevalier de Boufflers, who had recently returned from Senegal, presented Antoinette with a three year old Senegalese boy. Antoinette had him baptised and renamed Jean Amilcar, and saw to it that he was well-cared for in her household under the supervision of her page, Jean Müller.[3] When the Royal Family was moved to the Tuileries Palace in Paris in October 1789, Jean Amilcar was placed in the care of a tutor, Quentin Beldon; Antoinette sent monthly payments to provide for his upkeep. When she was moved from the Tuileries to the Temple prison in August 1792, she was unable to keep up the payments. For several months, he and his tutor were destitute amid the turmoil of the Reign of Terror. When Beldon found work, he paid for Jean Amilcar's education at the prestigious École Liancourt at Saint-Cloud, where there were other children of African descent. At school, Jean studied painting. However, he died at age fourteen in 1796, probably of malnutrition.[4]

On December 19, 1778, Louis and Antoinette, after eight years of marriage, were finally blessed with a child of their own. No longer awkward teenagers, they were aged twenty-four and twenty-three respectively; the Queen's menstrual cycle, referred to by her mother as *la*

Générale Krottendorf, had finally become regular. Antoinette certainly was better prepared psychologically and physically for motherhood than when she was first married. Nevertheless, the Queen had a long, difficult labor which she had to endure in public, with courtiers standing on chairs to see her pain, and the crowd so dense that she almost suffocated. Louis famously tore open the windows of her bedroom to give her air. Antoinette suffered some gynecological damage during the birthing process, which resulted in severe hemorrhaging. We do not know how permanent the damage was and if it caused discomfort in her marital relations and future preganancies. Empress Maria Theresa was convinced that someone had injured the Queen on purpose, to keep her from having more children.[5]

It was with great joy that they welcomed Marie-Thérèse-Charlotte. The baby was baptized immediately and given the title *Madame la Fille du Roi* which by age five had become *Madame Royale*. She was named after her maternal grandmother the Empress, who was also her godmother. She was called "Charlotte" after Antoinette's favorite sister, Maria Carolina, the Queen of Naples, as well as her godfather, Charles III, the King of Spain. Louis' brother the Comte de Provence stood in for Charles III at the baptism, and caused a stir when he loudly inquired who was the father of little Marie-Thérèse. At the time, it may have been seen as a moment of jest. However, it was around that time that the rumors began that Antoinette's children were fathered by men other than the King. Marie-Thérèse herself soon gave lie to the rumors as she so closely resembled her Papa in more ways than one.

Louis and Antoinette had become a devoted couple, ready for their parental duties. Louis' manners and appearance had improved. As King, no doubt due to

Antoinette's influence, he had two tubs of which he made daily use, one for washing and one for rinsing. Their relationship deepened following the birth of their Madame Royale. When the Queen came down with measles, she secluded herself at Petit Trianon. Louis, missing her, came one evening to the Trianon and stood under her window as she leaned out, whispering his devotion into the night. No one else ever knew what was said, except the Queen, who sent back her own words of tenderness.[6]

In the meantime, Antoinette greeted her baby with the words: "Poor little one, you are not what was desired, but you will be none the less dear to me! A son would have belonged to the state—you will belong to me!"[7] The baby soon became a lovely little girl, with blonde curls and blue eyes accompanied by a quiet but forceful personality. Her governess was the Princesse de Guéménée, who had brought up her aunt Madame Élisabeth, although the person who supervised her care the most was the Alsatian sub-governess, Madame de Mackau. Madame de Mackau had also taken care of Madame Élisabeth and her daughter, the Marquise de Bombelles, was Élisabeth's closest friend. Rose Bertin described the tiny Madame Royale as being always *une grande dame, bien grande dame* and never a child.[8] By age four, the little girl's serious expression gained for her the nickname *Mousseline la sérieuse* from her Uncle Artois, who would someday be her father-in-law. Antoinette's greatest fear for her child was that she would be spoiled, and so she was firm with her during childish tantrums.

At four years old, Marie-Thérèse went through a stage where she discovered she made a huge sensation in the adult world when she expressed dislike of her mother. The Marquis de Bombelles recorded in his journal how, when told by Abbé Vermond that the Queen had fallen

Marie-Antoinette, Daughter of the Caesars

from her horse and could have died, Madame Royale said that it would please her because then her mother would no longer keep her from doing whatever she liked. The outspoken toddler went on to say how she liked her papa better than her mother because her papa always held her hand whereas her mother made her walk behind. No doubt the Queen was trying to teach her daughter about precedence, which governed court life. During the course of the Madame Royale's outrageous speech, Antoinette ran in tears to her friend Madame de Polignac, who surely explained that the little one did not know what she was saying, but merely enjoyed the attention she was receiving.[9] Some authors have taken the incident to indicate a deep, lasting dislike of Madame Royale for her mother, as well as an irreparable character flaw in the little princess. Those of us who have had dealings with the realm of toddlerhood are aware of the potential for socially unacceptable conduct and know not to take certain behaviors too seriously. Madame Royale grew up accompanying her mother everywhere; her lessons were overseen by the Queen herself. The care for the poor which Antoinette showed her by example was to become one of the hallmarks of the princess' adult life. The few occasions the child was sick, Antoinette hardly left her side. There can be no doubt, however, that Marie-Thérèse especially adored her father, as was evident to the court when Louis returned from a trip in June of 1786, and the princess dragged her two little brothers onto a balcony shouting: "Papa! Papa!" The King leaped out of his coach and ran up the stairs to them.[10] There are few kings who so completely loved and enjoyed their children as much as did Louis XVI. He tried to make time for them every day, helping with their lessons and telling them stories at bedtime.

On October 22, 1781 the long-awaited heir to the

throne of France was born to Louis XVI and Antoinette. The birth of the Dauphin Louis-Joseph brought unprecedented popularity to the Queen as well as increasing her political clout. While Antoinette was not involved in politics at the time, being the mother of a future king made her more dangerous to the enemies of the crown, and therefore a target for increasingly lurid calumnies. Nevertheless, the first days of Louis-Joseph's short life were those of unmitigated bliss for his parents. The King had ordered that the crowd was not to be allowed in the Queen's room while she was giving birth, a break with tradition that many resented, but people still massed in the rooms, stairwells, and galleries nearby. Present in the room were Monsieur, the Comte d'Artois, the Mesdames Tantes, as well as the Queen's ladies: Mesdames de Lamballe, de Chimay, de Mailly, d'Ossun, de Tavannes, and de Guéménée. It had also been decreed that Antoinette should not be told the sex of the child until she was out of harm's way. However, Antoinette thought that everyone's restrained silence meant that the child was a girl. Louis, having seen his son washed and dressed before being handed over to the governess, Madame de Guéménée, could not contain himself and said to Antoinette with tears in his eyes: "Monsieur le Dauphin requests permission to enter."[11] The child was brought; he was strong, healthy, and reputedly quite beautiful for a newborn; Antoinette kissed her baby boy with tears of happiness, then handed him back to Madame de Guéménée, saying: "Take him, he belongs to the State; but I shall have my daughter." Those present later described the scene at Versailles as being one of infectious joy, as friends, enemies and strangers embraced each other with tears. While Louis' brothers tried to look happy in spite of themselves, feeling themselves disinherited, their sister Madame Élisabeth laughed and wept with happiness. The archbishop wished to adorn the baby with the *cordon-bleu*, but Louis XVI declared the he must be made a Christian first. The afternoon of the day of his birth, the baby was baptized Louis-Joseph-Xavier-François in the chapel of Versailles by the Cardinal de Rohan, the Grand Almoner. He was presented with both the *cordon-bleu* and the Cross of St. Louis, followed by a solemn *Te Deum*, and fireworks in the Place d'Armes.

In Paris the raptures of the court were echoed by people of all stations, and indeed throughout all France. When Monsieur Croismare, lieutenant of the guards, announced the news of the birth at the Hôtel de Ville de Paris, the citizens embraced one another in the streets. The joy caused by a small boy, whose birth indicated to the people that the monarchy would continue, shows that most of the French people were happy with having a king; they were not groaning with misery under an oppressive tyrant as some would later portray them. Versailles was flooded with gifts from the various guilds and fifty market women of Les Halles came to pay their respects wearing their best black silk dresses. There was dancing in the streets as a universal holiday was declared in France. When the President of the Court of Accounts and the President of the Court of Aid came to pay their compliments, the latter said to the Dauphin, "Your birth is our joy; your education will be our hope; your virtue our happiness."[12] In years that followed, Louis XVI cultivated a vegetable garden at Versailles in which he worked in with his oldest son, Louis-Joseph. He felt it important for his heir to have an appreciation for how the food in France was grown. Later, at the Tuileries, his second son Louis-Charles also had a little garden.

Although Antoinette had tried to breastfeed Madame Royale herself, for the Dauphin they had found a healthy peasant mother to be the nurse. She was from Sceaux and her legal name was already "Madame Poitrine" or

"Mrs. Chest." She swore like a trooper, in spite of the prim lace caps she was given to wear; as she nursed the royal child she sang an old lullaby, *"Malbrouk s'en va-t'en guerre."* What may have originated as an Arab tune, brought to Europe by the medieval crusaders, had been known in France for quite some time. Known to us today as "The Bear Went Over the Mountain," or "For He's a Jolly Good Fellow," the song was named after one of France's greatest enemies, John Churchill, 1st Duke of Marlborough (1650-1722), whose military exploits under James II, William III and Queen Anne were infamous. Written in 1722 when Marlborough died, it began triumphantly with "Marlborough, he's gone to the war, I don't know when he'll be back." The Queen heard the tune being sung by Madame Poitrine, and began humming it herself. Soon the entire court, even the King, was singing *Malbrouk.* It rapidly spread to Paris, where the song was sung everywhere, as an expression of the people's joy over having a Dauphin. To commemorate the national exultation, Antoinette built a small tower in her gardens at Trianon, called the *tour de Malbrouk*. The Dauphin Louis-Joseph often played there before he died at age seven in 1789. Later, the verse *Madame à sa tour monte* ("My Lady climbs into her tower") was used to mock Antoinette as she was imprisoned in the tower of the Temple Prison in 1792. As Louis-Joseph grew he displayed a precocious intellect far beyond his years; he was slender, frail and delicate, with chestnut hair and vivid blue eyes.

Before and after Louis-Joseph's birth, the Queen suffered miscarriages but then on Easter Sunday, March 27, 1785, she gave birth to Louis-Charles, the Duc de Normandie. There is a legend that at the moment the attending *accoucheur*, Monsieur Vermond, brother of the Abbé Vermond, announced that the birth was imminent, saying *"La Reine va accoucheur"* a crown from the moulding of the bed decoration fell down and shattered on the ground.[13] Louis-Charles was a robust and husky little lad, resembling his papa; a "peasant child," his mother described him. Others said he looked like Louis XV, as well as the King's mother, Marie-Josèphe de Saxe.[14] He had golden hair, blue eyes and plump rosy cheeks. Antoinette called him her *chou d'amour*. He was mischievous and curious, with a tendency to be high-strung, just like his mother.

Madame Sophie, the youngest, was born on July 9, 1786 during the Diamond Necklace scandal when Antoinette was under excruciating stress. Baptized Sophie-Hélène-Béatrice, she was the last royal child to be born at Versailles but not the last royal child to die there. She was never really healthy and died in June 1787 at eleven months old. In her grief, Antoinette turned to her deeply spiritual sister-in-law Élisabeth for consolation. "She might have grown up to be a friend," said the Queen, who was feeling that the number of her enemies was increasing.[15] But as her sorrows grew, so did her faith, and she turned to religious devotion.

In October of 1793, when on trial for her life, Antoinette was accused by the revolutionary tribunal of sexually abusing her eight-year-old son, Louis-Charles. When the Queen failed to answer, she was badgered for a response. She rose to her feet and faced the crowded courtroom, saying: *"Si je n'ai répondu, c'est que la nature se refuse à répondre à une pareille inculpation faite à une mère. J'en appelles à toutes celles qui peuvent se trouver ici."* "If I do not respond, it is because nature refuses to answer such a charge made to a mother. I appeal to all the mothers who are here!" [16] The spectators, especially the women, applauded the Queen and hissed at the revolutionaries, who had overplayed their hand. The infamous charge elicited disgust even from those deeply committed to the

Revolution. Whatever else her faults may have been, Antoinette was a devoted mother. As Maxime de la Rocheterie writes: "There is not a letter to Marie-Antoinette's friends, not a letter to her brothers, which does not abound in details of the health and a thousand incidents in the life of her dear little ones. She goes to see them at every hour of the day and night...."[17]

To the governess Madame de Tourzel, who took the place of Madame de Polignac in the summer of 1789, she gave detailed instructions concerning the care of each of her children, saying:

> I have always accustomed my children to have great confidence in me, and, when they have done wrong, to tell me themselves; and then, when I scold them, this enables me to appear pained and afflicted rather than angry. I have accustomed them to regard 'yes' or 'no' once uttered by me as irrevocable, but I always give them reasons for my decisions, suitable to their ages....[18]

Antoinette and Louis decided early in the Revolution never to allow themselves to be separated from their two surviving children. However, after the King's death, little Louis-Charles was taken away from his mother in August 1793 and infamously brutalized by his captors. In the fall of the year, the Queen was removed from the Temple prison to the Conciergerie, away from her fifteen-year-old daughter Madame Royale, whom she never saw again. When interrogated in prison as to whom she regarded as her enemies, the Queen replied: "My enemies are all those who would bring harm to my children."[19] In her last letter she wrote to her sister-in-law: "I feel profound sorrow in leaving my poor children: you know that I only lived for them and for you, my good and tender sister....My God, how heart-rending it is to leave them forever! Farewell! Farewell!"[20]

"Dauphin Louis-Joseph of France"

Marie-Antoinette, Daughter of the Caesars

"Madame Royale with her nurse"

"Churching of Marie-Antoinette at Notre Dame de Paris after birth of Dauphin Louis-Joseph, 1781."

Marie-Antoinette, Daughter of the Caesars

"Dauphin Louis-Charles, Louis XVII"

Marie-Antoinette, Daughter of the Caesars

"Gabrielle de Polignac, Royal Governess, in Court Dress with Flowers"

15 MARIE-ANTOINETTE AND FRIENDSHIP

Portait charmant, portait de mon amie
Gage d'amour par l'amour obtenu
Ah viens m'offrir le bien que j'ai perdu
Te voir encore me rappelle à la vie.
—"*Portraint charmant*" by Marie-Antoinette

In her last letter, Antoinette wrote to her sister-in-law Madame Élisabeth: "Happiness is doubled when shared with a friend...."[1] In those words are expressed the value she placed on friendship as being intrinsic to her happiness. In this she was participating in the eighteenth century's "cult" of friendship, which idealized friendship as the highest and purest of relationships.[2] Indeed, the Queen had a great capacity for friendship, although she was not always prudent in her choice of companions. Some of her friends were ladies of virtue and sterling character, such as the Princesse de Chimay and the Duchesse de Fitz-James. There were others, however, like Madame Dillon, mistress of the Prince de Guéméné, who was always asking for money, and Madame de Polignac, herself indifferent to honors but weak when it came to the importunities of her family and friends. In some cases, especially in regard to Madame de Polignac, the friendship spilled over into girlish infatuation on the part of the Queen. Her enemies seized upon it to feed the false rumors that Antoinette had lovers of both sexes. No serious biographer of the Queen gives credence to the scandalous stories. Nevertheless, in Dena Goodman's collection of essays much is made of the Queen's friendships with women, especially in Terry Castle's essay, where it maintains that not only was Antoinette a homosexual but people who are interested in her are also latent homosexuals. Such a contention tells us nothing about Antoinette but plenty about the obsessions of such writers who insist upon making unfounded pseudopsychological claims.[3]

The French court itself, after years of being ruled by Madame de Pompadour and Madame du Barry, was the sort of setting that overshadowed innocent relationships with tawdry connotations. Antoinette, with her beauty, naiveté and sentimentality, was the perfect target for every sort of calumny. In an age famous for florid and exaggerated expressions, the Queen was especially gushing and emotional when revealing her feelings. It speaks of the loneliness and isolation that she experienced as a young girl, sent away from home to a foreign land. To some extent, her emotions remained fixed at age fourteen, with all the intensity of early adolescence, as can be seen in the lyrics she wrote for a song, "Portrait Charmant":

> *Portait charmant, portait de mon amie*
> *Gage d'amour par l'amour obtenu*
> *Ah viens m'offrir le bien que j'ai perdu*
> *Te voir encore me rappelle à la vie.*
>
> *Oui les voilà ses traits, ses traits que j'aime*
> *Son doux regard, son maintien, sa candeur*
> *Lorsque ma main te presse sur mon coeur*

Marie-Antoinette, Daughter of the Caesars

Je crois encore la presser elle-même

Non tu n'as pas pour moi les mêmes charmes
Muet témoin de nos tendres soupirs
En retraçant nos fugitifs plaisirs
Cruel portrait, tu fais couler mes larmes

Pardonne-moi mon injuste langage
Pardonne aux cris de ma vive douleur
Portait charmant, tu n'es pas le bonheur
Mais bien souvent tu m'en offres l'image.[4]

Translation:

Charming portrait, portrait of my friend
Token of love, by love obtained
Ah come and give me back the good I have lost
To see you again brings me back to life.

Yes here they are, her features, her features I love
Her sweet looks, her bearing, her ingenuousness
When I press you to my heart
I think I still embrace her herself.

No you don't have to me the same charms
Silent witness of our tender sighs
By recounting our fleeting pleasures
Cruel portrait, you make my tears fall.

Forgive me for my unfair language
Forgive the cries of my bitter woe
Charming portrait, you are not happiness
But so often you give me the image of it.[5]

"Portrait Charmant" was written by the Queen for one of her close friends, perhaps Madame de Lamballe. It

235

would be unwise to interpret the lines in terms of contemporary American culture, so colored by Puritanism yet ready to see sensuality where it does not belong. In the existence the Queen tried to design at Petit Trianon, life was beautiful, love was pure, everything was rustic, pristine, and natural, a place for small children to play in innocence. In her letters she was always covering everyone with kisses, completely unaware of any *double entendres*, of any sordid misinterpretation.

Why did Antoinette have such a need for close friendships? In the vast palaces where she was born and brought up, amid a many-peopled court, where she often went for ten days at a time without seeing her busy mother, the Archduchess Antoine's closest family member was her sister, Maria Carolina, three years her senior. Maria Carolina was bossy but very motherly and extremely protective of her little sister. When Antoine was about twelve, Carolina married and the two sisters never saw each other again. Later, Antoinette, far away in France, separated from her mother, who was always highly critical of her anyway, tried to find a friend, a "big sister" to take Carolina's place. Antoinette was accused of having friends too young and silly and when she defended herself by saying most of her friends were older people she has been accused of lying.[6] However, most of her circle were older, some much older, than herself. Both of her closest friends, Madame de Lamballe and Madame de Polignac, were a few years older and, especially Madame de Polignac, were highly maternal. The Queen seemed to grow in emotional maturity and balance after she herself became a mother and had to fight for the survival of her family.

The fact that her marriage had so many difficulties getting started, and that her husband Louis XVI, although a worthy man, was known to be moody, the

Queen gravitated to her girlfriends for emotional support. Louis XVI had high regard for Madame de Polignac and encouraged his wife to befriend her, seeing her as someone who could guide Antoinette into her wifely and motherly duties. Throughout her life, Antoinette had many friends from all walks of life, including artists, musicians, and theater people; her maid Madame Campan describes the Queen as being "too much in an equality with the people of the court."[7] In the last few years, she grew closer to her pious sister-in-law Madame Élisabeth; it was to Élisabeth that the Queen, about to die, expressed her last thoughts and her restrained agony. "I had friends," she wrote. "The idea of being forever separated from them and from all their troubles is one of the greatest sorrows that I suffer in dying. Let them at least know that to my latest moment I thought of them."[8]

Several of Antoinette's friends were in her service, and had come to greet her at the French border with Madame de Noailles in May, 1770. It should be noted that a post at the royal court, or even at a lesser princely or wealthy bourgeois household, were salaried positions. Although the modern view is that women had no professions available to them outside the nunnery or motherhood other than prostitution, the reality is that Versailles, and any number of other palaces and great households, functioned only because of the women who worked there. At Versailles, many ladies wielded power and influence solely through their duties in the Queen's household, or even in the households of one of the princesses, and were able to have their own income.[9] The higher positions demanded intelligence, discretion and the social graces, for a lady-in-waiting often had to appear in public with her mistress, or mingle at parties and balls. If the lady were unmarried, the Queen, or whoever her patroness was, would help arrange a marriage for her. If she were married and a mother then the Queen might arrange marriages for her children. Pensions in old age were usually provided for those who had served faithfully. At any rate, an office at court was an honorable way in which many women were able to supplement their income, or even provide for their families.

I want to mention a few of the Queen's less famous ladies so as to put her relationships in perspective; she was not just clinging to one or two people but had a wide circle of friends. Several of Antoinette's ladies had served the late Queen Marie Leszczyńska and were, for the most part, virtuous and devout like the Polish Queen. A few of them were closely related or had similar names, so it can be difficult to keep track of them. For instance, there are two Duchesses de Gramont and two Duchesses de Maillé, as well as a Madame de Mailly. When each lady died or retired, their places in Antoinette's household were often filled by their daughters. Like everything else at Versailles, such positions were hereditary, which is why when Antoinette brought in people who were not part of the old court families, there was much indignation. There remained, however, many from the traditional families until the Revolution and even throughout the Restoration.

Laure-Auguste de Fitz-James, the **Princesse de Chimay** (1744-1815), was one of Antoinette's first close friends at Versailles and her chief lady-in-waiting from 1775 until 1789. The Princesse was a great granddaughter of James II of England, and thus distantly related to Antoinette through the Stuarts. Proud of her royal Stuart blood, Laure's family was one of the several Scottish and Irish noble Catholic families who had been transplanted to France in order to have the freedom to practice their faith. Married to the Prince de Chimay, Philippe d'Alsace-Hénin-Liétard, the Princesse had served Queen Marie Leszczyńska. She was one of the ladies sent to greet Antoinette at the French border; the Dauphine befriended the Princesse at once and found her worthy of her confidence. When Antoinette became Queen she promoted her friend to first Dame d'Honneur, supplanting Madame de Noailles. The childless Princesse was known for her piety and religious devotion as well as for her love of music and opera. She kept a monkey as a pet which she would dress in a suit and let him scamper through the gardens of Versailles. Highly favored by Antoinette as Queen, she was given a suite of twelve rooms at Versailles. She stayed at the Queen's side through many troubles until the Royal Family was carried away from Versailles to Paris; then the Queen asked the Princesse to escape for the Queen's ladies were being targeted for harassment by the Revolutionaries. She left France with her husband and lived in exile abroad for many years, returning when law and order were restored after the Revolution, living a life devoted to prayer and charitable works.

Marie-Claudine-Silvie de Thiard de Bissy, **Duchesse de Fitz-James** (1752-1812), was the sister-in-law of the Princesse de Chimay, married to her older brother, Jacques-Charles, Duc de Fitz-James (1743-1805). Like the Princesse, she was one the the ladies chosen to attend the Dauphine upon her arrival in France, although she probably was not present at the handing-over ceremony due to pregnancy. The mother of four children, she was highly esteemed by Antoinette, and served her until 1790. Her daughter, Henriette-Victorine de Fitz-James, joined the Queen's ladies as a *dame du palais* in 1781. Henriette became known as the **Duchesse de Maillé** when she married Charles-François de Maillé de la Tour Landry, Duc de Maillé. The Duchesse de Fitz-James' father, Henri de Thiard, Comte de Bissy, died on the guillotine during the Terror. The Queen encouraged

Marie-Claudine to flee to Rome with her family in 1790, writing a letter of recommendation for the Duchesse to the Duc de Fitz-James' cousin, Henry Stuart, Cardinal York, brother of Bonnie Prince Charlie.[10] The Queen also wrote to her friend the Duchesse de Polignac, asking her to take care of the Duchesse de Fitz-James and ask the protection of Cardinal de Bernis. The Queen corresponded with Marie-Claudine as long as she was able, sending her a lock of hair which was kept as a relic by the Fitz-James family for generations. The Duc de Fitz-James died in exile, but the Duchesse de Fitz-James survived to return to France, where she died in 1812 at age sixty. The other **Duchesse de Maillé** was Madeleine de Bréhant, second wife of Charles de Maillé de la Tour Landry and mother-in-law of Henriette de Fitz-James. Madeleine served Antoinette as a *dame du palais*, displaying enormous courage by staying at the Queen's side throughout the attacks on the Tuileries until separated by imprisonment in August 1792. She escaped the guillotine only through the death of Robespierre, and lived to see the Restoration, dying in 1819.

Another former lady-in-waiting to Queen Marie Leszczyńska, Marie-Jeanne de Talleyrand-Périgord, **Comtesse de Mailly** d'Haucourt (1747-1792), was also present at the handing over ceremony of the Arduchess Antoine in May 1770. Known for her wit, wisdom and vivacity, she and the Dauphine became friends immediately. Happily married, with children, Madame de Mailly was popular at Versailles as well as a relative of the famous bishop-diplomat, Charles-Maurice de Talleyrand. When she lost her son in 1770, Antoinette rushed to her side to comfort her. The Comtesse died during the Revolution, in 1792, a year before Antoinette herself. Close to the Comtesse was Marie-Paule d'Albert de Luynes, **Duchesse de Chaulnes-Picquigny** (1744-1781), who was part Italian like the Princesse de

Lamballe. She had been a *dame du palais* of Queen Marie Leszczyńska, as had her mother. She traveled across France with Madame de Noailles in 1770 to become a lady-in-waiting of the new Dauphine. Marie-Paule's was an unfortunate case; her husband the Duc de Chaulnes was a horticulturist from an eccentric family. For some reason he refused to consummate his marriage. The Duchesse de Chaulnes always wore white to show that she was still a virgin. She died in 1781 at age thirty-seven.

Thérèse-Lucy de Rothe, **Comtesse Dillon** (1751 – 1782), was the wife of her second cousin General Arthur Dillon, both the descendants of several noble Irish families. She was one of Antoinette's first ladies-in-waiting, closer to her in age than the others, but without their spotless reputations. She and the Queen were great friends at first but Antoinette drifted away as she was known to do when people bored or disappointed her. Madame Dillon's husband, known at court as *le beau Dillon*, was away fighting most of the time. Beautiful and vivacious Madame Dillon became the mistress of the Prince de Guéméné, whose wife was the Royal Governess. According to her daughter, she was also good friends with the Swedish Count Axel von Fersen, who came to their house every day.[11] Madame Dillon died of tuberculosis in her early thirties. Later, her daughter, Henriette-Lucie Dillon, **Madame de la Tour de Pin de Gouvernet** (1770-1853), entered the Queen's service. Lucie had been brought up in Paris by her grandmother at the house of her great uncle, who was a bishop, and came to court as a young married woman. As an old lady, Lucie wrote her memoirs, which remain an excellent source of information about Versailles and the French Revolution. She is often critical of Antoinette in her writings so when she praises the Queen, we know it is genuine. Lucie and her husband Frédéric truly loved each other and had several children. They escaped the guillotine and went to Albany, New York where they operated a dairy farm. They experienced a deep religious transformation after they lost two of their children to death. They later returned to France and were there for decades of political ups and downs, which ended with them in exile again. Lucie died in Italy in 1853.

Among the thousands murdered during the French Revolution, one of the most notorious cases was that of the death of Marie-Thérèse-Louise de Savoie-Carignan, **Princesse de Lamballe** (1749-1792). The fury of the new order of Liberty, Equality, and Fraternity vented itself upon her frail form in a manner of extreme violence. It was as strange as it was hideous, because other than being a confidante of the Queen's, Madame de Lamballe could be counted among the more liberal, "enlightened" aristocrats, devoted to works of charity and civil improvements. Contrary to the standard depiction of Madame de Lamballe as a lovely but simpering idiot, the princess was intelligent as well as cultured. She was the Grande Maitresse of all the French masonic ladies' lodges, for she saw freemasonry as a tool for creating a better world, as did many of her contemporaries. Her liberal politics were one of the reasons that King Louis XVI encouraged his wife towards the Polignacs, and away from Madame de Lamballe and her Orleanist salon. Madame de Lamballe discovered before the end that utopian politics that seek to create an earthly paradise inevitably lead to social chaos.

Marie-Thérèse-Louise was born in Turin on September 8, 1749. In 1767 she was married to Louis Alexandre de Bourbon, Prince de Lamballe, heir to one of the greatest fortunes in France. He was the son of the kindly Duc de Penthièvre, a grandson of Louis XIV by

Madame de Montespan. Marie-Thérèse-Louise had been chosen for her piety and beauty, with the hope that she could reform the wild libertine young bridegroom. He soon grew restless, however, and a few months into their marriage he ran away with his mistress. He contracted a venereal disease from which he died, in his wife's arms, having returned to her in his illness. Antoinette pitied the young widow and took her sleigh-riding. According to Madame Campan, the Queen's chambermaid:

> It was at the time of the sleighing-parties that the Queen became intimately acquainted with the Princesse de Lamballe, who made her appearance in them wrapped in fur, with all the brilliancy and freshness of the age of twenty,–the emblem of spring, peeping from under sable and ermine. Her situation, moreover, rendered her peculiarly interesting; married, when she was scarcely past childhood, to a young prince, who ruined himself by the contagious example of the Duc d'Orleans, she had had nothing to do from the time of her arrival in France but to weep. A widow at eighteen, and childless, she lived with the Duc de Penthievre as an adopted daughter. She had the tenderest respect and attachment for that venerable Prince; but the Queen, though doing justice to his virtues, saw that the Duc de Penthievre's way of life, whether at Paris or at his country-seat, could neither afford his young daughter-in-law the amusements suited to her time of life, nor ensure her in the future an establishment such as she was deprived of by her widowhood.[12]

Antoinette made Madame de Lamballe, known for her benevolence, the Superintendent of her household, which was controversial at the time since there were other courtiers who felt the position was due to them. There was also the small matter of the expense of the salary due the Superintendent, as Mercy warned. In spite of the furor, the two women became good friends. However, the Princesse tried at times to monopolize the Queen. Once the Princesse invited the Queen to a party at her house; Antoinette, having dressed with care, arrived to find that no party had been planned but only a private supper. No doubt the dinners of Madame de Lamballe had a tendency to focus on lengthy discourse, as that was the way of Freemasonry. Annnoyed, Antoinette left and went on to a party at the Palais Royale. Overall, Madame de Lamballe was too intellectual for Antoinette and so the Queen, with Louis' approval, eventually became closer to the Polignacs. She always remained friends with Madame de Lamballe, though.

When the Revolution erupted in 1789, Madame de Lamballe returned to France from the safety of England in order to be share the troubles of the Royal Family. She became closer than ever to the King's devout sister, Madame Élisabeth of France, and was horrified at how the masonic principles she had thought to be so constructive had contributed to such a violent revolution. When the Royal Family was arrested and sent to the Temple prison in August 1792, Lamballe was separated from them and sent to the prison of La Force. When the September Massacres broke out, in which thousands were killed and the streets ran with blood, Madame de Lamballe was asked to renounce her loyalty to the King and the Queen. She refused, and was delivered over to the mob. She was bludgeoned and stabbed to death, and by some accounts raped and mutilated. She was definitely decapitated, and the valet of Louis XVI, Hanet-Cléry, gave an account of how the mob brought her head on a pike to the Temple prison for the Queen to kiss.

> We were hardly seated before a head at the end of a pike was presented at the window. Tison's wife screamed loudly; the murderers thought it was the queen's voice, and we heard the frantic laughs of those barbarians. Thinking that Her Majesty was still at table, they had raised the victim's head so that it could not escape her sight; it was that of the Princesse de Lamballe. Though bloody, it was not disfigured; her blond hair, still curling, floated around the pike.[13]

Such excesses became typical of the French Revolution, stirred up by propaganda which played upon the fears of frightened people. The Princesse de Lamballe was a bit misguided but ultimately heroic and loyal, and the grisly death to which she was subjected exemplified the misogyny of the new order.

At the French court in the Old Regime the office of governess of the royal children was among the most coveted and influential in the land. *La Gouvernante des Enfants de France* had the duty of bringing up the heir to the throne which meant that in the future she —and her family—would have a unique connection to the King. The royal governess was the only woman in France who would swear loyalty directly to the King.[14] Now before the reign of Louis XVI the royal governess was only chosen from certain high families. Victoire-Armande-Josèphe de Rohan, **Princesse de Guéménée** (1743-1807) was originally made the governess of the young Madame Élisabeth, chiefly because she was born a Rohan. The Rohans were a tremendously important family and their members were usually picked for the chief positions in the royal household. Cardinal Louis de

Rohan was appointed Grand Almoner in spite of his scandalous personal life and the Queen's repugnance for him. It was among one of the more frustrating traditions which Louis and Antoinette sought to abolish, to the outrage of many courtiers.

Although it might seem like an inefficient practice to install someone in an office based upon their family connections rather than their qualifications, Madame de Guéménée proved capable of guiding the education of Madame Élisabeth. She was appointed in 1775, when her aunt Madame de Marsan retired after Madame Clothilde's marriage. Madame de Guéménée was a charming and elegant lady, with several of her own children. She was concerned that Élisabeth's upbringing under Madame de Marsan had been too rigid and stifling. She encouraged Élisabeth to take part in dancing and outdoor games in the park of Montreuil, which belonged to the Guéménés before they went bankrupt. When Madame Élisabeth no longer needed a governess and when Madame Royale was born, Madame de Guéménée continued as royal governess but of the King's children rather than of his sister.

However, the Guéménés were part of a fast set. Both the Prince and the Princesse had lovers outside of marriage, the Prince with Madame Dillon and the Princesse with the Duc de Coigny, a friend of the Queen's. In her careless youth, Antoinette frequented Madame de Guéménée's extravagant card parties because the stakes were high and the crowd boisterous. Thus the Guéménés were seen as belonging to the Queen's circle of friends, although Antoinette had no deep affection for them.[15] Madame de Guéménée, a disciple of Mesmer, had some odd views, such as her conviction that spirits communicated with her through her dogs. According to a biography of the Austrian ambassador Comte de Mercy:

The Royal Governess was the Princesse de Guéménée, who received this appointment by virtue of her relationship to Madame de Marsan, the function of instruction being considered vested in the family of de Rohan. There was no doubt that the Princesse de Guéménée was capable of instructing upon many matters. She was a great lover of little dogs, and invariably appeared surrounded by a multitude of them. 'She offered to them a species of worship, and pretended, through their medium, to hold communication with the world of spirits.' She had been convicted of cheating at cards on several occasions. She was distinguished for the urbanity of her manner towards the ladies honoured by her husband's preference, paying the most delicate attentions to each in turn; thus she compelled admiration for her exemplary fulfillment of a wife's highest duty. She entertained magnificently, royally, outshone the whole Court by her dress, and paved the way for the greatest bankruptcy known in France—the failure that affected all classes of society and plunged France into ruin; for all, from dukes to poor Breton sailors, had invested their moneys in the house of de Guéménée. 'Only a King or a Rohan could have made such a failure,' was the consoling sentiment of the Princesse, as she contemplated her bootmaker's bill of 60,000 *livres* [£2,400], or the amount of 16,000 *livres* [£640] owed to her paper-hanger. And the ruin of the Rohans hastened the Revolution.[16]

After the Guéménés left court, the Queen insisted upon choosing a governess for her children not from one of the great families but from an impoverished, unknown family called the Polignacs. Madame de Polignac had by that time become Antoinette's best friend, a friendship encouraged by Louis XVI, since Madame de Poliganc had a calming and steadying influence upon the high-strung and easily distracted Queen. The choice of Madame de Polignac as the new royal governess and the subsequent rise of her family to power caused outrage among the nobility, especially those who thought they had a better claim upon the job. Trouble would come of the Queen's choice, unfortunately.

The closest confidante of Antoinette's was Yolande-Martine Gabrielle de Polastron, **Duchesse de Polignac** (1749-1793). Gabrielle is usually portrayed in books and films as Antoinette's "bad girl" friend, responsible for leading the young Queen of France into a wild, decadent lifestyle. Often depicted as a greedy, spendthrift slut, Gabrielle preferred simplicity, was a devoted mother and loyal friend of both Louis and Antoinette. Part of the rehabilitation of Antoinette's reputation is a careful look at her relationship with Gabrielle. Gabrielle, born on September 8, 1749, came from an old family of Languedoc. After her mother's death when she was three, Gabrielle was given to the care of an aunt, Madame d'Andlau, who had once been a governess to the daughters of Louis XV. As a small child, Gabrielle was placed in a convent school, where she was reared by the nuns. Girls of high and low estate were educated by nuns in those days, including Louis XV's mistress, Madame du Barry. In Gabrielle's case, perhaps because she was separated from her family at such an early age, there seems to have been some influence of the religious life on her personal habits. She chose simple, tasteful clothes, and never wore perfume or diamonds. One of the only pictures of her in formal court attire shows her wearing fresh flowers in place of jewelry. Cheerful and discreet, a lover of music and the outdoors, Gabrielle emerged from the convent as a lady with polished manners and a straightforward demeanor. With delicate features, violet eyes, ivory skin and black curling hair, Gabrielle was petite and well-proportioned. Her defining trait was a lack of pretense; she had a gentle, forthright manner of speaking, totally at odds with the highly sophisticated wit so valued by high society. Her enemies would later attribute to her powers of great cunning and manipulation, but her strength was in her honesty, and most of all, in her discretion. The same cannot be said of her relatives, however.

At the age of eighteen, La Belle Gabrielle was given in marriage to Comte Jules be Polignac of an ancient clan of Auvergne, as impoverished as her own family, as many nobles were in France at the time. Since the twenty-two year old bridegroom was a captain in the Royal Pologne regiment, they moved to Paris. The young couple had a small fortune from the recent harvest, besides the Comte's pay, with which they had to support not only themselves but the indigent members of their large families. They most certainly could not afford to present themselves at court or even live in the town of Versailles, so they dwelt in Paris at an apartment at the Louvre, or at the family property at Claye with Madame d'Andlau. Gabrielle always preferred the country to the city.

In the meantime, Comte Jules' sister, Diane de Polignac, had managed to acquire a position in the household of the Comtesse d'Artois, Antoinette's sister-in-law. In the late summer of 1776, Diane invited Jules and Gabrielle to visit Versailles. There, in the Hall of Mirrors, they met Antoinette and, as Diane had hoped, Gabrielle's charming, easy-going manner fascinated the twenty-year-old Queen, who was struggling with the iron restraints of the court etiquette. Antoinette wrote at once to her mother, saying she had found a new friend whom she "infinitely loved," that is "*une femme que j'aime infiniment*."[17] Mercy also dashed off a letter to the Empress, expressing his fears that Gabrielle would be an adverse influence on the Queen, for Madame de Polignac was the niece of the Comtesse d'Andlau, a governess who had once let Madame Adélaïde read a naughty book *Le Portier de Chartreux* at Mass and had been banished from court by Louis XV. Mercy passed on the gossip that Gabrielle had a lover, her cousin the Comte de Vaudreuil; that she was equivocal in matters of dogma—she was indeed a Freeemason. Furthermore, Mercy reported, Dr. Lasonne had told Vermond that she would attaint the piety of the Queen. A year later in 1777, Mercy complained to the Empress that the Queen gave all her confidences to Gabrielle, a protegée of Maurepas. She had gained the Queen's favor for Maurepas whom she even invited to Petit Trianon.[18] Mercy's main problem with Gabrielle is thus exposed; it was not her character he disliked but the fact that she had replaced himself as the Queen's confidante, she who was also in league with Maurepas, Louis' minister. It becomes clear that Gabrielle was a pawn at the center of a political chess game of intricate stragedy, and through her Louis defeated Mercy in his efforts to gain political influence over the Queen of France.

Now, it must be recalled that Antoinette had been sent to France as Louis' bride in order to further Austrian interests. Louis XVI, however, did not want his wife to meddle in politics, knowing that as a foreigner it could lead to her unpopularity. He also feared to replicate the pattern of his grandfather Louis XV's reign, in which at times it seemed like Madame de Pompadour was ruling France. As it might be gathered by now, Louis felt that Antoinette needed watching over, and by a non-Austrian; not because he thought she was bad, but because she was impulsive and imprudent. He could not watch her himself because of business and hunting, so he found someone else that could. He wanted to keep Antoinette from manipulation by the various factions at court, especially the liberal Orleanist clique, to which the Princesse de Lamballe belonged. Maurepas, Louis' minister, was an uncle of Gabrielle de Polignac. Louis XVI and Maurepas encouraged the Queen to befriend Gabrielle, and thus created for her a circle of politically "safe" friends, who owed their social success to the King alone. Gabrielle thus became a sort of governess for Antoinette. At Antoinette's request, Louis happily gave Gabrielle's husband a lucrative position at court so the Polignacs could afford to live at Versailles. Over the next few years, he gave Polignac relatives high positions that traditionally went to other, more prominent families. Diane de Polignac became Madame Élisabeth's first lady-in-waiting. Gabrielle herself became Royal Governess, after the Princesse de Guéménée retired from court due to bankruptcy. Jules and Gabrielle, who had a growing family of young children, were given a thirteen room apartment at Versailles; over the years they became good friends of both Louis and Antoinette. As the royal family increased, the King and Queen continued to entrust Gabrielle with their children, being that she had showed herself to be an exemplary mother of her own three. Gabrielle influenced the Queen to adopt simpler styles. In 1780, Gabrielle's twelve-year-old daughter Aglaé married the Duc de Gramont de Guiche; the Queen called her "Guichette." Guichette, a replica of her mother, had her first child in the summer of 1789, just as the Revolution was breaking out, making Gabrielle a grandmother even as she fled the country.

In 1780, Mercy mentions to the Empress that the King had visited Madame de Polignac at her house after giving birth to her son Jules, who would someday become prime minister of France.[19] The Queen provided the baby's layette. Jules was elevated to the rank of Duc and given Bitche, a county in Lorraine; hence Gabrielle was known as the Duchesse de Polignac. Madame de Polignac was the only person Louis XVI ever visited in a private home; he sat with her at the opera, and wrote to her when she left Versailles. His letter to her is quite affectionate, and he refers to Antoinette as "*votre petite soeur*," "your little sister."[20] Some people believe Gabrielle was Loius' mistress, but the reason for his high regard for her is obvious the more one understands Antoinette's temperament.[21] Let us recall that as a little child she experienced convulsions when distressed. Antoinette needed a calm, motherly companion, older than herself, to advise her about the difficulties in her intimate marital life, her possible fears about pregnancy and childbirth, which she may have had due to tales from her sister Maria Carolina and the horrific death of her sister-in-law, Isabella of Parma. Gabrielle was such a friend, soothing the Queen in her moments of hysteria and depression. At Gabrielle's suite and with her family, Antoinette said, "Here I can be myself."

However, the Polignac salon, called *la société Polignac* soon provoked envy and calumny among the courtiers who felt excluded from the Queen's intimate circle, which often met for supper and cards at Petit Trianon. Among the men in the circle, Vaudreuil, Gabrielle's much older Creole cousin, held the first place. Not handsome in the least due to a pock-marked countenance, he was witty and entertaining, as well as devoted to Gabrielle, according to the standards of chivalry. Rumors and gossip spread through the court and to Paris, growing in venom with each year, fed by the pamphlets and the Diamond Necklace scandal, convincing many that the Queen and her friend were loose women. Antoinette grew more and more distressed. Madame Campan told what happened when she entered the Queen's room at Trianon one morning. To quote:

> There were letters lying on the bed and she was weeping bitterly. Her tears and sobs were occasionally interrupted by exclamations of 'Ah ! That I were dead!— wretches! monsters!What have I done to them?... If you love me, it would be better to kill me at once!'I suggested sending for the Duchess de Polignac...In less than ten minutes,
> she was at the queen's door...The queen stretched her arms towards her, and the Duchess rushed towards her. I heard her sobs renewed and withdrew."[22]

The Polignacs were accused of greediness, but they were probably not greedier than any other family. Most courtiers received much more from the royal purse. The calumnies grew uglier as the propaganda machine, aimed at provoking the Revolution, produced pornographic pamphlets depicting Antoinette and Gabrielle as lesbian lovers, engaged in orgies at Trianon. Gabrielle became universally detested and was blamed for depleting the royal treasury, although it was war that had caused the bankruptcy. She often asked to retire from the court. 'I am not made for living at Versailles,' she kept repeating.[23] The friendship cooled, as Gabrielle's relatives became more grasping. Antoinette became more politically involved as Louis began to struggle with depression. Furthermore, Antoinette could no longer tolerate Vaudreuil, and asked Gabrielle to send him away, and Gabrielle refused. Antoinette and Gabrielle also disagreed on politics, especially the fall of the Polignac-backed Calonne, whom Antoinette blamed for making France's financial situation worse than it already was.The Duchess withdrew more into her private life, and there were rumors about her health. The Queen, who found the Polignacs ungrateful, began to spend her evenings elsewhere. My sense is that Gabrielle was torn between family loyalty and loyalty to Antoinette.

After the Diamond Necklace fiasco, Gabrielle went to England with Comtesse Diane, Guichette, and Monsieur and Madame de Vaudreuil. Gabrielle had traveled to England occasionally over the years, once with the Princesse de Lamballe; she visited with her friend Georgiana, Duchess of Devonshire. Georgiana had visited France several times and had been received by the Queen at Versailles. Georgiana and her friends called the Duchesse de Polignac "Little Po" and Gabrielle had carried on a correspondence with the Duchess for many years. Gabrielle's charge the Dauphin Louis-Joseph was in bad health, but the sub-governess Madame de Mackau had him in her care. Gabrielle's official purpose was to go to Bath to "take the waters" which was considered a remedy for many indispositions. She also went on private business for the King and Queen, attempting to purchase the defamatory "memoir" by the notorious Madame de la Motte, which calumniated Antoinette to an obscene degree. She managed to buy the manuscript, but the La Mottes had another copy and published the book anyway. She returned to find France on the edge of the abyss.

The King wished to reform the feudal tax system and eliminate the deficit by taxing the nobility, and so he called the Estates-General in May 1789. The opening of the Estates-General coincided with the death of the King and Queen's seven year old son, the Dauphin Louis-Joseph. The royal couple was devastated; with difficulty they met the escalating crisis. When violence erupted on July 14, 1789, Antoinette implored Gabrielle to leave, fearing that she would be assassinated. Gabrielle begged to stay with Louis and Antoinette in their hour of need, but the Queen said, "Remember that you are a mother." On July 16, the Polignac clan left Versailles for a life of exile. They went to Rome but ended up in Vienna as Gabrielle's health deteriorated. She had cancer as well as being consumed with horror and anxiety as she heard of the imprisonment and tragedies that befell Louis and Antoinette.

> One of her friends wrote: 'She did not stop crying. For six months, a deep sadness, great sufferings without certain causes weakened her each day more.' A last blow hit her when they were forced to announce to her this horrible news: on October, 16th, 1793, Marie-Antoinette had been beheaded in Paris. This was the true beginning of Madame de Polignac's agony. She could not survive the queen, and she herself died on December, 9th, 1793, one month and a half, precisely, after her friend. A witness told of her death: 'Her last sigh was but her last breath, and to tell this in one word, her death was as sweet as she herself had been. She was buried in Vienna and they wrote on her tomb her name only, followed by this mention: "Dead from suffering" on December 9th, 1793.'[23]

I am more and more convinced that Gabrielle has been just as maligned as the Queen. What went on with the Polignac relations and friends was a common occurrence at every court of Europe: when you rose, your family rose with you, it was almost expected. If there had been no Revolution, no one would have given a second thought to the Polignacs, except perhaps to find them annoying, as many did. But with the complete upheaval of society in the Revolution, contemporaries and historians alike were grasping at straws to see what the Queen did that made herself so hated by the French people. They think it must have been the problems with La Barry, or the Queen's dress allowance, or her Trianon, or Gabrielle's greedy relatives, etc, etc.

Be that as it may, Antoinette was hated because she was deliberately maligned by a careful campaign on the part of political enemies, which included dissimulating false and exaggerated rumors to the people, as well as every form of the vilest pornography. Gabrielle was routinely included in the pornographic depictions. People were scandalized and believed that some of it must be true. Gabrielle must have done something wrong. To this day Gabrielle is seen as the naughty, greedy friend, when in reality she probably saved Antoinette's sanity. The powerful tools used to destroy the French monarchy and transform society into a totalitarian state are with us still, but on a much larger and more pervasive scale through technology and the media.

Geneviève de Gramont, **Comtesse d'Ossun** (1751-1794) was another close friend of the Queen's and her *dame d'atours*, the Mistress of the Robes or lady-in-waiting in charge of her clothes. Madame d'Ossun was a niece of Choiseul and the older sister of the Duc de Gramont de Guiche, who married Aglaé de Polignac. Having charge of Antoinette's wardrobe was a challenging occupation, but Madame d'Ossun was up to the task, although the expenses often went over budget. While not posessing the wit or beauty of Antoinette's other friends, the Comtesse had the rare commodities of common sense and practicality. She was responsible for making sure all the merchants were paid. She was also genuinely loyal to the King and Queen. She directed a large staff in the maintenance of the Queen's clothing. As Antoinette became disillusioned with the Polignac set for their avarice, she began to enjoy quiet musical evenings at

Madame d'Ossun's apartments, which were close to her own at Versailles. The King even gave Madame d'Ossun money to defray the expenses of entertaining the Queen, but most of it Madame d'Ossun paid for out of her own pocket. Such simple recreational evenings, and the fact that the Queen was imposing strict economies on herself and her household, caused some of the Polignac clan to complain and make up slanderous verses. However, Madame d'Ossun conducted herself with great dignity and would not speak against the Polignacs to the Queen. She continued to serve the Queen through many dangers until she was told to leave when the Royal Family tried to escape to Montmédy in June 1791. She fled to her *château* in the country. The revolutionaries tried to implicate her in the flight of the Royal Family but to no avail. They did eventually arrest her as a counter-revolutionary. She was guillotined in July of 1794, just as the Terror was about to end.

Louise Emmanuelle de Châtillon, **Princesse de Tarente** (1763-1814) was one of the younger ladies-in-waiting, succeeding the Princesse de Chimay as *première dame d'honneur* to the Queen in 1785. In 1781, she married Charles, Prince de Tarente, later Duc de la Trémouille. They had one child, a little girl who died as an infant. The marriage was unhappy and broke down eventually. The Princesse, greatly esteemed by Antoinette, stayed with the Royal Family until the fall of the monarchy on August 10, 1792, when they were all arrested. The Princesse was thrown into the Abbaye prison for refusing to testify against the Queen. She managed to disguise herself in order to avoid being massacred in the September massacres. She was released and escaped to England. She eventually went to Russia, where she served the Russian Imperial Family for many years, being especially favored by the wife of Alexander I,

Empress Elisabeth Alexeyevna, who thought she was a saint. It was with a noble Russian family, the Golovines, that she returned to France at the time of the Restoration in 1814. The Princesse joined the suite of Antoinette's daughter, the Duchess d'Angoulême, for a brief time, returning to her friends the Golovines in Russia, when her health failed. The Golivines, whom she had helped convert to Catholicism, were with her when she died in July of 1814.

Marie Louise d'Esparbès de Lussan, **Vicomtesse de Polastron** (1764-1804) was the sister-in-law of Gabrielle de Polignac, married to her younger half-brother, Denis de Polastron. After losing her mother shortly after birth, Louise was reared by a grandmother. At the age of twelve, she was sent to the convent of Panthemont to prepare for her First Communion, as was the custom. Shy, sweet and well-mannered, Louise was a favorite pupil of the nuns. She remained with them until age seventeen, when a marriage was arranged for her by her father, the Comte d'Esparbès, to the Vicomte de Polastron. The Vicomte's sister Gabrielle de Polignac brought her brother to the convent to interview Louise. Gabrielle was at the time the governess of the royal children as well as being confidante of Queen Antoinette; an alliance with her family was seen as an excellent match for Louise. Gabrielle was charmed by the young girl's modest demeanor and thought she was the perfect bride for her brother. In the memoirs of Madame de Gontaut, a cousin of both Louise and the Polignacs, and later governess of Charles X's grandchildren, Gabrielle is quoted as saying:

> Now that everything is settled, and the young people like each other, we must begin to make preparations for the marriage. It will take place at

Versailles. I have obtained the position of lady-in-waiting to the queen for my charming sister-in-law, with an apartment in the palace. We shall be always together; she shall be not only a sister to me, but a cherished child. I love to think that with us she cannot fail to be happy. [24]

The wedding was simple and small for Versailles and the bridegroom, elevated to the rank of colonel, departed to take command of his regiment immediately after the ceremony, and was gone for a year. As Madame de Gontaut says: "In those days, this was often the way young couples made each other's acquaintance."[25] The Duchesse de Montaut-Navailles (mother of Madame de Gontaut) "idolized" Louise and was resolved to watch over her at court, as was the kind-hearted Duchesse de Guiche (Madame de Polignac's daughter), for Louise had a "gentle spirit" and "the splendors held out before her had not the power to dazzle her."[26]

After the marriage, preparations began for Louise to be formally presented to the Queen. Her gown was designed by Mademoiselle Bertin and her hair dressed by Monsieur Léonard, as she was instructed in the etiquette of the proper manner of curtsying to the Queen. Louise was presented to Antoinette by the Duchesse de Polignac, along with her daughter the Duchesse de Guiche and Madame de Montaut-Navailles. However, disaster struck. The new young Vicomtesse de Polastron forgot everything she had learned and froze before the Queen, the princes, and all their entourages. She stood stiff and motionless, even when Antoinette came forward to embrace her. This was an unspeakable disgrace which set all of the courtiers whispering and tittering. But the Comte d'Artois was moved by her timidity and gentle manner. He spoke to her the next day when everyone else was avoiding her. Artois was the

King's handsome, charming, youngest brother. He chased women, gambled, and spent exhorbitant amounts of money on his country-house, the Bagatelle. He was unhappily married to Marie-Thérèse de Savoie, whose heart he had broken many times by his infidelities. Used to easy conquests, he was enchanted by Louise's virtue and restraint, and fell deeply in love with her. As Madame de Gontaut describes:

> Madame de Polastron was very agreeable, without being pretty; her figure was slender and supple, and her expression was mournful and touching. She was too timid to speak very loud; her voice had a wonderful charm, and she expressed herself with dignity and grace. She was neither humble nor arrogant, but very retiring; and to know her it was necessary to make an effort to draw her out. The Prince, who felt compassion for her, sought her out and made this effort.[27]

In 1782 Louise became a *dame du palais* in the service of the Queen. Artois caused a great stir at court by hovering around Madame de Polignac's apartments so as to be close to Louise, unable to hide his admiration. Antoinette noticed and cautioned Louise about Artois' attentions. Louise was too guileless and innocent to fully understand. Madame de Gontaut relates in her memoirs that her mother, the Duchesse de Montaut-Navailles, who had been given the special charge of watching over Louise de Polastron, was herself too naïve about life to protect her from the amorous advances of the Comte d'Artois. Madame de Montaut-Navailles saw that the prince held Louise in high regard, which was obvious to the entire court, but "feeling that [Louise] merited it by her noble and simple conduct, she would have felt that as though she were committing a sin if she had attached to this regard the slightest suspicion of gallantry."[28] Thus Louise continued to be constantly thrust into the prince's presence and being the focus of his disturbing but highly flattering flirtatious behavior.

Louise's husband the Vicomte de Polastron finally returned to Versailles after being with his regiment for a year. Polastron lacked his sister Gabrielle de Polignac's charm and people did not like him. He did not care for the royal court and longed to be back with his regiment. Nevertheless, he managed to get his wife with child and they had a son named Louis, to whom Louis XVI and Antoinette stood as godparents. Motherhood brought Louise great happiness and, although her husband could be surly and disagreeable, she slowly grew in confidence. Soon she had a small circle of friends, while continuing to wait upon the Queen.

The prince only became more enraptured with Louise and constantly sought her company, so that tongues were wagging. He finally wrote her a passionate love letter, promising to make any sacrifice in order to win her. Louise, deeply touched but filled with confusion, showed the letter to the Duchesse de Montaut-Navailles, who insisted that she send it back to the prince with no reply. Then Louise opened her heart to the Queen and to her sister-in-law the Duchesse de Polignac. Antoinette encouraged her to withdraw from the palace and move to Paris, returning only on the days when she was in waiting. Soon it was all over Paris that Madame de Polastron was exiled and that the prince was in despair. According to Madame de Gontaut:

> The Comte d'Artois was dejected and hurt by this removal which the queen had sanctioned; the more obstacles he encountered, the more ardently he tried to overcome them. He took care to let Louise know that he would seize every opportunity to meet her,

that even if he could not speak to her he would at least see her at any price.[29]

Artois discovered what night Madame de Montaut-Navailles would visit the opera, accompanied by Louise. He vested himself in an outlandish disguise, huge wig, embroidered cravat, and a voluminous riding coat. He took a taxi to the theatre instead of his own coach, but in spite of his pretenses, everyone recognized him, and his presence caused a great commotion at the Opera. He dramatically cast aside the wig and great coat, hoping to catch Louise's eye. Louise, humiliated, hid in the back of her cousin's opera box. Gossip had already declared her to be his mistress; many who spread such false rumors were themselves compromised in illicit situations and did not understand Louise's determination to be a faithful wife.

Louise tried to resist temptation, continuing to avoid the prince while always praying for him, but her married life was difficult and the times were full of foreboding. Artois found himself in the thick of the political controversy because of his conservatism and resistance to all revolutionary ideas. In July of 1789, after the disturbances following the capture of the Bastille, Artois and his family were obliged to flee the country, as well as the Polignacs. Louise returned to Versailles to be at the Queen's side, but Antoinette implored her to escape while she could and join the Polignacs abroad. Louise's husband had already departed to be with his regiment.

Louise journeyed with her son to Turin where the Polignacs were temporarily staying. Word then came to her from Germany of the Comte d'Artois with his colony of *émigrés*, that they had no money and were low on supplies. Louise begged her grandfather for her dowry money which had never been paid. With her son and two servants, she traveled by coach to Coblentz, through many dangers and difficulties, hardly even knowing where to go. At last she found the army of the Prince de Condé, also at Coblentz, along with the Comte d'Artois. There was quite a sensation as she arrived, and a crowd gathered. Artois, who had thought that he would never see her again, slowly walked towards her coach in a daze. As Madame de Gontaut describes:

> Monseigneur did not understand what had brought her, and questioned her; astonished at finding so much devotion, resolution, and courage in that timid soul, he was greatly touched, and overwhelmed with gratititude. But already he foresaw for her the consequences of her imprudence....[30]

The people fell silent as the prince doffed his hat and bowed, asking what her orders for him were. "To find some shelter," Louise replied, wearily. Artois immediately arranged for quarters to be prepared for her, but as she was being escorted there, someone from the crowd cried out, "Whore!"[31]

After Madame de Polignac died of cancer in Vienna in 1793, her family and friends scattered; many eventually found their way to Scotland, where Artois was holding court at Holyrood Palace in Edinburgh, courtesy of the English monarch. He was openly living with Louise de Polastron in the castle which had seen many dramatic episodes in the life of Mary Stuart. Madame de Montaut-Navailles, when visiting after many years of exile, found Louise sad and unhappy; she felt deep pity for her. Louise had for so long borne the stigma of being a fallen woman, in spite of her innocence, that when she surrendered at last to the passion of the Comte d'Artois, being censured by the world was nothing new to her. However, being a woman with a strong sense of honor, a lifestyle which violated her religious beliefs and moral principles could not bring her happiness. Nevertheless, having become so emotionally attached to Artois, and he to her, she found it beyond her strength to leave him. Louise reared her son and sent him to college; she was not reunited with her husband, nor Artois with his wife, who remained on the continent. Artois' younger son the Duc de Berry was often with them in Scotland; the older son the Duc d'Angoulême, who had married the King and Queen's daughter, remained in Mitau in Courland with Louis XVIII, as is told in the novel *Madame Royale*.

As for Artois, he possessed at last the lady of his heart, and was content, although he had little income, and could only go riding on Sundays, for Scottish law forbade the arrest of debtors on the Lord's Day. Every evening he and his entourage played cards in Louise's salon. He made ends meet by gambling, occasionally traveling to London for bigger stakes. He took Louise with him and it was there in 1804 that she was reunited with her cousin Madame de Gontaut. Madame de Gontaut was shocked to find Louise coughing and pale. She never complained and those who surrounded her seemed to be unaware that she was sick; most especially Artois, who appeared oblivious. With great difficulty, Madame de Gontaut was able to get Louise at last to the physician of King George III, Sir Henry Halford, who diagnosed her as being in the last stages of consumption. When the doctor broke the news to Artois, telling him that the Vicomtesse de Polastron must be taken to the country and given total rest, the prince was shocked. "Do anything to save her!" he implored.[32]

Madame de Gontaut found a house in the country at Brompton for her dying cousin and had her moved there, where she cared for her tenderly. She especially was concerned about the lack of peace and interior despair that Louise revealed to her in their conversations. She sent for a priest, Abbé Latil. He heard Louise's confession and restored her tranquility, speaking to her of the goodness of God. He asked one sacrifice of her, however, that she not see Artois again. Louise agreed, asking only that she might see him at the hour of her death. The priest consented. Artois was beside himself with grief but departed from Louise's side as Abbé Latil demanded. It was only for a week, since Louise was failing fast. She said farewell to her son, her faithful servants, and her loyal remaining friends, asking their pardon for the public scandal she had given. All were present as the last moment drew near and knelt around the bed as she received the last rites and the prayers for the dying were recited. Artois rushed to the house when summoned. He paused in the doorway of Louise's room. Trembling and gasping for breath, she raised her hands to heaven and said: "A favor, Monsieur, grant me one request. Give yourself to God!"

Artois fell on his knees. "As God is my witness, I swear it!"

"Entirely to God!" Louise repeated, and her head fell on her cousin's shoulder as she breathed her last.

Artois cried out and lifted his arms as if to embrace her departing soul. "I swear it!" he promised again.

He asked Abbé Latil to receive him as a penitent; making his own peace with God. He took a vow of chastity, although, as the writer Lamartine recorded, "he was young, handsome, a prince, and a king." He kept his vow until his own death in 1836. [33]

Louise Elisabeth de Croÿ-Havré, **Marquise de Tourzel** (1749-1832) was a devout lady chosen by Antoinette to be governess of her children. Madame de Tourzel was a widow with five children whose husband, Louis François du Bouchet de Sourches, Marquis de Sourches de Tourzel had been *grand prévost* of France. He had died in 1786 while hunting with Louis XVI. After Madame de Polignac had to flee from the Revolution in July of 1789, Madame de Tourzel was chosen to replace her as *Gouvernante des Enfants de France*. There are many people who wonder why the Queen and her children did not also try to escape at that time. It is because Antoinette would not desert her husband., saying that it was her duty to die at the feet of the King and in the arms of her children.[34] Louis XVI, of course, would not abandon his people. Early in the crisis the King and Queen made the decision that they would not be parted from their children, but would keep them close at hand, not knowing what was going to transpire next in the tidal wave of events. So Antoinette chose as governess as trustworthy and reliable a person as she could find. "I entrusted my children to friendship," she remarked. "I entrust them now to virtue."[35] Madame de Tourzel was loving but strict; the Dauphin and Madame Royale playfully called her "*Madame Sévère*." The Queen wrote detailed and explicit directions about the care of her two surviving children for Madame de Tourzel, whose youngest daughter Pauline was a teenager. Pauline became a close friend of young Madame Royale. Both mother and daughter were devoted to Marie-Thérèse-Charlotte and the rambunctious Louis-Charles as well as to the saintly Madame Élisabeth.

Madame de Tourzel was with the Royal Family on the October night in 1789 when Versailles was stormed. It is she who reported in her memoirs how the Queen's bed was slashed by the mob. The governess and her daughter accompanied the Royal Family to Paris and shared their house arrest at the Tuileries. She recorded how one of the first actions of the Queen at the Tuileries was to build a staircase joining her room with the King's, so that the family could get to each other if the mob attacked again, which it did in June and in August of 1792. Madame de Tourzel was with the Royal Family when they tried to escape in 1791 and shared the long ordeal of the re-capture. When Louis and Antoinette and their family were imprisoned in the Temple, Madame de Tourzel and Pauline were not permitted to join them but were placed in one of the prisons in Paris. Somehow, they escaped the September Massacres, in which the Queen's friend Madame de Lamballe was torn to pieces.

Madame de Tourzel lived to see the Restoration in 1814 and in 1830 Charles X made her a duchess. She and Pauline were united with Louis XVI's daughter the Duchesse d'Angoulême, whom Pauline served as lady-in-waiting until the fall of the Bourbons in 1830.

In addition to ladies of the nobility, the French court was a place where women from a middle class background also found honorable and lucrative employment. Jeanne-Louise-Henriette Genet, **Madame Campan** (1752-1822) was the *première femme de chambre*, the first chamber maid, of Queen Antoinette. She is author of the famous memoirs, detailing life at Versailles. Madame Campan was an educated and cultured lady from a bourgeois family who began her career at Versailles as the Reader to the daughters of Louis XV, from whom she heard an earful of gossip. Married in 1774, she mentions her husband only once or twice in her memoirs; theirs was an unhappy marriage, although they had a son to whom Madame Campan was devoted. Monsieur and Madame Campan separated in 1790. In the same year of her marriage, Madame Campan received her post as the Queen's *femme de chambre*, which meant she probably spent more time around Antoinette than practically anyone else. As Antoinette's maid, she attended to the details of the running of the Queen's household. She stayed with the Queen until the flight of the Royal Family from the Tulieries on August 10, 1792. Madame Campan had to flee herself since the Tuileries was stormed amid a gruesome massacre. She went to her house in Paris to find it burning, and so had to escape to the countryside, where she went into hiding until the Revolution was over.

After the Revolution, Madame Campan opened a school for girls which was a success, and she included housekeeping skills as part of the curriculum. She also brought up her three orphaned nieces: Antoinette, Aglaé and Adèle Auguié. One of her pupils was Hortense de Beauharnais, Napoleon's step-daughter. In 1807 Napoleon placed Madame Campan at the head of an academy for the education of the orphaned daughters of members of his *Légion d'honneur*. The academy was closed at the time of the Restoration in 1814 and the return of the Bourbons. Madame Campan was never received at the court of Louis XVIII, due to her close connections with the Bonapartes. She died in 1822.

Madame Campan has often been accused of exaggerating her role in Antoinette's life, especially where the Diamond Necklace scandal is concerned. That may very well be; it is easy to picture Madame Campan as an old lady at the finishing school she ran for the daughters of revolutionaries, carried away by memories of a glittering past. I do not, however, think she deliberately softened her portrayal of Antoinette in order to get back into the good graces of the Queen's daughter, the Duchesse d'Angoulême. In that case, she would not have been so critical of Louis XVI, since it was well-known that the princess idolized her dead father. Here are some passages in which Madame Campan does not speak too highly of the Queen:

> Marie Antoinette took little pains to promote

literature and the fine arts....The most indifferent artists were permitted to have the honour of painting the Queen. A full-length portrait, representing her in all the pomp of royalty, was exhibited in the gallery of Versailles. This picture, which was intended for the Court of Vienna, was executed by a man who does not deserve even to be named, and disgusted all people of taste. It seemed as if this art had, in France, retrograded several centuries.

The Queen had not that enlightened judgment, or even that mere taste, which enables princes to foster and protect great talents. She confessed frankly that she saw no merit in any portrait beyond the likeness. When she went to the Louvre, she would run hastily over all the little 'genre' pictures, and come out, as she acknowledged, without having once raised her eyes to the grand compositions. [36]

It sounds like a fairly honest assessment, with which one is free to disagree. Madame Campan must not have thought much of Madame LeBrun, or even of the botanist Redouté, whose flower paintings delighted Antoinette. She made the following comments about Louis XVI:

Who would have dared to check the amusements of a queen, young, lively, and handsome? A mother or a husband alone would have had the right to do it; and the King threw no impediment in the way of Marie Antoinette's inclinations. His long indifference had been followed by admiration and love. He was a slave to all the wishes of the Queen, who, delighted with the happy change in the heart and habits of the King, did not sufficiently conceal the ascendency she was gaining over him.[37]

I fail to see how such observations, which make Louis sound like a weakling, were supposed to win the favor of the daughter of the murdered royal couple, who viewed her parents as holy martyrs. If Madame Campan was trying to ingratiate herself to the Duchesse d'Angoulême, she was taking the wrong tact. Her descriptions of the various personalities seem to be balanced, shrewd and detailed, rather than an attempt to curry favor.

Adélaïde-Henriette Genet, **Madame Auguié** (1758-1794) was one of the maids of Antoinette, and a younger sister of Madame Campan. As a young girl, she entered the Dauphine Antoinette's service as a *femme de chambre*. Antoinette was fond of Adélaïde, who had a charming and gentle manner. Because of her long, thick, curly hair, Antoinette dubbed Adélaïde *ma Lionne* or "my Lioness." A tall, shapely young woman, with a peaches and cream complexion, in 1779 she married Pierre-César Auguié whom Louis XVI made *Receveur Général des Finances de Lorraine*. The Queen provided her with a dowry of 7000 *francs*. Over the years the couple had three daughters: Antoinette, Aglaé and Adèle, the King and Queen being godparents of the eldest child. The artist Wertmüller painted Madame Auguié dressed as a dairy maid at the Queen's dairy at Petit Trianon.

Madame Auguié was one of the women who stayed outside the Queen's room on the night of October 5, 1789, helping Antoinette escape through the private passage when the mob tried to break into her room to kill her. She stayed with the Royal Family throughout the upheavals until they were forced to leave the Tuileries for the National Assembly, where they were arrested and sent to the Temple prison. But before the Queen departed, Madame Auguié discreetly gave her some of her own money, helping in the only way she could. She also burned any of the Queen's remaining compromising papers so the Revolutionaries could not get them. Poor Madame Auguié could not bear the horrors into which France was plunged, and the Queen's execution in October of 1793 caused her intense grief. She discovered that the money she had given to the Queen had compromised her, as well as her role in burning the papers. Hearing that she was going to be arrested, Madame Auguié threw herself out of a sixth story window to her death. Perhaps she also feared she would be treated with the same indignity as the Princesse de Lamballe.

The three Auguié girls were left in the care of their aunt, Madame Campan, who brought them up. Antoinette married respectably, Aglaé married Napoleon's general Marshal Ney, and Adèle became the Baronne de Broc. Adèle died in a tragic accident when she fell off a cliff in her twenties while traveling with Hortense Bonaparte. Aglaé was later presented to the Duchesse d'Angoulême at the Restoration in 1814 but it did not go well. The former Madame Royale gave great offense when she addressed Madame Ney, her childhood playmate, by her first name. What the daughter of Antoinette meant as a friendly familiarity was taken as a reminder of Madame Ney's former humble status as a daughter of the Queen's *femme de chambre*. Madame Ney had been ennobled by Napoleon and resented not being addressed by her new noble title. It is sad that the ties to the past had been so damaged that renewing certain connections were rendered futile.

At her trial in October of 1793, Antoinette was shown the portraits of two ladies, which had been found among her personal possessions. When asked to identify the women, she replied that they were "Mesdames de

Mecklenbourg et de Hesse" with whom she was brought up in Vienna.[38] Charlotte Wilhelmine Christiane Marie of Hesse-Darmstadt, **Duchess of Mecklenburg-Strelitz** (1755-1785) grew up with the Archduchess Antoine and, being the same age, shared studies and lessons, in spite of Charlotte being a Lutheran. It was the custom for the Imperial Family to bring noble children from around the empire to be brought up as companions for the Emperor's children; it was considered a privilege and an asset for the child's future opportunities. Charlotte was eventually joined by her younger sister Louise Henriette Karoline of Hesse-Darmstadt, the future **Grand Duchess of Hesse and by Rhine** (1761-1829). The sisters were the younger daughters of a younger son of the house of Hesse and so to be reared in the Imperial Court was an enormous advatange. Charlotte and Louise accompanied the Archduchess Antoine to the French border where they were parted from her with many tears. Antoinette wrote to both of them for many years. Charlotte married her oldest sister's widower, the Duke of Mecklenburg-Strelitz, becoming stepmother to his five children, her own nieces and nephews, among whom was the future great beauty and heroine, Louise of Mecklenburg-Strelitz, Queen of Prussia. However, Charlotte died giving birth to her only son in November of 1785. There exists a gentle letter from Antoinette to Charlotte from June of 1785, in which the Queen tries to calm of worries of her friend about giving birth to her first child at age thirty but Charlotte's fears proved be true.[39] By the time Charlotte died, the Queen was embroiled in the humiliations of the Diamond Necklace scandal. Louise had become Grand Duchess of Hesse by marrying her first cousin Louis I of Hesse in 1777. They had eight children; Louise exchanged letters with the Queen until 1792. She was admired by Napoleon for her intelligence and popular with the people of Hesse until her death in 1829.

The friend who would become the closest to Antoinette as her days darkened was her sister-in-law, **Madame Élisabeth of France**, Louis' youngest sibling. From the first moments at Versailles, Antoinette had been fond of her husband's littlest sister, whom she embraced as her own, playing lively games of hide-and-go-seek in the vast rooms of the *château*. In the summer of 1775, Antoinette wrote to her mother about the eleven year old Élisabeth: "*Je suis enchantée avec ma soeur Élisabeth*" or "I am enchanted with my sister Élisabeth.[40] Élisabeth, under the care of the pious Madame de Marsan, then the fun-loving, careless Princesse de Guéménée, and always under the wise sub-governess Madame de Mackau, blossomed into an ebullient, cheerful young woman, deeply Catholic and committed to a vibrant spiritual life. She had many friends, including Madame de Bombelles, the daughter of Madame de Mackau, whom she called *ma Bombe*. Plump and petite with chestnut blonde hair, she was not a great beauty but attractive due to her vivacity. Many princes sought her hand in marriage, including Antoinette's brother Emperor Joseph II, but Élisabeth wanted to become a nun. She longed to join her Tante Louise at the Carmelite monastery at Saint Denis, where she often visited and served the nuns at table. Louis XVI would not give his permission for her to enter, begging her to stay. "We will have need of you here," he said.[41]

So Élisabeth took on the challenge of living the single, consecrated life in the world, without the support of a community, and living it amid the splendors of Versailles. As Élisabeth grew older she more frequently joined Antoinette at Petit Trianon, and she remained close to her brother, Louis XVI. She adored her brother Artois, the rascal of the family, and tried to encourage him to reform his life, while comforting his forlorn and forsaken wife, Marie-Thérèse de Savoie. For her twenty-fifth birthday, Élisabeth was given Montreuil, the former estate of the Guéménés near Versailles, by the King and the Queen, where she started a dairy to provide milk for poor children. While she organized her ladies in devotions and charitable works, Élisabeth also enjoyed music, embroidery, clothes and especially pretty shoes. She loved to dance and was the last to leave any ball. She always remained strong-willed when it came to adhering to her principles, however. Like her Tante Louise before her, she lived a life of true devotion in the midst of the intrigues and vanities of the most worldly court in the world. After Antoinette lost Baby Sophie, she turned to the company of Madame Élisabeth, who influenced her towards the way of devotion.[42]

Marie-Antoinette, Daughter of the Caesars

MADAME ÉLISABETH DE FRANCE
SŒUR DE LOUIS XVI

Née au Palais de Versailles, le 3 Mai 1764.
Captive, avec la Famille Royale, dans la Prison
du Temple, après la journée du 10 Août 1792.
Morte sur l'échafaud,
le 10 Mai 1794, avec une admirable résignation.

(Reproduction interdite)

16 GENTLEMEN FRIENDS

"Who could see her, day after day, without adoring her?" —The Prince de Ligne on Marie-Antoinette

With all the misplaced emphasis on Antoinette's friendship with Count Fersen, it is forgotten that the Queen had many male friends in whom she confided and with whom she corresponded over the years. The focus on Fersen started after both their deaths when the nephew of the Count published the transcribed letters between the Queen and the Count during the Revolution, letters which dealt mainly with the precarious political situation. During her lifetime, there were a dozen men more likely to be accused of being her lover than Fersen. Then as now, there were people who insisted on seeing impropriety where none existed. The first and most frequent person accused of being Antoinette's lover was her own brother-in-law, Charles-Philippe, **Comte d'Artois** (1757-1836), who was destined to outlive all of his siblings, and be the last Bourbon to sit upon the throne of France. As has been established, Louis felt

Antoinette needed looking after, not because he thought she was immoral but simply because she was vivacious, headstrong and a magnet for mischief-makers. Where Louis was secretive and cautious, Antoinette was transparent and heedless. Artois was often told to be her escort or dance partner at parties and balls; Louis, who could not be everywhere, loathed dancing whereas Artois was as fluid and graceful a dancer as Antoinette herself. Artois was also a good actor and played opposite Antoinette at her many amateur theatricals at Trianon. However, Artois' companionship with Antoinette stirred up gossip. In March 1775, Mercy warned the Empress about the dangers of Antoinette keeping company with Artois, saying: 'M. le comte d'Artois, who cares for nothing but frivolities and whose behavior is that of a libertine....'[1] The Empress was upset and chided her daughter with the following words:

> You must know better than I that this Prince [Artois] is not at all respected and that you thus share his errors. He is so young, so giddy: that may still pass in a prince but these are very grave failings in an older Queen, of whom people thought better. Do not lose that estimable possession which you had so perfectly.[2]

The Empress refers to Antoinette's enormous popularity which was beginning to fade as the people began to see her as a hoyden. The mother's words fell on deaf ears since Antoinette did not see any impropriety in her behavior, being in the company of her sisters-in-law on most public occasions, plus the ever-watchful Provence, Louis' other brother, usually accompanied them as well.

One example of Artois' increasingly unacceptable public behavior was in February 1778 at the Mardi Gras

Ball at the Paris Opera, a masked ball, when he had a public foray with his mistress and cousin, the Duchesse de Bourbon. The couple were seen to be deep in heated conversation when the suddenly the Duchesse reached forward and lifted the Prince's mask, causing the string to break. Artois tore off the Duchesse de Bourbon's mask, punched her in the face with his fist, and then hit her again across the face with his mask. He then stalked away in a fury. The Duchesse, humiliated, injured and bleeding, was assisted by the Comte de Provence, who happened to be hovering nearby. A huge scandal erupted, since Bathilde d'Orléans was a Princess of the Blood. "From that moment the Princes of the Blood were in open mutiny," said Mercy.[3] She complained to her brother, the Duc de Chartres and to her father, the Duc d'Orléans, but they did nothing. Her father-in-law, the Prince de Condé, was outraged, and went to the King, who would not hear anything against his brother, Artois having been called colorful epithets by the Duchesse. The Duc de Bourbon, the estranged husband of the shamed lady, challenged Artois to a duel. In the meantime, all Paris was talking about nothing else, and everyone blamed the Comte d'Artois, whose bestial temper was well-known. The King had to call a family meeting, in which he instructed the Duchesse de Bourbon and Artois to apologize to each other. The Duchesse apologized, but Artois did not, and everyone ended up shouting at each other, including the King. So Artois and the Duc de Bourbon decided that the only way to settle the quarrel was by the sword. They met at the Bois de Boulogne one morning, Artois with his best sword. Removing their coats and spurs, they began to fight; Artois was scratched by the Duc, who then declared his honor satisfied. The cousins embraced and Artois rushed to the house of the Duchesse de Bourbon and apologized profusely. The Duc and Duchesse de

Bourbon were heartily applauded when they appeared together at the theater that night. The King exiled Artois and the Duc to the country for eight days as a punishment for dueling. Antoinette was met by a cold welcome in Paris, because of her known friendship with Artois, although she would never have approved of his brutal behavior, and saw him as a wayward younger brother.[4]

Artois and his wife had four children, two girls and two boys, but the girls Sophie and Thérèse, did not survive childhood. The boys, Louis-Antoine, **Duc d'Angoulême** (1775-1844) and Charles-Ferdinand, **Duc de Berry** (1778-1820), were playmates of Louis and Antoinette's children, and played important roles in the Restoration of 1814. Angoulême married his first cousin Madame Royale in 1799, as Louis and Antoinette had once planned.

One of the gentlemen whose name was first linked to the Queen's was Marie-François-Henri de Franquetot, **Duc de Coigny** (1737-1821), whose son the Marquis de Coigny served at Versailles at the same time. A lifelong soldier with a distinguished military record, the Duc also served loyally at court, and Louis XVI made him his First Equerry in 1774. The Duc's handsome, dignified and courtly bearing endeared him to the Queen, who invited him into her circle, where he displayed chivalrous regard for her. He was one of the four older gentlemen chosen to wait upon the Queen when she was recovering from measles at Petit Trianon in 1779. He was, however, not pleased with the favors shown to the Polignac clan and by his opposition to Madame de Polignac he alienated the Queen. In 1791 he fled France and joined the *émigré* army. Eventually, he spent Napoleon's reign serving in the armies of the King of Portugal. He returned to France during the Restoration.

Louis XVIII made him a Peer of France and Governor of Les Invalides, and in 1816 a Marshal of France. He died in 1821.

Adrien-Louis de Bonnières, **Duc de Guînes** (1735-1806) was another old soldier and handsome polished courtier, whom Antoinette allowed into her inner circle, mostly due to the fact that he was a *choiseuliste*. He was one of the four older gentlemen chosen to wait upon the Queen when she was recovering from measles at Petit Trianon in 1779. He was an accomplished flautist who hired Mozart to teach his daughter. Mercy disliked him since he was close to the Polignacs, and wrote of him to the Empress, worrying that his influence on Antoinette would supplant his own. In 1776, Louis XVI made him Ambassador to England, where it was later found that his secretary was misappriating funds. Guînes was held accountable but the Queen took his side and he was acquitted. Upon his return to France he was given the Order of the Holy Spirit. He continued to serve the King in many capacities but in the meantime he grew quite corpulent, so that he had to have special breeches made for sitting and others for standing. During the Revolution he escaped to England, to return in 1806 during the reign of Napoleon. He died shortly after his return to France.

One of Antoinette's most cultured, charming and cosmopolitan friends was indubitably Charles-Joseph Lamoral, **Prince de Ligne** (1735-1814), from the country now known as Belgium, once a province of the Habsburg Empire. Many of her closest friends were foreigners, who asked for less and were not embroiled in the court intrigues. The Prince de Ligne had fought in the Seven Years War on the Austrian side and later became a Field Marshal of the Empire. He was an intimate friend and distant relative of the Habsburg family, especially Emperor Joseph II. The Prince and his wife were the parents of seven children and immensely wealthy. They had vast estates in the Brabant, including marvelous gardens at Bel Oeil. The Prince knew a great deal about horticulture and was able to advise Antoinette when she was planning her gardens at Petit Trianon. Of Antoinette, whom he knew quite well, he said: "Her pretended gallantry was never any more than a very deep friendship for one or two individuals, and the ordinary coquetry of a woman, or a queen, trying to please everyone."[5] The Prince de Ligne was the author of several books, including works of military history. In his personal memoirs he wote extensively of Antoinette, praising her beauty and her virtue while defending her reputation; he must be quoted in his own words:

> The charms of her face and of her soul, the one as white and beautiful as the other, and the attraction of that society hence made me spend five months of every year in her suite, without absenting myself for a single day....
>
> As for the queen, the radiance of her presence harmed her. The jealousy of the women whom she crushed by the beauty of her complexion and the carriage of her head, ever seeking to harm her as a woman, harmed her also as a queen. Fredegonde and Brunehaut, Catherine and Marie de Medici, Anne and Theresa of Austria never laughed; Marie Antoinette when she was fifteen laughed much; therefore she was declared 'satirical.'
>
> She defended herself against the intrigues of two parties, each of whom wanted to give her a lover; on which they declared her 'inimical to Frenchmen;' and all the more because she was friendly with foreigners, from whom she had neither traps nor importunity to fear.

An unfortunate dispute about a visit between her brother the Elector of Cologne and the princes of the blood, of which she was wholly ignorant, offended the etiquette of the Court, which then called her 'proud.'

She dines with one friend, and sometimes goes to see another friend, after supper, and they say she is 'familiar.' That is not what the few persons who lived in her familiarity would say. Her delicate, sure sense of the becoming awed them as much as her majesty. It was as impossible to forget it as it was to forget one's self.

She is sensible of the friendship of certain persons who are the most devoted to her; then she is declared to be 'amorous' of them. Sometimes she requires too much for their families; then she is 'unreasonable.'

She gives little *fêtes*, and works herself at her Trianon: that is called 'bourgeoise.' She buys Saint-Cloud for the health of her children and to take them from the malaria of Versailles: they pronounce her 'extravagant.' Her promenades in the evening on the terrace, or on horseback in the Bois de Boulogne, or sometimes on foot round the music in the Orangery 'seem suspicious.' Her most innocent pleasures are thought criminal; her general loving-kindness is 'coquettish.' She fears to win at cards, at which she is compelled to play, and they say she 'wastes the money of the State.'

She laughed and sang and danced until she was twenty five years old: they declared her 'frivolous.' The affairs of the kingdom became embroiled, the spirit of party arose and divided society; she would take no side, and they called her 'ungrateful.'

She no longer amused herself; she foresaw misfortunes: they declared her 'intriguing.' She dropped certain little requests or recommendations she had made to the king or the ministers as soon as she feared they were troublesome, and then she was 'fickle.'

With so many crimes to her charge, and all so well-proved, did she not deserve her misfortunes? But I see I have forgotten the greatest. The queen, who was almost a prisoner of State in her *château* of Versailles, took the liberty sometimes to go on foot, followed by a servant, through one of the galleries, to the apartments of Mme. de Lamballe or Mme. de Polignac. How shocking a scandal! The late queen was always carried in a sedan-chair to see her cousin, Mme. de Talmont, where she found a rather bad company of Polish relations, who claimed to be Leczinskis.

The queen, beautiful as the day, and almost always in her own hair, — except on occasions of ceremony, when her toilet, about which she never cared, was regulated for her, — was naturally talked about; for everybody wanted to please her. The late Leczinska, old before her time and rather ugly, in a large cap called, I think, 'butterfly,' would sometimes command certain questionable plays at the theatre; but no one found fault with her for that devout ladies like scandals. When, in our time, they gave us a play of that sort we used to call it the queen's repertory, and Marie Antoinette would scold us, laughing, and say we might at least make known it was the queen before her. No one ever dared to risk too free a speech in her presence, nor too gay a tale, nor a coarse insinuation. She had taste and judgment; and as for the three Graces, she united them all in herself alone.[6]

The Queen was cautious about gossip due to the

infatuations which many gentlemen cherished for her. As the Prince penned many years after her death:

> Who could see her, day after day, without adoring her? I did not feel it fully until she said to me: 'My mother thinks it wrong that you should be so long at Versailles. Go and spend a little time with your command, and write letters to Vienna to let them know you are there, and then come back here.' That kindness, that delicacy, but more than all the thought that I must spend two weeks away from her, brought the tears to my eyes, which her pretty heedlessness of those early days, keeping her a hundred leagues away from gallantry, prevented her from seeing. As I never have believed in passions that are not reciprocal, two weeks cured me of what I here avow to myself for the first time, and would never avow to others in my lifetime for fear of being laughed at.
>
> But consider how this sentiment, which gave place to the warmest friendship, would have detected a passion in that charming queen, had she felt one for any man; and with what horror I saw her given in Paris, and thence, thanks to their vile libels, all over Europe, to the Duc de Coigny, to M. le Comte d'Artois, M. de Lamberti, M. de Fersen, Mr. Conway, Lord Stratheven, and other Englishmen as silly as himself, and two or three stupid Germans. Did I ever see aught in her society that did not bear the stamp of grace, kindness, and good taste? She scented an intriguer at a league's distance; she detested pretensions of all kinds. It was for this reason that the whole family of Polignac and their friends, such as Valentin Esterhazy, Baron Bezenval, and Vaudreuil, also Segur and I, were so agreeable to her. She often

laughed with me at the struggle for favour among the courtiers, and even wept over some who were disappointed.[7]

The Prince de Ligne's refusal to help the Belgians rebel against the Empire led to the loss of his estates in his native land. He died in Austria in 1814.

Count Bálint (Valentin) Miklos Esterhazy (1740-1805) was a scion of one of the most powerful and well-known noble families in Hungary, but he himself never spoke Hungarian and never lived there. His family had immigrated to France after the lost Hungarian revolt earlier in the century; Maria Theresa never forgot that his grandfather had been a rebel. After his father's death in 1743, little Valentin was brought up in France by a Count of Bercsényi (Bercheny), a Hungarian immigrant. He grew up to become an officer in the French army and found favor at the royal court. It was Valentin who conveyed the portrait of the Dauphin Louis-Auguste to the Archduchess Antoine in Vienna. A *choiseuliste*, he served as colonel of a French regiment until the dismissal of Choiseul in 1774, when he resigned. He was a very brave and loyal friend of the King and the Queen, and had a beloved wife to whom he remained loyal and wrote hundreds of letters to her. He was one of the four older gentlemen chosen to wait upon the Queen when she was recovering from measles at Petit Trianon. As the Dauphine Marie-Antoinette wrote to her Mother in December of 1772:

> Esterhazy was at our ball yesterday. Every one was greatly pleased with his dignified manner and with his style of dancing. I ought to have spoken to him when he was presented to me, and my silence only proceeded from embarrassment, as I did not know

him. It would be doing me great injustice to think that I have any feeling of indifference to my country; I have more reason than any one to feel, every day of my life, the value of the blood which flows in my veins, and it is only from prudence that at times I abstain from showing how proud I am of it....[8]

Esterhazy, who was in the favor of the Comte d'Artois, was made a *maréchal de camp* in 1780 and placed in charge of inspecting the troops. He continued to be devoted to his Fanny and their several children. During the Revolution he helped the French *emigrés* to escape by way of Namur, then hastened back to Paris to assist the King. He later joined Artois and the *emigrés* in Coblenz; they sent him to Russia to seek the help of Catherine II against the forces of the Revolution. He failed in his mission but gained an estate in Russia, where he died in 1805.

Pierre Victor, **Baron de Besenval** de Brünstatt (1722–1791), the last commander of the Swiss Guards in France, belonged to the Polignac circle and was thus one of Antoinette's friends. He was one of the four older gentlemen who waited upon the Queen when she was recovering from measles in 1779. He was a wealthy bachelor, spending a great deal of money on *objets d'arts*. According to Madame Campan:

> The Baron de Besenval added to the bluntness of the Swiss all the adroitness of a French courtier. His fifty years and gray hairs made him enjoy among women the confidence inspired by mature age, although he had not given up the thought of love affairs. He talked of his native mountains with enthusiasm. He would at any time sing the 'Ranz

des Vaches' with tears in his eyes, and was the best story-teller in the Comtesse Jules's circle.[9]

The Baron de Besenval was unique among Antoinette's friends for his skill in yodeling, although his family originally came from Savoy not Switzerland, and his mother was Polish, a kinswoman of Queen Marie Leszczyńska. Beneath his *bonhomie* and charm was insolence and disdain. Antoinette, being innocent of the ways of the world, surely thought that his age and white hair made him beyond the slightest romantic pretensions, but she was mistaken. It was the yodeling Swiss who described the Queen as having "a wonderful elegance in everything."[10] Unfortunately, his infatuation with her caused her much harm, due to his careless vanity and romantic fantasies. Madame Campan describes a time when Antoinette, trying to stop the duel between the Comte d'Artois and the Duc de Bourbon, had Monsieur Campan escort the Baron into a small room attached to her private chambers so she could relay him a message from the King to pass on to Artois. The Baron later exaggerated his descriptions of the encounter, making it sound as if the Queen had invited him into some private love nest. The Queen, furious at his overtures towards her, ordered him out of her presence. She did not tell the King, fearing a scandal. Besenval secured his own petty revenge by making cowardly insinuations in his memoirs. As Madame Campan later wrote:

> I read with infinite pain the manner in which that simple fact is perverted in M. de Besenval's memoirs. He is right in saying that M. Campan led him through the upper corridors of the *château*, and introduced him into an apartment unknown to him; but the air of romance given to the interview is equally culpable and ridiculous. M. de Besenval

says that he found himself, without knowing how he came there, in a plain apartment, but very conveniently furnished, of the existence of which he was till then utterly ignorant. He was astonished, he adds, not that the Queen should have so many facilities, but that she should have ventured to procure them. Ten printed sheets of the woman Lamotte's impure libels contain nothing so injurious to the character of Marie Antoinette as these lines, written by a man whom she honoured by kindness thus undeserved. He could not possibly have had any opportunity of knowing the existence of these apartments, which consisted of a very small ante-chamber, a bedchamber and a closet. Ever since the Queen had occupied her own apartment this had been appropriated to Her Majesty's lady of honour in cases of confinement or sickness, and was actually in such use when the Queen was confined. It was so important that it should not be known the Queen had spoken to the Baron before the duel that she had determined to go through her inner room into this little apartment to which M. Campan was to conduct him. When men write upon times still in remembrance they should be scrupulously exact, and not indulge in any exaggerations or constructions of their own.[11]

The Baron died in 1791, a year before the infamous massacre of the Swiss Guard at the Tuileries.

Armand Louis de Gontaut Biron, **Duc de Lauzun** (1747–1793) was a military hero and author of a memoir as well as being a courtier at Versailles during the reign of Louis XVI. He could easily have been the model for Valmont in *Dangerous Liaisons* in that no woman was free from his advances, not even the Queen of France.

His mother died giving birth to him; he was brought up by his aunt, the Duchesse de Choiseul, wife of the Choiseul. Therefore it can be said that Lauzun was brought up in the boudoir of Madame de Pompadour, his aunt and uncle being part of her inner circle. Lauzun joined the Swiss Guards while still a teen. At nineteen he married a fourteen year old girl, Amélie de Boufflers, granddaughter and heiress of the Maréchal de Luxembourg, but he never cared for her; the marriage was a failure. A friend of Madame de Guémenée's, Lauzun managed to have the Princesse introduce him to the Queen. He invited Antoinette to see his horse in a race, which she found thrilling, and so he arranged other races. The Queen soon discovered his bad reputation, revealed to her by Mercy and the Abbé Vermond; it was not to her liking. However, she continued to allow him access to her presence, which was perhaps unwise on her part. She once admired the heron plume on Lauzun's hat; he gave it to her, which was awkward, because she wanted to refuse it, but did not wish to offend. She wore it once, hoping he would see her gratitude, and let the matter pass. Instead, he came to see her, making unwanted overtures so that she had to order him from the room. "That man shall never again come within my doors," she said to Madame Campan.[12] Antoinette, knowing what he was, prevented him from positions of power in the military. Neither would she intervene on his behalf when Madame de Guémenée importuned her for *lettres d'etat*, to save him from his creditors. Lauzun went from being an admirer of the Queen to being her enemy, joining the faction of the Duc d'Orléans, and eventually the Revolution, along with his close friend Talleyrand. Lauzun fought in the Vendée against the Royal and Catholic Army. Nevertheless, his fellow revolutionaries disliked his aristocratic *hauteur*. He was arrested and guillotined in January 1794; his neglected wife was guillotined a few months later.[13]

"Count Hans Axel von Fersen"

17 THE FERSEN LEGEND

> "I have made inquiries and sought information with zeal aud caution, and asked persons attached to the Court and the Queen, and found my veneration for her virtue confirmed in every respect."—Comte d'Hézècques, former page at Versailles

Too often in the many articles and books about Antoinette, Count Axel von Fersen is referred to as the "Queen's lover" or as her "probable lover." Surfing the internet anyone can see that the Fersen myth is deeply entrenched in the public mind. This is due to major publishers yearly churning out sensational biographies and novels, which focus on the legend rather than on the facts, scouring letters and diaries for the slightest indication that Antoinette and Count Fersen may have slept together. It is repeatedly disregarded that according to the reliable historical evidence Count Fersen and Antoinette were merely friends, and that he was as much her husband's friend as he was hers. People are free to speak of Louis XV and Madame de Pompadour as "lovers" since they openly lived together for many years, as well as Louis XV and Madame du Barry, or Philippe Égalité and Madame de Genlis. There are many famous lovers in history: Antony and Cleopatra, John of Gaunt and Katharine Swynford, Napoleon and Josephine, Lord Nelson and Lady Emma Hamilton and for all of them abundant facts determine that they were, indeed, lovers. In the case of Antoinette and Fersen, innuendo is passed off as fact and supposition is accepted as truth. To speak that way of Antoinette, who was known for her chaste behavior and moral rectitude among her circle of close friends, of whom the Prince de Ligne, said: "Her soul was as white as her face," who lost her life because she chose to stay at her husband's side, is the height of irresponsibility.[1]

The accounts of those whose personal knowledge of the Queen, or deep study of her life, reveal her virtue, as well as her fidelity and devotion to her husband, are continually ignored. To quote the words of her page, the Comte d' Hézècques:

> She was always a most tender mother, and always retained the affections of her husband, as an unfaithful wife can never do. The duties of religion always had her full attention, not following them as vigorously as her mother, but taking example by the King, and he was as attentive as possible amid the turmoil of Royalty. Childless during the earlier part of her union to a spouse who professed to devote his leisure from royal duties to hunting and study, the Queen collected companions of her own, and among them were some young men. Thence arose the shocking stories put down to the credit of that unhappy princess. And yet vice lurks concealed while these visits were quite in public; besides, if

the Count de Fersen and MM. de Vaudreuil and de Coigny were admitted to her society, old Besenval was summoned there as well. All these calumnies have come to an end these ten years, for they have lost their purpose. And though by this time all danger that might have arisen from the publication of a criminal intrigue with the Queen has vanished, and all the actors in these fictitious scenes of shame are yet alive, not one of the anecdotes that were propagated at the beginning of the Revolution has been confirmed, and all the dreadful stories are buried in complete silence. I have made inquiries and sought information with zeal aud caution, and asked persons attached to the Court and the Queen, and found my veneration for her virtue confirmed in every respect.[2]

Count Fersen was in the service of his sovereign King Gustavus III and his presence at the French court needs to be seen in the light of that capacity. The Swedish King was a devoted friend of Louis XVI and Antoinette and Gustavus, even more than the Queen's Austrian relatives, worked to aid the King and Queen of France in their time of troubles. Fersen was the go-between in the various top secret plans to help Louis XVI regain control of his kingdom and escape from the clutches of his political enemies. The diplomatic intrigues that went on behind the scenes are more interesting than any imaginary romance. However, books and movies continue to add this sensationalism to the Queen's life, as if anything could be more sensational than the reality. Serious modern and contemporary scholars, however, such as Thomas Carlyle, the Goncourts, Imbert de Saint-Amand, Maxime de le Rocheterie, G. Lenôtre, Pierre de Nolhac, Paul and Pierrette Girault de Coursac, Hilaire Belloc, Nesta Webster, Simone Bertière, Philippe

Delorme, Jean Chalon, Desmond Seward, Jean Petitfils, Frances Mossiker and Simon Schama are unanimous in saying that there is no conclusive evidence to prove that Antoinette violated her marriage vows by dallying with Count Fersen.

The origins of the legend of Antoinette's affair with Fersen began not with her revolutionary foes, who certainly would have picked up on anything of that nature to discredit the Queen at her trial. Fersen's name came up at the trial only in regard to the fact that he had driven the Royal Family's coach out of Paris in June 1791 as they tried to escape to Montmédy. It was a courtier, the Comte de Saint-Priest, who made insinuations about the Queen and Fersen in his memoirs, probably to cover the humiliation that Fersen had slept with Madame de Saint-Priest, his wife. Madame de la Tour du Pin, a former lady-in-waiting of the Queen, in her memoirs mentions that "the Count de Fersen, said to be Queen Marie-Antoinette's lover, also came to see us everyday." She says this in a paragraph about her childhood where she is discussing the various men who, according to gossip, were "considered" to be in love with with her own mother, Madame Dillon. So the Fersen affair is lumped in with what must be seen as frivolous court gossip.[3]

As Jean Chalon points out in his biography *Chère Marie-Antoinette*, Fersen, who had many mistresses, saw the Queen as an angel, to whom he offered reverent and chaste homage. According to Chalon, Antoinette knew about sex only through conjugal love, where she found her "happiness," her "*bonheur essentiel*," as she wrote to her mother.[4] Petitfils, in his biography of Louis XVI, quotes the Queen's brother Joseph, who said Antoinette was a "font of honesty and virtue."[5] Petitfils asserts that there was no affair but a romantic pact, like a courtly novel, for the Queen was too religious to have an affair.[6]

If there had been any cause for concern about Count Fersen's presence at the French court as regards the Queen's reputation, the Austrian ambassador Count Mercy-Argenteau would surely have mentioned it in one of the reams of letters to Antoinette's mother Empress Maria Theresa, to whom he passed on every detail of the young Queen's life. Count Mercy had spies whom he paid well to gather information, but Fersen was not worth mentioning. Neither is he mentioned in a romantic way by other people close to the Queen in their memoirs, such as her maid Madame Campan and the Baron de Besenval.

Much has also been made of the following passage from a letter from M. Creutz, the Swedish ambassador, to King Gustav III:

> *Je dois confier à Votre Majesté que le jeune comte de Fersen a été si bien vu de la Reine que cela a donné des ombrages à plusieurs personnes. J'avoue que je ne puis m'empêcher de croire qu'elle avait du penchant pour lui: j'en ai vu des indices trop sûrs pour endouter. Le jeune comte de Fersen a eu dans cette occasion une conduite admirable par sa modestie et par sa réserve et surtout par le parti qu'il a pris d'aller en Amérique. En s'éloignant il écartait tous les dangers; mais il fallait évidemment une fermeté au-dessus de son âge pour surmonter cette séduction. La Reine ne pouvait le quitter des yeux dans les derniers jours; en le regardant ils étaient remplis de larmes.*[7]

Here is a translation:

> I must confide to Your Majesty that the young Count Fersen is so well received by the Queen that it has given offence to several persons. I admit that

I cannot refrain from thinking that she has a fondness for him: I saw signs of this that were too clear to leave any doubt. The young Count Fersen's behavior on this occasion was admirable in its modesty and restraint and especially in his decision to go to America. By leaving, he removed all dangers, but of course wisdom and resolve beyond his years were required to overcome this seduction. The Queen could not take her eyes off him these last few days; as she watched him they filled with tears. I beg Your Majesty to keep this a secret for her sake and Senator Fersen's.

Although the letter of Creutz is dated 1779 it was in August of 1778 that Fersen returned to Versailles; Antoinette was six months pregnant at the time with her first child. She may have been a bit weepy as are many women with child. It could also be that *le beau Fersen* did indeed impress her with his charm and masculine beauty, which seemed to be his usual effect on women. She was not made of wood. But what must be remembered here is that the Austrian ambassador Comte de Mercy, who constantly spied on Antoinette, reporting everything to her mother, did not think the incident with Fersen was worth mentioning. He was much more upset about the influence of Madame de Polignac on the young Queen. The Spanish ambassador Count Aranda, who paid servants to inspect the royal sheets so that he knew when the King and Queen had marital relations, also did not think anything of the Queen's friendship with Fersen. Creutz was an adroit minister who knew it would please his king to know that a Swede was in favor at the French court. His probable exaggerations of Fersen's impact on the Queen need to be viewed in that light.

Antoinette and Count Fersen first met at the opera ball

during Carnival on January 30, 1774, when she chatted with him behind her mask, in the presence of her husband and in-laws, but no eyebrows were raised by this playful incident. Later in 1778 when the Queen was pregnant with her first child, Fersen was admitted to the Queen's circle of friends. There is no record, in the various records of guest lists and visitors, that Fersen ever visited Petit Trianon.[8] He returned in 1783, coming and going over the next few years, and every time he arrived Antoinette was already pregnant, which is an important point for those who try to claim that Fersen fathered Antoinette's younger children.[9] He once asked the Queen to write letters on his behalf to his king, as she did for another Swedish aristocrat as well. Some biographers claim that in March 1780 when the Queen sang the aria, "*Ah! Que je fus inspirée...*" from the opera *Didon* by Picinni, she did not take her eyes from the count. However, that opera did not premier until October 1780, while the count was in America, so it is probable that the story is apocryphal. At any rate, it is not evidence of a liaison.[10]

Some biographers assert that in the 1780's Antoinette may have become sexually involved with Count Fersen; other authors see this as ridiculous. As Chalon notes, she had found her *bonheur essentiel* in her marriage. Also, she was in those years having babies, miscarriages, caring for sick and dying children, and after the death of her daughter Sophie in 1787, becoming more observant of Catholic devotional practices. In 1788, she gave orders that the fasts of the Church be more carefully observed at her table than previously. She also began making public devotions and prayers with her household in the Royal Chapel.[11] Acording to Desmond Seward in his biography of Antoinette: "Post-Freudian biographers all tend to ignore Marie-Antoinette's intensely devout personal religion which, as with her mother, was the real source of her strength."[12] From 1785 onward, she had to deal with the stress of the Diamond Necklace scandal, the growing political crisis, the death of her baby, the long slow death of her oldest son due to tuberculosis, all the while experiencing nervous problems as a result, including dizziness and headaches. Nesta Webster quotes the memoirist Laure Junot, the Duchesse d'Abrantès, who said:

> The Queen was so seriously engaged at the period when she is accused of this liaison with M. de Fersen that it is unbelievable that she could have long hours to consecrate to love. How could one love during the infernal existence this unhappy Princess was then leading?[13]

Nesta Webster in *Louis XVI and Marie-Antoinette during the Revolution* shows how the Queen would have found it impossible to have had an affair even if she had been so inclined. At Versailles, she lived in public, and even at Petit Trianon there were servants and family members around. Even when she was alone, she was not really alone; there were people around every corner. Both the Austrian and Spanish ambassadors, and other diplomats as well, wrote meticulous reports to their respective monarchs on the Queen's private life based on their spy rings, questioning maids and footmen. As Webster writes in her two volume study:

> Yet not once in the vast correspondence of Mercy is Fersen's name mentioned, nor amidst the malicious gossip of the other ambassadors do we find so much as a hint that he was regarded with particular favor by Marie-Antoinette. After the royal family had been brought to the Tuileries she was even more closely surrounded, with one National Guard

sleeping in her antechamber and others keeping watch on her all day. In a letter to her sister... she herself had written on this: 'I defy the universe to find any real wrong in me; indeed, I can only gain by being guarded and followed so closely.'[14]

Some authors claim that not only was Antoinette sleeping with Fersen, but she was also sleeping with the King. To be shared by two men is completely at odds with the modest, prudish, innocent image of Antoinette built by biographers such as Cronin, Delorme, Webster, and Bertière. Antonia Fraser insists that Louis fathered all of his wife's children because Fersen would have been clever enough to use condoms.[15] Nevertheless, she cites an instance when Fersen impregnated one of his mistresses; condoms were not always reliable.[16] There are those that have Antoinette throwing Louis out of bed while running off to sleep with Fersen. Indeed, Simone Bertière mentions how Louis and Antoinette refrained from marital relations after the birth of Sophie in 1786.[17] Antoinette's brother Joseph II was scandalized that she wanted to space the birth of her children, which was becoming fashionable among young mothers, he lamented.[18] He was used to the women in the Habsburg clan who would have sixteen, seventeen and eighteen children in as many years. But Antoinette wanted to regain her health so she could devote herself to bringing up the children she already had. Louis and Antoinette's abstinence was surely due to the Queen's health and fragile emotional state. For one thing, she was in her thirties which was considered middle aged in those days. The year 1786 was a difficult year for her: Louis-Joseph's health was failing, the baby Sophie was not thriving. Antoinette, aware of the abominable calumnies being spread about her in the wake of the Diamond Necklace scandal, declared to Madame Campan in

September of 1786, "I want to die!" When Madame Campan brought her orange flower water for her nerves, she said, "No, do not love me, it is better to give me death!"[19] She may have had post-partum depression or even on the verge of a breakdown. Louis himself was also in a state of collapse by 1787, due to the ongoing financial disaster.[20]

While Antoinette might have been in love with Count Axel von Fersen at some point, there is no evidence of an extramarital affair, and to over speculate on the Queen's personal feelings is to violate the sanctuary of the human heart. Whatever her sentiments, they did not interfere with her duties as wife, mother, and Queen. Adultery for a Queen of France was high treason and if any of her many enemies at court discovered such a situation, had it existed, Louis XVI would have been forced to take her children away from her and banish her to a convent. Even the most basic knowledge of her temperament suggests that she was devoted to her children and would never have risked being separated from them. Those who claim that Louis XVI "knew" about his wife's "affair" with Fersen, but looked the other way, are ignoring the moral scruples and religious principles of *le Roi très chrétien*. He would never have permitted the mother of his children to carry on with another man.

A passage written by Lady Elizabeth Foster in her diary, claiming that Antoinette and Fersen were lovers, has sometimes been used as proof of an affair, even in Lady Antonia Fraser's otherwise worthy biography. It is no proof at all; Bess Foster was not part of the Queen's inner circle, although she was briefly Fersen's mistress when they met abroad. Furthermore, according to Amanda Foreman's acclaimed biography of Georgiana, Duchess of Devonshire, Bess' version of events in her diary "was more fantasy than truth."[21] Georgiana's daughter Harriet described Bess thus: "...More perverted than deceitful...I really believe she hardly knows herself the difference between right and wrong now."[22] Bess is not a reliable source concerning Antoinette.

The myth of Axel von Fersen as Antoinette's lover evolved after the deaths of both the count and the Queen. The count himself carelessly sowed the seeds of the legend because being "the Queen's lover" added to his prestige; so much for his reputation for discretion. In 1822 an Irishman named O'Meara published *Napoleon in Exile* in which he repeated gossip that had been rampant at Bonaparte's court, about Fersen and the Queen, attributed at the time to the Queen's maid Madame Campan. [23] The rumor was proved to be false by British historian John Wilson Croker, who in October 1822 wrote in the *Quarterly Review* that Madame Campan had not been present at court when certain allegations were said to have occurred.[24] Madame Campan herself refuted any such stories when she said of Antoinette:

> I who for fifteen years saw her attached to her august consort and her children, kind to her servitors, unfortunately too polite, too simple, too much on an equality with the people of the Court, I cannot bear to see her character reviled. I wish I had a hundred mouths, I wish I had wings and could inspire the same confidence in the truth which is so readily accorded to lies.[25]

Other writers allege that Madame Campan fabricated this statement in order to return to the good graces of Antoinette's daughter, who was annoyed with her for having taught Napoleon's sisters at her finishing school. But then, if Madame Campan was a liar, of what value would her testimony be at all, for anything? But people more easily believe stories of scandals than they do stories of virtue. If she deliberately softened her portrayal of Antoinette, in order to get back into the good graces of Madame Royale, she did not do a good job. In that case, she would not have been so critical of Louis XVI, since it was well-known that the princess idolized her dead father.

For many years following, most historians and biographers, including Carlyle, the Goncourts, Imbert de Saint-Amand, Rocheterie, Bimbinet, Lenôtre and Nolhac did not take the Fersen story seriously and ignored it. When the letters of the Queen and Count Fersen were published by his great nephew Baron von Klinckowström in the late nineteenth century, they proved the nature of the Queen and Fersen's relationship to be principally a diplomatic one. And anyone can read the extant latters now, transcribed by Fersen from the cypher used, and see that they are almost entirely political. His letters to her are particularly cold and business-like. According to Nesta Webster in *Louis XVI and Marie-Antoinette during the Revolution t*he Fersen letters were "written in a very difficult cipher to which a particular edition of *Paul and Virginie* provided the key....In certain of the letters, mainly those from the queen to Fersen, passages have been erased and are indicated by rows of dots in the printed text."[26] The Baron himself wrote that "the Fersen family has retained the greatest veneration for those holy and august martyrs, Louis XVI and Marie-Antoinette, and there is nothing among the papers remaining from the Comte de Fersen which can cast a shadow on the conduct of the Queen."[27] The passages erased were most likely sensitive diplomatic issues, not declarations of love, as some romantics have claimed. They concealed allusions to the Queen's disagreements with her brothers-in-law Artois and Provence, or references to the Duc d'Orléans and other revolutionaries, or even mentions of spies or persons whose families would have been compromised had the letters fallen into the wrong hands. The original letters are lost; some say the Baron burned them in order to keep the cipher from being imitated and used for forgeries; others say he burned them to keep people from discovering proof of a love affair, but there was no love affair to be found, by his own admission.

In the 1930's Alma Söderhjelm published the letters of Count Fersen to his sister Sophie, hoping to prove from those letters that the Count and the Queen had had a love affair. It is upon Söderhjelm's book that most of the modern romances about Antoinette are based. Now in the spring of 1790, Fersen was having a passionate affair with an Italian lady named Eleonore Sullivan, who had been the mistress of several aristocrats, including Antoinette's brother Joseph II. She was married to an Irishman but as of 1790 she was the mistress of a Scotsman named Quintin Crawford. She was kept by Monsieur Crawford in an elegant house in Paris, where she had a maid named Josephine, and a hideaway for Fersen in the attic. Later authors would claim that when Fersen mentioned "Josephine" in his letters, it was always a code name for Antoinette, forgetting the Fersen knew sat least three women with that name.[28] It cannot be ignored that Fersen gave "Josephine" menial instructions about a stove; in that instance he was more than likely referring to Mrs. Sullivan's maid and the cold room in the attic. Likewise, the woman Fersen writes ardently about to his sister at this time, who is honored by Sophie's attentions, is most likely Mrs. Sullivan, whom he refers to as "El" or "elle." Some try to make the Queen the subject of his ecstatic passages, but why would the Queen of France, in the midst of so many political intrigues, threatened by death, have wanted to ingratiate herself to Fersen's sister? "Elle" (capitalized), however, is what Fersen uses when referring reverently to the Queen, *la Reine*, whom he usually mentions in conjunction with the King. Baron Klinckowström quotes Fersen's letter to his father in Feb 1791, in which he writes of his service to Louis XVI and Antoinette: "I am attached to the King and the Queen and I owe it to them for the kindness they showed me when they were able, and I should be vile and ungrateful if I deserted them now that they can do nothing for me...."[29] As the Duchesse de FitzJames, a great-niece of Fersen, is quoted by Webster from a 1893 French periodical *La Vie Contemporaine*:

> I desire first of all to do away with the lying legend, based on a calumny, which distorted the relations between Marie-Antoinette and Fersen, relations consisting in absolute devotion, in complete abnegation on one side, and on the other in friendship, profound, trusting and grateful. People have wished to degrade to the vulgarities of a love novel, facts which were otherwise terrible, sentiments which were otherwise lofty.[30]

Much has been made of the letters Antoinette wrote to her friend Count Esterhazy, and the ring which she sent to Fersen via Esterhazy. In August 1791, after the failure of the escape to Montmédy the royal couple were isolated and cut off from news about relatives and friends since Fersen, the principle channel for conveying the news, had been silent for almost two months. The Swedish count was in Vienna at King Gustavus' request on a secret mission, consulting with the Emperor about the possible rescue of the French royal family. The Queen wrote to Esterhazy: "If you write to him [Fersen] be sure to tell him that many leagues and many countries can never separate hearts: I feel this truth more everyday."[31] In September 1791, the Queen sent Esterhazy two gold rings which, according to Webster, bore the motto: *Domine, salve fac regem et regina.* (God save the King and the Queen.) Other authors say the motto was *Lâche qui les abandonne.* (Coward be the one who lets them down.) She wrote:

> I am delighted to find this opportunity to send you a little ring which will surely give you pleasure. They have been sold in prodigious quantities during the last three days and one has all the difficulty in the world to find them. The one surrounded with paper is for him [Fersen], it will just fit him; I wore it for two days before packing it. Tell him it is from me. I do not know where he is; it is a dreadful torment to have no news and not even know where the people one is fond of [*qu'on aime*] are living.[32]

Of course, a ring once worn by a queen is of great value, just like a cap once worn by the Pope. Nesta Webster's commentary on the rings and letters must be quoted in its entirety:

> These letters have again been quoted as evidence that there was a liaison between Antoinette and Fersen, and that Esterhazy being in on the secret, the Queen did not hesitate to confide in him on the subject. But in reality, what do they prove? Nothing more than that she had great affection for him. That a captive Queen should send royalist rings to two of her oldest and most faithful friends is nothing extraordinary, that she should have referred to Fersen as "him" was only in accordance with the plan of avoiding all names in writing. As to the words "*qu'on aime*," aimer is a verb that in French…may mean either to like, to be fond of, to

love with affection or to be in love with. It cannot have been in the last sense that Marie Antoinette employed it here, since she applies it in the plural—"*les gens qu'on aime*"—that is to say, her friends in general....If she had used it in the amorous sense of one whom Esterhazy knew to be her lover, would she not have said, "*celui qu'on aime*?"[33]

There is much controversy over a certain night in February 1792, when some biographers, including Stanley Loomis and Vincent Cronin, think that Antoinette and Count Axel von Fersen may have finally consummated their passion in her suite in the Tuileries palace. The theory has occurred over a smudged out phrase in Fersen's diary. However, no one knows for certain if the erased phrase was indeed *Resté là*, Fersen's usual term indicating that he had slept with a lady. Also, the Queen, following her escape attempt, was more closely guarded than ever, with a sentry keeping watch at her door all night, and checking every once in awhile to see if she was in her room—how could she have entertained a lover?[34] The purpose of Count Fersen's final visit to his friends Louis and Antoinette was to discuss the dire political situation and persuade them to try to escape again, which Louis would not do. Fersen may have had to linger in the palace overnight in order to avoid the revolutionary authorities, but not in the Queen's bed. At his earliest convenience, he made his way to the welcoming arms of his mistress Eleonore Sullivan and stayed at her house in the attic hideaway.

According to the Queen's maid Madame Campan, Antoinette spent her nights at the Tuileries reading in order to calm her agitated mind. Madame Campan also writes in her memoirs of how the Queen found a confessor who had not taken the constitutional oath, whom she would secretly receive. For Easter of 1792, she would not make her Easter duty in public but arranged to hear Mass privately with a non-juring priest. As Madame relates:

> The Queen did perform her Easter devotions in 1792; but she went to the chapel attended only by myself. She desired me beforehand to request one of my relations, who was her chaplain, to celebrate a mass for her at five o'clock in the morning. It was still dark; she gave me her arm and I lighted her with a taper. I left her alone at the chapel door. She did not return to her room until the dawn of day.[35]

So instead of liaisons with a lover, Antoinette was at that season of her life preparing her soul for the sufferings and death which lay ahead, of which her keen sense of the escalating events gave her a strong premonition. I see no reason why Madame Campan would have fabricated such events, which are similar to other reports of the Queen's religious beliefs and practices, especially her own final testament. Furthermore, at the Tuileries, as at Versailles, a private passage linked the Queen's room to her husband's. According to Madame de Tourzel, the royal governess, in her memoirs, one of the first things the Queen did after being forcibly dragged to the Tuileries was to have a private staircase constructed between her room and the King's. It would not be very convenient to dally with a lover when a husband might walk in at any moment from behind the hidden door in the paneling.[36]

The psychology of Count Fersen in his later years must also be taken into account. He was proud of his daring and initiative which had intially delivered Louis XVI, Antoinette and their family from the Tuileries in June, 1791. However, the failure of the Royal Family to escape to Montmédy he blamed on the fact that he had not accompanied them after they left Paris; he was haunted by the night of Varennes for the rest of his life. Indeed, he was murdered by a mob in Stockholm about twenty years later on the exact anniversary of the Royal Family's escape, June 20. He saw his failure as not only costing the lives of his dear friends, but also for destroying what would have been the glory of his career, to have been the one responsible for the rescue of the French Royal Family. Webster maintains that the count seemed to be always looking for signs that the Queen had loved him. He pinned in his diary a scrap of a letter that she had written to someone else, that was passed on to him after her death by Madame de Korff, the Russian lady whose passport Madame de Tourzel had used in the foiled escape. The scrap contained the words: *Adieu, mon coeur est tout à vous*, "Farewell, my heart is all yours."[37] The Queen expressed herself in such a gushing style to all of her friends and family and although the words were in her handwriting there is no indication to whom it was written. There is evidence, however, that Fersen transcribed known letters of the Queen into his journal, and at least in one case altering the original text to make it more personal. He claimed that the Queen had once used his seal with the motto: *Tutto a te mi guida*. "Everything leads me to thee." Webster claims that she had also used the seal of the monarchist Quentin Crauford in her correspondence – using other people's seals was a subterfuge employed in sensitive diplomatic correspondence, but Fersen thought the words were meant as a message for himself. As Webster says: "Everything could certainly not be guiding her to Fersen when she was imprisoned in the Temple and had just refused Jarjayes' plan of escape, saying she could have no happiness apart from her children and therefore she abandoned the idea without even feeling any regret."[38]

A phrase from the Queen's final letter of October 16,

1793, written a few hours before her death to her sister-in-law Madame Élisabeth, has often been interpreted as referring to Fersen. "I had friends. The idea of being separated for ever from them and their troubles forms one of my greatest regrets in dying. Let them know that up to my last moment I was thinking of them...."[39] While the count was probably included among the "friends," it is more likely that the Queen was thinking specifically of the Polignac family. Antoinette had often referred to the Duchesse de Polignac as her "dear heart," and had entrusted her children to her care. The two families had been close, with Louis XVI writing to Madame de Polignac and confiding in her, and they had been rearing their children together. Antoinette had a great capacity for friendship, and the persistence of authors in interpreting her friendly interactions in terms of sex and romance is to obscure what was a beautiful aspect of her personality in itself. As she wrote to Élisabeth of her children in her last letter:

> Let them learn from our example how much the consolation of our affection brought us in the midst of our unhappiness and how happiness is doubled when one can share it with a friend—and where can one find a more loving and truer friend than in one's own family?[40]

For in those last days of Antoinette it is vital to understand her as a mother who had been violently separated from her children. They were the chief subject of her thoughts, and while she showed indifference to her own fate, the mention of them would reduce her to tears. She was in anguish over her eight year old son, as would any parent whose child had been torn from their arms. Not only was she, like any mother, concerned for his diet and hygiene while in the hands of his captors, but she knew that they were beating him, giving him excessive alcohol, teaching him lewd songs, and subjecting him to other forms of unspeakable abuse. Any mother would almost lose her mind; as for the Queen, she only wanted to survive and so someday be united with her son and put her arms around him. What parent would not be tormented if a beloved child was ill in the hospital and they could not be at his side? And yet, in a recently published novel about the Queen, I was sickened when the author with extreme mawkishness portrayed the desperate Antoinette wrapped up in Fersen fantasies while in prison. Such sentimentality and romanticism are obscene, considering the actual bitter and tragic circumstances, expressed by the Queen herself to Élisabeth in her last letter: "I embrace you with all my heart, together with those poor dear children. My God! What agony it is to leave them forever! Adieu! Adieu! I shall henceforth pay attention to nothing but my spiritual duties." [41]

I would just like to add that Antoinette being a Catholic martyr has nothing to do with whether or not she had an affair with Count Fersen. Since genuine martyrdom wipes away all past sins then if the Queen did truly die a martyr's death her martyrdom would blot out past offenses. An extramarital affair may keep one from being officially beatified but there are many whose martyrdom is known only to God. However, those of us who do not believe the Queen and Fersen were lovers do so not because we are trying to prove she was a martyr; we do so because of the historical evidence or lack thereof.

18 PALACES, CHÂTEAUX, AND GARDENS

> "They walked together to the Belvedere. To Madame Élisabeth, coming to Trianon was like entering another world. At Montreuil she had gardens which were quite beautiful, but there was something magical about Antoinette's arcadian retreat. One always had a sense of expectation, as if there were some hidden enchantment only waiting to be discovered. She experienced a repose in the solitude of its groves and winding paths, where one could easily and happily become lost." —from *Trianon* by Elena Maria Vidal

Shortly after her husband's succession to the throne of France in 1774, Antoinette was given the **Petit Trianon** as a refuge from the public life at the main palace of Versailles. Part of the reason for Louis XVI's generous gift was that he wanted to keep his Austrian born wife from meddling in politics. Early on, he may at times have seen her as a foreign spy from whom he had to hide state secrets. He also thought by secluding her, she would be safe from her enemies at court. By giving her Trianon, he was only following a royal tradition. His grandmother Queen Marie used to frequently retire to the nearby Grand Trianon in order to escape the court, as did Louis XIV and Louis XV. Yet when Antoinette sought privacy it was seen as a dereliction of duty.

Antoinette loved nature, gardening and solitude. She wanted her domain at Petit Trianon to have a natural landscape, albeit a fabricated one. She remodeled the Trianon gardens in the informal English-style and she started a farm. Every Sunday the Queen would open the gardens of Trianon to the public; she had large tents erected where all were welcomed to dance and listen to music. She herself would join the dancing, which often included square dancing. Many parents and nannies would bring their small children, and Antoinette, clothed in white linen, would receive them, making conversation regardless of rank or social class. Occasionally, the gardens were used for entertaining foreign guests, in a simple manner which did not add overmuch to the national debt. As consort of the most powerful monarch in Europe, it was expected that the Queen entertain foreign visitors in grand style. The French government was nearly bankrupt due to the help given by King Louis XVI to the American colonists in their war for independence from Britain. To save money, Antoinette would use her private gardens as the site of the entertainments by illuminating the gardens and having everyone wear white. As Baroness Oberkirch remarked, "…The gardens of many private individuals have cost more."[1] Most of the nobles had very extravagant gardens and unlike theirs, the Queen's were not just for pleasure, but had a purpose.

The eighteenth century saw the popularity of gardens that resembled nature as closely as possible. To achieve the effect of rusticity, artificial waterfalls and grottoes were constructed. Antoinette's gardens, designed by Mique and Hubert Robert, were where she enjoyed the outdoors with her family and friends. The Belvedere was also called "the music pavilion," perfect for small concerts, suppers and teas. Nearby was a Grotto on the lake, also designed by Mique. The Grotto, more than any place else, was a spot where the Queen would go for solitude. As Maxime de la Rocheterie describes:

> Not far from the Belvedere, and half hidden in a narrow ravine shaded by thick masses of trees, was a grotto which was only reached after a thousand turnings by a sombre stair cut in the rock. The rivulet which traversed it exhaled a delicious freshness; the light penetrated but dimly through a crack in the roof; a bushy growth concealed it from indiscreet eyes; the moss which carpeted the walls and ceiling prevented the noises of the outer world from entering. It was a place for retirement and rest until the day when the queen was to hear the first murmurs of October 5.[2]

As Madame Campan relates:

> On the evening of the 5th of October, the King was shooting at Meudon, and the Queen was alone in her gardens at Trianon, which she then beheld for the last time in her life. She was sitting in her grotto absorbed in painful reflection, when she received a note from the Comte de Saint-Priest, entreating her to return to Versailles.[3]

We hope that in those quiet moments of repose she found the strength to face the storm.

In May of 1782 Paris was in a flurry over the visit of the "Comte and Comtesse du Nord," the pseudonyms adopted by Grand Duke Paul and Grand Duchess Maria Feodorovna, future Tsar and Empress of Russia. The imperial couple traveled incognito so as to lessen the formality of their European tour, which otherwise would have entailed a variety of stiff state receptions. As it was, the young pair were able to meet with other royals, such as Louis and Antoinette, on a more informal basis. They even won the approval of the Orléans clan by sending calling cards to all the Princes of the Blood the day after their arrival in Paris. Although Paul was called a "Tartar," Maria's tact and wit made the visit of the Russian heirs a social success.

Grand Duke Paul, the son and heir of Empress Catherine the Great, was known for his mercurial temperament and general oddness. He was loved, however, with unconditional and endless devotion by his second wife, Sophie Dorothea of Württemberg, who upon her conversion to Orthodoxy became "Maria Feodorovna." When Maria married Paul in 1776 she was hailed as "an angel incarnate." They made family life a priority and had ten children, two of whom later became Tsars of Russia. Maria Feodorovna had a tenuous relationship with her mother-in-law Empress Catherine, whom she rivaled in both intellect and sense of style. Maria was a skilled horticulturist and the gardens she created at the imperial palace of Pavlovsk lasted for generations to come. She came to Paris with her childhood friend Baroness Oberkirch, whom she called "Lanele." In her memoirs, the Baroness wrote a detailed account of every single event she witnessed with her Imperial friends in Paris and at the French court.[4]

Like many who traveled to the court of Louis XVI and Antoinette, "the Nords" were impressed with the magnificence of the royal palace and the gracious conduct of the sovereigns. Antoinette was uncomfortable at first, since she had heard that the Grand Duchess was an intellectual. And Maria Feodorovna asked, "Am I as beautiful as the Queen?"[5] As one biographer describes the meeting:

> At first sight the grand-duchess, who had a beautiful figure, though somewhat too fat for her age, and who was stiff in her bearing, and fond of displaying her learning, had displeased [Marie-Antoinette]. By an unusual accident, the queen, whose manners were easy, and who had always an amiable word to say, had been embarrassed before these imperial visitors; she had retired to her chamber as though overcome with faintness, and had said, on asking for a glass of water, that she had just discovered that the role of queen was more difficult to play in the presence of other sovereigns, or of princes destined to become sovereigns, than before courtiers. This embarrassment, however, was but momentary; and her reception of her new guests was, on the whole, as affable and gracious as usual....
>
> The first interview was cold; the Queen, as we have said, was disturbed; the King appeared timid. That evening, at dinner, all embarrassment disappeared. The grand-duchess exhibited wit; the grand-duke, who was extremely ugly, and had a face like a Tartar, made up for his ugliness by the vivacity of his eyes and conversation. The queen, 'beautiful as the day,' animated all by her presence.[6]

Antoinette and the Grand Duchess were soon getting along as if they had known each other all of their lives. Louis and Paul found much in common as well, after

Louis' initial shy muttering. They were both religious men who valued family life and simple pleasures; neither was known to have been unfaithful in marriage. Antoinette displayed her usual kindness and thoughtfulness which charmed Maria and Paul. They wanted to see the Children of France; Grand Duke embraced the Dauphin Louis-Joseph and questioned his governess as to his progress, while the Grand Duchess spoke kind words to him. Little Madame Royale sat on the lap of the Grand Duke, and in her outspoken way declared that she liked him and planned to come see him in Russia. Ironically, as an adult Marie-Thérèse-Charlotte would indeed seek refuge in the Russian empire, and Tsar Paul, remembering her sweetness, would readily offer asylum.

Antoinette received Baroness Oberkirch who, it may be recalled, had been present at the border to greet the new Dauphine in 1770. "Madame," said the Queen, "I do not know which I ought to envy most, you the friendship of the Countess du Nord, or her the possession of so faithful a friend, as I understand you to be." The Baroness later penned in her memoirs: "Never shall these words be effaced from my remembrance, nor the gentle glance by which they were accompanied. The Queen made me sit behind her and the Countess du Nord, between Madame de Beckendorf and Madame de Vergennes, and did me the honour of addressing me five or six times during the concert."

The Queen also said: "You come from a province, Baroness, that I thought very beautiful and very loyal when I passed through it. I never can forget that I was there first greeted by the French; that it was there they first called me their queen."[7]

Entertaining heads of state was an expensive enterprise, even when they visited incognito. After treating the imperial couple to an opera and a ballet,

Zémire et Azor by Grétry and *Jean Fracasse au sérail* by Gerdet, and to supper, Antoinette opened her gardens at Trianon; she had musicians playing amid the shrubbery, so that it seemed that the music was wafting through the gardens in an ethereal manner. It was spring; the air was warm and the gardens, fragrant. The shrubbery, the Belevedere and the Grotto were illuminated; everything looked like a fairy land. "How much I should like to live with her!" the Comtesse du Nord exclaimed of the Queen. "How glad I should be if Monsieur le Comte du Nord were dauphin of France!"[8]

Madame Campan's remarks on such occasions are always worth a glance. As recorded in her infamous memoirs:

> Brilliant entertainments were given at Court in honour of the King of Sweden and the Comte du Nord. They were received in private by the King and Queen, but they were treated with much more ceremony than the Emperor [Joseph], and their Majesties always appeared to me to be very cautious before these personages. However, the King one day asked the Russian Grand Duke if it were true that he could not rely on the fidelity of any one of those who accompanied him. The Prince answered him without hesitation, and before a considerable number of persons, that he should be very sorry to have with him even a poodle that was much attached to him, because his mother would take care to have it thrown into the Seine, with a stone round its neck, before he should leave Paris. This reply, which I myself heard, horrified me, whether it depicted the disposition of Catherine, or only expressed the Prince's prejudice against her.[9]

During the course of the Nords' visit, in which they

dined at least once with every member of the Royal Family as well as the Princes and Princesses of the Blood, Maria Feodorovna paid a call on Madame Élisabeth. As one biographer of the Tsarina Maria writes:

> One afternoon Marie Feodorovna paid a visit to Madame Élisabeth the King's sister, a lady who was renowned for her charm of mind and person, and whose tragic ending has caused her name to be remembered with infinite pity. At the conclusion of the visit, the Countess [Diane]of Polignac, lady-in-waiting to the Princess, was ordered to conduct the Grand Duchess to her carriage. As they proceeded down the corridor together, Marie Feodorovna spoke with admiration of Madame Élisabeth, and praised not only her grace and amiability, but her charming face.
> 'She has beauty, certainly,' replied [Diane] de Polignac, 'but her *embonpoint* spoils her appearance altogether.'
> This was not only in extreme bad taste on the part of one of her own ladies in the Royal Palace itself, but it was doubly rude, as the Grand Duchess was also inclined to stoutness, though with her fine carriage it was less noticeable. She was consequently much offended, and, drawing herself up in a stately manner, replied drily, 'I admire Madame Élisabeth immensely. Madame, she could not be prettier, and I did not notice the defect you speak of.'[10]

The Comte and Comtesse du Nord eventually took leave of France and visited several other countries before returning to Russia. They had made themselves beloved by the people of Paris through their generosity to the poor, in which they were also fulfilling the wishes of the Empress Catherine, who had commanded that largesse be given in her name.[11] Before saying farewell, Antoinette gave the Grand Duchess a diamond-studded fan with opera glasses built into the handle. "I know," she said to Marie Feodorowna, "that, like myself, you are short-sighted. Permit me to give you this fan, which may be a convenience to you, and which I trust you will keep as a souvenir of me."

"I will keep it all my life," answered the Grand Duchess.[12]

In 1796 Paul and Maria became Tsar and Empress at the death of Catherine the Great. Maria Feodorowna's life was shattered when her husband Paul was brutally murdered in 1801. Not someone to be swept out of the way, she continued to exert considerable influence as dowager Empress and as a patroness of the arts and of many charities. Her combination of beauty, grace and brains even into old age made her a force with which to be reckoned, although she tempered majesty with gentleness, kindness and wit. Empress Maria died in 1828 at the age of sixty-nine at her beloved Pavlovsk, where she had brought up most of her children with the husband whom she found immensely lovable even if no one else did.

In June of 1784, King Gustavus III of Sweden arrived under the alias of the "Comte de Haga." Antoinette did not care for him, for political reasons as well as for what she had heard concerning his private life. Gustavus was known for his male favorites; some have suggested that Count Fersen was one of them.[13] As Madame Campan relates:

> The Queen, who was much prejudiced against the King of Sweden, received him very coldly. All that

was said of the private character of that sovereign, his connection with the Comte de Vergennes, from the time of the Revolution of Sweden, in 1772, the character of his favourite Armfeldt, and the prejudices of the monarch himself against the Swedes who were well received at the Court of Versailles, formed the grounds of this dislike. He came one day uninvited and unexpected, and requested to dine with the Queen. The Queen received him in the little closet, and desired me to send for her clerk of the kitchen, that she might be informed whether there was a proper dinner to set before Comte d'Haga, and add to it if necessary. The King of Sweden assured her that there would be enough for him; and I could not help smiling when I thought of the length of the menu of the dinner of the King and Queen, not half of which would have made its appearance had they dined in private. The Queen looked significantly at me, and I withdrew. In the evening she asked me why I had seemed so astonished when she ordered me to add to her dinner, saying that I ought instantly to have seen that she was giving the King of Sweden a lesson for his presumption. I owned to her that the scene had appeared to me so much in the bourgeois style, that I involuntarily thought of the cutlets on the gridiron, and the omelette, which in families in humble circumstances serve to piece out short commons. She was highly diverted with my answer, and repeated it to the King, who also laughed heartily at it.[14]

The Swedish king, however, was charmed with both Louis XVI and Antoinette, in spite of various misunderstandings. He enjoyed their warmth, informality and sense of humor. Gustavus was especially enchanted by the illuminated gardens of Trianon, which he thought resembled the Elysian fields. A Swedish scholar once told me that because of Louis and Antoinette, Gustavus was seriously considering becoming a Catholic; I have not yet substantiated that information, but it would not surprise me. He certainly did all he could to save their lives, especially through his delegate, Count Fersen; his attempts to save them ended only with his atrocious murder at a masked ball. Gustavus said of the French king: "Louis XVI is the best and most benevolent prince in existence. His soul radiates serenity. I am filled with admiration."[15]

Trianon was not just for merrymaking and entertaining. It was also a place for repose. The chapel at Petit Trianon was used by Marie-Antoinette during her stays there. Sometimes she would visit her country house for an afternoon but other times she would remain there for a month. The 1774 altar painting by Joseph-Marie Vien portrays Saint Louis IX and Queen Marguerite de Provence visiting Saint Thibauld, whom they were asking to pray for them to have a child. Saint Thibauld of Marly was a thirteenth century saint of royal blood who joined the austere Cistercian order and was known for his great devotion to the Blessed Virgin Mary. The picture depicts the saint handing the King and Queen a branch with eleven white lilies; they would go on to have eleven children. What a very appropriate subject for the chapel of a Queen who spent many years praying for a child. The statues on either side of the altar are of "St. Anne" and "Christ in the Garden of Olives" by Jacques-Augustin Dieudonné, added by King Louis-Philippe in the mid-nineteenth century. The chapel is decorated in a simple style so cherished by Marie-Antoinette, as is the rest of Petit Trianon. There is a tiny onion dome over the chapel roof reminiscent of Austrian architecture. Unfortunately, people referred to all of Trianon as "Little Vienna."

The house itself, that is, Petit Trianon, was a simple affair, with clean strong lines, purely neo-classical. The bare, white walls of the vestibule accentuated the exquisite workmanship of the bronze and blue enamel lantern that hung from the ceiling. The black wrought iron banisters had a curling designs of lyres, caduceus and the gilded monogram "M.A." The antechamber led into the dining room, with its carvings of fruits, nuts and trees entwined with mythological animals and cornucopia, then into the billiard room, with its colored panels portraying sylvan and pastoral scenes. It opened into the large salon. The sea-green panels, on which the white carvings, accented with gold, made a striking contrast with the furniture of red and gold-striped silk. The Queen kept her harpsichord on one side of the room. On the other was a pianoforte, a harp and a music stand. In the next room, the boudoir, the ceiling became very low, as in a true country house. Roses were carved everywhere, entwined with ribbons, doves, quivers and lyres. The Queen's gilded initials appeared here and there, bordered on each side by two torches, symbolizing the flame of love. The boudoir, known as *la petite chambre de la reine*, was also called "the cabinet with moving mirrors." To quote Pierre de Nolhac:

> It contained a mechanical contrivance by which mirrors were slid up from the floor, and concealed the windows. The apparatus was destroyed and the fragments were sold during the Revolution; but the white marble mantel-piece has been preserved, and also the panels which were carved for the Queen. These, with the panels of the Versailles cabinets, are the most perfect remaining from her reign....The narrowest are encircled by rose blooms

on their branches; on the others, the shield, bearing *fleurs-de-lys*, supported by ribbons, appears among lightly—smoking cressets, doves, wreaths and quivers: above these pretty emblems is a lyre, and here and there the Queen's gilded cipher shines in the midst of the roses, between two torches, symbolical of the flame of love. Flowers, as we see, play a large part, suggested by its gardens, in the decoration of Little Trianon. One flower above all has supreme charm for the artist, and on leaving this boudoir, which might be called the rose cabinet, we shall find it, mingled with jasmine and narcissus, in the adjoining room.[16]

The boudoir led into the Queen's bed chamber. Except for the carvings of roses, jasmine and narcissi, it was very simple and plain, with the low ceiling and narrow bed which had muslin hangings embroidered in silk. There was a bronze clock on the mantelpiece, with its Austrian eagles, birds, roses, and shepherds. The King was often with the Queen when she was at Trianon; they were apart only during the time that Antoinette had measles in the late seventies. Here is a quote from one of the royal pages, the Count d'Hézeques:

Louis XVI had the affection of a kind husband for his wife, and was tender and caressing. Far from avoiding her, he came to see her as often as his occupations permitted. Besides their meeting at supper, he visited her many times a day. When the Queen was at the Trianon, the King spent part of the day there. Scandal never attributed little quarrels to them, such as few establishments are without. Their mutual attachment was only augmented by several years that elapsed without children, and in course of time a charming family came to draw their bonds of union closer. Can it ever be believed that the Queen, being a mother, would impoverish France, and injure her own son for her brother's advantage, by sending large sums to him, as was reported? Surely maternal affection is a thousand times stronger than any other natural feeling."[17]

Trianon became the setting for family gatherings as well as time alone. Although Louis did not usually sleep there all night, he often visited Antoinette in the early hours of the morning, walking or riding over from the *château*.[18] In the summer, they usually had their family suppers at Trianon, including Louis' brothers and their wives.

In 1783, Antoinette commissioned the architect Mique to build a village and farm on the grounds of Petit Trianon. The *hameau* was a working farm, managed by the peasant Valy-Busard and his wife; it was not just a folly for amusement. Horticultural and agricultural experiments were tried there, including the potato, introduced to France at Trianon in 1785, for the benefit of all the people. The "little hamlet" was to provide food for the royal family, thus giving an example of self-sufficiency to other nobles, as well as celebrating the traditional agricultural life of the French people. The Queen invited twelve destitute families to live and work in the *hameau*. She saw the farm as a way that her children could experience the healthiness of country life, without actually leaving Versailles. Life in the palace had little or no privacy for the Royal Family; Antoinette wanted her children to have one place where they could be themselves. Louis XVI and Antoinette did not want their children to grow up too isolated from the real world. The farm was an environment where they could get an idea of how ordinary people lived, see the livestock, and learn about plants and nature.

The farm has often been cited as an example of decadence on the part of Antoinette, particularly the dairy with the porcelain milk pitchers. It did provide food for the royal household, however. It must be taken into account that wealthy people all over Europe were building "follies" in their gardens, such as a fake ruined castles, ornate mosques, Chinese tea houses, solely for decoration. At least, Antoinette's *hameau* had a practical purpose. Of course, she would not wear an elaborate court gown when spending time on the farm; she would wear a simple cotton dress and sometimes an apron. Therefore she is still accused of "playing dairy maid." How visiting the livestock with her children and friends can be regarded as extreme frivolity does not make sense; it seems like a fairly innocent pastime. In the main "farm house" there was elegant furniture, a billiard table and such amenities for entertaining in the manner expected of a queen. Foreign guests and ambassadors were occasionally given hospitality at the *hameau*, although it was mainly just for the family and the peasants who lived there permanently. There was also an orchard, berry bushes, and lots of vegetables in the garden, as well as fish in the lake. Her orange trees produced bushels of blossoms every spring from which was produced fragrant orange-flower water; Antoinette gave bottles of it to Louis and her entire entourage. Everyone needs a refuge, a place to be quiet. In our busy world there seems to be more of an appreciation of Antoinette's creative way of carving out a retreat for herself and her family, one which patronized and exulted French craftsmanship while simultaneously helping the poor.

In 2015 Christie's auctioned a drawing by a teenaged Antoinette.[19] As an Austrian Archduchess Antoinette learned how to draw and paint. It seems she was always interested in the work of ordinary people, for she drew a scene of people working at a tavern with a church, a walled town and mountains in the background. In September, 1777 Marie-Antoinette had a farmers' market in the park at Trianon to inaugurate the opening of her new gardens. The Queen wore peasant attire and served at an outdoor tavern. Pierre de Nolhac describes the market thus:

> A market-place was set up on the lawn...where the baker, the confectioner, and the purveyor of charcuterie dispensed their wares...and even the cook's shop was busy in the open air. All these stalls were connected by a garland of roses....There were shows of all sorts....Actors...gave several performances on an improvised stage....The avenues leading to Trianon were lined with the booths of Paris shopkeepers who had been engaged to come, their expenses being paid. [20]

The Queen always sought ways to celebrate the life of the ordinary French people, particularly the peasants, whose industry fed the nation. Far from keeping her beloved Trianon for herself, she shared it with the public on several occasions, although many then accused her of being too democratic and not putting enough distance between herself and the people.

The ***château* de Saint-Cloud**, a country estate owned by the Orléans family on the outskirts of Paris, was bought by Louis XVI for Antoinette in 1785. The king sold properties owned by the crown in the south of France in order to pay for the *château*. Antoinette thought it was vital to get her children away from the unhealthy environment of Versailles, and Petit Trianon was not far enough way. So many members of the royal family, including Louis himself as a child, had become ill with tuberculosis over the years, and so the Queen wanted to bring her children into cleaner, healthier air. As it was their youngest daughter and oldest son would die of tuberculosis in 1787 and 1789. The King put the *château* of Saint-Cloud in the Queen's name, which outraged many French people, since a Queen owning property in her own right and having complete control of it was something that had not happened since the Middle Ages.

After the Royal Family was taken prisoner in October 1789, they were still permitted at times to go to Saint-Cloud for the country air and some exercise. During the Restoration of 1815-1830, the Royal Family used Saint-Cloud as a summer residence, and it was put in the name Antoinette's daughter Marie-Thérèse even as it had been owned by Antoinette. Marie-Thérèse would often walk from Saint-Cloud to her sanctuary at Villeneuve l'Étang. During the Commune of 1871, the palace was destroyed, and no longer stands. Only the gardens remain, and the chapel built by Antoinette.

The *château* of **Marly** was built in 1679 as a place for Louis XIV to stay while he was building Versailles. He continued to use it as a retreat from the protocol of the main royal residence, while constructing a fabulous garden that would offer summer recreation to the court for years to come. The *machine de Marly* was a feat of hydraulic engineering which pumped the waters of the Seine into a grand cascades, fountains, ponds and canals at Marly, with the water flowing on to the park at Versailles a few miles away. Even in the days of Louis XVI and Antoinette, Marly was a place for the court to recreate in grand style and a special costume was required. The *château* itself was small and so were the surrounding pavilions, which were supposed to make for a casual environment, although plumes, powder and jewels were *de rigueur*. The King had to pay for the food and entertainments; Louis XVI hated the cost and Antoinette disliked the stiffness of being formally dressed while promenading and playing cards. The arrangement of the gardens sounds like an Incan, Mayan or Aztec shrine to the sun but then Louis XIV always lived up to his name of Sun-King. In the words of Madame Campan:

> Every age has its peculiar colouring; Marly showed that of Louis XIV even more than Versailles. Everything…appeared to have been produced by the magic power of a fairy's wand. Not the slightest trace of all this splendour remains; the revolutionary spoilers even tore up the pipes which served to supply the fountains. Perhaps a brief description of this palace and the usages established there by Louis XIV may be acceptable. The very extensive gardens of Marly ascended almost imperceptibly to the Pavilion of the Sun, which was occupied only by the King and his family. The pavilions of the twelve zodiacal signs bounded the two sides of the lawn. They were connected by bowers impervious to the rays of the sun. The pavilions nearest to that of the sun were reserved for the Princes of the blood and the ministers; the rest were occupied by persons holding superior offices at Court, or invited to stay at Marly….During half of Louis XV's reign the ladies still wore the *habit de cour de Marly*, so named by Louis XIV, and which differed little from, that devised for Versailles. The French gown, gathered in the back, and with great hoops, replaced this dress, and continued to be worn till the end of the reign of Louis XVI. The diamonds, feathers, rouge, and embroidered stuffs spangled with gold, effaced all trace of a rural residence; but the people loved to

see the splendour of their sovereign and a brilliant Court glittering in the shades of the woods. After dinner, and before the hour for cards, the Queen, the Princesses, and their ladies, paraded among the clumps of trees, in little carriages, beneath canopies richly embroidered with gold, drawn by men in the King's livery. The trees planted by Louis XIV were of prodigious height, which, however, was surpassed in several of the groups by fountains of the clearest water; while, among others, cascades over white marble, the waters of which, met by the sunbeams, looked like draperies of silver gauze, formed a contrast to the solemn darkness of the groves.[21]

Antoinette eventually talked Louis out of spending time at Marly, seeing it as a boring waste of money. In spite of Marly being a popular spot for the public to come and watch the Royal Family "recreate" it was destroyed with a particular vengeance by the revolutionaries. Nothing of the *château* remains although parts of the gardens have been restored in recent times.

Montreuil was given to Madame Élisabeth of France in 1781 by Louis XVI and Antoinette. Since life at the royal palace afforded little or no privacy, the King and the Queen decided to give the seventeen year old princess a place to call her own. Built in 1776 for the Princesse de Guemènée when she was Royal Governess, Louis XVI bought it when the Guemènés went bankrupt. Élisabeth had played there as a child so the estate already had happy connotations for her. There were paths amid the shady groves; from the property one could glimpse Paris glittering in the distance. According to Imbert de Saint-Amand's *Marie-Antoinette and the*

End of the Old Regime:

> In spite of her love of solitude, she was the only princess of the royal family who had no country-house. One day in 1781, Marie Antoinette and Madame Élisabeth were driving along the Avenue de Paris. 'If you like,' said the Queen to her young sister-in-law, we will stop at that house in Montreuil, where you used to like to go when you were a little girl.'
> 'I shall be delighted,' answered Madame Élisabeth; 'for I have spent many happy hours there.'
> The Queen and the Princess got out of their carriage, and just as they were crossing the threshold, Marie Antoinette said, 'Sister, you are now in your own house. This is to be your Trianon. The King has the pleasure of offering this present to you, and has given me the happiness of informing you.' Madame Élisabeth was then but seventeen years old. The King decided that she should not sleep at Montreuil until she was twenty-five....The first thing that Madame Élisabeth did with her new property was to give to Madame de Mackau [the sub-governess] a little house adjacent, upon the estate. She thought that the best way of inaugurating her taking possession was by sharing it with her former instructress. The Baroness of Mackau, who was not rich, accepted gratefully the gift of the Princess, and established herself at Montreuil with her daughter, Madame de Bombelles, whom Madame Élisabeth treated like an old friend.[22]

Henceforth, the princess spent all her days at Montreuil, living an almost monastic existence with her household. After morning Mass in the Royal Chapel, they would walk or ride to her estate, where the day was strictly regulated into hours of prayer, work and recreation. She and her ladies would dine together at the same table; in the evening they would recite the night prayer of Compline before returning to the palace for the night. Like Petit Trianon, Montreuil had a grotto, an orangerie, and a dairy. Madame Élisabeth donated the milk to poor children. One of her maids was a Swiss girl who had left the man she loved behind in Switzerland. When Antoinette heard of the girl's plight, she sent for the fiancé, called Jacques Bosson, and paid for the wedding. The incident inspired a popular song, Pauvre Jacques.

> *Pauvre Jacques, quand j'étais près de toi*
> *Je ne sentais pas ma misère;*
> *Mais à présent que tu vis loin de moi*
> *Je manque de tout sur la terre.*

> Poor Jack, while I was near to thee,
> Tho' poor, my bliss was unalloyed;
> But now thou dwell'st so far from me,
> The world appears a lonesome void.

Madame Élisabeth was at Montreuil on October 5, 1789 when word came that the mob was marching on Versailles. Although she had many opportunities to leave France, she chose to be imprisoned with Louis XVI, Antoinette and their children. She shared all of their humiliations and hardships in the Temple prison, without regret. The following incident is recorded from December 1792:

> On 7th December a deputation from the Commune brought an order that the royal family should be deprived of 'knives, razors, scissors, penknives, and

all other cutting instruments.' The King gave up a knife, and took from a morocco case a pair of scissors and a penknife; and the officials then searched the room, taking away the little toilet implements of gold and silver, and afterwards removing the Princesses' working materials. Returning to the King's room, they insisted upon seeing what remained in his pocket-case. 'Are these toys which I have in my hand also cutting instruments?' asked the King, showing them a cork-screw, a turn-screw, and a steel for lighting. These also were taken from him. Shortly afterwards Madame Élisabeth was mending the King's coat, and, having no scissors, was compelled to break the thread with her teeth.

'What a contrast!' he exclaimed, looking at her tenderly. 'You wanted nothing in your pretty house at Montreuil.'

'Ah, brother,' she answered, 'how can I have any regret when I partake your misfortunes?' [23]

Bellevue was a country estate originally built by Louis XV for Madame de Pompadour. It was on a hill overlooking the Seine and the forest of Meudon; the view was said to be truly magnificent. In 1775, after he had become king, Louis XVI gave Bellevue to his maiden aunts Adélaïde, Victoire, and Sophie, the surviving daughters of Louis XV, known as Mesdames Tantes. Madame Louise having already entered the Carmelite monastery, Louis thought it would be good for his other aunts to have a retreat from the court, a house they could call their own. For all their genuine piety, Mesdames Tantes had manipulated Louis and gossiped about Antoinette in the early years of their marriage, coining the term *L'Autrichienne*, an epithet that would later be taken up by the revolutionaries. It probably helped maintain the peace at court for Antoinette to be at her Trianon while the Aunts were at their Bellevue. According to the Comte d'Hézecques, who in his capacity as a page at Versailles witnessed the inner workings of the court:

> The position of Mesdames at Court being obscure and unsatisfactory, they were seldom seen there. They spent the chief part of the year either at Bellevue, on that splendid height that commands the proud city and the charming country around it...Madame Adélaïde and Madame Victoire were the only survivors of the four daughters of Louis XV who outlived their father. The third, Madame Sophie, had died two years before....Mesdames the Aunts only came to Paris in the winter, as they had been able to stay at Bellevue up to the 5th of October. Seeing that they were of very little use to their nephew, unable to enjoy his confidence, and fearing measures opposed to their religious opinions, they at last decided on going to Rome. Possibly in their solitude, standing in a position whence they could form a better judgment of the course of events, theirs was the surer presentiment of all the trouble that hung over their family; therefore, they separated themselves from it for life, but they could not prevail on Madame Élisabeth to leave her brother and accompany them. . . . No doubt Mesdames did not find themselves happy at Rome. The news of the fall of the throne of their fathers and the sorrows of their family came to disturb the peace they might have enjoyed in the Eternal City. They could at least carry their tears and prayers for their guilty country to the foot of the altar, till the day when they were forced to quit the hospitable city that had received them, by conquests

that the noble head of the Church could neither arrest nor foresee. So they left Rome to retire to Naples; and, after several changes of their place of refuge, Madame Adélaïde, had the sorrow of seeing her younger sister die at Trieste. Her own mournful existence was shortened by grief, and she soon died herself at Klagenfurth. [24]

In the 1780's Mesdames Tantes had Mique create an English-style garden at Bellevue, complete with a tower, a lake, a mill, a dairy and a grotto, similar to what Antoinette had at Trianon. It is fascinating that while they did not always approve of the Queen they imitated her in that for which she was greatly criticized, the creation of fanciful gardens. The tower and some other structures of the gardens of Bellevue survived well into the twentieth century; little is left of it today. The palace was looted during the Revolution. In 1823, it was demolished.

Miniature palaces surrounded by elaborate gardens being the style of the 1770's and 80's, the Comte d'Artois, youngest brother of Louis XVI, and prince of the fashionable world, was not to be outdone. Artois' **Bagatelle** was in the Bois de Boulogne on the outskirts of Paris, which made it immensely convenient for a prince who so enjoyed the night life of the capital. Indeed *Parva sed apta* "small but convenient" were the words which Artois had graven over the entrance of his new house. Originally built as a small hunting lodge for Maréchal d'Estrées, Artois bought the property in 1775, tearing down the old house. He hired the architect François-Joseph Bélanger to build a small neo-classical structure which he called "Bagatelle" from the Italian word "bagatella" which meant "trifle." Antoinette wagered that the house could not be finished within three months; Artois won the bet. The house and the gardens cost around two million livres. The park of Bagatelle was designed by the Scotsman Thomas Blaikie, with sham ruins, ponds, primitive hermits' huts, a pagoda, waterfalls and grottoes. It became the site of many parties and entertainments held by the Artois family. While Artois lost his Bagatelle during the Revolution, along with everything else, he regained it during the Restoration. It stayed in his family until the Revolution of 1830.

The gardener Thomas Blaikie also worked for Antoinette at times; it seems she enjoyed his outspoken, curmudgeonly ways. She came to see him at the Bagatelle immediately after the Royal Family was brought to live in the Tuileries in October 1789. Blaikie had not been paid everything that Artois and the Duc d'Orléans owed him and was in need of funds. The Queen visited him in his cottage which she found quite clean and neat; they talked about the Revolution and she told him she would never forget him.[25] Later, he worked for Joséphine at Malmaison. He was eventually given a pension by the son of Orléans, Louis-Philippe the Citizen-King.

While the young Artois is usually dismissed as being a shallow and decadent character he had a deeper side. Later in life, after the death of his last mistress Madame de Polastron, Artois (Charles X) became so devout that his enemies accused him of having been secretly ordained a priest. He was falsely rumored to be secretly offering Mass at the Tuileries, a deed no one would have tried to pin on the young Artois. The *château* and gardens of Bagatelle still exist and are open to the public.

The **Palais de Luxembourg** was built in 1615 by Henri IV's widow Queen Marie de Médicis during her regency on behalf of her son, Louis XIII. Decorated in an elaborate Florentine style, its long galleries were perfect for displaying the gigantic canvases painted by Peter Paul Rubens of Queen Marie's life and her husband's. The gardens were vast and magnificent. She bequeathed the palace to her second son, Gaston d'Orléans; it passed through many hands until it came to Louis XIV in 1694. Louis let his scandalous grand-niece, Marie-Louise Élisabeth d'Orléans, live there, giving the place a bad name, until her death in 1719. The palace became a museum in 1750, a function later taken by the Louvre. In 1778, Louis XVI made it the property of his brother, the Comte de Provence. It became the Paris residence of the Comte and Comtesse de Provence and thus the center of much political plotting and intrigues. At the heart of the cabal was Madame de Balbi. While Louis XVI broke with tradition and refused to take a mistress, it was not so with his brothers. When the Comtesse de Provence became inordinately attached to one of her ladies-in-waiting, Madame de Gourbillon, the Comte de Provence, the future Louis XVIII, sought the company of a certain Madame de Balbi. Anne Jacobé Nompar de Caumont La Force, Comtesse de Balbi, born in 1758, was not a beauty but her biting wit kept Provence entertained. She had once been the governess of the children of the Comte d'Artois. She soon gained ascendancy over his circle, known for its political plots. According to *The Nation*:

> The Countess de Balbi, who first became the favorite of the Count de Provence, was the daughter of Bertrand de Caumont La Force and of Madeleine de Galard de Brassac de Béarn. M. de Caumont was one of the Count's gentlemen, and his daughter was appointed *'dame pour accompagner'* and afterwards *'dame d'atours'* of the Countess, who

was called Madame. M. de Balbi, her husband, was of a Genoese family and served as Colonel in the regiment of Bourbon. Madame de Balbi was tolerably pretty, was a great coquette, and was feared for her wit, which spared nothing and nobody. She pleased the Count de Provence by her conversation more than by her charms. The Count de Balbi was a jealous husband (a rare being at that time), but he was exiled to Senlis; he afterwards emigrated and returned to France at the beginning of the Consulate. Madame de Balbi became the great power in the house of the Count de Provence. 'She was a sort of Dubarry, but well born.'[26]

Some historians have claimed the relationship between Provence and Madame de Balbi was strictly platonic; others claim the contrary. Whatever it was that went on between them, other than conniving at late night suppers and having lively games of backgammon, Provence installed Madame de Balbi in apartments at both the Petit Luxembourg and at Versailles. He also named some gardens after her. She no longer lived with her husband but remained a fixture in the household of Provence until the emigration. She was ridiculed by the Revolutionary pamphleteers for her influence over a prince who was politically liberal but who clung to his royal dignity in hopes for someday gaining the throne. It was Madame de Balbi who, quite ironically, counseled Provence on certain matters of conscience in regards to receiving Holy Communion from constitutional priests. In *Essays on the Early Part of the French Revolution*, John Wilson Croker remarks:

> In stating the motives that induced [Provence] to quit France he mentions his reluctance to accept the services of the revolutionized clergy:— 'I was

convinced,' he says, 'that I had no choice between apostasy and martyrdom; the former revolted me, and I will own I felt no great vocation for the latter. I talked a great deal with Madame de Balbi on this subject, and we agreed that there was a third course open to me, which was to abandon a country where the usual exercise of our religious duties was about to be proscribed.' Now Madame de Balbi (*née* Caumont de la Force) was a lady separated from her husband, and supposed to be higher in Monsieur's favour than she ought to be; and we wish we could only smile at the simplicity with which the Prince makes a public confession that, though he would not accept the ministration of a Constitutional priest, he consulted Madame de Balbi on the spiritual concerns of his conscience! [27]

I suppose we should be edified that Provence contemplated the possibility of martyrdom, in light of some of his other behaviors. His own account of events dwells a great deal on what he had to eat and drink in the inns at which he stayed during his escape. He was a Bourbon, after all; the Bourbons appreciated good food, Provence perhaps more than the others. As for Madame de Balbi, they parted during Louis XVIII's years of exile, when he had to endure poverty and humiliation, which he expected his wife and family to share with him but not his mistress. Besides, Madame de Balbi gave birth to twins who were not fathered by Louis XVIII. She returned to France during Napoleon's reign and lived in the provinces. She died in 1842, long after the Bourbons had been restored and exiled again.[28]

One of the Revolutionary leaders and greatest adversaries of Louis and Antoinette was their mutual cousin Philippe d'Orléans. He was married to the lovely and devout Adélaïde de Bourbon-Penthièvre, the sister-in-law of the Princesse de Lamballe, and sole heiress of one of the greatest fortunes in France. Philippe and Adélaïde, who were then the Duc and Duchesse de Chartres, had six children in eight years, one of whom was Louis-Philippe, the future Citizen-King. In spite of her devotion to him and their offspring, Philippe grew bored with his wife and took up with the writer Madame de Genlis, who liked to be counter-cultural by not wearing make-up. To the surprise of Paris, he made his mistress, who was also his wife's best friend, the governess of his children. She had them chop firewood and other menial chores in an effort to make them democratic. Although Philippe Égalité, as he came to be called during the Revolution, liked to portray himself as a man of the people, he was not averse to creating his own stately gardens. The **Parc Monceau** was in the English style, like the gardens of Trianon; while Antoinette was criticized for her gardens, Orléans was not. The Parc Monceau was designed by Louis Carrogis Carmontelle, at the request of the Duc de Chartres, later the Duc d'Orléans, on a small parcel of land he had purchased. The Scottish gardener Thomas Blaikie also worked on parts of it. The landscaping included a pavilion as well as a windmill, a pyramid, and some Corinthian pillars near the pond. There are said to be many masonic references in the designs of the park, which is not surprising since Philippe was Grand Master of the Grand Orient de France, the governing body of French freemasonry. The Parc Monceau is featured in the novel *Madame Royale* as the setting of the picnic to which Louis-Philippe invites Marie-Thérèse-Charlotte.

19 THE DIAMOND NECKLACE

> "Fatal moment! in which the Queen found herself, in consequence of this highly impolitic step, on trial with a subject, who ought to have been dealt with by the power of the King alone." —Madame Campan

On August 15, 1785, the "Affair of the Necklace" broke upon France, just as Louis XVI and Antoinette were about to assist at the Mass of the Assumption, the patronal solemnity of the realm. Cardinal Prince Louis de Rohan, who was supposed to offer the Mass, was publicly arrested in his pontifical robes for his part in the debacle. The Diamond Necklace scandal was one of the events which precipitated the French Revolution of 1789 and the fall of the monarchy. After perusing the internet I think it becomes necessary to affirm once again that Antoinette, according to several major biographers, was an innocent victim in one of the most sordid intrigues in history. She never sought to possess the necklace. For one thing, it was not to her liking; she preferred light, aerial creations. A few scholars even doubt that Madame du Barry, whom the jewelers had in mind when they originally designed the huge, garish necklace, called a "Slave's Collar," would have cared for it, her taste being not quite so grotesque as is generally assumed. Also, by 1785 Antoinette had cultivated simpler tastes; she was under the influence of Madame de Polignac, who never wore diamonds. It is known that when Boehmer tried to sell her the necklace, she remarked that France needed ships, not diamonds.[1]

The fault of the King and Queen was in attempting to be too democratic and open in the handling of the proceedings. Instead of trying to settle the disaster quietly, there was a public trial of the Cardinal, for whom Antoinette harbored resentments; her mother the Empress had called him *ce vilain eveque* or "that villain bishop."[2] Not only had Cardinal de Rohan rudely infiltrated one of her garden parties, but a letter he had written to one of Louis XV's ministers was found by Madame du Barry and turned into a joke about Antoinette's mother. He had many mistresses; he symbolized the worst decadence of the French nobility and the corrupt higher clergy. He was Grand Almoner of Versailles due to his ancestral prerogatives, but neither the King nor the Queen had any use for him. The scandal rid them of him, but at a very high price. They could never have known at the onset the cast of bizarre characters with whom the Cardinal was involved, who were brought into the light of day. The Queen's name was dragged through the mud by being associated with such people in the gazettes, people who were complete strangers to her. Biographer Maxime de la Rocheterie affirms that even had the King and Queen tried to suppress the scandal, the results would have been disastrous nevertheless.[3]

How did it all come about? Through a woman who lied. Each lie told by Madame de la Motte was more outrageous than the last, yet individuals motivated by lust or ambition or greed believed her tales. She told people that she was an intimate friend of the Queen, who had never even heard of her. The swindle was tragic for all involved, especially for the innocent Antoinette, for it confirmed in the popular imagination all the salacious gossip which portrayed her as a loose, extravagant woman.

Jeanne de Valois-Saint-Rémy, later known as the Comtesse de la Motte, was from a destitute family with an alcoholic father who claimed to be descended from an illegitimate son of Henri II, and therefore claimed to be the last of the royal Valois. Jeanne was sent out to beg in the streets at age four and was brutally beaten by her mother when she did not return with enough money. Her father died and her mother eventually abandoned Jeanne and her siblings, who were found begging and stealing to fend off starvation. A noble family took them in, Jeanne was fed and cared for but her personality was already fixed; she was amoral to a sociopathic degree, and a convincing liar. Jeanne married Nicolas de la Motte, from the lower untitled nobility, and soon they were calling themselves "Comte and Comtesse." She had managed to secure a royal pension based upon her Valois antecedents. She gained another when she visited Versailles and pretended to faint in Madame Élisabeth's antechamber. But she needed much more money than two pensions to live in the princely style she felt she deserved. Jeanne reached out to Cardinal de Rohan. She told him that she was a confidante of the Queen. The Cardinal believed it, knowing the Queen was fairly democratic with her friendships. He gave Jeanne more money and saw that her husband was given a post as a bodyguard of the Comte d'Artois.

The Cardinal was infatuated with the Queen, and had tried in a thousand ways to win her attention, even by coming uninvited to one of her *fêtes* at Trianon, which only infuriated her more. He wanted to belong to her inner circle at Trianon, not understanding that both Louis and Antoinette disliked playboy prelates. His infatuation is the only thing that explains why he was taken in by a woman like Jeanne de la Motte, whose airs of grandeur could not hide her crudeness and lack of education. Knowing about the necklace which Boehmer and Bassange had offered to the Queen but had been refused, she and her lover, the forger and gigolo Rétaux de Villette, began passing notes on to the Cardinal. The forged notes were on gold-edged writing paper and signed "Marie-Antoinette de France" and asked the Cardinal to be the intermediary for her secret purchase of the famous necklace. He agreed, secured the necklace from the jewelers, and gave it to the La Mottes, who broke it up and sold the diamonds.

Meanwhile, at Versailles months passed since the Queen had told Boehmer that she had no intention of buying the "Slave's Collar." Suddenly, the Queen began to receive strange notes from the jeweler, thanking her for her "purchase," and hinting that her first "payment" was due. She assumed the man had become deranged and discarded the notes without another thought. Then Boehmer began to pester Madame Campan, while the latter was on holiday in the country. Madame Campan persuaded her mistress to receive him. On August 12, 1785, he came to Versailles in a state which bordered on hysteria. He claimed that the Queen had secretly bought the diamond necklace from him, using Cardinal de Rohan, the Grand Almoner of France, as an intermediary. The necklace was delivered to the Cardinal in February, but he, Boehmer, had not yet been paid the first installment, due August 1. As he saw the Queen's blank expression, and realized she knew nothing of any such transaction, he fell to his knees, sobbing, declaring himself to be ruined.

It is ironic that the tragedy exploded on the patronal feast day of the kingdom, the Assumption of the Blessed Virgin Mary, which was also kept as the feast day of the Queens of France. It is an additional irony that a Cardinal of the Roman Church was instrumental in the culmination of the scandal through his own unworthy and imprudent conduct. Here is Madame Campan's account of the Cardinal's arrest:

> On the following Sunday, the 15th of August, being the Assumption, at twelve o'clock, at the very moment when the Cardinal, dressed in his pontifical garments, was about to proceed to the chapel, he was sent for into the King's closet, where the Queen then was.
>
> The King said to him, 'You have purchased diamonds of Boehmer?'
>
> 'Yes, Sire.'
>
> 'What have you done with them?'
>
> 'I thought they had been delivered to the Queen.'
>
> 'Who commissioned you?'
>
> 'A lady, called the Comtesse de Lamotte-Valois, who handed me a letter from the Queen; and I thought I was gratifying her Majesty by taking this business on myself.'
>
> The Queen here interrupted him and said, 'How, monsieur, could you believe that I should select you, to whom I have not spoken for eight years, to negotiate anything for me, and especially through the mediation of a woman whom I do not even know?'
>
> 'I see plainly,' said the Cardinal, 'that I have been duped. I will pay for the necklace; my desire to please your Majesty blinded me; I suspected no trick in the affair, and I am sorry for it.'

He then took out of his pocket-book a letter from the Queen to Madame de Lamotte, giving him this commission. The King took it, and, holding it towards the Cardinal, said:

'This is neither written nor signed by the Queen. How could a Prince of the House of Rohan, and a Grand Almoner of France, ever think that the Queen would sign Marie Antoinette de France? Everybody knows that queens sign only by their baptismal names. But, monsieur,' pursued the King, handing him a copy of his letter to Boehmer, 'have you ever written such a letter as this?'

Having glanced over it, the Cardinal said, 'I do not remember having written it.'

'But what if the original, signed by yourself, were shown to you?'

'If the letter be signed by myself it is genuine.'

He was extremely confused, and repeated several times, 'I have been deceived, Sire; I will pay for the necklace. I ask pardon of your Majesties.'

'Then explain to me,' resumed the King, 'the whole of this enigma. I do not wish to find you guilty; I had rather you would justify yourself. Account for all the manoeuvres with Boehmer, these assurances and these letters.'

The Cardinal then, turning pale, and leaning against the table, said, 'Sire, I am too much confused to answer your Majesty in a way—'

'Compose yourself, Cardinal, and go into my cabinet; you will there find paper, pens, and ink,– write what you have to say to me.'

The Cardinal went into the King's cabinet, and returned a quarter of an hour afterwards with a document as confused as his verbal answers had been. The King then said, 'Withdraw, monsieur.' The Cardinal left the King's chamber, with the

Baron de Breteuil, who gave him in custody to a lieutenant of the Body Guard, with orders to take him to his apartment. M. d'Agoult, *aide-major* of the Body Guard, afterwards took him into custody, and conducted him to his hotel, and thence to the Bastille....

The moment the Cardinal's arrest was known a universal clamour arose. Every memorial that appeared during the trial increased the outcry. On this occasion the clergy took that course which a little wisdom and the least knowledge of the spirit of such a body ought to have foreseen. The Rohans and the House of Condé, as well as the clergy, made their complaints heard everywhere. The King consented to having a legal judgment, and early in September he addressed letters-patent to the Parliament, in which he said that he was 'filled with the most just indignation on seeing the means which, by the confession of his Eminence the Cardinal, had been employed in order to inculpate his most dear spouse and companion.'

Fatal moment! in which the Queen found herself, in consequence of this highly impolitic step, on trial with a subject, who ought to have been dealt with by the power of the King alone. The Princes and Princesses of the House of Condé, and of the Houses of Rohan, Soubise, and Guemenée, put on mourning, and were seen ranged in the way of the members of the Grand Chamber to salute them as they proceeded to the palace, on the days of the Cardinal's trial; and Princes of the blood openly canvassed against the Queen of France.[4]

In the months that followed, the squalid affair was brought to public trial. The Queen desired everything to be as open as possible, but the Parisian lawyers were delighted that the case proved to doubly besmirch the Church and the Crown. As the story unraveled, it came to light that the Cardinal had often consulted a Sicilian alchemist named Joseph Balsamo, who styled himself the "Comte de Cagliostro," a dabbler in the occult. Cagliostro claimed not only to be two thousand years old, but to possess prescience of future events. He had even conjured up a vision of the Queen in a carafe for the benefit of the Cardinal. The motto of Cagliostro was *Lilia pedibus destrue*, "Tread underfoot the Lilies." The implications of Cagliostro's involvement horrified the King and Queen, as much as did the Cardinal's story about a nocturnal rendezvous with the Queen in the palace gardens. Most people believed the tale about his encounter with a lady in white, who handed him a rose, since it was common knowledge that Her Majesty loved to take walks in the moonlight. However, the Cardinal had been duped again. The LaMotte woman had paid a streetwalker to impersonate the Queen, attired in a white dress and veiled hat.

In the end, the Cardinal was acquitted of all guilt, and was allowed to go free. He was hailed as a hero by the French people for escaping the clutches of the evil, lustful *L'Auchrichienne*. When Louis refused to have the man back at Versailles, he was accused of tyranny. Meanwhile, Antoinette's reputation was soiled beyond repair. Many thought the Cardinal was her lover, and that she had used him to procure the necklace for her, afterwards abandoning him to his fate. The La Motte woman, after being publicly branded as a thief, escaped from jail to England, where she wrote and published a "memoir" about the Queen's "private life." It was the manuscript of the "memoirs" that the Polignacs had gone to England to buy, but Monsieur de la Motte had it published anyway. Louis tried to buy up every copy, but one copy came into the wrong hands, and was republished. The book was a sensational best seller. Antoinette's good name was destroyed. She was hissed at the Opera, and compared to every wicked and wanton queen who had ever lived, including Jezebel and Messalina. In 1791, Jeanne fell, or was pushed, from an upstairs window in London and died, two years before the Queen herself was killed.

In spite of Cardinal de Rohan's acquittal, the King banished him to the Benedictine monastery at Chaise-Dieu. The Cardinal was elected to the Estates-General and sat in the National Assembly in 1789. However, after the 1790 Civil Constitution of the Clergy was passed, Rohan refused to take the oath denying the papal supremacy and left France for Germany. He opened his house at Ettenheim to faithful Catholics and non-juring priests displaced by the Revolution. He embraced a life of penance and gave all of his money to helping the poor. He died in 1803 in the odor of sanctity.[5] The Rohan family was paying off the debt of the stolen necklace until the 1890's.[6]

20 THE REVOLUTION

> "I saw everything, knew everything, and have forgotten everything." —Marie-Antoinette, Queen of France

Of Louis XVI, Nesta Webster writes: "As Soulavie says again, under former kings the monarch was the idol of the nation, under Louis XVI, on the contrary, the nation was the object almost of adoration of the King."[1] She discusses the painting by Hersent of "Louis XVI relieving the Afflicted" of which an eye-witness later said that art completely imitated reality in that case: Louis did indeed go among the peasants distributing alms, including firewood.[2] The many reforms of Louis XVI began in 1774 at the beginning of his reign, including the abolition of torture, civil rights for Jews and Protestants, the abolition of servitude and *lettres de cachet*, and many more. By July of 1789, with the problems with the Estates-General and the death of his oldest son, he was essentially having a nervous breakdown. Indeed, the King had a series of physical and mental collapses in the last turbulent years of his life; it is amazing he was able to function at all. Beginning in 1787, he contracted a painful case of the skin disease erysipelas. He began drinking heavily as well. He was known at times to have crying jags, which some historians try to attribute to Louis possibly "discovering" his wife's "affair" with Fersen, but Louis had much graver issues to worry about. Indeed, Antoinette became his strength, and therefore more than ever became the target of the pamphleteers and of those who wanted control of the throne. Louis XVI did not want to leave his people in the hands of extremists and the Queen, of course, would not leave his side. "I will die at his feet" she was heard to say repeatedly, when it was suggested that she try to escape on her own during the Revolution's dark days.[3]

On several occasions, when attacked by the mob, it had been the hope of the revolutionary leaders, especially the Duc d'Orléans, that the royal couple would either flee or be killed. The fact that Louis and Antoinette were able to ride the tide of total upheaval for four years can be attributed to their courage, which gained the respect even of those intent upon tearing them to pieces. The King and especially the Queen had the gift of turning enemies, such as Mirabeau, Barnave, and Toulan, into friends. As the revolutionary leader Barnave found, according to Beaulieu, "the Queen treated him with that affectionate politeness which had led her to being given the title of 'Mary, full of grace (*Marie, pleine de graces*).'"[4] The blunders of the far right, that is, the *émigrés* abroad, led to the destruction of Louis, Antoinette and their family as much as did the malice of their enemies on the left. Nevertheless, the King, Queen and Madame Élisabeth were distinguished for their profound courtesy, kindness and forgiveness, even in the most desperate situations. Their trials forged Louis and Antoinette into one. At the beginning of their imprisonment in the Temple in August 1792, the Queen shed tears, saying to her husband:

> 'I weep less for myself than for you.'
>
> Louis XVI replied: 'Our eyes were not given us to weep with, but to look up to Heaven, the source of all our consolations....'
>
> At these words, the Queen dried her eyes and faced the situation with the magnificent courage that sustained her to the end. It was now that she entered the fifth phase of her life. Once, a light-hearted child—then a pleasure-loving woman—a mother—a politician—she fulfilled her tragic destiny to the last and became that great figure revered by all noble minds of posterity—the Queen Martyr.[5]

Louis' childhood struggles with tuberculosis came back to haunt him as the political crisis escalated for both his baby daughter Sophie and his oldest son were infected with consumption. I think seeing Louis-Joseph die just as he had watched his older brother die long ago revived a lot of the childhood trauma. Death from tuberculosis is not pretty to watch. I am of the opinion that since the death of his oldest son, which coincided with the beginning of the Revolution in 1789, Louis XVI was suffering from clinical depression. In the past, he had acted with much more energy and decision. It is one of the reasons Antoinette had to become more involved in the political arena during the Revolution. He was deprived of much of his riding after October 1789 and it had a devastating effect upon his health and state of mind. Losing two of his children, his authority, his home, seeing his people and family suffer, and being deprived of the exercise and fresh air vital to his health, left him in a very bad condition. If we consider the courage with which Louis XVI faced the worst moments of crisis, including his death, then he is to be admired, especially in the light of everything else. The Queen is to be admired as well, for she could have slipped out of the country with her surviving children and left Louis to his doom—there were many plans for her escape—but she refused to budge from Louis' side. She would not leave him to face the disasters alone.

Throughout the reign of Louis XVI there were crop failures in different parts of the country due to adverse weather conditions. The year 1788 was especially bad in every way. In July, an incredible hailstorm swept through the countryside; the hailstones destroyed crops across many provinces. This caused there to be a poor harvest, followed by a winter with freezing temperatures. In Provence and Languedoc not only was the olive crop destroyed but one third of the trees as well. The chestnut trees and a variety of crops in southern France also suffered from the cold and the frost. People began to die of starvation as well as illnesses brought on by the extreme physical hardships. As has been seen, Louis and Antoinette dedicated themselves to relieving the sufferings of their people, by charitable works and also by economizing in the royal household. Many extraneous court posts were deleted; the Queen began refurbishing her clothes and shoes, and she and Louis sold their flatware so as to have money for famine relief. They took to eating cheap barley bread at Versailles. The King bought grain for the people from the Netherlands. However, the efforts of the King and his minister was counteracted by persons such as the Duc d'Orléans, whose grain speculation made the bread shortages more catastrophic than they already were.[6]

In the meantime, Louis had been through a succession of ministers who sought to salvage the government and economy from total bankruptcy but to no avail. At the advice of his liberal minister Turgot, Louis implemented deregulation of the grain market but it led to inflated bread prices. Turgot and Malesherbes put radical financial reforms in place, which angered the nobles and were blocked by the *parlements* who insisted that the King did not have the legal right to levy new taxes. In 1776, Turgot was dismissed and Malesherbes resigned, to be replaced by the Swiss banker Jacques Necker. Instead of raising taxes, Necker took out large international loans. In 1781, in an attempt to pander to popular opinion, he published the Crown's first financial statement, called *Compte rendu au roi*. As the situation failed to improve, Louis dismissed Necker and appointed Calonne in his place in 1783. Calonne increased public spending in an effort to stimulate the economy. The project was a disaster; Louis convoked the Assembly of Notables in 1787 to discuss a revolutionary new fiscal reform proposed by Calonne. However, the nobles rejected the plan since they felt it chipped away at their ancient prerogatives, one of which was to be exempt from taxation. At this point, Antoinette became involved and she persuaded Louis to appoint as finance minister the Archbishop of Toulouse, Lomenie de Brienne, who was head of the Assembly of Notables. Louis did not like Brienne because he was an atheist in spite of being a bishop; he also had a loathsome skin disease and Louis refused to touch any papers that he had handled. But Brienne became finance minister and succeeded in making the *parlement* register edicts dealing with internal free trade. When the *parlement* refused to register edicts on the stamp duty and the proposed new general land-tax, Louis XVI held a *lit de justice*, to enforce the registration of his edicts. When his cousin the Duc d'Orléans, leader of the opposition, insisted it was illegal, Louis replied: "It is legal because I wish it."[7] In August 1787, Louis exiled the *parlement* to Troyes.

He also exiled his cousin Orléans to the country. A further attempt by Brienne to force the *parlement* to register an edict for raising a loan of 120 million *livres* met with determined opposition. The struggle between *parlement* and Brienne ended in its voting for its own abolition, under the condition that the Estates-General be summoned as a remedy for the disordered financial affairs of the state. Brienne resigned on August 25, 1788. Louis began to prepare for the Estates-General, while struggling with discouragement as well as health issues. Of course, the Queen was blamed for all of France's problems, although her expenditures over eighteen years were miniscule compared to the massive expense of the American War which had pushed France over the edge into an economic freefall.[8]

From the beginning of her marriage there was a preoccupation in the court in particular and in France in general with Antoinette's body: with her beauty, her clothing, her sex life, her ability to bear children. The initial adulation and infatutation had turned to violent disappointment. From her first days as Queen, her enemies began to circulate pornographic depictions of her. Of course, if people had not been so eager to look at it, it would have had no effect whatsoever. People did look at it and, as is the way with pornography, it altered the way many of them perceived reality. It is often wondered at how such a civilzed nation as France could have degraded itself with the extreme violence which came to characterize the Revolution. Contrary to the popular notion of the Revolution being led by starving peasants, the real instigators were well-fed artistocrats and *bourgeois*. They were able to play upon the fears of the lower classes who were genuinely suffering as a result of famine and unemployment. However, the French Revolution has been more and more revealed as an era of great misogyny, as expressed in the pornographic pamphlets which were circulated in vast quantities. The sheer volume of pornographic material attests to the fact that there was a demand for such filth. Perhaps the century and a half of Jansenism in France can be blamed for the mass addiction to porn, Jansenism being a rigorist, puritanical heresy which had infiltrated French Catholic piety. When everything is forbidden, then nothing is forbidden. Considering that there have been found to be psychological links between porn and violence, particularly sexual violence, then it is not surprising how vicious the sadism came to be, which should surprise no one, since the convicted sex offender the Marquis de Sade was one of the pornographers.

The lewd drawings targeted Antoinette and her circle with particular fury. In her book *The Wicked Queen*, historian Chantal Thomas emphasizes the fact that the pamphlets had no connection with the real Antoinette at all, except to use her name and her face. "Any reading that credits the caricature of the pamphlets with a modicum of reality falls into...confusion."[9] She was most often depicted as a lesbian, in the drawings as in the lewd plays and false "memoirs" which often accompanied them. Homosexuality was the eighteenth century replacement for witchcraft and was the worst thing one could be accused of, although the word "homosexual" did not yet exist. Other words, such as "sodomite" or "tribade" were used. The Queen herself ignored the pamphlets as much as possible, believing that such trash was beneath her notice and that the truth would prevail. Louis XVI, more aware of the danger to the monarchy, attempted to have them bought up and destroyed. The pamphlets did irreparable harm to the Queen's image and led many people to believe that not only was she a nymphomaniac but that she hated the French people with a vampire-like frenzy. Such lies led to a conflagration of savagery.

Some of the pornographic pamphlets were printed at the order of Louis' brother, the Comte de Provence, and his cousin, the Duc d'Orléans.[10] Both men were involved in their own struggles for power. They ridiculed the marriage of Louis and Antoinette and the seven years it took for them to have a child, accusing Louis of impotence. However, after the Queen had children, and in particular, a son and heir, the vitriolic attacks on her chastity became more heated and widespread from those who wished to destroy the monarchy. The Queen as the mother of a future king was a formidable enemy who had to be destroyed. Enough people were obsessed with Antoinette that she had to be constantly shown in the nude and engaged in copulation. It was the closest thing to having the Queen stripped and violated. True, the images had nothing to do with her actual behavior, but everything to do with the twisted fantasy life of too many citizens; it goaded them to madness. It made the unthinkable believable, which is why Hébert was embolded at the Queen's trial to accuse her of incest with her own son. Another of the most common ways to attack the Royal Family was to depict them as animals or mythological beasts. Animal caricatures were not only a humiliation, but a way to dehumanize the King and his family—or anyone else the Revolution needed to attack.

Many authors have accused Freemasonry of having a subversive, potent role in the distribution of pornography as well as in the planning and organization of the Revolution. It is well known of course, that the King's main enemy, Philippe d'Orléans, was head of the Grand Orient Lodge. In 1738, Pope Clement XII prohibited Catholics from becoming Freemasons, on the grounds that the order required secret oaths, involved pagan rituals, and encouraged religious indifferentism. But like papal decrees before and after, many Catholics blithely decided to ignore the prohibition and joined the masons, anyway. They thought that those who took such bans seriously were being stuffy and getting in the way of progress. Lawyers, doctors, merchants, artists, writers, ladies, aristocrats, kings and emperors, who were otherwise practicing Catholics, were initiated into various lodges, lodges which often rivaled each other with different goals and endeavors. In the family of Antoinette there were some members who were masons, including her father, Emperor Francis I. Her mother, Empress Maria Theresa, was vehemently against masonry. The Empress sent the police to raid one of the lodges while her husband the Emperor was at a meeting, and he had to escape by a back staircase.

Freemasonry was so popular among European aristocracy in the 18th century that some ladies joined a bizarre offshoot called the Mopses which was supposed to bypass the papal ban. It involved kissing the backside of a pug dog but other than that gross peculiarity it seemed to be nothing but a ridiculous waste of time. While there is no evidence that Antoinette was herself ever initiated into a lodge, she went through a phase when she was favorable to Freemasonry.[11] Her close friend, the virtuous Madame de Lamballe, presided over the Lodge of the Social Contract, one of the ladies' lodges or *loges d'adoption*. In 1781, Madame de Lamballe eventually became Grand Mistress of all of the Lodges of Adoption in France. That same year, Antoinette wrote to one of her friends, praising the good works of the masonic sisterhood, and how they provided dowries for poor girls and were very pious. She also praised them in a letter to her sister Maria Christina, saying: "It is only a society of benevolence and pleasure."[12] She and Louis XVI both saw the masons as a means of charitable works to benefit society, and they both may have at one point visited certain lodges, so that to this day, some masonic groups claim them as their own. There is also evidence that Antoinette's best friend Madame de Polignac was a member of a ladies' lodge, along with Louis XVI's Orléans cousin the Duchesse de Bourbon.[13] Nesta Webster, who blames the masons for practically everything, said that the Lodges of Adoption were harmless enough ladies' clubs. They were probably one step away from the Mopses, but Catholics should not have joined, since masonry was forbidden by the Church.

As for Louis XVI, there has long been a debate as to if he was ever formally initiated into a lodge as his brothers probably were. When he ascended the throne, Louis XVI was quite liberal and progressive; like all young progressives at the time he saw the masons not only as harmless, but as a group who would benefit society by active good works. Some of this explains his initial acquiescence to certain measures in the beginning of the Revolution which were damaging to the Church, especially the Civil Constitution of the Clergy. He admits as much in the Vow to the Sacred Heart which he made under house arrest in the Tuileries in 1791.[14]

It is true that many monarchists were masons and many revolutionaries were not masons. However, in the years preceding the Revolution of 1789, masonic lodges formed a network that fomented discord, spread propaganda against the King and especially against the Queen. The lodges were used by a core of aristocrats and politicians who wanted to secularize society, and destroy the Church, or at least enervate it, by destroying or by seizing the crown. Antoinette came to see this quite clearly. On August 17, 1790 she wrote to her brother Emperor Leopold II of Austria: "Be well on your guard where you are with regard to all associations of Freemasons. You must already have been warned that it is by this means that all monsters here count on attaining the same end in every country. Oh, God, preserve my

Fatherland and you from such misfortunes."[15] For Antoinette and Louis XVI, the warnings had not been heeded, until it was too late.

The internet is crawling with various sites with phrases such as "Marie-Antoinette obstinately fought for the divine right of kings." Yes, it seems to be the general consensus that Antoinette did not support the French Revolution; she even had the temerity to think that monarchy was a good idea. How could anyone expect the "Daughter of the Caesars" to see things differently? Her father was the Holy Roman Emperor, her mother an autocratic sovereign in her own right, and yet people censure Antoinette for not rejoicing when France became a Republic. It should be kept in mind that the Revolution was introduced to her in a manner of extreme violence, with herself and her family being dragged to Paris with the heads of guards on pikes before them. That the Queen would dedicate herself to trying to save her family from further violence by working against the Revolution should not come as a great shock.

There are several points that need to be considered here. First of all, Antoinette was indeed an Austrian Archduchess, raised to be the consort of the European ruler. She had it instilled in her mind from early on that she was meant to be a queen, although it was not until late in her childhood that it was decided that she was to be the bride of the Dauphin of France. Therefore, Antoinette was brought up with the idea that it was the monarchy which protected the rights of the people, particularly from the excesses of greedy nobles and barbarous invaders. Without the monarchy's protection, the people would become pawns in games between politicians who would take power for themselves and become dictators. Or so she was taught to see it.

Among European monarchs who were contemporaries of Louis XVI and Antoinette, the more "enlightened" ones, such as Antoinette's brother Joseph II, and Catherine the Great of Russia, open to the teachings of the deists and *philosophes*, were also the most despotic. The enlightened despots loved to talk about the rights of man but in actuality ruled with iron hands, especially in contrast to the benevolence of Louis XVI. Antoinette herself was not closed to the new ideas; she read Rousseau and was favorable to the civic contributions of the masons; both she and Louis were great advocates of reform and progress. However, the escalating violence of the Revolution and the laws against the Church, as promulgated by the Civil Constitution of the Clergy in 1790, killed any support the Queen might have had for the Revolution. Nevertheless, she corresponded with prominent revolutionaries such as Barnave, in order to have some influence on the course of events. She called the constitution passed on September 14, 1791 "a tissue of impracticable absurdities," as she wrote to the Austrian ambassador; even the revolutionaries came to regard it so, and scrapped it.[16] She wanted the foreign powers, particularly her brother the Emperor, to form a congress which would put pressure on the revolutionaries and restore order. However, she thought that any attempts of military invasion on the part of the Louis XVI's brothers would lead to more violence against the crown and her fears were proved to be right.[17][18]

The calling of the Three Estates was the last recourse open to the King in his effort to correct the situation of unequal taxation in France. If his reforms could have become law, it would have reversed many of the country's economic problems. The *parlements* had resisted registering his edicts. By summoning the Third Estate, which was comprised of the elected representatives of the common people, he hoped to appeal directly to those citizens whom his programs would most benefit. By doing so, he was taking a tremendous risk, because many of the people's elected representatives were disciples of Voltaire and Rousseau. Not only that, but the powerful nobles and clergymen, who would lose money from Louis' tax reforms, sought to agitate the bourgeois representatives against their King. Meanwhile, Louis had decided that the Third Estate should have as many deputies as the clergy (First Estate) and the nobility (Second Estate) combined, extending the franchise to all male tax payers over twenty-five. He was giving concessions that no king had ever granted before, hoping to win the commoners to his side. He was determined to make the Estates-General a success, and devoted all of 1788 to preparing for it. If successful, he believed it would have meant a new era of prosperity and civil peace for France. In accordance with the character of his reign, he planned to protect religion and the good traditions, while pruning away what was cumbersome and obsolete. But he needed to have the nation behind him.

Louis XVI and Antoinette led the Eucharistic procession that opened the Estates-General on May 4, 1789. The Dauphin Louis-Joseph was desperately ill; he and his sister sat with Madame de Polignac on a balcony above the stables so they could watch the magnificent procession. The procession wound from the Royal Chapel, across the vast courtyard of the palace, through the streets of the town of Versailles, to the Church of Saint Louis. The monstrance, in the hands of a bishop, was under a rich canopy carried by Provence, Artois, Berry, and Angoulême. Everyone held a candle, except for the standard bearers, with the fluttering silken banners, and the royal falconers, with falcons on their wrists, looking both noble and fierce. The Duc d'Orléans, member of the Jacobin club, walked among the members of the Third Estate, even though he was a

Prince of the Blood. The King, with a lighted taper, walked directly behind the monstrance. He wore a cloth of gold mantle and a plumed hat with the famous Regent diamond. He was wildly applauded by the crowds that lined the route. But when Antoinette, who with her ladies followed the King's household, passed by in her gown of gold and silver tissue, every tongue fell silent. When passing beneath the balcony where Louis-Joseph was, she glanced up to blow him a kiss. The cry "Long live Orléans!" was at that moment taken up by the crowd, intended as an insult to the Queen.[19] The Queen stumbled; Princesse de Lamballe steadied her. During Benediction at the Church of Saint Louis, the bishop preached against the luxury of the court which, he said, was causing the martyrdom of the French people. After the services, back in her rooms, she collapsed in a fit of convulsions. She trembled so violently, her pearl necklace and diamond bracelets broke. They had to cut off her dress in order to get her to bed.[20]

She recovered enough the next day to be at the King's side in the Hall of Lesser Pleasures at Versailles, where he gave his welcoming address to the deputies. Louis XVI, in his golden robes, was heartily applauded, while Antoinette, in her lavender-blue silk gown covered with silver spangles, received a few weak cheers. The King spoke and then His Keeper of the Seals, Monsieur de Miromesnil, then presented the King's program of reform to the deputies: he wanted the clergy and nobility to share in the burden of taxation. The day appeared to be a success, in spite of a long, sonorous speech by the finance minister, Monsieur Necker. But in the following weeks, the King's worst fears were realized. The deputies demanded more than the King thought it was possible to give. The Third Estate wanted to abolish all class distinctions and privileges of rank. They were not really interested in economic reform, but demanded the restructuring of society, the only society France had ever known, and they wanted it to happen immediately. On June 17, without the King's permission, they created what they called the National Assembly—the basis of what they hoped would become a constitutional monarchy. And there were some who wanted no monarchy at all.

While the fate of France was being decided, the Dauphin Louis-Joseph was dying an agonizing death, in great physical and mental torment. On June 2, Forty Hours devotion began, and the bell of Notre Dame tolled, summoning the people to pray for the dying heir of the Bourbons. In all the churches of Paris, the Blessed Sacrament was exposed. On June 4, the curtain of the Théatre Français was lowered after the first act. At one o'clock that morning, his agony came to an end. He was dressed in a golden crown and spurs, laid in a white coffin, and carried in procession to the Cathedral of Saint Denis, where he was buried in the royal crypt with his ancestors. Custom did not permit the bereaved parents to follow their son to his tomb. Instead, they went alone to the *château* of Marly, to mourn together for a week, until duty recalled them to Versailles. The King, incessantly badgered by deputies, was overcome by his son's death, and cried out to them: "Are there no fathers in the Third Estate?" [21] He and Antoinette arranged for a thousand Masses to be said for the soul of Louis-Joseph, paying for the stipends with what was left of their silver plate.

While the King and Queen mourned a dead child, their enemies were busy. Orléans devoted himself to stirring up the people. By the end of June, there was rioting in the streets of Paris. The King saw to the replenishment of the grain supply, but the citizens were not appeased. To protect Paris and Versailles, and restore law and order, Louis summoned six regiments from the eastern frontier. He was accused of tyranny, and on July 14 an enraged mob stormed the Bastille. Monsieur de Launay, the Governor of the Bastille, who treated with great benevolence the seven criminals who were housed therein, was tricked by the leaders of the mob, and decapitated. When word reached Versailles of the bloody events, the reaction was shock and horror. Many courtiers left, including the Polignacs. The Artois family decided to leave as well. Louis and Antoinette considered leaving. Louis wanted Antoinette to go with the children but she refused to leave him. Provence advised them all to stay and they did, although Louis later regretted it deeply.[22]

On July 17, Louis arranged to go to Paris to be reconciled with the citizens of Paris. He made his will before he left. Antoinette was in a panic while he was gone, and insisted that horses be kept in readiness for her to be taken to her husband in case he was made a prisoner. She read Madame Campan a short speech she had prepared to give before the National Assembly: "Gentlemen, I come to put in your hands the wife and family of your sovereign. Do not suffer those who have been united by Heaven to be put asunder on earth."[23] She seemed to have a deep fear of being separated from Louis, as she also displayed great anxiety when he journeyed to Cherbourg. When he returned, she and her children, along with Madame Élisabeth, ran to greet him as he stepped out of his coach. According to an eyewitness account:

> This princess, as virtuous as she was amiable, whom monsters later on accused of having never loved her husband, was absolutely in despair. As soon as she heard the King's carriage entering the Cour Royale she ran towards him holding the Dauphin in her arms, then breathless and almost

fainting she fell into those of the King who was no less moved than she was. Holding out one hand to his children who covered it with kisses, with the other wiping the tears from the eyes of Marie-Antoinette and Madame Elisabeth, Louis XVI smiled again...he kept on repeating: 'Happily no blood was shed, and I swear that not a drop of French blood will ever be shed on my orders.'[24]

The King recalled Necker, who was popular with the people. The peace was short-lived, as tumults erupted in Paris throughout the summer. From Normandy, Alsace and Provence there were horrific reports of the country estates being attacked by the populace and innocent men, women, and children being tortured, raped and murdered. In other provinces, however, the local authorities immediately put down the social unrest.[25] In the National Assembly, all tithes and noble privileges were abolished. There was a movement led by Orléans and Mirabeau to overthrow Louis and replace him on the throne with Orléans. In the middle of September a rumor came to Versailles that an attack was being planned to achieve the removal of Louis, or at least bring him back to Paris where he would be under the thumb of the Assembly. Louis sent for more troops to come to protect Versailles. On October 1, the Royal Bodyguards at Versailles gave a banquet at the palace opera for the Flanders regiment, who had recently arrived as reinforcements to protect the Royal Family. Four-year-old Louis-Charles, the new Dauphin, was eager to see the soldiers. Against their better judgment the King and Queen decided to take him, and Madame Royale, too. They walked over to the opera with both of their children, and the troops welcomed them with thunderous cheers and acclamations. "Long live the King! Long live the Queen! Long live the Dauphin!" Then the soldiers began to sing a song from Grétry's opera *Richard Coeur de Lion*:

*O, Richard, O mon Roi
L' univers t'abandonne.
Sur la terre il n'est donc que moi
Qui m'intéresse à ta personne.*

The little Dauphin went with one of the soldiers, and proudly walked the length of the large horseshoe table without upsetting a single glass. Unfortunately, within a couple of days, the banquet was turned into a story of a wild orgy in which Antoinette, the evil Austrian woman, trampled on the red, white and blue revolutionary cockade, inciting the soldiers to cry: "Down with the Assembly!" It was a far cry from the truth, but people were ready to believe anything bad about the Queen.[26]

On the afternoon of October 5, 1789, the Queen was relaxing in her grotto at Trianon, when the Comte de Saint-Priest sent word that a huge mob was marching on Versailles. As it started to rain, Antoinette rushed back to the main palace where her children were. The King was hunting in the forest of Meudon; he was found and galloped home. The Comte de Saint-Priest, who was Minister of the Royal Household, had carriages made ready to take the Royal Family to Rambouillet. Louis could not make up his mind; he wanted Antoinette and the children to go but once again the Queen would not leave her husband. The mob arrived, led by fishwives armed with pikes and all manner of sharp objects, as well as men dressed like women. They were demanding bread, and saying they had come for the "Baker, the Baker's wife and the Baker's boy" meaning the King, the Queen and the Dauphin.They were also shouting for the Queen's intestines, in order to make cockades of them, as well as other gruesome terroristic threats. Louis refused to allow his soldiers to fire upon women; he met with a delegation of them inside the palace and the clamor seemed to calm down when he assured them they would have bread. The Marquis de Lafayette, hero of the American Revolution, was in charge of securing the safety of the palace inhabitants, but for some reason he went to sleep in a house in town, leaving the palace poorly guarded, with only two Swiss Guards to guard the Queen's staircase. He trusted the word of the Revolutionary leaders that peace would be preserved. Around 5:30 am a huge crowd found an unguarded entrance and began raging its way through the palace, dismembering any guards they happened upon, on their way to Antoinette's room. They were shouting "Long live the Duc d'Orléans!" which showed whose cause they were supporting.[27] It seems they were determined to kill the Queen. Although she had sent her ladies away, Madame Thibaut and Madame Auguié "the Lioness" insisted on keeping watch outside the Queen's bedchamber. It was a good thing they did because when they heard the mob they leaped up and woke the Queen, throwing a yellow dressing gown around her and fleeing with her down the passage to the king's room. The door was locked; they banged on it in a panic until a valet finally opened it.[28] Louis was not there; he had been rescuing the Dauphin and his governesses, who followed him down a dark subterranean passage to avoid the mob. At last, the family was safe in the King's room, including the Mesdames Tantes and Madame Élisabeth. As one biographer describes the ordeal:

> Louis XVI...always calm and self-controlled, he called the ministers together in the Council Hall. The Queen, the Dauphin, Madame Royale, Madame Elisabeth, the Count of Provence, the aunts, were all collected in the King's bedroom. The Dauphin

said to his mother, 'Mamma, I'm hungry.'

'Be patient,' answered Marie Antoinette; 'this will soon be over.'

The palace courtyards were filled with battalions of the National Guard and with the populace. Marie Antoinette stood, perfectly calm, at a window, looking out on the vast throng. While everyone about her was giving way to tears or despair, she did not lose her head for a moment, but consoled and encouraged everyone. Louis XVI went out on the balcony, with the same air of confidence and kindness that he always wore. Cries of 'The Queen, the Queen!' were heard. La Fayette advised Marie Antoinette to show herself; he said it was the only way to allay the excitement.

'Very well,' answered the Queen, 'if I have to go to my execution, I shall not hesitate; I will go.'...Marie Antoinette, pale, with disheveled hair, appeared at the balcony of the King's room, accompanied by La Fayette, and holding the Dauphin with one hand, her daughter with the other. The cries redoubled; shouts of 'No children! No children! The Queen alone!' arose from all sides...Without thinking about the probable evil significance of these shouts, Marie Antoinette gave the Dauphin and his sister to their father; then she came out alone, fearless, heroic, and calmly letting her eyes run over the multitude, folded her arms. It was the daughter of the Caesars who appeared. The noble haughtiness of her brow, the dignity of her bearing, wrung from the crowd a shout of admiration and surprise. Even those who, a moment before, wanted to kill her, joined in the cry. A loud roar of 'Long live the Queen!' burst forth. Marie Antoinette was not the dupe of this greeting; she heard the crowd shouting another alarming cry: 'To

Paris with the King!' and, leaving the balcony, she went up to Madame Necker, and said sadly, 'They are going to make the King and me go to Paris, with the heads of our guards carried before us on the ends of their pikes.'[29]

The mob stabbed at the Queen's bed and smashed up her room,[30] which they had been told was hung with black satin and burned black candles. Lafayette asked Antoinette what her personal intentions were and she replied: "I know the fate which awaits me but my duty is to die at the feet of the King and in the arms of my children."[31] The same night saw the church of St. Louis, the parish church of Versailles, the site of sacrilege as well as vandalism, until the vicar came and offered Mass, which stopped the commotions.[32]

In the morning, the Royal Family was packed up and taken to Paris, surrounded by hostile crowds, with heads of decapitated guards on the pikes carried in front of them. The bloodcurdling journey took most of the day; it was late in the afternoon of October 6 when they arrived at the Tuileries palace. What had once been a royal residence had been broken up into apartments for retired retainers and other private persons, who were summarily asked to vacate the premises. It was crowded, untidy, and in a state of disrepair. Four-year-old Louis-Charles exclaimed: "But it is so ugly here, Maman!" The little boy was extremely anxious after the terror to which he had been subjected. Antoinette decided to keep her family as close to her as possible, with the governess Madame de Tourzel sleeping in the same room with the Dauphin. Some of the doors could not be locked and had to be barricaded for privacy. The next day, a noisy crowd gathered under their windows. Louis-Charles asked: "Is it still yesterday?' as he threw himself into his mother's arms, frightened and sobbing.[33] The next few years would see Antoinette frightened not of the mob nor of popular opinion but of being separated from her husband and children. She was especially anxious about having her son taken away from her. However, when asked to give a statement on the ordeal of being attacked in her bedroom and then dragged from Versailles to Paris, the Queen responded: "I saw everything, knew everything, and have forgotten everything,"[34] meaning that she held no rancor against the people, whom she knew were being used as tools by men who wished to seize power. In was in her nature to look ahead and hope for the best. She refused to give in to despair.

Marie-Antoinette, Daughter of the Caesars

"Louis XVI and Marie-Antoinette in profile"

Marie-Antoinette, Daughter of the Caesars

"Marie-Antoinette as Vesta, based on painting by Dumont."

21 AT THE TUILERIES

"Calumny kills much more quickly, and they will use calumny to kill me." —Marie-Antoinette to Madame Campan

The next few moths saw major redecorating of the state appartments at the Tuileries as the Royal household was reorganized to suit the new conditions. In the summer, while still at Versailles, Antoinette composed a letter to her children's new governess, Madame de Tourzel, about the details of their upbringing. It is worth reading in its entirety due to the prudence which the Queen displays when it came to her children:

July 24, 1789.

My son is four years and four months less two days old. I say nothing of his figure or of his appearance; you have only to see him. His health has always been good; but even in the cradle we perceived that his nerves were delicate, and the slightest unusual noise affected him. He was backward in cutting his first teeth, but they came without illness or accident. It was not until with the last—I think it was with the sixth—that he had a convulsion at Fontainebleau. Since then he has had two,—one in the winter of 1787 and 1788, and the other at the time of his inoculation; but this last was very slight. As a result of his sensitive nerves, any noise to which he is not accustomed frightens him; for example, he is afraid of dogs, because he has heard them bark near him. I have never forced him to see them, because I believe that as his reason develops, his fears will subside. He is, like all strong and healthy children, very quick and violent in his anger; but he is a good child, tender, and caressing even, when his impulsiveness does not carry him away. He possesses inordinate vanity, which, if well directed, may some day turn to his advantage. Until he is quite at ease with any one he will control himself, and even stifle his impatience and anger, that he may appear gentle and amiable. He is most trustworthy when he has promised anything, but he is very indiscreet; he repeats readily anything he has heard, and often, without meaning to lie, he adds what his imagination has made him see. This is his greatest fault, and one which it is most necessary to correct. Nevertheless, I say it again, he is a good child; and with kindness, and at the same time with firmness, but not too great severity, any one can make of him what one will. Severity, however, drives him to rebellion, because for his age he has a great deal of character: to give an example, from his babyhood the word 'pardon' has always been offensive to him. He will do and say all that one may wish when he is in the wrong; but he will not pronounce the word 'pardon' without tears and great reluctance.

My children have always been accustomed to feel great confidence in me, and when they have done wrong, to tell me of it themselves; consequently in scolding them I have appeared more troubled and grieved than angry at what they have done. I have trained them all to believe that a 'yes' or 'no' pronounced by me is irrevocable; but I always give them a reason within the reach of their comprehension, that they may not think it caprice on my part.

My son cannot read, and learns with great difficulty, for he is too heedless to apply himself. He has not the slightest idea of haughtiness in his head, and I am most desirous that this should continue. Our children always learn soon enough what they are. He loves his sister well and heartily. Whenever anything gives him pleasure,— whether it be to go somewhere or to be given something,— his first act is always to ask the same for his sister. He was born light-hearted. He has need for the sake of his health to be much in the open air; and I believe it is better for his health to let him play and dig in the ground on the terrace than to take him a greater distance. The exercise which children get in running and playing out of doors is more wholesome than when they are forced to walk, which often tires their backs.

I will now speak of those who surround him. Three undergovernesses,—two Mesdames de Soucy (mother-in-law and daughterin-law) and Madame de Villefort. Madame de Soucy, the mother, is an excellent woman, very lenient and exact, but vulgar. The daughter-in-law has the same air, — there is no hope for her. For several years she has not been with my daughter, but with the little boy there is no risk. In other respects, she is faithful and even a little severe with the child. Madame de Villefort is just the opposite, and spoils him. She is also quite as vulgar, and even more so in appearance. They all get along well together. The first two women are both strongly attached to the child. Madame Lemoine, however, is an insufferable gossip and chatterbox, telling everything she knows in the room, whether before the child or not,—it makes no difference. Madame Neuville has an agreeable exterior, intelligence, and polite manners; but she is said to be ruled by her mother, who is very intriguing. Brunier, the physician, has my entire confidence whenever the children are ill; but beyond that he must be kept in his place. He is familiar, ill-tempered, and boastful. The Abbé d'Avaux may be very good to teach my son his letters; but in other respects he has neither the tone nor any of the qualifications necessary for the charge of my children. It is for this reason that I have at present decided to withdraw my daughter from under him. You must take great care that he does not settle himself in my son's apartments outside of lesson-hours. The intercourse with the under-governess was one of the things which gave Madame de Polignac the greatest trouble, and with all her efforts she could not always control it. Ten days ago I heard of some ungrateful remarks by this Abbé, which displeased me greatly.

My son has eight waiting-maids. They serve him with zeal, but I cannot count much upon them. Lately there has been much evilspeaking in the prince's chamber, but I cannot say exactly by whom. There is, however, one—a Madame Belliard—who does not hide her sentiments. Without suspecting any one, you can be on your guard. All of the men-servants are faithful, devoted, and quiet.

My daughter has two first women, and seven waiting-maids. Madame Brunier, wife of the physician, has been with her since her birth, and serves her with zeal. Though I have no objections to her personally, I would never intrust to her more than attendance on the princess; she has the same disposition as her husband. In addition, she is avaricious and greedy of the small gains which are to be made in the small chamber.

Her daughter [Madame Fréminville] is a person of real merit. Although only twenty-seven years of age, she possesses all the qualities of mature years. She has attended my daughter since her birth, and has never lost sight of her. I [arranged her marriage]; and the time which she does not spend with my daughter she gives up entirely to the education of her three little girls. She has a gentle, pliable disposition, is highly cultivated, and it is she whom I choose to continue the lessons in place of the Abbé d'Avaux. She is well fitted for the task; and since I have the good fortune to be sure of it, I find her preferable to all the others. Besides, my daughter loves her, and has confidence in her. Seven other women are excellent persons, and this chamber is much more tranquil than the other. There are also two very young girls, but they are supervised by their mother, — one belonging to my daughter, and the other to Madame Lemoine. The men have served her since her birth. They are absolutely insignificant creatures; but as they have nothing to do but wait upon her, and do not remain in her room except for that, this is of no importance to me.[1]

Here is a letter Antoinette wrote in August 1789 to

Madame de Tourzel concerning Louis-Charles' temper. It is interesting that she addresses Madame de Tourzel as "dear heart" which was usually reserved for Madame de Polignac. "My dear heart, our tenderness for this child should be stern. We must not forget that we are educating him not for ourselves, but for the nation. The first impressions of childhood are so strong that I am, in truth, frightened when I think that we are bringing up the king."[2]

In Paris, the Royal Family were surrounded by their enemies and exposed to the fickleness of popular opinion with its violent demonstrations. The Royal Family endured a life of virtual house arrest from October of 1789 until August of 1792. The following passages from Imbert de Saint-Amand describe the tightening of security around the family after their escape attempt in June 1791. The Queen, especially, was closely guarded; as anyone can see, it would have been impossible for her to have privately entertained Count Fersen, as some authors claim. To quote from Baron Saint-Amand's *Marie-Antoinette at the Tuileries*:

> It had been resolved that [the queen] should have no personal attendant except the lady's maid who had acted as a spy before the journey to Varennes. A portrait of this person was placed at the foot of the staircase leading to the Queen's rooms so that the sentinel should permit no other woman to enter. Louis XVI was obliged to appeal to Lafayette in order to have this spy turned out of the palace where her presence was an outrage on Marie Antoinette. This espionage and inquisition pursued the unfortunate Queen even into her bedroom. The guards were instructed not to lose sight of her by night or day. They took note of her slightest gestures, listened to her slightest words. Stationed

in the room adjoining hers they kept the communicating door always open so that they could see the august captive at all times.[3]

The family continued to assist at daily Mass, albeit with difficulty.

> The precautions taken were so rigorous that it was forbidden to say Mass in the palace chapel because the distance between it and the apartments of Louis XVI and Marie Antoinette was thought too great. A corner of the Gallery of Diana, where a wooden altar was erected, bearing an ebony crucifix and a few vases of flowers became the only spot where the son of Saint Louis, the Most Christian King, could hear Mass.[4]

However, their fortitude was admirable.

> The royal family endured their captivity with admirable sweetness and resignation and concerned themselves less about their own fate than that of the persons compromised by the Varennes journey, who were now incarcerated....Louis XVI, instead of indulging in recriminations against men and things, offered his humiliations and sufferings to God. He prayed, he read, he meditated. Next to his prayer book his favorite reading was the life of Charles I either because he sought, in studying history, to find a way of escaping an end like that of the unfortunate monarch, or because an analogy of sorrows and disasters had established a profound and mysterious sympathy between the king who had been beheaded, and the king who was soon to be so.[5]

The unfolding of events revealed that the attack on the royal sovereignty coincided with an attack on Church authority. In November of 1789 all Church property was confiscated by the government. The legislation was backed by anti-clerical propaganda, including plays which either ridiculed the Church, or portrayed priests and nuns as being wicked and licentious. In July of 1790 the National Assembly voted to nationalize the Catholic Church in France under the Civil Constitution of the Clergy. Henceforth, bishops and priests would be elected by the State, and no longer invested by the Pope. On November 27 of the same year, the Assembly passed a decree mandating every priest and bishop to swear an oath to the Civil Constitution of the Clergy, and the King was pressured to sign the decree. The King appealed to the Pope for advice, and the Holy Father appointed two archbishops to guide him. When his two advisors urged him to sign the decree, the King did so out of obedience to the representatives of the Vicar of Christ, but against his conscience. While the worldly clergy freely took the oath, the more fervent priests and bishops refused; they began to be hunted and turned out of their parishes. The King's aunts, Mesdames Adélaïde and Victoire, would have nothing to do with the new national church, and escaped to Rome, in spite of public indignation.

On March 31, 1790, Wednesday of Passion Week, Madame Royale, age eleven, made her First Holy Communion at the church of Saint Germain de l'Auxerrois, which was the parish church of the Tuileries. Before the ceremony Antoinette told her daughter to kneel before the King and ask his blessing. Louis blessed her and then gave her a talk about the great mystery she was about to receive.

> It is from the bottom of my heart that I bless you, my child, while praying Heaven to grant you a full

realization of the great act which you are about to accomplish. Your heart is innocent in the eyes of God; your vows should be acceptable to him; offer them to him for your mother and for me. Ask him to accord me the grace necessary to bring about the happiness of those over whom he has given me empire, and whom I should consider as my children. Beg of him that he deign to preserve religious purity in the kingdom; and remember, my daughter, that our holy religion is the source of all happiness, and our support in the adversities of life. Do not believe yourself secure from them. You are very young, but you have already more than once seen your father in affliction.

You do not know, my daughter, to what Providence destines you: whether you are to remain in the kingdom, or whether you are to go to live in another. To whatever place the hand of God may lead you, remember that you must teach others by your example, and do good whenever you find the opportunity; but, above all, my child, relieve the unfortunate as much as is in your power. God has placed us in this rank of life only that we may work for their happiness, and console them in their sorrows.[6]

The ceremony was one of extreme simplicity, with the princess accompanied only by her governess Madame de Tourzel and her sub-governess Madame de Mackau. The Queen, who had made her Easter communion two days before, attended incognito, dressed like a *bourgeoise*, sitting in the shadows, but those present saw her reverence and devotion and how her eyes did not move from her child.[7]

The King became gravely ill. His illness was undoubtedly the result of the stress of the upheavals which he had tried to prevent, as well as the fact that his conscience was troubling him about signing the Catholic Church in France over to the revolutionary government, severing the ties with Rome. With the guidance of his non-juring confessor, a Eudist priest Abbé Hébert, he drafted a Vow to the Sacred Heart of Jesus. In the 1600's a Visitation nun, Saint Margaret Mary, had claimed that Jesus had requested that the King of France consecrate France to His Sacred Heart. The consecration had never been performed. So, with the help of Abbé Hébert, Louis promised that he would perform the solemn consecration should he be restored to his former power. He sealed the Vow in the walls of his apartments at the Tuileries. The Vow was not found until the palace had been partially burned by the Commune and was being torn down in 1871. It was discovered still sealed in the wall of the King's room. Louis was a locksmith and was fascinated with construction, so building a hiding place for his papers would not have been beyond him. He was known for his penchant for secrecy and his hiding of private papers from prying eyes. The fact that the Vow was not discovered until the 1870's demolishes the claim of some that it was merely a product of pious forgery during the 1814-1830 Restoration. The methodical legality of the document is typical of Louis XVI, who as an amateur cartographer was characterized by his precision and attention to detail. Here is the Vow:

Dedication of France to the Sacred Heart of Jesus by King Louis XVI

You see, O my God! all the wounds which tear my heart, and depth of the abyss into which I have fallen. Evils without number surround me on all sides. My personal misfortunes and those of my family, which are dreadful, overwhelm my heart, as well as those which cover the face of the kingdom. The cries of all the unfortunate ones, the moaning of oppressed religion resounds in my ears, and an interior voice still informs me that perhaps Your justice reproaches me with all these calamities, because, in the days of my power, I did not repress the license of the people and the irreligion, which are the principal sources; because I served the weapons of heresy which triumphed, by supporting it by laws which doubled its forces and gave it the audacity to dare all.

I will not have temerity, O my God! to justify to myself before You; but You know that my heart was always subject to faith and morals; my faults are the fruit of my weakness and seem worthy of Your great mercy. You forgave King David, who caused your enemies to blaspheme You and King Manassès, who had involved his people in the idolatry. Disarmed by their penitence, you restored them one and the other on the throne of Juda; you made them reign with peace and glory. Would You be inexorable today towards a son of Saint Louis, who takes these penitent kings for models, and which, with their example, wishes to repair his faults and to become a King according to Your Heart?

O Jesus Christ! divine Redeemer of all our iniquities, it is in Your Adorable Heart that I want to deposit the overflowing of my afflicted heart. I call upon the help of the tender Heart of Mary, my majestic protector and my mother, and the assistance of Saint Louis, my most famous patron and of my ancestor. O adorable Heart, by the so pure hands of my powerful intercessors, receive with kindness the wishes that confidence inspires in me and that I offer to You like the humble expression of my feelings. If, by an effect of the infinite kindness of God, I recover my freedom, my crown and my royal power, I promise solemnly:

1. To revoke as soon as possible all the laws which will be indicated to me, either by the Pope, or by a Council, or by the four Bishops chosen among most enlightened and most virtuous of my kingdom, with the purity and the integrity of the faith, the discipline and the spiritual jurisdiction of Holy Catholic, Apostolic Church, Roman, and in particular to revoke the Civil Constitution of the Clergy.

2. To take, in a one year interval, in union with the Pope and the Bishops of my kingdom, all measurements necessary to establish, according to the canonical forms, a solemn festival in honor of the Sacred Heart of Jesus, which will be celebrated in perpetuity in all France, on the first Friday after the octave of the Blessed Sacrament, and always followed by a general procession, in repair of the insults and profanations made in the time of the disorders, by the schismatics, the heretics and the bad Christians.

3. To go myself in person, within three months from the day of my delivery, to the church of Notre Dame of Paris, or in any other principal church of the place where I will be, and to pronounce, one day of Sunday or festival, at the foot of the high altar, after the offertory of the Mass, and between the hands of the celebrant, a solemn act of dedication of my person, my family and my kingdom to the Sacred Heart of Jesus, promising to give to all my subjects, the example of the worship and the devotion which are due to this adorable Heart.

4. To set up and to decorate at my own expense, in the church which I will choose for it, within one

year from the day of my delivery, an altar which will be dedicated to the Sacred Heart of Jesus, and which will be used as an eternal monument of my recognition and my confidence without end in the infinite merits and in the inexhaustible treasures of grace which are contained in this Crowned Heart.

5. Finally, to renew every year, in the place where I will be, on the Feast of the Sacred Heart, the act of dedication expressed in the third article, and to attend the general procession which will follow the Mass of this day. Today I pronounce only in secrecy this promise, but I would sign it my blood if it were needed; and the most beautiful day of my life will be that where I will be able to aloud publish it in the temple. O Adorable Heart of my Savior! Let my right hand be forgotten and let me curse myself, if I forget Your blessings and my promises, if I cease to love You, finding my confidence in You and all of my consolation. Amen.[8]

On March 10, 1791, the bull *Charitas* of Pope Pius VI condemned the Civil Constitution of the Clergy as being schismatic. The Holy Father declared all bishops elected by the State to be invalid and their consecrations a sacrilege. He suspended every priest and bishop who had taken the oath. When the bull was made public, the persecution began in earnest, with the burning of the Pope in effigy in Paris. Grey Nuns were beaten in the streets by fierce *poissardes*. In so many ways, however, *Charitas* came as a relief. Now all faithful Catholics knew exactly where they stood, including the King, who would not now receive Holy Communion from a juring priest. "Juring" meant that they had sworn an oath to the Civil Constitution of the Clergy. Underground Masses became the norm. On March 17, 1791, a week after the papal bull was published, the Abbé Henry Edgeworth de Firmont, an Irish ex-patriate, made his first visit to the Tuileries Palace as the new confessor and spiritual director to the King's sister, Madame Élisabeth of France. Her former confessor had taken the oath. Like the Queen, who could be seen about Paris visiting hospitals, orphanages, factories, and mental asylums, Madame Élisabeth occupied herself in charitable works. The Queen also dismissed her juring confessor and found one who had not taken the oath.

By Passiontide of 1791 it became clear to the King that his only recourse was to escape from Paris. He was no longer a free man, as he discovered on Monday of Holy Week when, with his family, he tried to leave for Saint-Cloud, where he planned on privately receiving his Easter communion from a non-juring priest. A mob surrounded the coach and would not let it leave the courtyard of the Tuileries. They had to give up going anywhere that day, and returned to the palace. Plans for an escape were made. Why did the Royal Family flee Paris? Because the increasing violence undermined the authority of the King, who was being treated as a prisoner. Furthermore, Louis, having privately made his Vow to the Sacred Heart, could no longer tolerate the recent legislation passed by the Revolutionary government against the Catholic Church which nationalized church lands and made all priests swear an oath to the state. It was decided to escape to Montmédy near Metz where Louis had supporters and would be able to take a firm stand against the fanatics who had gained control of the government A few days after Trinity Sunday, the Royal Family slipped out of the Tuileries in the middle of the night, and fled to the countryside, with the help of Count Axel von Fersen. Fersen, with the aid of the Scotsman Quentin Crauford, supplied a huge berlin with enough room for the royal party, including

Madame de Tourzel, who pretended to be the Russian aristocrat Madame de Korff. The real Madame de Korff provided the funds for the escape as well as her own passport, including papers for children and servants. Louis disguised himself as a steward, the Queen as a governess, and Madame Élisabeth as a maid. Madame Royale and the Dauphin were supposed to be Madame de Korff's daughters, so Louis-Charles had to dress like a girl. When the Royal Family's absence was discovered, the Parisians went wild, tearing the *fleur-de-lys* off of all public buildings. The King, however, had no intention of leaving France; believing the citizens of the provinces to be faithful, he planned to go to Montmédy near Metz, where he meant to rally all loyal troops and subjects in order to hold the revolutionary government at bay. Before he departed from the Tuileries with his family, Louis XVI left a message for the people of France. Here is an excerpt of the declaration:

> Frenchmen, and above all Parisians, you inhabitants of a city which his majesty's ancestors were pleased to call the good city of Paris, disabuse yourselves of the suggestions and lies of your false friends; return to your king; he will always be your father, your best friend. What pleasure will he not have in forgetting all his personal injuries, and in being returned among you, while the Constitution, which he will have accepted freely, will cause our holy religion to be respected, the government to be established on a firm foundation and useful in its actions, the property and the status of each one no longer to be troubled, the laws no longer to be disobeyed with impunity, and finally liberty to be established on firm an immovable foundations. In Paris, 20 June 1791, Louis.[9]

On June 21, 1791, Louis XVI, Antoinette, and their family were captured at the town of Varennes. The King begged the the grocer Sauce and his family not to hand them over to the authorities, saying:

> I am your King; this is the Queen and the royal family. Surrounded in the capital by daggers and bayonets, I have come to the country, into the midst of my faithful subjects, to seek the peace and liberty you all enjoy. I could not stay in Paris; it would have been death to myself and my family. I have come to live among you my children, whom I will not forsake....Save my wife, save my children.[10]

His entreaties fell on deaf ears; the Royal Family were sent back to Paris where they all, except for young Madame Royale, met their deaths. Some people find it interesting how a quatrain in the prophecies of Nostradamus appears to allude to the capture of the Royal Family at Varennes.

> *De nuict viendra par le forest de Reines,*
> *Deux pars, vaultorte, Herne la pierre blanche,*
> *Le moyne noir en gris dedans Varennes:*
> *Esleu Cap. cause tempeste, feu, sang, tranche.*

> By night shall come through the forest of Reines
> Two parts, face about, the Queen a white stone,
> The black monk in gray within Varennes.
> Chosen Cap. causes tempest, fire, blood, slice.[11]

Whether the prophecy genuinely refers to the night of Varennes or not, it was indeed the night that spelled the end of the monarchy. The unfortunate family was brought back on the Vigil of Corpus Christi surrounded by a bloodthirsty throng. The people viciously murdered an old nobleman, who had had the courage to salute the King. The berlin slowly creaked passed altars set up on the roadside, adorned with flowers, ready to receive the Saving Victim in the monstrances, borne in the Corpus Christi processions. Meanwhile, the men along the road kept their hats on, and soldiers reversed their arms, pointing the barrels of the muskets to the ground, as signs of disdain for the King and Queen. It was a miracle they were not all dragged from their coach and killed.

After returning to the Tuileries, the Royal Family was under a closer guard, with two gendarmes sleeping in the antechamber of the Queen's bedroom. One needed a special pass in order to enter the royal apartments. It was with great difficulty that Abbé Edgeworth occasionally managed to see Madame Élisabeth in order to hear her confession. He found it easier to enter in the mornings, when many tradesmen were going in and out of the palace. Madame Élisabeth disagreed with the conciliatory policies of her brother Louis XVI and the political maneuverings of Antoinette. She saw the Revolution as pure evil, as an attack upon the Church and Christendom and thought that it should be stopped with fire and sword if necessary. There were many heated arguments at the Tuileries and as author Simone Bertière points out in *L'Insoumise*, Antoinette could hardly stand her sister-in-law at times.[12] However, misfortune would bond the two women together as if they had been blood sisters. Meanwhile, the Pope had written to the King and Queen, imploring them to take refuge in his dominions. But they were now too closely watched to be able to escape together. They begged Madame Élisabeth to go, but she refused to leave them, not even with her brother Provence and his wife, who managed to get away. The King tried to get the Queen to leave, but she would not go without him. The moderate revolutionary Mirabeau and loyal Count Fersen then implored the King to flee with the Dauphin, but he did not want to leave the rest of his family alone at the hands of the mob. And so the summer of 1791 slipped away.

In August, the King of Prussia and the Emperor of Austria declared that they were ready to help the King if his life was threatened, much to Madame Élisabeth's joy, although they made it clear they were not eager to invest too many of their resources in restoring France to her former prestigious position. The *emigrés*, aristocrats who had fled abroad, snickered at Louis, calling him "King Log." They did not think he was dealing energetically enough with the Revolution, but from a place of safety it was easy for them to criticize the King, who was left with only a handful of loyal supporters, and was for all practical purposes a prisoner in his own palace. On September 14, 1791, the Feast of Exaltation of the Holy Cross, the King was forced to sign the new constitution, in which he had very few powers, except that of the veto. Afterwards, he staggered into Antoinette's room. Madame Campan describes the scene thus:

> 'Ah! Madame,' cried he, his voice choked by tears, 'why were you present at this sitting? to witness—' these words were interrupted by sobs. The Queen threw herself upon her knees before him, and pressed him in her arms. I remained with them, not from any blamable curiosity, but from a stupefaction which rendered me incapable of determining what I ought to do. The Queen said to me, 'Oh! go, go!' with an accent which expressed, 'Do not remain to see the dejection and despair of your sovereign!' I withdrew, struck with the contrast between the shouts of joy without the palace and the profound grief which oppressed the

sovereigns withins.[13]

In the months that followed Louis sank into a silent stupor, so that he did not even recognize his own children; once he asked who Louis-Charles was.[14] Eventually, he extracted himself from such a depressed state, and with renewed courage was able to face the fresh gale of tragedy that broke upon them in the months that followed. He unflinchingly used his right to veto on November 29, 1791, when the Assembly decreed that priests who had refused to take the oath were to be punished. The Jacobins, the radical party of the Revolution, so named because they congregated at the Dominican monastery of Saint Jacques, were livid. They increased the campaign of calumny and slander against the King and Queen, calling them Monsieur and Madame Veto, and worse. Especially vicious was the procurator Hébèrt's gazette *Père Duchesne*, which urged the people to crime and violence while showing the Queen in obscene poses.

On April 20, 1792, the violent feelings were somewhat pacified when the Assembly voted to have the King declare war on Austria. It showed, at least, that he was not in league with his wife's relatives. France was in no condition to fight, but the Assembly was eager to spread the principles of the Revolution to other lands. Madame Élisabeth hoped that now the Austrians and the French *émigrés* would come to rescue them. But the King feared that with war, all was lost for them, because if anything went wrong for the French, the Queen would be accused of sending military secrets to her nephew the Emperor. The past spring, they had lost their staunchest supporter, King Gustavus III of Sweden, stabbed to death at a masked ball. On Good Friday, 1792, the Assembly passed a decree forbidding priests to wear clerical dress, and prohibiting Christian emblems. The worldly, juring clergy had long abandoned priestly garb; while the devout had already gone underground.

There was an article published not long ago entitled "Ciphers of Marie-Antoinette and Fersen" by S. Tomokiyo[15] which sheds light upon the royal family's desperate years of virtual imprisonment at the Tuileries palace between October 6, 1789 and August 19, 1792. Author Jean Chalon in his biography *Chère Marie-Antoinette* dubs the Queen *la Sévigné des Tuileries* after the famous Madame de Sévigné, known for her prodigious letter writing.[16] In her determination to save the lives of her family, restore the royal authority, and preserve the throne for her son, Antoinette wrote hundreds of letters, not only to Count Fersen, the representative of King Gustavus III of Sweden who was trying to save them, but to her relatives and friends, to Comte Mercy the Austrian ambassador, to fellow monarchs such as the Queens of Spain and Portugal, and to moderate revolutionaries, the Girondins, such as Barnave.[17] One must remember that from any careful study of her correspondence it appears that the Queen was balancing precipitously between opposing parties as she attempted to persuade Fersen, Barnave, and Mercy into doing what she needed them to do. Many of the letters were written in cipher, that is, in a secret code, which could be broken only by using certain key words. The complexity of the ciphers should destroy forever the myth that Antoinette was not intelligent; indeed, she must have had a very high I.Q. in order to adroitly master so many puzzles. Writing in code could be challenging. As Antoinette wrote to the Comte de Provence: "At length I have succeeded in deciphering your letter, my dear Brother, but it was not without difficulty. There were so many mistakes [in the use of the cipher]. Still, it is not surprising, seeing that you are a beginner and that your letter was a long one...."[18] Sometimes white or invisible ink was also used, about which the Queen complained, saying: "Little accustomed to writing in this manner, my writing will be indecipherable."[19] The Queen burned most of the letters she received but many of those she sent to others have been preserved. The relatives of Axel von Fersen saved some original manuscripts of the letters from the Queen to Fersen, although not always in her hand-writing but in Fersen's after he had decoded it. S. Tomokiyo quotes extensively from a 2009 paper by Jacques Patarin and Valérie Nachef based upon a study of the cipher used by Marie-Antoinette and Count Fersen for French television.[20] According to Tomokiyo:

> Patarin and Nachef found in the French National Archives some encrypted letters with the keyword written on it. The manuscript letters were edited and published in 1877 by Baron von Klinckowström, a grandson of an elder sister of Fersen. The manuscript letters, long believed to have been destroyed, were auctioned by descendants of Baron von Klinckowström in 1982 and purchased by the French National Archives. Two exemplary manuscript sheets are reproduced in the paper of Patarin and Nachef.
>
> The first one is from a letter dated 8 July 1791 from Marie-Antoinette to Fersen. The keyword courage is written below the ciphertext and deciphered plaintext is written above the ciphertext. This letter is printed in, e.g., Klinckowstrom p.147, according to which the deciphering is in the hand of Fersen. (In this manuscript, Fersen writes keyword letters below the ciphertext, contrary to the above example, in which we wrote keyword letters above the ciphertext.)

Marie-Antoinette, Daughter of the Caesars

The second one is from a letter dated 10 October 1791 from Fersen to Marie-Antoinette. This shows the plaintext and keyword letters below it. Probably, this sheet was used by Fersen for enciphering. This letter is printed in, e.g., Klinckowstrom p.193, according to which this is a minute in the hand of Fersen. (The actual letter received by Marie-Antoinette was probably lost during the French Revolution.)[21]

The paper by Patarin and Nachef is focused totally on the correspondence of the Queen and Count Fersen. While some of their interpretations are questionable, they include pictures of the original manuscripts which make one realize the complexity of discerning the hidden meaning of the letters. There is no question that Patarin and Nachef's treatise "I will love you to the death" is like something right out of a romance novel. I do think that the passages written to Fersen have suffered from extrapolation while undergoing decryption. In the words of the authors:

> Most of the time, these letters show that Marie-Antoinette is trying to find alliances with foreign countries in order to restore the Monarchy in France. But some parts of her letters are devoted to expressing her love for the count. A French TV channel asked us to explain Marie-Antoinette's encryption algorithm. This led us to the study of some letters. There are very few letters written by the queen which are still available. Most of them were destroyed. Fersen kept the letters he received and deciphered, and also the letters he wrote himself to Marie-Antoinette. These archives were kept by his nephews and great-nephews. In 1877, Baron von Klinckowstrom published all the letters,

but some parts were missing or crossed out. In 1982, some descendants of Baron von Klinckowstrom auctioned letters that were supposedly destroyed, and the French Historical Archives bought them. It is surprising to notice that on one hand, historians who published Marie-Antoinette's letters always chose the deciphered version published by Baron von Klinckowstrom....[22]

When the letters of the Queen and Count Fersen were published by his great nephew Baron de Klinckowström in the late nineteenth century, they proved the nature of the Queen and Fersen's relationship to be principally a diplomatic one, especially on the part of the Count, whose letters are coldly businesslike. In certain of the letters, mainly those from the Queen to Fersen, passages have been erased and are indicated by rows of dots in the printed text. The Coursacs, Webster, and Delorme believe that Fersen erased certain passages himself. The erasures of Fersen were most likely sensitive diplomatic issues, not declarations of love, as some authors have claimed. They concealed allusions to the Queen's disagreements with her brothers-in-law Artois and Provence, or references to the Duc d'Orléans and other revolutionaries, or even mentions of spies or persons whose families would have been compromised had the letters fallen into the wrong hands. Also, it must be noted that most letters from the era, all handwritten of course, have sentences scribbled out or erased; it does not mean that every scribbled out or erased passage were words of forbidden love.

In 1907 a certain Monsieur Lucien Maury published in *Revue Bleue* what he claimed to be a fragment of a love letter of the Queen to Fersen. Some collections of Antoinette's letters include it although it has never been verified to actually be from the Queen:

July 29, 1791

> I can tell you that I love you and indeed that is all I have time for. I am well. Do not worry about me. I hope you to be well too. Write me cipher letters and send them by mail to Mrs Brown's address, in a double envelope to Mr. de Gougens. Send the letters by your manservant. Tell me to whom I should send the letters I could write you. I cannot live without that. Farewell, the most loved and the most loving of men. I kiss you with all my heart.[23]

The letter had no signature, was not in the Queen's handwriting, only in the cipher she used, jotted down by Fersen in cipher, as Maury himself admitted. There is no proof it was from the Queen but could have been from one of the many ladies with whom Fersen dallied over the years. Patarin and Nachef also include the same dubious letter in their study although they admit that Maury did not give any details about the decryption and that there is no corresponding cipher text in existence. I also question the reliability of the claims of Patarin and Nachef that the hidden phrases they have discovered are sweet words from the Queen to the Count. For instance, the letter of June 18, 1791 is supposed to be a letter to Fersen with a request to send a letter to...Fersen? Its decryption reads thus:

> Do not worry about us. It seems that the chiefs of the Assembly want to behave more softly. Talk to my parents about foreign approaches (6 encrypted letters). If they are afraid it is necessary to come to compromise with them. Burn all that is (10 encrypted letters) and send the remainder of the letter to M. von Fersen. He is with the king of

Sweden. [24]

Therefore I take the "love letter" from Marie-Antoinette which Patarin and Nachef have "discovered" with a grain of salt. Even if the romantic words were absolutely proved to be genuinely penned by the Queen, it must be remembered that she also wrote loving words to many of her friends of both sexes, calling them "*mon cher coeur*" that is "my dear heart" and saying such things as "*je vous embrasse très fort*" which means "I kiss you hard."[25] Such was her manner of expression with those of whom she was fond. It must also be kept in mind that Antoinette absolutely needed the help for the royal cause that only Fersen could give in the outside world; it should not be surprising if her words to him were especially tender, if we are going to believe Patarin and Nachef's interpretation.

Although Tomokiyo says that the work of Patarin and Nachef have proved that the hidden passages were romantic and not diplomatic, here is one of their decryptions from a letter of Antoinette to Fersen, dated July 8, 1791, which indeed appears to be about diplomacy:

> There is no doubt that a foreign power could get into France, but the armed people would flee the borders and the troops from outside. Then they would make use of their weapons against their fellow citizens that they have been considering as enemies for two years. In our trip and especially since our return we have made every day the sad experiment to be considered as enemies. The king thinks that a full unlimited power as it composed even by dating it on June 20th, would be dangerous in its current state.[26]

Marie-Antoinette, Daughter of the Caesars

The Tomokiyo article provides a great service by discussing the ciphers used by Marie-Antoinette when writing coded letters to other persons such as Comte de Mercy. To quote:

> Marie-Antoinette's use of cipher was not limited to her correspondence with Fersen. Marie-Antoinette is also known to have written in cipher to her brother Leopold II (Arneth1). Feuillet de Conches1 mentions a particular cipher arranged between Marie-Antoinette and Mercy (Vol.2, p.95). (When in Paris as Austrian minister, the Comte de Mercy had worked to strengthen the alliance between France and Austria, which materialized as the marriage of Marie-Antoinette into the France in 1770. He was instructed by Maria-Theresa to act as a mentor of the young princess. In 1792, he became governor-general of the Austrian Netherlands.) On the other hand, Marie-Antoinette appears to have used the cipher with Fersen also in her correspondence with the Comte de Mercy.... Marie-Antoinette had relatives in many courts in Italy, including her elder sisters Maria Carolina, Queen of Naples, and Maria Amalia, Duchess of Parma. Marie-Antoinette's cipher with them is recorded in Secret memoirs of the royal family of France, during the revolution, Vol. 2. The author is an English lady-in-waiting to Princess of Lamballe, a confidante of Marie-Antoinette. The author says Marie-Antoinette carried on a very extensive correspondence with Edmund Burke through the medium of Princess of Lamballe and she frequently 'deciphered' letters (presumably from Burke) (p.140). Princess of Lamballe was sent to England by the Queen in 1791 to seek help to the French royal family. Twice during her residence in

England, the author was sent by Marie-Antoinette with papers communicating the result of the secret mission to the Queen of Naples. On the second of these trips, after reaching the destination after travelling night and day, she was immediately compelled to decipher the papers with the Queen of Naples in the office of the secretary of state (p.140). On 2 August 1792, when the situation was becoming critical, she left Paris with Marie-Antoinette's letters to the Queen of Naples, the Duchess of Parma, and other relatives in Italy. She was entrusted with the cipher and the key for the letters (p.304-326).[27]

Madame Élisabeth of France, the sister of Louis XVI, also used a cipher when communicating with her friend the Marquise de Raigecourt. It appears, however, that the princess did not make use of ciphers as often as Antoinette did, since some of Élisabeth's letters were later used against her at her trial.

While I may question some of the interpretations of the articles I have been quoting, I applaud the marvelous efforts of Tomokiyo and of Patarin and Nachef in giving us a glimpse into the extraordinary way in which people communicated sensitive information in the days before telephones and telegraphs, not to mention computers and cell phones.

As of this writing, the media has reported so-called new discoveries of scribbled passages in letters between the Queen and Fersen. A great deal of excitement has been elicited by those who think that they finally have proof that the Antoinette and Fersen were lovers, not only that they were lovers, but that Fersen fathered the Queen's two youngest children. How odd, since every time Fersen visited Versailles, the Queen was already pregnant by her husband. Nevertheless, beneath the scribble in a letter from the Queen to Fersen, some researchers have claimed to have discovered the phrase "I love you madly." The letter was written on January 4th, 1792. Here is the entire phrase, which someone covered with ink: "I am going to close, but not without telling you, my dear and very tender friend, that I love you madly and never, ever could I exist a moment without adoring you." (Or in French: *Je vais finire, non pas sans vous dire mon bien cher et tendre ami que je vous aime à la folie et que jamais jamais je ne peu être un moment sans vous adorer.*) The ink of the scribble is different from that of the original pen, so the Queen probably is not the one who blackened the sentence in question. It indicates she felt she had nothing to hide. Perhaps because she spoke about so many others in the same manner, including her children, saying of Louis-Charles "*je l'aime à la folie*" or "I love him madly" as she wrote to Madame de Polignac in December of 1789.[28] According to Marie-Antoinette scholar Anna Gibson:

> Critically, the claim that 'I love you madly' is for lovers only does not hold up when you compare it to other contemporary letters from that time period. The claim also wavers when you take into consideration Marie Antoinette's personal style of writing. 'I love you madly' does not differ very much from phrases Marie Antoinette regularly wrote to people she genuinely adored. The intensity with which Marie Antoinette wrote to people she considered her cherished companions cannot be overstated. Her letters to these few — people she knew from childhood, people she brought into her intimate 'Trianon' circle, and those who remained loyal to her during the Revolution — contain such gushing phrases as 'I kiss you tenderly,' 'It would

be a great pleasure for me to kiss you,' 'My feelings for you are tender and grow every day,' 'my tender heart,' 'my dear heart,' 'I kiss you with all my heart,' 'I embrace you with all my soul,' 'I will never cease to love you,' 'I kiss you hard,' and other flourishes that would easily be considered romantic today. Marie Antoinette even wrote to Yolande de Polignac saying that 'nothing but death could make me stop loving you.'

Could lovers have used the phrase? Of course. But in the context of Marie Antoinette and Fersen, it's not some outlier phrasing that is totally incongruous with Marie Antoinette's normal style. It shows that she considered him an intimate, loved companion who wasn't just loyal to her but was, by all her accounts, fighting for her life and the life of her family. If there was any point where Marie Antoinette was going to use her trademark tender, romantic phrases, the years where Fersen was an almost sole outside devotee when she was living in a country that was increasingly hostile to her is definitely that point. And remember: 'I love you madly' was not hidden by the queen. It was written plainly in her letter to Fersen, as were her romantic phrases in letters to her other cherished loved ones. If this was a phrase reserved for lovers, it is extremely unlikely that Marie Antoinette would ever risk everything (her security, the future of her children, the stability of the monarchy, her reputation to the European powers, to name a few things) by so casually revealing something that was considered treasonous. So what does the phrase mean? The answer is genuinely simple: Marie Antoinette wrote passionately, romantically, even gushingly to people she considered intimate friends. Before and after the revolution. And she knew how to use that flattering language to keep people on her side, when she needed to do so, and she definitely needed to bring Fersen back around after his recent criticisms and fears, which I will get more into below.

The role that Fersen played in the last years of Marie Antoinette's life was an intense one, that in all likelihood bonded them emotionally in a way that is difficult to imagine today. He was, in the queen's estimation, working to save their lives. He was one of the few people who was willing to take an active role in saving the royal family and the crown, beyond vague promises by foreign rulers or the dangerous behavior of the emigrated Artois and Provence elsewhere in Europe or the moderates in France that Marie Antoinette never fully trusted. Is it any wonder that Marie Antoinette wrote to him as she did other intimates like Polignac, so favored that she had to flee France? No, it is not. As with the use of gossip as evidence, using this phrase and similar phrases as evidence that the two were physical lovers does not stand up to an extrapolating critical view. Marie Antoinette wrote this way — many women of that time period wrote this way.

If 'I love you madly' proves that Marie Antoinette and Axel Fersen were physical lovers, then it stands to reason that 'Nothing but death can make me stop loving you' should be used as proof that Marie Antoinette and Yolande de Polignac were also physical lovers. Yet once again, I doubt historians would claim that because the Queen wrote romantically to Polignac, they were lovers, physical or otherwise, due to the context of Marie Antoinette's personality and the general romantic writing style of her contemporaries.[29]

The circumstances in which the Queen found herself must also be looked at carefully. Gibson continues her analysis, saying:

> For the last several months, Marie Antoinette and Louis XVI had been embarking on course of action that none of their allies...had really approved. That course of action was to play both sides: ally themselves with Barnave and other constitutionals, all the while keeping up their correspondence with Fersen, Craufurd, Breteuil, and various European monarchs. In September of 1791, Louis XVI had also accepted the Constitution and the royal couple decided to outwardly support the Constitution, not just to appease the rumblings in the government but to, as Louis XVI put it, show the people that the Constitution could not work by following it to the letter. Abroad, this had the effect of sending the émigrés, the king's brothers and European monarchs into a war-minded frenzy. The king's brothers were stirring the pot by spear-heading the raising of *émigré*-based armies with the intention of sending those armies into France to take back control over the country. On December 14th, 1791, Louis XVI —without consulting or notifying Fersen and the others in contact with the queen—addressed the Assembly and declared that any European powers which did not disband *émigré*-based troops by January 15th, 1792 would be considered enemies of France. Furthermore, he declared that he wrote to Leopold II and informed him that he was fully prepared to declare war on Austria if those troops were not disbanded.
>
> Eight days later, Fersen wrote Marie Antoinette a lengthy letter which contained what the queen

later referred to as 'scoldings.' In this letter, Fersen admonished the queen for not being openly affectionate towards people he was trying to get on their side....Yet the 'scoldings' in this letter did not stop there. Fersen then wrote that he was astounded and grieved by the king's unsupported decision and the fact that Marie Antoinette did not tell him about it....Fersen went on to suggest that Marie Antoinette should not have acted without consulting Fersen and Breteuil, and that by doing so she invited disastrous consequences. He also questioned the queen's confidence in him....Is it any wonder that Marie Antoinette, who had excelled at charming people from an early age, knew how to reassure Fersen — who, by the tone of this letter and those leading up to it, was becoming increasingly critical of her and wary of her decisions? Fersen himself said it best: 'Do you not think that it would be well to show persons of good-feeling and good-will certain marks of kindness?' Fersen wanted reassurance that the queen trusted him, that she accepted his devotion, and that she considered his confidence worthy of respect. And she did just that, as she had throughout the last year to this years-long friend who she saw as fighting for the salvation of her family and for her country.[30]

Other experts also remain unconvinced that the tender phrases indicates a love affair. To quote from an interview in an online journal:

> According to Fanny Cosandey, a French historian and a professor at the School for Advanced Studies in the Social Sciences in Paris, while the count and the queen may have shared a love story, it likely only unfolded on the page, not in the bedroom.

'Personally, I don't think it was possible for Queen Marie Antoinette to have had an actual physical relationship with Fersen,' Cosandey told *The Daily Beast*. 'Maybe it was a platonic love, maybe it was a stronger relationship… but I don't think these documents are going to tell us much more.'[31]

On June 19, 1792, the King vetoed the Assembly's decision to deport twenty thousand priests to the jungles of Guiana for slave labor because they had refused to deny the papal supremacy. The next day, Paris marched on the Tuileries, chanting, "Down with the veto! Down with the priests!" The Royal Family was again in danger. Madame Élisabeth clung to her brother's coat, refusing to leave him, and together they went to the first floor to meet the mob. Both men and women were armed with everything from axes and pikes to sticks and paring knives. Many of the intruders were already rampaging through the palace, looking for the Queen. They were determined this time to kill her, but she was hiding in a secret passage with the children. She had to leave her hiding place when the mob began hacking at the doors and walls with axes, so a nobleman dragged her into the Council Room, where she and the children were barricaded behind a table. She begged her ladies and the guards to let her go to the King. "It is only with me the people are angry. I am going to offer them their victim. Let me go the King, my duty calls me there!" Of course, the guards prevented her from going. Meanwhile, the rabble thought Élisabeth was the Queen, and she begged: "Do not undeceive them," hoping to die in the Queen's place. Louis held the bulk of them at bay for almost two hours, in spite of their insults. They were amazed that he did not appear to be afraid, or even the least bit shaken. "Put your hand on my heart, and see if it beats any faster," he said to them. Eventually they stopped shouting, "Down with the veto!" and several unspeakable descriptions of the Queen. They handed the King a bottle of wine and a red cap, which he put on, drinking to the health of the nation. At last, the mayor of Paris, Pétion, arrived and told the people it was time to leave. The King calmly asked if they would like to see the State apartments, and so in a procession that could almost be called orderly, they traipsed through the Palace, filled with awe. Eventually, they came upon Antoinette and her children, but did no harm except for one fierce old fish wife, who screeched, 'You vile woman!' at the Queen. Antoinette calmly replied, "What harm have I ever done to you?" Soon, the people filed out of the palace, and the Royal Family was reunited.[32]

Louis began quietly strengthening the defense of the Tuileries, in preparation for the next attack. On July 14, 1792 on the Champs de Mars, Louis renewed his oath to the constitution, surrounded by another violent, cursing horde of people. Yet they ended by shouting, "Long live the King!" Louis' courage seemed to affect them that way. In the meantime, the Jacobins under Danton planned on seizing the government and declaring a republic, using the Brunswick Manifesto as propaganda. The Duke of Brunswick had recently declared that if any harm came to the Royal Family he would use military force on Paris, to Louis XVI's horror. He disavowed the manifesto before the Assembly. The King and his sister tried to convince the Queen to flee to Vienna. At one point she agreed to go with Princesse de Lamballe. She secretly confessed and received Holy Communion, and packed, but at the last minute changed her mind. She could not bring herself to leave the King or her children. Meanwhile, the family was insulted even while at Mass or at Vespers, with the chapel musicians playing the revolutionary song *Ça ira* when the King and Queen entered. People congregated outside the Queen's windows with lewd drawings and placards, sometimes even exposing themselves in indecent ways. The King and Queen were advised to wear special iron vests under their clothes to protect them from assassination attempts, but both refused. "Whoever assassinates me will be releasing me from a truly wretched existence," said Antoinette.

On the morning of August 10, 1793, there could be heard the tramp of feet, along with the *Marseillaise* and *Ça ira*. A mob was again marching on the Tuileries. It was the Feast of Saint Laurence, who had been roasted on the gridiron. The revolutionary authorities advised the King, for the sake of his wife and children, to leave the palace, the champions of liberty being either unwilling or unable to control the people. Accompanied by their most faithful attendants, the Royal Family escaped through the palace gardens, where very strangely the premature shedding of leaves had already made deep piles on the ground, to the National Assembly, where they took refuge in the stenographer's box, called the Logographe. Louis had ordered the Swiss to lay down their arms, thinking that if they surrendered there would be no bloodshed. The servants and Swiss guards who remained in the palace were butchered and mutilated by the indignant citizens. Even children threw heads in the air and caught them on sticks. The enraged populace poured into the National Assembly, and screamed at the beleaguered family, who had little to eat except what the English ambassador's wife sent over. They spent three days in the cramped box behind the President's chair, and three nights in a deserted convent, where they were always within earshot of the screeches of: "No more kings!" or "Down with the Fat Pig!", and especially things like "Death to the Austrian whore!" The crowd had plundered the palace, and mocked the Queen with her possessions they had rifled, including some jewels.

They had also stolen a golden ciborium full of consecrated Hosts from the palace chapel which were publicly desecrated. After long debates, it was finally decided by the Assembly to imprison the family in the medieval fortress known as the Temple. The Temple was the former headquarters of the Knights Templar, who had been disbanded by the Church in the 1300's because of accusations of occult practices, for which they were later absolved by the Holy See. The knights had been tortured and killed at the hands of the French King Philip the Fair, who was himself rebellious towards the Pope. And now Philip's dethroned descendant was to be humbled on the very site of the former infamy.

In August 1792, Louis XVI, Antoinette, their children, and Louis' sister Madame Élisabeth were incarcerated in the Temple Prison. Marie-Thérèse-Charlotte later described their experiences in her memoirs:

> The following is the way our family passed their days. My father rose at seven, and was employed in his devotions till eight. Afterwards he dressed himself and my brother, and at nine came to breakfast with my mother. After breakfast, my father taught my brother his lessons till eleven. The child then played till twelve, at which hour the whole family was obliged to walk in the garden, whatever the weather might be; because the guard, which was relieved at the time, wished to see all the prisoners, and satisfy themselves that we were safe. The walk lasted till dinner, which was at two o'clock. After dinner my father and mother played at tric-trac or piquet, or, to speak more truly, pretended to play, that they might have an opportunity of saying a few words to one another. At four o'clock, my mother and we went up stairs

and took my brother with us, as my father was accustomed to sleep a little at this hour. At six my brother went down again to my father to say his lessons, and to play till supper-time. After supper, at nine o'clock, my mother undressed him quickly, and put him to bed. We then went up to our own apartment again, and the King did not go to bed till eleven. My mother worked a good deal of tapestry: she directed my studies, and often made me read aloud. My aunt was frequently in prayer, and read every morning the divine service of the day. She read a good many religious books, and sometimes, at the Queen's request, would read aloud.[33]

"Incarceration of the Royal family in the Temple, August, 1792."

Marie-Antoinette, Daughter of the Caesars

"Murder of the Princesse de Lamballe"

22 LES ADIEUX

"I will drink the chalice to the dregs." —Louis XVI

In the Temple, the Queen and Madame Élisabeth managed to send messages to friends and relatives wrapped in balls of silk. They were separated from all of their attendants except for the steward Hüe, the valet Cléry and two footman, Chamilly and Turgy. The Princesse de Lamballe had been separated from the other prisoners, and was held in the dreaded prison of La Force. In the Temple, they were constantly derided by the guards. The King and Queen responded to the mockeries with either silence or courtesy, forbidding their children to complain, and insisting that they be polite to their captors, who reacted by writing graffiti on the wall which read "Strangle the cubs."[1] Louis and Antoinette focused on the education of Madame Royale and Louis-Charles. Antoinette instructed her daughter in Bible studies and music while Louis taught both children Latin, history, geography, and literature. Madame Élisabeth was the math teacher, although the guards confiscated the table she used for teaching arithmetic because they thought it was a secret code. The guards harassed the family a good deal, blowing tobacco smoke into their faces as they walked by. They threatened both the King and Queen in front of their children, describing how they would torture them to death, which frightened both children and reduced the Dauphin to tears.[2]

The Temple tower had, until the Revolution, belonged to the Knights of Malta, of whom the honorary Grand Master had been Artois' son the Duc d'Angoulême, and housed a library with 1400 books. The King pointed to books by Voltaire and Rousseau and said to his steward Hüe: "Those two men have been the ruin of France."[3] The King spent much of his time reading. Between August 1792 and January 1793 he read 250 books in several different languages. As always, he favored Shakespeare, Erasmus, and the classics of antiquity, as well as *The Imitation of Christ*. The Queen also read daily from *The Imitation of Christ* by Thomas à Kempis. The King taught his son a new prayer to say every day:

> God all-powerful, you have created me and redeemed me. I adore you. Preserve the days of the King my father, and those of my family. Protect us against our enemies. Give Madame de Tourzel the strength she needs to sustain herself through the pain she endures because of us.[4]

On September 2, 1792 there began five days of carnage unlike anything Paris had experienced since the days of the Wars of Religion. The streets ran with blood, as the prisons were emptied, and the hapless inmates thrown to a sea of knives, pikes, and cudgels. Fourteen hundred people were slaughtered, and the murderers were seen to dip their baguettes into the blood of the victims. After refusing to renounce her allegiance to the King and Queen, the Princesse de Lamballe was handed over to two lines of criminals with sharp instruments.

The first man to strike was a former protegé of the princess, whose baptism and religious instruction she had provided, but whom she had been forced to send from her service when he took to immoral ways. The blow killed her; her corpse was mutilated and raped. The princess' head was borne to a hairdresser who, under duress, arranged and powdered the luxuriant, blood-splattered tresses. The head was then carried in triumph to the Temple, where the maniacs vowed to make the Queen kiss the cold face of her friend. Among the garments that had been stripped from the dead princess' body were found a red moroccan volume of *The Imitation of Christ* and a Sacred Heart badge.

In late November 1792, the King was separated from his family. This was a hardship especially for the little Dauphin because Louis played with him and kept his active mind engaged with lessons, games and stories. Louis found it particularly traumatic to have his son taken away. The King and the Dauphin had had their own quarters, separate from the women of the family. As Cléry recorded:

> At eleven o'clock, while the king was giving his son a reading-lesson, two municipals entered and told His Majesty that they had come to fetch young Louis and take him to his mother. The king wished to know the reason of this removal; the commissioners replied that they executed the orders of the council of the Commune. His Majesty kissed his son tenderly, and charged me to go with him. When I returned to the king, I told him I had left the young prince in his mother's arms, and that seemed to tranquillize His Majesty. One of the commissioners entered to inform him that Chambon, mayor of Paris, was in the council-chamber and was coming up to see him.

'What does he want of me?' asked the king.

'I do not know,' replied the municipal.

His Majesty walked hastily up and down his room for some moments; then he seated himself in an arm-chair close to the head of his bed; the door was half closed and the municipal dared not enter, to avoid, as he told me, questions. Half an hour passed thus in the deepest silence. The commissioner became uneasy at not hearing the king; he entered softly, and found him with his head on one of his hands, apparently deeply absorbed.

'What do you want?' asked the king, in a loud voice.

'I feared you were ill,' replied the municipal.

'I am obliged to you,' said the king, in a tone of the keenest sorrow, 'but the manner in which my son has been taken from me is infinitely painful to me.'

The municipal said nothing and withdrew.[5]

On Christmas Day, Louis XVI, alone and still separated from his family, made his will.

> The last Will and Testament of Louis XVI, King of France and Navarre, given on Christmas day, 1792.
>
> In the name of the Very holy Trinity, Father, Son and Holy Ghost.
>
> To-day, the 25th day of December, 1792, I, Louis XVI King of France, being for more than four months imprisoned with my family in the tower of the Temple at Paris, by those who were my subjects, and deprived of all communication whatsoever, even with my family, since the eleventh instant; moreover, involved in a trial the end of which it is impossible to foresee, on account of the passions of men, and for which one can find

neither pretext nor means in any existing law, and having no other witnesses, for my thoughts than God to whom I can address myself, I hereby declare, in His presence, my last wishes and feelings.

I leave my soul to God, my creator; I pray Him to receive it in His mercy, not to judge it according to its merits but according to those of Our Lord Jesus Christ who has offered Himself as a sacrifice to God His Father for us other men, no matter how hardened, and for me first.

I die in communion with our Holy Mother, the Catholic, Apostolic, Roman Church, which holds authority by an uninterrupted succession, from St. Peter, to whom Jesus Christ entrusted it; I believe firmly and I confess all that is contained in the creed and the commandments of God and the Church, the sacraments and the mysteries, those which the Catholic Church teaches and has always taught. I never pretend to set myself up as a judge of the various way of expounding the dogma which rend the church of Jesus Christ, but I agree and will always agree, if God grant me life the decisions which the ecclesiastical superiors of the Holy Catholic Church give and will always give, in conformity with the disciplines which the Church has followed since Jesus Christ. I pity with all my heart our brothers who may be in error but I do not claim to judge them, and I do not love them less in Christ, as our Christian charity teaches us, and I pray to God to pardon all my sins. I have sought scrupulously to know them, to detest them and to humiliate myself in His presence. Not being able to obtain the ministration of a Catholic priest, I pray God to receive the confession which I feel in having put my name (although this was against my will) to acts which might be contrary to the discipline and the belief of the Catholic church, to which I have always remained sincerely attached. I pray God to receive my firm resolution, if He grants me life, to have the ministrations of a Catholic priest, as soon as I can, in order to confess my sins and to receive the sacrament of penance.

I beg all those whom I might have offended inadvertently (for I do not recall having knowingly offended any one), or those whom I may have given bad examples or scandals, to pardon the evil which they believe I could have done them.

I beseech those who have the kindness to join their prayers to mine, to obtain pardon from God for my sins.

I pardon with all my heart those who made themselves my enemies, without my have given them any cause, and I pray God to pardon them, as well as those who, through false or misunderstood zeal, did me much harm.

I commend to God my wife and my children, my sister, my aunts, my brothers, and all those who are attached to me by ties of blood or by whatever other means. I pray God particularly to cast eyes of compassion upon my wife, my children, and my sister, who suffered with me for so long a time, to sustain them with His mercy if they shall lose me, and as long as they remain in his mortal world.

I commend my children to my wife; I have never doubted her maternal tenderness for them. I enjoin her above all to make them good Christians and honest individuals; to make them view the grandeurs of this world (if they are condemned to experience them) as very dangerous and transient goods, and turn their attention towards the one solid and enduring glory, eternity. I beseech my sister to kindly continue her tenderness for my children and to take the place of a mother, should they have the misfortune of losing theirs.

I beg my wife to forgive all the pain which she suffered for me, and the sorrows which I may have caused her in the course of our union; and she may feel sure that I hold nothing against her, if she has anything with which to reproach herself.

I most warmly enjoin my children that, after what they owe to God, which should come first, they should remain forever united among themselves, submissive and obedient to their mother, and grateful for all the care and trouble which she has taken with them, as well as in memory of me. I beg them to regard my sister as their second mother.

I exhort my son, should he have the misfortune of becoming king, to remember he owes himself wholly to the happiness of his fellow citizens; that he should forget all hates and all grudges, particularly those connected with the misfortunes and sorrows which I am experiencing; that he can make the people happy only by ruling according to laws: but at the same time to remember that a king cannot make himself respected and do the good that is in his heart unless he has the necessary authority, and that otherwise, being tangled up in his activities and not inspiring respect, he is more harmful than useful.

I exhort my son to care for all the persons who are attached to me, as much as his circumstances will allow, to remember that it is a sacred debt which I have contracted towards the children and relatives of those who have perished for me and also those who are wretched for my sake. I know that there are many persons, among those who were near me, who did not conduct themselves towards me as they should have and who have even shown ingratitude, but I pardon them (often in moments of trouble and turmoil one is not master of oneself), and I beg my son that, if he finds an occasion, he should think only of their misfortunes.

I should have wanted here to show my gratitude to those who have given me a true and disinterested affection; if, on the one hand, I was keenly hurt by the ingratitude and disloyalty of those to whom I have always shown kindness, as well as to their relatives and friends, on the other hand I have had the consolation of seeing the affection and voluntary interest which many persons have shown me. I beg them to receive my thanks. In the situation in which matters still are, I fear to compromise them if I should speak more explicitly, but I especially enjoin my son to seek occasion to recognize them.

I should, nevertheless, consider it a calumny on the nation if I did not openly recommend to my son MM. De Chamilly and Hüe, whose genuine attachment for me led them to imprison themselves with me in this sad abode. I also recommend Clery, for whose attentiveness I have nothing but praise ever since he has been with me. Since it is he who has remained with me until the end, I beg the gentlemen of the commune to hand over to him my clothes, my books, my watch, my purse, and all other small effects which have been deposited with the council of the commune.

I pardon again very readily those who guard me, the ill treatment and the vexations which they thought it necessary to impose upon me. I found a few sensitive and compassionate souls among them – may they in their hearts enjoy the tranquillity which their way of thinking gives them.

I beg MM. De Malesherbes, Tronchet and De Sèze to receive all my thanks and the expressions of my feelings for all the cares and troubles they took for me.

I finish by declaring before God, and ready to appear before Him, that I do not reproach myself with any of the crimes with which I am charged.

Made in duplicate in the Tower of the Temple, the 25th of December 1792.

LOUIS [6][7]

The King was brought to trial before the Commune of the new republic on December 26, 1792. The charges leveled against him were quite flimsy; the trial was a mockery. Among other things, he was accused of distributing money to the poor for the purposes of "enslaving the nation."[8]

"I always took pleasure in relieving the needy," he candidly answered, "but I never had any treacherous motives." When accused of shedding the blood of his own people, his composure, it was reported, clouded with pain and disbelief, since he had avoided violence at great cost to himself and his family. The dignified resignation of his manner, the straightforward honesty of his replies, the serenity in his eyes, brought even his most virulent enemies to a confused and admiring silence, so that even a cry of "Long live the King!" would not have seemed out of place. With the help of his lawyers, Messieurs de Séze and de Malesherbes, he insisted that he had always upheld the Constitution, he had not broken any of the new laws, and could not be held responsible for his political actions before his acceptance of the Constitution.[9] At the end of his defence of the King, Raymond de Sèze stated:

Louis ascended the throne at the age of twenty,

and at the age of twenty he gave to the throne the example of character. He brought to the throne no wicked weaknesses, no corrupting passions. He was economical, just, severe. He showed himself always the constant friend of the people. The people wanted the abolition of servitude. He began by abolishing it on his own lands. The people asked for reforms in the criminal law... he carried out these reforms. The people wanted liberty: he gave it to them. The people themselves came before him in his sacrifices. Nevertheless, it is in the name of these very people that one today demands... Citizens, I cannot finish... I stop myself before History. think how it will judge your judgment, and that the judgment of him will be judged by the centuries.[10]

When the Commune voted for his death, the deciding vote was cast by the King's own cousin, the Duc d'Orléans, now known as Philippe Egalité, a fervent revolutionary. To everyone's disgust, he voted when he could have legally abstained. On January 18, 1793, the King was sentenced to death. Abbé Edgeworth was sent for, the King having heard of him through the recommendation of Madame Élisabeth. His own confessor, a Eudist priest, had been killed during the September massacres. In the streets of Paris, young boys were hawking copies of *The Trial of Charles I.*

On January 20, 1793, Louis XVI said farewell to his family. He was to be guillotined the next morning. Madame Royale later recorded their last meeting; it is said that she fainted when saying good-bye to her father.

About seven o'clock in the evening we learned the sentence by the newsmen, who came crying it under our windows: a decree of the Convention permitted us to see the King. We ran to his apartment, and found him much altered; he wept for us, not for fear of death; he related his trial to my mother, apologizing for the wretches who had condemned him; he told her, that it was proposed to attempt to save him by having recourse to the primary assemblies, but that he would not consent, lest it should excite confusion in the country. He then gave my brother some religious advice, and desired, him above all, to forgive those who caused his death and he gave him his blessing, as well as to me.

My mother was very desirous that the whole family should pass the night with my father; but he opposed this, observing to her how much he needed some hours of repose and quiet. She asked at least to be allowed to see him next morning, to which he consented. But, when we were gone, he requested that we might not be permitted to return, as our presence afflicted him too much. He then remained with his confessor till midnight, when he went to bed....

Such was the life of my father during his rigorous captivity. In it were displayed piety, greatness of mind, and goodness; — mildness, fortitude, and patience, in bearing the most infamous insults, the most malignant calumnies; — Christian clemency, which heartily forgave even his murderers; — and the love of God, his family, and his people, of which he gave the most affecting proofs, even with his last breath, and of which he went to receive the reward in the bosom of his almighty and all-merciful Creator.[11]

The Abbé received permission from the authorities to say Mass first thing in the morning, with one of the officials bringing what was needed from a neighboring church. In the meantime, he heard the King's confession and gave him spiritual assistance. At dawn on January 21, 1793, Abbé said the Mass of the virgin-martyr Saint Agnes. The King knelt throughout the liturgy on a flat cushion that he habitually used at his prayers. He received Holy Communion with the greatest devotion. The Abbé left him in silent prayer as the mass ended, and he went to remove his vestments. Then he sat with the King and together they recited the Divine Office. The King used not only the breviary of the archdiocese of Paris, but was accustomed to praying the Office of the Order of the Holy Spirit on a daily basis. "My God," said the King," how blessed I am in the possession of my religious beliefs! Without my faith, what would I now be? But with it, how sweet death appears to me. Yes, there dwells on high an incorruptible Judge, from Whom I shall receive the justice refused to me on earth." [12]

The King spoke to his valet Cléry. "You will give this seal to my son, and this ring to the Queen." He removed his wedding ring and handed it to Cléry. "Tell her that I part from her with pain. This little packet contains locks of the hair of my family; you will give her that also. Tell the Queen, my dear sister, and my children that, although I promised to see them again this morning, I have resolved to spare them the ordeal of so cruel a separation. Tell them how much it costs me to go away without receiving their last embraces once more. I bid you to give them my last farewell."[13] He returned to the priest but they were frequently interrupted in their discussion by the guards. When the bells of Paris tolled eight o'clock there came a loud knock on the door. It was the commissary Santerre, the head of the National Guard, who had escorted the Abbé up to the King's room the night before. "Monsieur, it is time to go," he announced.

"I am busy," said the King, firmly and abruptly. "Wait for me. In few minutes I shall be with you." Louis XVI closed the door on Santerre. At that moment, his calm seemed to vanish. He threw himself at the Abbé's feet. "*Tout est consommé*," he cried, quoting John 19:30, which can be translated as "It is finished" or "It is consummated." "Monsieur, please give me your final benediction and pray God that He will sustain me until the end."[14] The Abbé made the sign of the cross over the prostrate King. He got to his feet, composed and collected, and opened the door. Several guards and commissaries were standing there; none of them removed their hats. The King, who wore a white jacket and grey breeches, refused the offer of an overcoat, but put on his three-cornered hat with its red, white, and blue cockade. He said good-bye to Cléry who, bathed in tears, unabashedly asked for the King's blessing.

"Messieurs," said the King, "I wish that Cléry might stay with my son, who is used to his care." The only response was a stony silence. He handed his last will and testament to an official who refused to take it.

"I am charged only with conducting you to the scaffold," the man proclaimed. Another official quietly took the document.

"I hope Cléry may be allowed to enter into the Queen's . . . into my wife's service," the King said. They did not reply. "Let us proceed," said the King.[15]

They left the tower. As they crossed the courtyard, the King twice looked back at the prison where his family was confined. They climbed into a coach. Two gendarmes insisted on riding with them, so they could have no private conversation. The King sank into a profound silence, until the Abbé offered him his breviary. Together they recited the seven penitential psalms. The streets of Paris were ominously quiet, except for the sound of the drums. All windows were shuttered and doors closed along the route of the King's *via dolorosa*. Cordons of soldiers, standing four deep, lined the streets. They came to the Place de la Révolution, formerly called Place de Louis XV, after the King's grandfather. A statue of the old King had once stood there. The Royal Family had been forced to watch the dismemberment of the statue, before being imprisoned in the Temple.

Thousands of people had come to see the execution of the King. A large space had been left around the scaffold, the crowd spilling out from it as far as the eye could see. The coach stopped. The King spoke to the two gendarmes before they jumped from it.

"Gentlemen, I recommend to you this good man." He was referring to Abbé Edgeworth. "Take care that no one insults him after my death. I charge you to prevent it." He spoke in majestic tones.

"Yes, yes, we will take care of him," one said, in a tone which the Abbé said made him freeze. [16]

As Louis XVI climbed out, the crowd began to buzz, "There he is! There he is!" At the foot of the scaffold steps, three guards came towards the King, trying to remove his jacket. He shook them off, and himself removed his hat, his jacket and neckcloth, unbuttoning his shirt and arranging it so his neck was exposed. The guards then made as if to seize his hands.

"What are you attempting?" cried the King, pulling away from them.

"To bind you," they answered.

"To bind me!" exclaimed the King. "No, I shall never consent to that! Do what you have been ordered, but you shall never bind me!" A knight must never be bound like a criminal, as if he might try to run in terror from the face of death. The guards called on others to help them. The Abbé feared they might strike the king, which for him would be worse than dying. The King looked steadily at the priest, mutely begging for a word of advice.

"Sire," said the priest, "in this new insult, I see only another trait of resemblance between Your Majesty and the Savior Who is about to be your reward."

According to the priest, the King raised his eyes to Heaven, as if his gaze had pierced the clouds and glimpsed the Kingdom which awaited him. "You are right," he said. "Nothing less than His example should make me submit to such a degradation." He turned to the guards. "Do what you will. I must drink the chalice to the dregs."[17]

They bound him, and the executioner Sanson cut his hair. With the Abbé holding his arm, he mounted the scaffold. At the top of the stairs, he suddenly left the Abbé, and strode with a firm step to the edge of the platform. With a nod, he silenced the drummers. He began to speak, his words ringing throughout the square. "I die innocent of all the crimes of which I am accused. I pardon those who have occasioned my death, and I pray to God that the blood you are going to shed will never fall upon France . . . ." The drums began again. The executioners grabbed the King, dragged him over to the guillotine, and threw him roughly upon the plank. The blade fell.

Abbé Edgeworth cried, "Ascend to Heaven, Son of St. Louis!" He afterwards did not recall saying it, being in a state of shock. The crowd was silent as the King's head was held high for them to see. While the executioner walked around the scaffold with the head raised aloft, he made obscene gestures. Then cries of "Long live the Republic!" were heard, and hats were thrown into the air. People rushed forward, dipping handkerchiefs into the blood of Louis XVI. The Abbé, dazed, noticed that some of the blood from the severed head had splashed upon his clothes. Meanwhile, Sanson was selling locks of the King's hair, pieces of his jacket, his buttons, his hat. Someone began to play the *Marseillaise*, and people joined hands, dancing and cavorting around the guillotine. Abbé Edgeworth was able to slip through the crowd and found his way on foot through the streets of Paris to the house of the King's lawyer and faithful friend, Malesherbes. The priest gave him an account of the King's death, and the old man wept.[18]

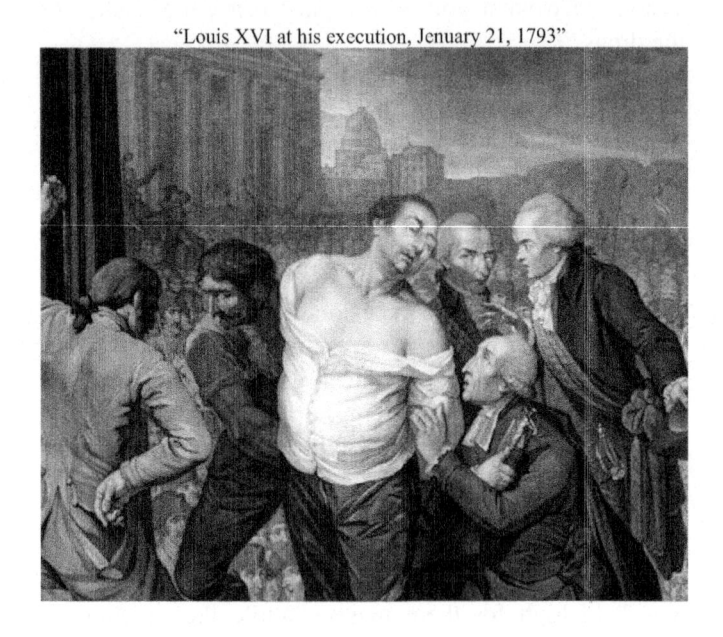

"Louis XVI at his execution, Jenuary 21, 1793"

Marie-Antoinette, Daughter of the Caesars

"Marie-Antoinette on trial"

"Marie-Antoinette and Madame Royale in prison"

23 THE AGONY

> "I ask you priests of God, to please say a Mass for my soul's salvation. I beg all of you standing here to forgive me the harm that I may have done you. Please pray for me." —Saint Joan, the Maid of Lorraine

During Louis' trial, Antoinette was unable to eat, and rapidly lost weight, so that her dresses had to be taken in. The morning of the King's execution, the Queen, Élisabeth, Thérèse, and Louis-Charles were up at dawn waiting for the King to come once more, but by ten o'clock, the beating of drums and distant cheers told them they had waited in vain. As they recovered their shattered composure, the Queen led her daughter and her sister-in-law in kneeling before Louis-Charles, and saying together: *Vive le Roi!* By March of 1793, far away in the Vendée, the seven year old was also being proclaimed king by the peasants and nobles who rebelled against the Revolution; the leaders of the Revolution took note of it. She who had once longed for a lack of etiquette now insisted upon her son sitting at the head of the table and having him served first because he was King. Her actions did not pass unnoticed.

Upon her husband's execution, Antoinette petitioned for mourning garments for herself, her children and her sister-in-law. She devoted her days at the Temple to the education of her children, along the curriculum laid down by her husband before he was taken away. However, she never accompanied them on their daily walk in the garden, because to do so meant she would have to pass Louis' door, which she could no longer bring herself to do. They continued to be forbidden to hear Mass or receive the sacraments. The Queen would ask her sister-in-law Madame Élisabeth, to read the words of the Mass to her from the missal. Madame Royale later wrote of that difficult time:

> We had now a little more freedom; our guards even believed that we were about to be sent out of France; but nothing could calm my mother's agony. No hope could touch her heart; and life and death became indifferent to her. She would sometimes look upon us with an air of pity which made us shudder. Fortunately my own affliction increased my illness to so serious a degree, that it made a diversion in the mind of my mother. My physician Brunier, and Lacase, a surgeon, were sent for. They cured me in the course of a month.[1]

By the time spring came, Louis-Charles had fallen ill, due to the unnatural confinement of prison life, and the limited amount of fresh air he was allowed to take, he who was accustomed to being so often outdoors. The first time he became ill, it was probably from worms, due to the unsanitary conditions of the tower. Also, the family was suffering the loss of Louis XVI. The King had played games with the little boy; he felt his father's loss keenly. In May, Louis-Charles began to have a pain in his side, and headaches. Antoinette was anxious, remembering her Louis-Joseph, who had died at seven years old. When summer came, Louis-Charles recovered, and soon Temple rang once more with the sounds of his exuberance. In June, however, he injured himself on a stick he was using as a hobby horse. Maman asked the guards to summon a physician at once, which they did, a Doctor Pipelet, who carefully examined him, scrupulously recording the cause of the accident, which had caused some bruising to his private parts. Unfortunately, the accident would be used against Antoinette in the course of her trial as evidence that she was abusing her son.

Meanwhile, one of the municipal guards, named Toulan, had become infatuated with Antoinette. She had once shown him the locks of hair of her two children who had died. He was transformed from a hardened Jacobin to the most devoted champion of the crown. It was a good thing, because other than faithful Cléry, the only servants they had were a certain Monsieur and Madame Tison, who were very coarse people and spies of the Committee of Public Safety. The other guards mocked them, blowing smoke in the faces of the Queen and Madame Élisabeth as they walked by. Toulan managed to get her husband's wedding ring and seal, which the commissaries had confiscated from Cléry. Toulan retrieved them from the Council Chamber, afterwards shouting, "Thief! Thief!" louder than anyone else. At Antoinette's request, he arranged for the ring and seal to be smuggled from the country to the Comte de Provence. Toulan, who also supplied her with information about the war, was eventually reported to the Committee of Public Safety by Madame Tison, and arrested. With every Austrian victory, with every French defeat, Antoinette was coming closer to her condemnation.

One day in late June 1793, Madame Tison burst in upon the Queen, throwing herself at her feet. "Madame, I ask your Majesty's pardon! How miserable I am! I have caused your death, and that of Madame Élisabeth!" Antoinette tried to raise the distracted woman from the ground, and calm her but the woman was beyond hysterical. The guards dragged her away. The next day she was incarcerated in a mental asylum.[2] On July 3 they prepared for bed, completely unsuspecting. Around ten o'clock that night came a loud pounding at the door. A group of commissaries burst into the room. One began very officiously to read a long decree, announcing the decision of the Committee of Public Safety to remove "Charles Capet" from his mother's care. The Queen ran to her little boy, who was asleep in his bed. He woke up, crying, and clung to her. In a few seconds, Élisabeth and Thérèse joined her, and with their arms they formed a barricade around the child. For an hour, they held them off. She screamed, begged, and pleaded. Then the intruders threatened to kill both of her children before her eyes if she did not give Charles to them. The Queen decided it was better to let him go peacefully rather than be injured or killed. His aunt and sister dressed him. Antoinette said to him: "My child, they are taking you from me; never forget the mother who loves you tenderly, and never forget God! Be good, gentle, and honest, and your father will look down on you from heaven and bless you."

"Have you done with this preaching?" said the chief commissioner.

"You have abused our patience finally," said another; "the nation is generous, and will take care of his education." Louis-Charles kissed his mother, Marie-Thérèse and Élisabeth. He was still sobbing as the men led him into the darkness.[3] His sister Madame Royale later described the scene thus:

> On the 3d of July, they read to us a decree of the Convention, that my brother should be separated from us, and placed in the most secure apartment of the tower. As soon as he heard this sentence pronounced, he threw himself into the arms of my mother, and entreated, with violent cries, than to be separated from her. My mother was stricken to the earth by this cruel order; she would not part with her son, and she actually defended, against the efforts of the officers, the bed in which she had placed him. But these men would have him, and threatened to call up the guard, and use violence. My mother exclaimed, that they had better kill her than tear the child from her. An hour was spent in resistance on her part, and in prayers and tears on the part of all of us.
>
> At last they threatened even the lives of both him and me, and my mother's maternal tenderness at length forced her to this sacrifice. My aunt and I dressed the child, for my poor mother had no longer strength for any thing. Nevertheless, when he was dressed, she took him and delivered him herself into the hands of the officers, bathing him with her tears, foreseeing that she was never to see him again. The poor little fellow embraced us all tenderly, and was carried off in a flood of tears. My mother charged the officers to ask the council-general for permission to see her son, were it only at meals. They engaged to do so. She was overwhelmed with the sorrow of parting with him, but her horror was extreme when she heard that one Simon (a shoemaker by trade, whom she had seen as a municipal officer in the Temple), was the person to

whom her unhappy child was confided. She asked continually to be allowed to see him, but in vain. He, on his side, cried for two whole days, and begged without intermission to be permitted to see us.[4]

The horror of the women prisoners knew no bounds when they heard Louis-Charles singing drunken obscene ditties about the Queen. Antoinette was in a state of panic and near despair. The royal women were able to climb a narrow staircase to the very top of the tower. There Antoinette would stand for hours staring through a narrow crack in the partition, hoping for even the tiniest glimpse of her child. The dread of what might be happening to him at any moment almost drove her out of her mind. Only her faith kept her going, and her determination to survive in case they might all be rescued by the Austrians. In the meantime, she turned to prayer and trust in God, following the Church calendar through the daily Mass readings in her missal.

Late on the night of August 1, 1793 officials and guards arrived to take Antoinette from the Temple to the Conciergerie, the prison which was the antechamber to the guillotine. The guards made the Queen dress in their presence. After embracing Élisabeth, she clasped Marie-Thérèse in her arms, encouraging the teenager to have courage and faith, obey her aunt, and take care of her health. Before leaving, she hurriedly gathered a few belongings into a large handkerchief, including a glove belonging to Louis-Charles, and a lock of his hair. The guards made her empty her pockets before taking her away. As she left the room Antoinette bashed her head on the door frame. One of the commissioners asked her if she was hurt and she replied "Nothing can hurt me now."[5]

Antoinette was placed in a particularly cold, damp

cell in the medieval fortress on the Seine. It had been a royal palace, the Palais de la Cité, in the days of Saint Louis IX, who had built the gothic masterpiece called the Sainte-Chapelle to house the Crown of Thorns. The Palais de Justice was there, where for centuries the Paris parlement met, to be replaced by the Revolutionary Tribunal during the French Revolution. Men and women were kept separately, although the women were at liberty during the day. The Queen was held apart from all, although anyone could come and watch her; once again in her life she found herself with little privacy. The conditions of the cell were calculated to break her health.

Nevertheless, Antoinette was not completely forsaken. In spite of the high security, she almost escaped, due to the resourcefulness of Michonis, the chief of police, who was sympathetic towards her, and the Marquis de Rougeville. The concierge and his wife, Monsieur and Madame Richard and their maid Rosalie Lamorlière (1768 – 1848), prepared the Queen's cell as well as they could; Rosalie even donated tapestry stool and a hand mirror for Antoinette's use. The damp soon destroyed her clothes, especially her undergarments. Michonis sent for clean chemises and a pair of shoes to be sent over from the Temple. The Queen received them with gratitude, recognizing in the carefully folded linens "the work of my sister Élisabeth." Michonis also made certain, at Élisabeth's request, that Antoinette had bottles of the Ville d'Avray water to drink, since she did not drink wine and the water of the Seine made her sick.[6]

The Richards provided good meals on pewter dishes while Rosalie helped the Queen with her hair and did her best to discreetly assist her without drawing the attention of the authorities. Rosalie was from a poor cobbler's family; her life was one of great hardship; nevertheless she showed a kindness and mercy to Antoinette that makes her a shining star in the stories of the French

Revolution. Once Madame Richard had brought her youngest son to cheer the desolate prisoner, but instead of being cheered, she burst into tears at the sight of one who so resembled her own boy. She gathered him into her arms, covering his face and hair with embraces.

After the escape attempt, the Richards were implicated and replaced with the Baults. Monsieur Bault had the appearance and manner of a *sans-culotte* hiding the soul of a knight. He made certain the Queen was not harassed by the guards, whose language could be foul, and personally brought her meals to her to make certain they were not poisoned. However, Fouquier-Tinville, the public prosecutor, had the royal prisoner transferred to a veritable dungeon, too dark for reading or sewing; she was no longer able to work on the stockings she was knitting with two quills for the little King. She had been denied knitting needles; the authorities thought she might try to kill herself. It was very cold, and the walls dripped with moisture. Monsieur Bault asked for an extra quilt for her but Fouquier-Tinville denied the request. Instead, Bault was able to procure a mattress as a covering. Rosalie continued to do her best for the Queen, making her a nourishing, medicinal soup every morning for breakfast. At the market, the market women often gave their best fruits to the concierge's wife, knowing it was for the Queen, passing along words of encouragement to her. For dinner she also had soup, fowl, or mutton chops, never drinking wine, only water like her mother the Empress. Nevertheless, her health continued to fail, and the prison conditions aged her prematurely. She began to have trouble with her eyes, either through an infection or a more serious affliction. After the capture at Varennes her hair was already white at the temples; now she rapidly dropped weight. There have been speculations that she was suffering from uterine cancer, due to the hemorrhaging she endured, but it has never been proven. There was always a gendarme outside her door, and another looking in the window, so she never had any privacy.

A fellow prisoner at the Conciergerie was the *ci-devant* Duc d'Orléans, or "Philippe Egalité," as he had been calling himself, in order to be in the good graces of the new order. He had nevertheless fallen out of favor with his Jacobin friends, and been thrown into the Conciergerie. He lived in his cell with many comforts and an elaborate wardrobe, including satin dressing-gowns, and silver plate. What a contrast to the Queen, whose shoes were soon dilapidated from mildew; who was so grateful when Rosalie brought her a cardboard box for her meager toiletries. Philippe was eventually guillotined as well.

Two of her guards were practicing Catholics, and had permitted the non-juring priest Abbé Magnin to twice hear her confession, and once even say Mass in her cell. She had been able to receive Holy Communion for the first time in more than a year. The guards had assisted at Mass with her, along with a local woman, Mademoiselle Fouché, who made the necessary arrangements. Two nights before her trial began, another non-juring priest secretly brought her Holy Communion. On October 12, the Abbé Emery, former superior of Saint Sulpice and himself a prisoner in the Conciergerie sent her a message, telling her he would pass by her cell door at a certain time and say the words of absolution.

Unlike Louis XVI, who had been given several months to prepare his case with his lawyers, Antoinette and the two men who were chosen to defend her— Guillaume Troncon Ducoudray (1750-1798) and Claude François Chauveau-Lagarde (1756-1841)—were given only a few hours on the evening before the trial to prepare for her defense. As Chauveau-Lagarde who as later to defend Madame Élisabeth, related:

Marie-Antoinette, Daughter of the Caesars

...I happened to be in the country when I received the news that I had been named with M. Tronson Ducoudray to defend the Queen before the revolutionary tribunal, and that the trial was to start on the following morning at eight o'clock. I immediately set out for the prison filled with a sense of the sacred duty which had been imposed on me, mingled with an intense feeling of bitterness. The Conciergerie, as is well known, is the prison in which are confined persons due to be judged or those due to be executed after sentence. After passing through two gates one enters a dark corridor which one could not locate without the aid of a lamp that lights up the entrance. On the right are the cells, and on the left there is a chamber into which the light enters by two small barred windows looking on to the little courtyard reserved for women. It was in this chamber that the Queen was confined. It was divided into two parts by a screen. On the left, as one entered, was an armed gendarme, and on the right the part of the room occupied by the Queen containing a bed, a table and two chairs. Her Majesty was attired in a white dress of extreme simplicity. No one capable of sympathetic imagination could fail to realize my feelings on finding in this place the wife of one of the worthiest successors of St. Louis and the august descendant of the Emperors of Germany, a Queen who by her grace and goodness had been the glory of the most brilliant court in Europe and the idol of the French nation. In presenting myself to the Queen with respectful devotion, I felt my knees trembling under me and my eyes wet with tears. I could not hide my emotion and my embarrassment was much greater than any I might have felt at being presented to Her

Majesty in the midst of her court, seated on a throne and surrounded with the brilliant trappings of royalty. Her reception of me, at once majestic and kind put me at my ease and caused me to feel, as I spoke and she listened, that she was honoring me with her confidence.

I read over with her the bill of indictment, which later became known to all Europe. I will not recall the horrible details. As I read this satanic document, I was absolutely overwhelmed, but I alone, for the Queen, without showing emotion, gave me her views on it. She perceived, and I had come to the same conclusion, that the gendarme could hear something of what she said. But she showed no sign of anxiety on this score and continued to express herself with the same confidence. I made my initial notes for her defense and then went up to the registry to examine what they called the relevant documents. There I found a pile of papers so confused and so voluminous that I should have needed whole weeks to examine them. When I observed to the Queen that it would not be possible for us to take cognizance of all these documents in such a short time and that it was indispensable to ask for an adjournment to give us time to examine them, the Queen said, 'To whom must we apply for that?'

I dreaded the effect of my reply, and as I replied in a low voice: 'The National Convention,' the Queen, turning her head to one side said: "No, never!"

I added that we had to defend in the person of Her Majesty not only the Queen of France, but also the widow of Louis XVI, the mother of his children and the sister-in-law of our Princess, who were accused with her in the bill of indictment. This final consideration overcame her scruples. At the words sister, wife and mother natural feelings rose superior to a sovereign's pride. Without uttering a single word, though she let a sigh escape her, the Queen took up her pen and wrote to the Assembly in our names, a few lines full of noble dignity in which she complained that they had not allowed us time enough to examine the evidence and claimed on our behalf the necessary respite. The Queen's application was transmitted to Fouquier-Tinville, who promised to submit it to the Assembly, But, in fact, he did nothing with it or, at least, nothing useful for the next day ... the hearing began at eight in the morning.[7]

The Queen was tried in the Grande Chambre of the Palais de Justice, renamed the "Hall of Liberty," overflowing with people who had come to see the trial. Preceding her trial had been preliminary hearings, which according to revolutionary custom had occurred in the middle of the night. In the name of liberty, the famous Crucifixion scene by Dürer had been replaced by a large reproduction of the Declaration of the Rights of Man and Citizen. In the galleries were the *tricoteuses*, the rugged women of Paris, who hovered about at every revolutionary event, bringing their knitting with them. At eight o'clock in the morning of October 14, 1793, Antoinette was led to a raised platform, where she could be heard and seen by all, in front of a long table, at which sat young Nicolas Hermann, the President of the Revolutionary Tribunal, and five other judges. Hermann was a great friend of Robespierre, whose Committee of Public Safety now ruled France. As it was commonly known, once Robespierre decided someone needed to be gotten out of the way the person was usually abandoned to Mother Guillotine, bribes and pleas having no effect on the "incorruptible." Robespierre and his friends thought France was overpopulated and needed to be thoroughly purged, of peasants as well as aristocrats, the peasants being the ones who clung so adamantly to superstitions like Christianity. The public prosecutor Fouquier-Tinville was a pale man with thick black eyebrows. Both he and Hermann wore medals on which were inscribed the words *La Loi*, "the law." The men were clothed in the deepest black; even their round hats, turned up in front, had black ostrich plumes. The wretched woman was made to stand while forty-one witnesses took their oaths. Then Hermann said: "The accused may be seated!" Antoinette slowly sat in the chair that had been provided for her. "What is your name, surname, age, position, place of birth and residence?" asked Hermann.[8]

She replied, steadily. "My name is Marie-Antoinette of Lorraine-Austria, aged about thirty-eight, widow of the King of France, born in Vienna. At the time of my arrest I was in the session hall of the National Assembly." A clerk then began to read the eight page indictment about orgies and elaborate feasts, of extravagances, of engineering a famine, of printing pamphlets slandering herself so as to gain sympathy, of dominating her husband, of being a counterrevolutionary, of dissipation and waste. Behind her chair stood her lawyers Troncon Ducoudray and Chauveau-Lagarde.

When the clerk finished reading the accusation, Hermann spoke. "This is what you are accused of. You will now hear the testimony against you. First witness to the stand!" The first witness was a deputy of the convention, formerly second in command of the National Guard at Versailles. He began to testify about orgies he had witnessed at the palace. He went on for two hours, turning the banquet for the Flanders regiment at the Versailles Opera into a bacchanalian revel, in which the Queen had presided like a harpy, stamping on the red, white and blue revolutionary cockade. Hermann addressed the Queen. "Have you anything to say about the testimony?" he asked.

"I have no knowledge of the majority of the incidents mentioned by the witness," she replied. "As for the bodyguards' feast, we briefly visited them while at table, but that is all." He accused her of inciting regiments against the Revolution. "I have nothing to say," she replied.

"How did you use the huge sums of money given to you by the various ministers of finance?"

"I was never given huge sums. My allowance I used to pay the people in my service."

"Why did you lavish gold upon the Polignac family and several others?"

"They had positions at court which supplied them with wealth," she replied.

The interrogation went on and on. The *tricoteuses* began shouting because they were having difficulty hearing the Queen's responses. "Make the Widow Capet stand up!" they cried.

The Queen sighed to her lawyers. "Will the people ever grow weary of my sufferings?"

The public prosecutor Fouquier-Tinville called to the stand the procurator Hébert, publisher of the raunchy gazette *Père Duchesne*. Hébert was one of the men responsible for removing Louis-Charles. He accused her of sexually molesting her own son. He declared that Louis-Charles, "Little Capet," had testified that she, his mother, had led him into unnatural vice in order to weaken his constitution, so she could rule France through him. Madame Élisabeth was likewise accused.

"What reply have you to Citizen Hébert's testimony?" asked Hermann.

"I have no knowledge of the incidents he speaks of," she replied.

Hébert then accused her of treating her son as if he were king.

"Did you witness it?" she calmly asked him.

"I did not, but the municipal guard will confirm it," affirmed Hébert. "You allowed your son to take precedence at table."

One of the jurors rose. "Citizen President, the accused has not fully replied concerning the incident mentioned by Citizen Hébert, regarding what allegedly happened between herself and her son."

The Queen rose to her feet. "If I did not reply, it was because nature recoils at such an accusation against a mother." She turned to the galleries. "I appeal to all the mothers who may be here!" A stir broke out among the spectators. The *tricoteuses* all began talking at once, and a few of them cheered her, with boos and hisses at Hébert. They were generally disgusted with him. The judges and jurors whispered among themselves. Hermann had to suspend the proceedings for two hours, after which they continued again until eleven o'clock at night. The Queen was led across the courtyard of the Palais de Justice to the Conciergerie and her damp, moldy cell.

The following day was Tuesday, October 15, the Feast of Saint Teresa, the name-day of her mother and her daughter. The Christian calendar having been abolished in France, the new republic celebrated the day as the feast of the Amaryllis. At nine o'clock there began eighteen hours of more cross-examination. At one point, Hermann had the usher display her personal belongings, holding up each one, and demanding an explanation from her. "A packet containing various colors of hair," he announced.

"They come from my dead and living children, and

from my husband," explained Antoinette.

"A paper with numbers on it."

"It is a table for teaching my son how to count." The Temple guards had confiscated the little arithmetic table, thinking she was teaching Charles how to send messages in secret code. The clerk displayed her sewing kit, her hand mirror, a ring with a lock of her mother's hair. Then he held up her prayer cards.

"A paper on which are two gold hearts with initials, and another paper on which is inscribed 'Prayer to the Sacred Heart of Jesus,' 'Prayer to the Immaculate Conception.' " Finally, he held up a portrait of Princesse de Lamballe.

"Whose is that portrait?" asked Hermann.

"Madame de Lamballe," answered the Queen.

"Two other portraits of women," announced the clerk.

"Who are they?" inquired Hermann.

"They are two ladies with whom I was raised in Vienna."

"What are their names?"

"Mesdames de Mecklembourg and de Hesse."

The clerk exhibited her scapular, which Fouquier-Tinville loudly denounced as being "counter-revolutionary." She was also vehemently denounced for the Sacred Heart badge that Hébert had found in her missal. Eventually they came to the subject of Trianon. "Where did you get the money to build and furnish the Petit Trianon, where you gave parties at which you were always the goddess?" asked Hermann.

"There were funds especially for that purpose," replied Antoinette.

"Those funds must have been extensive," said the judge, "for Petit Trianon must have cost immense sums." He was obviously not aware that she had not built Trianon; she was merely given it by her husband, keeping most of the original furnishings of the former chatelaine, Madame du Barry.

She answered with frankness: "It is possible that the Little Trianon cost immense sums, perhaps more than I would have wished. We were gradually involved in more and more expense. Besides, I am more anxious than anyone else that what went on there should be known."

"Was it not at the Little Trianon that you knew the woman called La Motte?" He was referring to the infamous thief of Boehmer's diamond necklace.

"I have never seen her."

"Was she not your victim in the infamous affair of the necklace?"

"She cannot have been, since I never met her."

"Do you persist in denying that you knew her?" asked the judge,

"It is the truth I have told and will persist in telling."

As the hours dragged by, they set out to prove she had been an unnatural wife. Fouquier-Tinville declared, "Through your influence, you made the King, your husband, do whatever you wished."

"There is an immense difference," said the Queen, "between counseling that something should be done, and having it carried out."

The prosecutor pointed threateningly at her. "You made use of his weak character to make him perform many evil deeds!"

"I never knew him to have such a character as you describe," she replied.

Again, they brought up the painful matter of her son. "I point out to you that your testimony is in direct opposition to your son's," challenged Fouquier-Tinville.

"It is easy to make a child of eight say whatever one wants."

"But he was made to repeat it several times and on several occasions," claimed the lawyer. "And he always said the same thing."

"Well, I deny it."

Finally, around half-past four in the afternoon, there was a short recess, and the Queen, who had eaten nothing since morning, was given a little soup, sent to her from the prison by Rosalie. All too soon, the session began once more, and she heard herself accused of practically everything from forgery to treason.

"At the time of your marriage to Louis Capet, did you not conceive the project of uniting Lorraine with Austria?"

"No," she replied.

"You bear its name."

"Because one must bear the name of one's country."

Around midnight, Fouquier-Tinville asked her if she had anything else to say for herself.

She stood up. "Yesterday, I did not know the witnesses, and I did not know what they would testify. Well, no one has uttered anything positive against me. I end by saying that I was only the wife of Louis XVI, and bound to conform to his will."

Her lawyers gave a zealous defense, begging that her life be spared, on the grounds that it was enough punishment for her to have lost her husband. Afterwards, Hermann gave a long summary of her accusation. She had aided and abetted the "last tyrant" of France, who had already been found guilty and executed. While the jury deliberated, she asked for a glass of water. One of the gendarmes hastened to fetch it for her. When the verdict of guilty was announced she did not display the slightest flicker of emotion. It was two o'clock in the morning of October 16, traditionally the feast of the French priest St. Gall. On the revolutionary calendar it was the feast of the Ox, an animal of the ancient Hebrew holocaust.

The same gendarme who gave her the water escorted

her back to her cell, respectfully removing his hat in her presence, and putting it under his arm. He did not seem to care that the gesture was noticed by many, and led to his arrest. The *tricoteuses* were silent as the Queen wearily limped out of the Hall of Liberty. She was almost too exhausted to walk. Her eyesight was worsened by fatigue and the darkness of the hour. As they came to the black entrance of the Conciergerie she said, "I cannot see." The young soldier took her arm. Nevertheless, she slipped on the rough staircase.

Soon she was back in her bone-chilling cell, but she did not sleep. In the light of two candles, her quill began to scratch across the page as she wrote to Élisabeth. The beauty of Antoinette's soul are captured in the lines in which she expresses her steadfast adherence to the Catholic religion and her concern for her friends and family. Note the delicate manner in which she refers to her little son's accusation of incest, wrested from him by his tormentors, showing more concern for Élisabeth's feelings than for her own agony. When she speaks of her children the words themselves fall like tears. Although it is known that she had previously received the ministrations of a priest faithful to the Holy See while in prison, in order to protect him she wonders aloud if there are any Catholic priests left in France. Also, in the last sentence she states her refusal to "speak," that is, to confess, to a juring priest, one who had denied the Pope by swearing an oath to the Civil Constitution of the Clergy. Robespierre kept the letter; it never reached Élisabeth.

> 16th October, 4.30 A.M.
> It is to you, my sister, that I write for the last time. I have just been condemned, not to a shameful death, for such is only for criminals, but to go and rejoin your brother. Innocent like him, I hope to

show the same firmness in my last moments. I am calm, as one is when one's conscience reproaches one with nothing. I feel profound sorrow in leaving my poor children: you know that I only lived for them and for you, my good and tender sister. You who out of love have sacrificed everything to be with us, in what a position do I leave you! I have learned from the proceedings at my trial that my daughter was separated from you. Alas! poor child; I do not venture to write to her; she would not receive my letter. I do not even know whether this will reach you. Do you receive my blessing for both of them. I hope that one day when they are older they may be able to rejoin you, and to enjoy to the full your tender care. Let them both think of the lesson which I have never ceased to impress upon them, that the principles and the exact performance of their duties are the chief foundation of life; and then mutual affection and confidence in one another will constitute its happiness. Let my daughter feel that at her age she ought always to aid her brother by the advice which her greater experience and her affection may inspire her to give him. And let my son in his turn render to his sister all the care and all the services which affection can inspire. Let them, in short, both feel that, in whatever positions they may be placed, they will never be truly happy but through their union. Let them follow our example. In our own misfortunes how much comfort has our affection for one another afforded us! And, in times of happiness, we have enjoyed that doubly from being able to share it with a friend; and where can one find friends more tender and more united than in one's own family? Let my son never forget the last words of his father, which I repeat emphatically; let him never seek to avenge our deaths.

I have to speak to you of one thing which is very painful to my heart, I know how much pain the child must have caused you. Forgive him, my dear sister; think of his age, and how easy it is to make a child say whatever one wishes, especially when he does not understand it. It will come to pass one day, I hope, that he will better feel the value of your kindness and of your tender affection for both of them. It remains to confide to you my last thoughts. I should have wished to write them at the beginning of my trial; but, besides that they did not leave me any means of writing, events have passed so rapidly that I really have not had time.

I die in the Catholic Apostolic and Roman religion, that of my fathers, that in which I was brought up, and which I have always professed. Having no spiritual consolation to look for, not even knowing whether there are still in this place any priests of that religion (and indeed the place where I am would expose them to too much danger if they were to enter it but once), I sincerely implore pardon of God for all the faults which I may have committed during my life. I trust that, in His goodness, He will mercifully accept my last prayers, as well as those which I have for a long time addressed to Him, to receive my soul into His mercy. I beg pardon of all whom I know, and especially of you, my sister, for all the vexations which, without intending it, I may have caused you. I pardon all my enemies the evils that they have done me. I bid farewell to my aunts and to all my brothers and sisters. I had friends. The idea of being forever separated from them and from all their troubles is one of the greatest sorrows that I suffer in dying. Let them at least know that to my latest moment I thought of them.

Farewell, my good and tender sister. May this letter reach you. Think always of me; I embrace you with all my heart, as I do my poor dear children. My God, how heart-rending it is to leave them forever! Farewell! Farewell! I must now occupy myself with my spiritual duties, as I am not free in my actions. Perhaps they will bring me a priest; but I here protest that I will not say a word to him, but that I will treat him as a total stranger.[9][10]

Her letter finished, she lay down on her bed, still fully dressed, weeping, while ignoring the guard who stood in the shadows watching her, as her last morning dawned. When Rosalie entered the Queen's dungeon, the Queen was still prone on her bed, weeping, with a small yellow glove pressed to her cheek. Antoinette could be seen fequently kissing the glove which belonged to Louis-Charles.

"Madame, you had no supper last night, and ate so little during the day. What shall I bring you this morning?" asked Rosalie.

"Nothing, my child, I need nothing. Everything is over for me."

"But Madame, I have been keeping some soup on the stove for you all night."

"Very well," the Queen said, "bring me some of your soup, Rosalie." Rosalie ran to fetch the soup. The Queen, with great effort, took a few spoonfuls, but it was obvious she had no appetite.

"Please, Rosalie, leave me. Return at eight to help me dress." Rosalie took the soup and left. She ran to a nearby café and bought a cup of chocolate. It was almost eight, and she went straight to the Queen, who was still prostrate, but much calmer. The little glove had disappeared. She sat up and drank the chocolate.

"It is time for me to dress," she said. She went into a corner by the bed and motioned to Rosalie, who came to stand between the Queen and the guard, making as much of a shield with her body as she could. But the man insisted on coming over to the bed, leaning over so he could watch. The Queen was bleeding due either to her period or to a serious health issue.

"Please, Monsieur," begged the Queen, "in the name of decency, allow me to change my linen without witnesses!"

"I am ordered to observe your every movement," he replied.

The Queen turned her back to him, and with the greatest delicacy possible changed her soiled linen and undergarments. She put on a clean chemise, and a black petticoat. Then she put on the white *piqué* gown that she usually used as a wrapper in the mornings. Around her neck and shoulders she wrapped a large, muslin *fichu*. Rosalie arranged the Queen's hair in a chignon, over which she placed a simple white cap, without the mourning veil. The authorities had forbidden her to wear black so she was to go to her death all in white. They had forgotten that white was the color of mourning for queens of France. The Queen gave Rosalie a white ribbon she had once used in her hair. "Keep it as a little remembrance of me."

The doors opened and a man in black clothes entered. It was a constitutional priest, Abbé Girard, the Curé of the parish of Saint-Landry. He was dressed as a layman. He asked the Queen if she wished for the services of his ministry. The Queen declined.

"What will people say when they hear that you refused the consolations of religion?"

Antoinette replied, "You will tell anyone who inquires that God in His Mercy provided for me."

"May I accompany you to the scaffold?" asked the

clergyman.

"If you wish," replied the Queen. "But do you think the people will allow me to go to the scaffold without tearing me to pieces?" The Queen turned away and kneeling by her bed, began to silently pray. Abbé Girard sat in a chair. The doors opened again, and Hermann entered, attired in his black suit and black plumed hat, with two other judges, and a clerk. The Queen was still kneeling by her bed. At the sound of their entrance, she slowly rose to her feet, and faced them.

"Attention!" announced Hermann. "Widow Capet, your sentence will be read to you!"

"It is not necessary," replied the Queen. "I know fully well what my sentence is."

"You must hear it again. It is the law."

The clerk read off the list of slanders. As he finished, Sanson the executioner strode in.

"Put out your hands," he ordered the Queen, who stepped away from him.

"Are you going to bind me?" she asked. "Louis XVI was not bound!" No one had told her of her husband's last moments.

"Do your duty, man," ordered Hermann.

Sanson roughly grabbed the Queen's arms, and lashed her hands and wrists together very tightly with cords, almost up to the elbow. She suppressed a small cry of pain. The executioner snatched off her little cap, and with a pair of huge shears roughly destroyed the neat, braided chignon, so that the Queen's hair resembled the ragged straw of a scarecrow. He replaced the cap, under which hung the frayed, uneven tendrils. When Abbé Girard offered her words of consolation, "Your death will expiate—"

She interrupted him, exclaiming, "Ah, faults! but no crime." [11]

Then the executioner pushed her out of the cell, and

she walked ahead of him as if on a leash. They walked to the entrance of the Conciergerie. Out of the arched, gothic portals could be seen the courtyard, and the vehicle in which Antoinette was to ride to her death, a rickety garbage cart. It would have been easy for violent hands to reach up and drag her into the street to be bludgeoned and hacked to death. Antoinette, seeing the cart, begged the executioner to loosen her hands, which he did, and she ran into a dark corner of the prison office where she squatted in order to relieve herself. Then Sanson bound her again. She straightened her back, lifted up her head, and walked towards the cart. Abbé Girard was at her side: "This is the moment, Madame, to arm yourself with courage."

"Courage?" she replied. "I have so long served an apprenticeship in it that it is not likely to fail me today." The priest continued his exhortations but the Queen silenced him by saying with firmness that "she was not of his religion, that she died professing that of her husband, and that she should never forget the principles so oft instilled in her."[12]

Thus the Queen of France rode to her death, sitting in the garbage cart, behind the horses' tails to show the people that she was nothing but dung, in her white wrapper and cropped hair, hands tightly tied behind her back. Two prostitutes were guillotined, one before and one after Antoinette, for in the eyes of the Revolution the Queen was just one more harlot. At the scaffold, she climbed the steps with her usual dignity and grace.

"I beg your pardon, Monsieur. I did not do it on purpose," she said to the executioner when she accidentally stepped on his hand. On the scaffold, Antoinette knelt down quickly and murmured a prayer. Standing, she glanced towards the towers of the Temple, saying, "Adieu, once again, my children. I go to rejoin your father." Then she was placed beneath the blade of the guillotine and it fell upon her. Sanson held up her head for the people to see. The Marseillaise played and many cheered, but some wept. Three individuals had rushed forward to dip their handkerchiefs in her blood, and were promptly arrested by the authorities. The Queen's body was tossed into a mass grave with other victims of the Revolution, head between the legs. Indeed, mass graves of multiple victims would become a part of the new world order, and would grow to mass proportions in other parts of the world in the wars and revolutions which would follow.

Marie-Antoinette, Daughter of the Caesars

"Sketch by J-L. David of Marie-Antoinette on her way to be executed"

Marie-Antoinette, Daughter of the Caesars

"Madame Royale in the Temple prison"

24 THE ORPHANS

"Marie-Thérèse is the most unhappy creature in the world. She can obtain no news of her mother; nor be reunited to her, though she has asked it a thousand times. Live, my good mother! whom I love well, but of whom I can hear no tidings. O my father! watch over me from heaven above. O my God! forgive those who have made my family die."—Marie-Thérèse-Charlotte of France, 1794 (scratched on the wall of the Temple prison)

Throughout the family's ordeals, there had been a steady stream of royalist plots to liberate them, beginning with the Favras plot as early as 1789. The Marquis de Favras raised a large sum of money to spirit the King, Queen and their children out of the country while making the Comte de Provence regent. The plot included starving the Parisans into submission in addition to the assassination of the mayor of Paris, Monsieur Bailly, as well as the assassinations of Necker and Lafayette. The plot was betrayed and Favras was captured and executed. Provence denied knowing anything about it. The plot of

Rougeville and Michonis almost succeeded in delivering Antoinette from the Conciergerie. There were other plots as well, and houses prepared in America to receive the Queen and her children, one in Edgecomb, Maine and another in Asilum, Pennsylvania. There was also a plot to spirit her away to Ireland.

Lady Charlotte Atkyns (1757–1836), a former actress of the London stage who had married an English knight, Sir Edward Atkyns. She was known before her marriage as "Mrs. Walpole" and she specialized in playing the part of boys. She became a spy for the British government, known as "the Little Sailor" because it was disguised as one that she traveled back and forth across the channel. The French police knew her as "Mrs. Williams of Liverpool" but they were never able to capture her. She claimed that she infiltrated both the Temple prison and the Conciergerie, dressed in the uniform of the National Guard, and twice spoke with the Queen, who begged her to rescue her son Louis XVII. After her husband's death in 1794, Lady Atkyns began to expend a great deal of money in an attempt to deliver the young King from his captors. A journalist in London put her in touch with a circle of French *émigrés*, who furnished her with contacts in Paris. She became entangled in such a web of espionage and counter-espionage, beyond anything she had ever imagined, all with the little King at the center. In 1794 Lady Atkyns and her agents became deeply involved in trying to rescue Louis-Charles from the Temple tower. Among her agents were many scoundrels, with the exception of the Comte de Frotté, a dedicated royalist. In her capacity as a spy, Lady Atkyns uncovered several royalist plots. Meanwhile, Lady Atkyns' agent, Monsieur de Frotté, wrote to her that he was convinced that Louis XVII had been replaced by another boy, and that the French government wished to do away with the replacement, who was becoming an embarrassment. Both the Spanish government and Charette, the leader of the Royal and Catholic army of the Vendée, were demanding the release and safe delivery of Madame Royale and Louis XVII, in exchange for peace. The Directoire of Barras badly needed peace from both its external and internal foes, but would not surrender Madame Royale until the child in the room below had died on June 8, 1795. Lady Atkyns did not believe that the boy who died on June 8 was Louis XVII. Her agents believed that Louis XVII was murdered by Robespierre's henchmen, possibly by Simon, and then replaced by another boy. Lady Atkyns merely says "a higher power than mine took possession of him." Lady Atkyns exhausted her fortune trying to rescue Louis XVII and later, during the Restoration, applied to Louis XVIII for money. He gave her a little. She spent the remaining years of her life persuing the various claimants to the identity of Louis XVII. She died in poverty in 1836.[1]

One of the most famous would-be rescuers was the Baron de Batz (1760-1814) who made a number of foiled attempts to rescue the Royal Family. He finally determined to rescue the Queen from the Conciergerie and had gold in order to bribe the National Guards. He was discovered but managed to escape. In 1795 he stirred up a Royalist revolt in Paris which died as soon as a young officer named Napoleon Bonaparte fired grapeshot into the crowd.

In the early spring of 1793, after her husband's murder, Antoinette was given an opportunity to escape from the Temple prison. Monsieur Jarjayes and the guard Toulan had a plan for her to get away, but she declined to leave her children and sister-in-law, although she knew that to stay meant her probable death. The following is a passage from the biography by Charles Duke Yonge:

But such a flight was forbidden alike by Marie Antoinette's sense of duty and by her sense of honor, if indeed the two were ever separated in her mind. Honor forbade her to desert her companions in misery, whose danger might even be increased by the rage of her jailers, exasperated at her escape. Duty to her boy forbade it still more emphatically. As his guardian, she ought not to leave him; as his mother, she could not. And her renunciation of the whole design was conveyed to M. Jarjayes in a letter which did honor alike to both by the noble gratitude which it expressed...It was written by stealth, with a pencil...Thus she wrote: 'We have had a pleasant dream, that is all. I have gained much by still finding, on this occasion, a new proof of your entire devotion to me. My confidence in you is boundless. And on all occasions you will always find strength of mind and courage in me. But the interest of my son is my sole guide; and, whatever happiness I might find in being out of this place, I can not consent to separate myself from him. In what remains, I thoroughly recognize your attachment to me in all that you said to me yesterday. Rely upon it that I feel the kindness and the force of your arguments as far as my own interest is concerned, and that I feel that the opportunity can not recur. But I could enjoy nothing if I were to leave my children; and this idea prevents me from even regretting my decision.' And to Toulan she said that 'her sole desire was to be reunited to her husband whenever Heaven should decide that her life was no longer necessary to her children.'[2]

In the September of 1793, Marie-Thérèse last saw her

brother Louis-Charles, in the council room of the Temple prison. He sat in a big chair, swinging his legs, reciting the calumny about how his mother and aunt had molested him. His eyes were bloodshot; he started to weep, and grasped for his sister's hand. Then they led him away. They interrogated the princess at length about her mother's behavior towards her brother but the innocent young girl could only vaguely comprehend what they were implying. It was only later that she fully understood. Nevertheless, her mental suffering was intense. To quote from the memoirs of Madame Royale:

> In the beginning of September, I had an indisposition caused solely by my anxiety about my mother: I never heard a drum that I did not expect another 2nd of September: every day I went upon the leads with my aunt. The officers visited us closely thrice a day, but their severity did not prevent our receiving now and then some hints of what was passing abroad, and particularly about my mother, which was our greatest concern.
>
> In spite of all the efforts and vigilance of these cruel men, we always found some compassionate hearts, who felt for us. We learned that the Queen was accused of having had a correspondence beyond the walls of the prison; we therefore hastened to get rid of our writings, our pencils, and whatever we had still preserved, fearing that we might be undressed and searched before Simon's wife, and that finding these things on us might endanger my mother; we had contrived, notwithstanding the most minute searches which were made in our chambers, and amongst all the furniture, to conceal ink, paper, and pens. We learnt too that my mother might have escaped from the Conciergerie. The wife of the keeper was not

insensible to her misfortunes, and paid her every possible attention.

The officers came again for linen for my mother, but they would not give us any account of her state of health. They even took away from us some pieces of tapestry which my mother had begun, and on which we were working, under pretence that these works might contain mysterious characters, and a secret mode of writing.[3]

Louis-Charles, in the meantime, was being devoured by the Revolution. The policy of revolutionaries so often seems to be that of taking children from their parents' care. After being forcibly removed from his mother the Queen in the summer of 1793, the eight year old was beaten and otherwise abused, especially when he refused to deny God. The Dauphin, when caught saying his prayers as his mother had taught him, was kicked in the face by Simon his jailer. He was taught to sing obscene songs and curse and swear. He was shown pornography. Since he had lost his father, the little boy had probably been chafing against being cooped up with weeping women, and being a sensitive and impressionable child who had already been traumatized by loss and violence, he was easily manipulated, as any child in such circumstances would be. We might also recall what the Queen wrote to Madame de Tourzel in 1789 when Louis-Charles was four years old:

> He is admirably faithful when once he has promised any thing, but he is very indiscreet; he is thoughtless in repeating any thing that he has heard; and often, without in the least intending to tell stories, he adds circumstances which his own imagination has put into his head. This is his greatest fault, and it is one for which he must be

corrected.[4]

Simon and the soldiers gave him alcohol so that he became drunk. It was in an intoxicated state that he signed the testimony that his own mother had committed incest with him, surely not fully understanding the connotations of the deed. One can see from his handwriting that he was not himself, especially when comparing it with his former schoolwork.[5]

Why did the builders of "liberty, equality, and fraternity" feel compelled to torment a child? Because they knew that children are the future. To manipulate and enslave a child's mind, to weaken his free will through alcohol, pornography and sexualization, is to make him a creature of the state, an automaton, a drone. The horror of the Temple prison has been replicated, in some degree at least, by every totalitarian dictatorship, by the communist and fascist regimes who wished to enslave Christianity and make a god of the nation-state. When the state becomes a god, it is insatiable, for every false god is a demon.

The orphaned daughter of Louis XVI and Marie-Antoinette was aware that her small brother Louis-Charles was in the room below, ill and abused with no one to care for him, especially after the Simons left the Temple, if what they did can be considered care. She was not permitted to see him and when he died of tuberculosis at the age of ten on June 8, 1795, she was not even allowed to keep vigil by his corpse. Only when his body was removed was Madame Royale allowed to go down into the garden. She ever after harbored doubts as to whether her brother had really died because of the rumors that he had been replaced by another boy.

The children of Louis and Antoinette were not the only innocents to suffer during the Revolution. Many French people, particularly the peasants of the Vendée, rebelled against the Liberty, Equality, and Fraternity that were being imposed upon them through bloodshed. They resented their churches being taken over and eventually closed by Republic, while the priests were killed or exiled. They took up arms; the Revolutionary government exercised the harshest brutality upon the uncooperative citizens, including torture, rape and mutilation. General Westermann and his *bleus* were especially notorious for their sadism towards children. There were atrocities all over the Vendée, in Lyon and other French towns and cities where the Revolution was not appreciated. It was the blueprint for the mass murders of the totalitarian regimes of later centuries. Many children died, many young lives were shattered at the dawn of the modern world. Madame Royale, who became known as the "Orphan of the Temple" was the living symbol of all the lost children of France.

A month after the Queen's death there began the *noyades* or "Republican marriages" in Nantes. Under the orders of the Republican Jean-Baptiste Carrier, those citizens who had resisted the Revolution were stripped naked, tied together, put in boats and drowned in the middle of the river. Many innocent, non-political persons, including young girls and nuns, were subjected to such grisly deaths. Usually it was a naked man and woman who were tied together and drowned. The practice was accompanied by other sadistic indignities as well. The Revolution showed no mercy in its macabre mockery of both marriage and baptism.

Madame Élisabeth had always been deeply aware of the danger to her own life by staying with Louis and Antoinette but she refused to leave her brother's family. She stood at Louis' side on June 20, 1792 when the mob stormed the Tuileries and hoped that the people would mistake her for the Queen so that her sister-in-law would be spared. When Louis XVI was killed and the Dauphin taken away and brutalized, Élisabeth comforted Antoinette and young Madame Royale, keeping them from despair. When a friend wondered if Madame Élisabeth could escape on her own, it was said, "Madame Élisabeth is inseparable from the queen; she would not leave her for the most splendid crown in the universe."[6] After the Queen's death in October 1793, the aunt and the niece remained in the Temple prison, enduring humiliations and taunts of the jailers. Élisabeth trained Marie-Thérèse how to survive in confinement, knowing that soon she would be alone. Élisabeth had instructed her niece not to ever let the jailers find her undressed or in bed.

Élisabeth was thirty years old when she was killed in May of 1794. Knowing she was to die, she offered to God the sacrifice of her life. At her trial she was condemned for plotting against the Revolution. In her memoirs, Madame Royale describes the last days of her aunt.

> In the beginning of spring we were refused candles, and we were obliged to go to bed as soon as it grew dark. Until the 9th of May nothing extraordinary happened. On that day, at the moment we were going to bed, the outside bolts of the doors were drawn, and a knocking was heard. My aunt begged of them to wait till she had put on her gown; but they answered that they could not wait, and knocked so violently, that they were near bursting open the door. When she was dressed, she opened the door, and they immediately said to her, 'Citizen, come down.' — 'And my niece?' — 'We shall take care of her afterwards.' She embraced me; and, in order to calm my agitation, promised to return. 'No, citizen,' said they, 'you shall not return:— take your bonnet, and come along.' They overwhelmed

her with the grossest abuse. She bore it all patiently, and embraced me again, exhorting me to have confidence in Heaven, to follow the principles of religion in which I had been educated, and never to forget the last commands of my father and mother. She then left me.

Down stairs they detained her a considerable time in searching her (though they found nothing), and in writing an account of their proceedings. At length, after a thousand insults, she was put into a hackney-coach, with the crier of the revolutionary court, and taken to the Conciergerie, where she passed the night. The next morning they asked her these questions.—

'What is your name?'

'Élisabeth, of France.'

'Where were you on the 10th of August?'

'In the palace of the Tuileries, with my brother.'

'What have you done with your jewels?'

'I know nothing about them; besides, these questions are wholly useless. You are determined on my death. I have offered to Heaven the sacrifice of my life; and I am ready to die—happy at the prospect of rejoining in a better world those whom I loved upon earth.'

They condemned her to death. She asked to be placed in the same room with the other persons who were to die with her. She exhorted them, with a presence of mind, an elevation of soul, and religious enthusiasm, which fortified all their minds. In the cart she preserved the same firmness, and encouraged and supported the women who accompanied her. At the scaffold they had the barbarity to reserve her for the last. All the women, in leaving the cart, begged to embrace her. She kissed them, and, with her usual benignity, said some words of comfort to each. Her strength never abandoned her, and she died with all the resignation of the purest piety. Her soul was separated from her body, and ascended to receive its reward from the merciful Being, whose worthy servant she had been.

It is impossible to imagine my distress at finding myself separated from my aunt. I did not know what had become of her, and could not learn. I passed the night in great anxiety, but, though very uneasy, I was far from believing that her death was so near. Sometimes I tried to persuade myself that they would only banish her from France, but, when I considered the manner in which she had been carried off, all my fears revived.[7]

While awaiting death, eyewitnesses reported how Élisabeth inspired the other prisoners: "She seemed to regard them all as friends about to accompany her to heaven....the tranquility of her mind subdued their anguish."[8] On May 10, 1794 she recited the *De Profundis* on the way to the guillotine. The princess was the last of a group of twenty-five people to be executed; they each knelt before her, asking her blessing. Some say she fainted in the process; the sound of so many decapitations was too much. When it was Élisabeth's turn, the executioner pulled her bodice down very low off her shoulders, and she begged for modesty's sake to be covered. There were no cheers when Élisabeth's head was thrown into a basket, the crowd was silent, and some reported the scent of roses filling the square, a miracle from the Middle Ages to disturb the dawn of modernity. Many regarded her as a saint, including Pope Pius VII, and perhaps someday her cause will be introduced.

Meanwhile, the guards were tormenting Louis-

Charles, awaking him at all hours of the night, torturing him by sleep deprivation. It became a game for them to call "Capet, are you awake?" and shout at the boy until he climbed out of bed and appeared at the door of his cell. In the streets of Paris, the Reign of Terror was at its height. On July 17, 1794, the sixteen Carmelite nuns of Compiègne were guillotined. Antoinette had sponsored the vocation of the prioress, Mother Thérèse de Saint-Augustin, by providing her with a dowry. Ten days later Robespierre was guillotined, and the Reign of Terror came to an end. 6,594 people had been executed by guillotine, including 2,639 just in Paris, and another 25,000 murdered in various ways in the rest of France. After the Thermidorians guillotined Robespierre, their leader Barras, who has been described as having the soul of a louse, visited the Temple, and appointed the young Creole Christophe Laurent to take charge of the orphans in the Temple. Laurent was polite and told Madame Royale that he had cleaned her brother's cell, and deloused him. But he never allowed her to see her brother, nor did he call a doctor. Neither child was allowed any fresh air.

In November Madame Royale was visited by Gomin, who brought matches, and candles, too, let us assume. He assured the princess that her brother was being nurtured, when in reality the child was ill, mute and covered with infectious sores. When Harmand, the chief of the metropolitan police, who had replaced Michonis after he was guillotined, visited the little prisoner in December, he found a dumb boy with rickets, covered with tumors, but still able to walk, and obviously able to obey simple commands. At the end of March 1795, Laurent was sent away from the Temple, to be replaced by Lasne. It was Lasne who at last summoned a physician for the unfortunate boy. On May 6, Dr. Pierre-Joseph Desault visited the boy and was shaken by his condition, the result of mistreatment and neglect, which he reported to the authorities. Within a month, the doctor died of a mysterious illness. There were those who thought he had been poisoned.[9] Two more doctors were sent to the Temple, Jean-Baptiste Dumangin and Philippe-Jean Pelletan, but they found the poor child too far gone for medical aid. They made certain he was cleaned up and made as comfortable as possible as he lay dying. Meanwhile, both the Spanish government and Charette, the leader of the Royal and Catholic army of the Vendée, were demanding the release and safe delivery of Madame Royale and Louis XVII, in exchange for peace. The Directoire of Barras badly needed peace from both its external and internal foes, but would not surrender Madame Royale until the child in the room below had died on June 8, 1795. Dr. Pelletan removed the heart of the boy and preserved it in alcohol and it was later used in the DNA tests of the 21st century to prove that the child was the son of a Habsburg princess.[10]

How dark must have been the thoughts of Marie-Thérèse-Charlotte de France on the midnight of December 18, 1795, the eve of her seventeenth birthday, as she prepared to be sent to her relatives in Austria. She had not only experienced a bloody revolution, but she had been subjected to verbal abuse and the constant threat of physical molestation. Since the guards would make surprise visits to her cell at all hours of the day and night, the teenaged princess, Madame Royale of Versailles, would sometimes spend the night in a chair, petrified. One by one, her parents, her brother, and her aunt had been taken away, until she was alone in the dreary Temple prison in Paris. After her brother died, she was sent a companion from the Barras government, a lady called Madame Renée de Chanterenne, who told her what had happened to her family and helped her to write her memoirs. Meanwhile, the citizens of Paris began to remember her. They stood on the roofs of neighboring houses so they could glimpse their princess when she went for a walk in the garden. Many wept for her, and public indignation rose against the government. Kindly Parisians sent her a dog and a baby goat for company. In October 1795, it was arranged that Marie-Thérèse de France would be exchanged for the four commissioners of the Convention delivered up to Austria by Dumouriez in April, 1793. She left the Tower of the Temple during the night of December 18, 1795. Madame de Tourzel and her daughter Pauline as well as Madame de Mackau came to be with her. They begged to travel with her to Austria but were not permitted. As she stepped out of the tower, she turned to the French minister who had come to escort her to the border. "I am grateful for your attentive and respectful manner," said the princess. "But even at the moment you are giving me liberty, how can I help thinking of those who crossed this threshold before me? It is just three years, four months, and five days since those doors were closed on my family and me; today I go out, the last and most wretched of all." The Temple was razed to the ground by order of Napoleon in 1811.

Maria Carolina, Queen of Naples, had a great deal to do with the Emperor and Empress, her nephew and her daughter, taking in the daughter of Antoinette. Maria Carolina would have welcomed her in Naples but Francis II wanted Marie-Thérèse to marry his brother Archduke Karl von Habsburg. Some gazettes were even announcing an engagement between them although when Madame de Tourzel and Madame de Mackau visited the princess she said she only had feelings for her cousin Louis-Antoine, the Duc d'Angoulême. Her uncle the Comte de Provence, now Louis XVIII, was afraid she was going to marry Karl. According to Louis XVIII,

Louis and Antoinette had originally wanted Marie-Thérèse to marry Artois' oldest son Louis-Antoine but when they had sons they lost interest in such a marriage. But now that their sons were gone he had no doubt that they would have returned to their original intention. On her journey to Austria, Marie-Thérèse was welcomed along the way by her Saxon relatives and by her mother's sister the Abbess, Archduchess Elisabeth, the one once intended as the bride of Louis XV.[11]

In the meantime, Marie-Thérèse received loving letters from Mesdames Adélaïde and Victoire, as well as from her cousin Charles-Ferdinand, Duc de Berry, all of whom she rejoiced to hear from. It seems that Marie-Thérèse was not a pauper, for not only were there Antoinette's diamonds which had been smuggled out of France, but money that Louis XVI had given to Mercy to keep for emergencies, as well as Antoinette's dowry which had never been paid in full by Austria. Marie-Thérèse displayed that she had inherited her parents' great facility for languages, for she was speaking fluent German after two months in Austria.[12] Her relations with Emperor Francis and his Empress, Maria Theresa of Naples, were cordial but cool; she became good friends with their daughters, Archduchess Marie Louise, who would marry Bonaparte, Archduchess Maria Leopoldina, the future Empress of Brazil. In the meantime, the Mesdames wrote to her again from Rome, telling her there had been a miracle before a statue of the Virgin, in which a dried, dead lily burst into bloom, which the aged princesses took as a sign that France had not been abandoned by God.[13] Louis XVI's other sister, Madame Clothilde, Queen of Sardinia, also corresponded with her orphaned niece, in whom she most certainly found a kindred spirit. But Francis II changed his mind about Madame Royale's marriage with Karl, since Bonaparte was growing more powerful and alliances with powerful rulers were needed. Some said the princess had become attached to the warrior Archduke and that her heart was broken, leading to an ongoing moroseness and depression in her character. Archduke Karl retired from active duty in 1812 and in 1815 married Princess Henrietta of Nassau-Weilburg by whom he had five children. Marie-Thérèse also received a letter from Count von Fersen, asking for a payback for Madame de Korff and her mother, who had given their money for the aborted escape attempt in June of 1791.[14] It was a cold letter, and extremely business-like. Marie-Thérèse paid the Korffs.

In 1799, Madame Royale left Vienna, and was conducted by several faithful retainers to Mitau in Courland in the Russian Empire, where Tsar Paul and Empress Maria had invited her and all the Bourbons to seek asylum. There she married her cousin Louis-Antoine, the son of the Comte d'Artois. At the ceremony she was given the wedding ring of her father, Louis XVI, which she wore until her own death. Here is a description which Louis XVIII wrote in 1799 of his niece to his brother Artois, calling her "our daughter" and comparing her to their sister Madame Élisabeth:

> The portraits you have seen of our daughter...cannot give you an accurate idea of her; they are not in the least like her. She so closely resembles both her father and her mother that she recalls them absolutely, together or separately, according to the point of view from which one looks at her. She is not pretty at first sight; but she becomes so as one looks at her, and especially as one talks to her, for there is not a movement of her face that is not pleasing. She is a little shorter than her mother, and a little taller than our poor sister. She is well made, holds herself well, carries her

head perfectly, and walks with ease and grace. When she speaks of her misfortunes her tears do not flow readily, owing to her habit of restraining them, lest her [jailers] should have the barbarous pleasure of seeing her shed them. It is no easy task, however, for her listeners to restrain theirs. But her natural gaiety is not quenched; draw her mind away from this tragic chapter of her life, and she laughs heartily and is quite charming. She is gentle, good-humoured, and affectionate; and there is no doubt that she has the mind of a mature woman. In private with me she behaves as our poor Élisabeth might have behaved with my father; in public she has the bearing of a princess accustomed to holding a Court. She not only says courteous things to everyone, but she says to each individual the most suitable thing that could be said. She is modest without being shy, at her ease without being familiar, and as innocent as on the day she was born. Of that I have been absolutely convinced by her manner with my nephew since Tuesday, the day of her arrival here. In fact, to put it briefly, I recognise in her the angel we have lost.[15]

When restored to France and the Tuileries in 1814, Marie-Thérèse was hailed as both the "Orphan of the Temple" and the "French Antigone" for her fidelity to her uncle Louis XVIII. She wanted everything to be exactly as it was when she had last been there with her family, which was of course, impossible. She was subject to nightmares and hysterical episodes when something would by chance remind her of her family's ordeal. Sometimes she would be heard pacing all night. She was known for her charitable activites, preferring hospitals and orphanages to the ballroom and the opera box. However, due to propaganda and the often dour expression she wore in public, by 1830 she was called *Madame Rancune* or "Lady Resentment." She was haunted by the fate of her brother and never completely certain that he had died in 1795. She never had any children but loved her niece and nephew, Louise d'Artois and Henri, Comte de Chambord, as her own. She did a lot to rebuild France after all the country had been through with the Revolution and Napoleonic wars. Marie-Thérèse lacked her mother's grace but carried herself with dignity and pride. She usually wore worn, mended dresses but on formal occasions, such as when she went to the opera, she arrayed herself in satins and velvets, covered with Antoinette's diamonds. She could be glamorous when she chose to be, emanating majesty as well as sorrow.

For many years scholars debated as to whether or not the marriage of the Duc and Duchesse d'Angoulême was consummated. From the fact that the matter was ever in doubt, we can guess that perhaps the marriage was not all it should have been. There were rumors that her husband was homosexual while others whispered that he was troubled by impotence.[16] According to the research of Dr. Susan Nagel, author of the most recent biography of Marie-Thérèse, the marriage was indeed consummated at some point and in 1813 the princess was pregnant for several months, although she had a miscarriage.[17] In 1820, at age forty-two, she thought she was pregnant but it turned out to be symptoms of menopause.[18]

Louis-Antoine loved the military; he actually distinguished himself as a soldier and even as a commander on several occasions. It was his courage that won Bordeaux to the side of the Bourbons in 1814. He was known to be a very devout and kindly man to those of his household, as was his wife, although they both had tempers and quarrelled with each other. He was closer to his uncle Louis XVIII than he was to his father Charles X (Artois). However, he and his father made the terrible blunders which led to the final collapse of the Bourbons and the rise of the House of Orléans to the throne in 1830, as is described in the novel *Madame Royale*. Louis-Antoine is often known as Louis XIX because he was king for about ten minutes after his father abdicated; then he himself signed the abdication as well. His wife, Marie-Thérèse, stayed with him to the end of his life (1844); they had become tender companions and best friends over the years in spite of many troubles, or perhaps because of them. Marie-Thérèse died at her estate at Frohsdorf in Austria in 1851, in the arms of her nephew Henri d'Artois, Comte de Chambord, the son of the Duc de Berry and his wife Caroline of Naples. As she died, Marie-Thérèse kissed the wedding ring of her father, which had engraved inside it the letters: "M.A.A.A" for "Marie-Antoinette, Archduchess of Austria."

Marie-Antoinette, Daughter of the Caesars

MADAME PREMIÈRE, DUCHESSE D'ANGOULÊME, DAUGHTER OF LOUIS XVI., BORN AT VERSAILLES ON DECEMBER 19TH, 1778

25 LEGACY

"You must have seen, on some fine summer's day, a black cloud suddenly appear and threaten to pour down upon the country and lay it waste. The lightest wind drives it away, and the blue sky and serene weather are restored. This is just the image of what has happened to me...." —Marie-Antoinette to Madame Campan

On January 21, 1815, under a tent on the Rue d'Anjou, eventual site of the expiatory chapel, the coffins of Louis and Antoinette reposed in state. After twenty-two years the former sovereigns were finally to receive Christian burial. The remains of the King and the Queen were carried by the Scottish company of the bodyguards, followed by rank upon rank of soldiers. Some members of the Royal Family were present, although the grieving Duchess d'Angoulême remained closeted in her private oratory at the Tuileries. The funeral procession wound across Paris to the Basilica of Saint Denis, where the requiem Mass was offered. Louis and Antoinette were then interred in the royal crypt; the Office of the Dead was recited. It was the same crypt which had been hideously rifled by the Revolutionaries in 1793, when the tombs of the kings and queens of France and their families were opened and the bodies thrown in pits, including that of the seven-year-old Dauphin Louis-Joseph.

Between 1816 and 1826, at the expense of Louis XVIII and the Duchess of Angoulême, the Chapelle Expiatoire was built on the place where the bodies of Louis and Antoinette had been buried after their murders. It was originally called the Madeleine cemetery because it was connected to the Madeleine church. When Louis and Antoinette were executed, they were obscurely buried there with many other victims. However, a Monsieur Descloseaux marked the exact spot where they were each buried. Descloseaux watched over the graves of the King and Queen for many years, going so far as to buy the property and plant an orchard and a garden there. Once a year a bouquet of the flowers from the graves of her parents was picked and sent to Marie-Thérèse in her exile. Although the bodies of the King and Queen were identified and reburied in Saint Denis, as has been described, the Chapelle Expiatoire marked the spot where they had lain for so long. The chapel is considered a model of late Neoclassicism. The statues of the monarchs are particularly unique. Marie-Antoinette is shown "supported by religion" while Louis XVI is portrayed as being "called to immortality."

Over the crypt where their tombs now lie are two magnificent statues of Louis and Antoinette, kneeling side by side in prayer at the Basilica of Saint Denis. Catherine Delors describes the statue of the Queen and how it reflects the transformation of Antoinette's relationship with Louis XVI. To quote:

> Here... she is pensive, humble, leaning forward and sideways towards her husband. This is very moving

in light of the evolution of the royal couple's complex relationship: mutual coldness at first, then disdain on her part, gradually followed by ever increasing closeness, respect and affection. During their last months together at the Temple, Louis XVI and Marie-Antoinette cared for each other in the deepest sense of the word. She was devastated by his death, and his last earthly concerns were for her and their children. I believe this sculpture beautifully captures this. There was definitely more than propaganda to the Saint-Denis reburials.[1]

After reviewing the life of Antoinette, with the heights of splendor and the depths of misery which characterize it, I must turn to the unpleasant subject of "Let them eat cake." That phrase, never spoken by any Queen of France, is the only thing the general public knows about our Antoinette. Of course, the Queen never said any such thing, as I hope readers have discovered by now. One theory about the origins of the legend of the phrase "Let them eat cake" is that it is the misunderstanding of a passage from the memoirs of the Comte de Provence (Louis XVIII), the brother of Louis XVI. Provence and his wife escaped from Paris to Coblenz by post-chaise in June, 1791. They stopped to eat and had meager provisions. Provence makes the allusion to a remark made by the queen of Louis XIV, Maria Theresa of Spain, in this passage: "We had a pie and some claret, but we had forgotten bread; and whilst we ate the crust with the pie, we thought of Queen Maria Theresa, who hearing one day the poor people pitied for being in want of bread, replied, 'But, dear me, why do they not eat pie-crust?' "[2] Pie-crust was often fed to the beggars, from the back doors of the *patisseries*. Antoinette, of course, never made any such remark in regard to starving people. Instead, she gave generously to the poor. There is also the phrase from Rousseau about *brioche*, the sweet bread of the French, *Qu'ils mangent de la brioche*, published in his *Confessions* in 1765, written when Antoinette was a child in Austria. What she did say, which is rarely quoted, is this: "It is quite certain that in seeing the people who treat us so well despite their own misfortune, we are more obliged than ever to work hard for their happiness."[3]

A mistake which many historians make is to project onto the past the popular issues of the present. We cannot judge Antoinette by contemporary political standards which exalt the democratic process or by modern norms of behavior according to feminist notions. There was no feminist movement, and the word "feminist" was not coined until the 1830's. There were a few women attached to the Revolution who championed social and political equality for the female sex; they tried to make the French Revolution their own, although in the end it betrayed them, and was indeed an orgy of misogyny. Mary Wollstonecraft, called the "Mother of Feminism," saw the Revolution as the dawn of a glorious new era, as she describes in an excerpt from her book *An Historical and Moral View of the Origin and Progress of the French Revolution; and the Effect it Has Produced in Europe*. When the book was published in 1795, thousands of people had already been killed; the genocide in the Vendée, including the torture, rape and murder of women and children, was at its height. Yet Mary Wollstonecraft dismisses the mass murders and extreme violence to be merely the result of "the desperate and engaged factions." Otherwise, she lauds the "grand theatre of political changes" which were leading France "from a state of barbarism to that of polished society...hastening the overthrow of the tremendous empire of superstition and hypocrisy, erected upon the ruins of gothic brutality and ignorance."

Marie-Antoinette, Daughter of the Caesars

I have no doubt that by "empire of superstition and hypocrisy" she was referring to the Catholic Church. She rejoices that the French were at last to "grasp the sentiments of freedom" while being delivered from the "servility and voluptuousness" of the *ancien régime*.[4] Mary Wollstonecraft, unfortunately, was not herself unfamiliar with "voluptuousness and servility," as she later became as famous for her stormy love affairs as for her writings. Mary was the brilliant and sensitive daughter of an abusive and improvident father; she had to protect her mother and sisters from beatings and heaven knows what else. She later became involved with men who used her then abandoned her, contributing to her struggle with depression and suicidal tendencies. Mary criticized Edmund Burke's lament for the fall of Antoinette and the end of chivalry; she hated chivalry and thought that women should be able to take care of themselves.[5] Poor Mary, however, could barely support herself and the child she had by one of her lovers. Finally, she found a man who sincerely loved her, William Godwin, and they married, but their happiness was short-lived. She died as so many other woman died in those days, from complications in childbirth. Nevertheless, before her death she found great satisfaction in her motherly role that she may not have found in other areas of her life. The child she brought into the world amid such great suffering became the gifted writer Mary Shelley, author of *Frankenstein* and wife of Percy Bysshe Shelley. All of which, of course, is a story in itself.

Antoinette was united with her husband in seeking the betterment of the French people; she championed women in her own way. Why did Antoinette so assiduously support women artists and writers? Perhaps because they were honorable professions by which women could support themselves and their children.

Antoinette did not see this as part of a feminist cause but rather as a way of protecting the virtue of women and their families. When left without income and deprived of the protection of a father, husband, or brother, women were more easily seduced into a life of concubinage. Impoverished women of the lower class, if they could not find work, often became prostitutes. That is why Antoinette generously gave dowries to girls so they could marry or become nuns. She patronized women with businesses as well as women in the arts. Antoinette was known to show special kindness to women with child. One of her ladies-in-waiting, Madame de la Tour du Pin, who does not refrain from criticizing Antoinette when she sees fit, remarks in her memoirs on the Queen's consideration towards her when she was expecting.[6] There is also the famous story, included in my novel *Trianon*, about how Antoinette got down on the floor to pick up the paints and brushes for Madame Vigée-Lebrun when the artist was pregnant.[7] The Queen also founded a home for unwed mothers called the Maternity Society.[8] She also supported foundling homes and orphanages for children who had been abandoned. How sad that so many of the genuine accounts of the Queen's charity are forgotten by history whereas falsehoods such as "Let them eat cake" are remembered forever.

As mentioned at the bginning of the book, there are some odd connections between Saint Joan of Arc and Queen Marie-Antoinette. At first glance no two people appear to be as different from each other as the Habsburg archduchess and the peasant girl from Domrémy, other than a shared love for children and needlework. Joan has often been referred to as the "Maid of Lorraine" or even as "Joan of Lorraine." Father Jean-Marie Charles-Roux, in building a case for the martyrdom of Antoinette in his book *Louis XVII: La*

Mère et l'Enfant martyrs and in articles, points out that the Queen's full name was Marie-Antoinette-Josèphe-Jeanne de Lorraine, even as the Maid was Jeanne de Lorraine. [9] Both women were called to their "mission" at age thirteen. At thirteen, Joan began to hear her voices; at thirteen, Antoinette was told she was to marry the heir to the French throne. Both were known for their staunch purity, and yet both were branded by enemies with the epithet of "whore." Both the Queen and the peasant have had their reputations despoiled beyond recognition. Both suffered the ordeal of a long imprisonment in which they endured outrages against modesty. Both were forced to defend themselves against calumnies and half-truths amid the scrutiny of a public trial. Both persisted in their loyalty to the Holy See. Both were condemned to an ignominious death and each was taken to the scaffold in a cart. Unlike Saint Joan, Antoinette never had a posthumous retrial. She was never officially vindicated and her name continues to be slandered in books and movies to this day.

Madame Clothilde, Queen of Sardinia, died in Rome in 1802 where she and her husband King Charles Emanuel had sought refuge from Napoleon. Clothilde died of typhoid fever, her saintliness recognized by many, especially by Pope Pius VII. In honoring Clothilde, it can perhaps be said that the pontiff indirectly paid homage to those members of her family who had died violent deaths. She is known as "Venerable Clothilde."

As her brother was hailed "Son of Saint Louis" at the moment of his death, so Madame Élisabeth could be called the "Daughter of Saint Louis" for she exemplified in her person everything that was fine, noble and magnificent about the House of France. It is sad that in so many novels and films, Élisabeth is either erased or minimized, when her presence was a source of comfort to the King and the Queen in their ordeals, even if she disagreed with them. She withstood the mob at her brother's side and encouraged the rest of the family in the darkness of imprisonment. She became a second mother to her niece Madame Royale, and comforted the condemned on the way to the scaffold.

Following their deaths, Louis and Antoinette were hailed by royalists and monarchists everywhere as the "King-Martyr" and the "Queen-Martyr." Objects that had belonged to them were often treated like relics, especially the bloody shirt of Louis XVI, which his daughter kept with her until her death. The last century saw the growth of the cult of Louis XVI, a cult which has existed since his execution, when people dipped handkerchiefs in his blood for souvenirs.[10] In his Allocution of June 17, 1793, Pope Pius VI called Louis a martyr of the Catholic faith.[11] The mystic Jeanne Le Royer (1732-1798) at the Poor Clares of Fougères declared that Jesus told her that Louis XVI was in heaven, saying: "*Il est glorieux!*"[12] In 1820, Marie-Thérèse de France tried to introduce the Cause of her father. She spoke to the Apostolic Nuncio, Vincenzo Macchi, who consulted Cardinal Consalvi. But Pius VII and the Sacred Congregation ruled that Louis XVI was not killed for hatred of the faith but for political reasons. She tried again in the reign of Charles X, gathering documents, but the Monsignor Clermont-Tonnerre said the King was killed for political reasons and also showed weakness by signing the Civil Constition of the Clergy. Under the Second Empire, Amedée Burion wrote *Louis XVI Martyr* with no success. During the Third Republic, a commission under Abbé Glaire tried again in 1874, but it went nowhere. In 1893, Abbé Ernest Rigaud tried to get Louis beatified with Joan of Arc.[11] There have been several other attempts, with Louis' biographers the Coursacs trying in 1991. Nothing came of it.[12] I would venture to speculate that the obstacles are mainly political. It took Saint Thomas More and Saint Joan of Arc hundreds of years before they were formally acknowledged as saints. We remember that there are many souls whose sanctity is known only to God and at the final judgment all shall be revealed.

"Royalist print of Louis XVI received by St. Louis IX in Heaven"

NOTES

Preface

1. Whaley, Joachim. *Germany and the Holy Roman Empire: Volume II: The Peace of Westphalia to the Dissolution of the Reich, 1648-1806*. Oxford: Oxford University Press, 2012, p. 347.

2. Charles-Roux, J.M. "Marie-Antoinette: The Martyred Queen of Christian Europe." *Royal Stuart Review*, Vol. 6, Number 3, 1987 and Number 4, 1988, pp. 55-62, 72-85.

3. Thomas, Chantal. *The Wicked Queen: The Origins of the Myth of Marie-Antoinette*, translated by Julie Rose. New York: Zone Books, 2001, pp. 41-42.

Introduction

1. Campan, Madame. *Memoirs of Marie-Antoinette*. New York: Collier and Son, 1910, pp. 81-82.

2. Marie-Thérèse d'Autriche et al. *Correspondance secrète entre Marie-Thérèse et le comte de Mercy-Argenteau, avec les lettres de Marie-Thérèse et de Marie-Antoinette, 2 Volumes*. Paris: Firmin-Didot, 1874, I, pp. 180-181.

3. Chalon, Jean. *Chère Marie-Antoinette*. Paris: Perrin, 1997, p. 187.

4. Montjoie, Félix-Louis Galart de. *Histoire de Marie-Antoinette-Josephe-Jeanne de Lorraine, archiduchesse d'Autriche, reine de France*. Paris: H.L. Perronneau, 1797, p. 107.

5. Croker, John Wilson. *Essays on the Early Period of the French Revolution*. London: John Murray, 1857, pp.

72-73.

Chapter 1: A Daughter of the Caesars

1. Rocheterie, Maxime de la. *The Life of Marie Antoinette, 2 Volumes*, translated by Cora Hamilton Bell. New York: Dodd, Mead and Company, 1906, I, pp.1-2. Translation: "I have lost: the august daughter has condemned me to pay. But if it be true that she resembles you, then all the world has won."
2. Yonge Charles Duke. *The Life of Marie Antoinette, Queen of France.* New York: Harper and Brothers, 1876, pp. 28-29.
3. Campan, p. 31.
4. Guéranger, Dom Proper, OSB. *The Liturgical Year, Volume I: Advent*, translated by Dom Laurence Shepherd, OSB. Powers Lake, North Dakota: Marian House, 1983, p. 385.
5. Bireley, Robert. *Ferdinand II, Counter-Reformation Emperor, 1578-1637.* New York: Cambridge University Press, 2014, p. 27.
6. Weber, Joseph. *Memoirs of Maria-Antoinetta, Queen of France and Navarre,* translated by R.C. Dallas. London: Rickaby, 1805, pp. 1-3.
7. Rocheterie, p. 2.
8. Cronin, Vincent. *Louis and Antoinette.* London: Harvill Press, 1996, p. 45.
9. Ibid.
10. Delorme, Philippe. *Marie-Antoinette: Épouse de Louis XVI, mère de Louis XVII.* Paris: Pygmalion/Gérard Watelet, 1999, p. 15.
11. Ibid, p. 11.
12. Cronin, p.47.
13. Rocheterie, I, p. 4.
14. Webster, Nesta. *Louis XVI and Marie-Antoinette before the Revolution.* London: Constable, 1937, p. 12.

15. Younghusband, Helen A. *Marie-Antoinette, Her Early Youth (1770-1774)*. New York: Macmillan, 1912, p. 104.

16. Rocheterie, I, p. 4.

17. Faulkner, Liam. "Johann Joseph Gassner – Exorcist Healer." *History in an Hour*, March 11, 2013. According to this online article, Fr. Gassner (1727-1779) was a Catholic priest and famous healer in Southern Germany and Austria during the reign of Empress Maria Theresa. He was reported to have cured hundreds of people from various diseases and afflictions, which included casting out devils and raising the dead. He was criticized by many physicians and scientists who thought he was using the same techniques as the notorious Mesmer. His healing ministry was condemned by Pope Pius IV in 1776 and he responded with obedience. Fr. Gassner was exiled to a remote region in Northern Austria by Emperor Joseph II, where he died in 1779.

18. Here is a list of the children of Emperor Francis Stephen and Empress Maria Theresa:

Archduchess Maria Elisabeth (1737-1740). Maria Theresa's heiress presumptive between 1737 and 1740.

Archduchess Maria Anna (1738-1789). Maria Theresa's heiress presumptive between 1740 and 1741.

Archduchess Maria Caroline (1740-1741).

Holy Roman Emperor Joseph II (1741-1790), married Infanta Isabel of Spain (1741-1763), then Princess Marie Josepha of Bavaria (1739-1767); no surviving issue. Holy Roman Emperor from 1765; Archduke of Austria, King of Hungary and King of Bohemia and from 1780.

Archduchess Maria Christina, Duchess of Teschen (1742-1798), married Prince Albert of Saxony, Duke of Teschen (1738-1822); no surviving issue.

Archduchess Maria Elisabeth (1743-1808).

Archduke Charles Joseph (1745-1761).

Archduchess Maria Amalia (1746-1804), married

Ferdinand, Duke of Parma (1751-1802); had issue.
Holy Roman Emperor Leopold II (1747-1792), married Infanta Maria Louisa of Spain (1745-1792); had issue. Grand Duke of Tuscany from 1765 (abdicated 1790); Holy Roman Emperor from 1790; Archduke of Austria, King of Hungary and King of Bohemia from 1790.
Archduchess Maria Carolina (1748).
Archduchess Johanna Gabriela (1750-1762).
Archduchess Maria Josepha (1751-1767).
Queen Maria Caroline of Naples and Sicily (1752-1814), married King Ferdinand IV of Naples and Sicily (1751-1825); had issue.
Archduke Ferdinand of Austria-Este, Duke of Breisgau (1754–1806), married Maria Beatrice d'Este, heiress of Breisgau and of Modena; had issue (Austria-Este). Duke of Breisgau from 1803.
Queen Marie Antoinette of France and Navarre, born Maria Antonia (1755-1793); married Louis XVI of France (1754-1793).
Archduke Maximilian Francis (1756-1801), Archbishop-Elector of Cologne: 1784.

19. Vovk, Justin C. *In Destiny's Hands: Five Tragic Rulers, Children of Maria Theresa.* Raleigh, North Carolina: Lulu.com, 2009, p. 14.
20. Schoenfeld, Hermann. *Women of the Teutonic Nations.* Philadelphia: Rittenhouse Press, 1908, pp. 278-282.
21. Löffler, Klemens. "Maria Theresa." *The Catholic Encyclopedia. Vol. 9.* New York: Robert Appleton Company, 1910.
22. Castelot, André. *Queen of France: A Biography of Marie Antoinette*, trans. Denise Folliot. New York: Harper & Brothers, 1957, p. 14.
23. Ibid. pp.14-15.
24. Lever, Evelyn, ed. *Correspondance de Marie-Antoinette (1770-1793).* Paris: Tallandier, 2005, p. 61.

25. Bicknell, Anna L. *The Story of Marie-Antoinette*. New York: The Century Company, 1897, p. 225.
26. Clegg, Melanie. *Marie-Antoinette: An Intimate History.* Amazon Digital Services LLC: Madame Guillotine, 2015, p. 138.
27. Mahan, Alexander J. *Maria Theresa of Austria.* London: Read Books Ltd, 2013, p. 270.
28. Clegg, p. 367.
29. Delorme, p. 21.
30. Ibid. p. 22.
31. Ibid. p. 19.
32. Jahn, Otto. *Life of Mozart, Volume 1*, translated by Pauline Townsend. London: Novello, Ewer & Company, 1882, p. 28.
33. Ibid. p.35.
34. Ibid.
35. Abert, Hermann. *W.A. Mozart*, translated by Stewart Spencer. New Haven: Yale University Press, 2007, p. 36.

Chapter 2: The Maid of Lorraine

1. Thomas, pp. 32, 34, 37.
2. Vidal, Elena Maria. "St. John the Baptist and the Durieux Sisters." *Tea at Trianon*, January 7, 2016.
3. Bicknell, p. 6.
4. Yonge, pp. 28-29.
5. Macleod, Margaret Anne. *There were Three of Us in the Relationship: The Secret Letters of Marie Antoinette, Vol I*. Irvine, Scotland: Isaac MacDonald, 2008, pp.10-11. Letter of Maria Theresa to Marie-Antoinette, April 21, 1770.
6. Bernier, Olivier, editor. *Secrets of Marie Antoinette: A Collection of Letters*. New York: Fromm International, 1986, pp. 31-32.
7. Delorme, p.37

8. Weber, Caroline. *Queen of Fashion: What Marie Antoinette Wore to the French Revolution.* New York: Henry Holt and Company, 2006, p. 30.
9. Oberkirch, Henriette Louise. *Memoirs of the baroness d'Oberkirch, countess de Montbrison*, ed. by her grandson, the count de Montbrison, 2 Volumes. London: Colburn and Company, 1852, I, pp. 41-43.
10. Mossiker, Frances. *The Queen's Necklace.* London: Phoenix, 1961, p.30.
11. Bertière, Simone. *Marie-Antoinette l'insoumise.* Paris: Editions de Fallois, 2002, p. 35.
12. Ibid. p. 33.
13. Matheson, Lister M. *Icons of the Middle Ages: Rulers, Writers, Rebels, and Saints*, Volume 2. Oxford: Greenwood, 2011, p. 424.
14. C. Weber, p. 77.
15. Ibid. p. 93.
16. Faÿ, Bernard. *Louis XVI ou la fin d'un monde.* Paris: La Table Ronde, 1981, p. 33.
17. Shriner, Charles Anthony. *Wit, Wisdom and Foibles of the Great: Together with Numerous Anecdotes.* New York: Funk and Wagnalls, 1920, p. 165.
18. *The American Catholic Quarterly Review*, Vol. 32, Jan- Oct, Philadelphia, 1907, p. 342.
19. Fraser, Antonia. *Marie-Antoinette: The Journey.* New York: Anchor Books, 2002, p. 69.
20. Petitfils, Jean-Christian. *Louis XVI.* Paris: Perrin, 2005, p. 60.
21. Younghusband, p. 198.
22. Rocheterie, II, pp. 23-24.
23. Campan, pp. 42-43.
24. Fraser, p. 70.
25. Yonge, p. 38.
26. Goodman, Dena, ed. *Marie-Antoinette: Writings on the Body of a Queen.* New York: Routledge, 2003, pp. 173-198.

27. Campan, pp. 41-42.
28. Ibid, p. 140.

Chapter 3: The House of Bourbon

1. Lever, ed., p.133. Letter from Marie-Antoinette to Maria Theresa on Feb. 15, 1773.
2. *The Court and Lady's Magazine, Vol. IV.* "Memoir of Isabella, Queen of Spain, Consort of Philip the Fourth." London: Dobbs and Company, 1839, p. 364.
3. Cronin, pp. 30-31.
4. Delpierre, Madeleine. *Dress in France in the Eighteenth Century.* New Haven: Yale University Press, 1997, p. 72.
5. Lever, *Madame de Pompadour*, p. 160.
6. Schmidt, Louise Boisen. "The King's Birdcage." *This Is Versailles,* May 7, 2013.
7. Stryienski, Casimir. *The Daughters of Louis XV*, translated by Cranstoun Metcalfe. New York: Brentano's, 1912, p. 7.
8. Cronin, p. 31.
9. *The American Catholic Quarterly Review*, p. 342.
10. Vidal, Elena Maria. "Marie-Josèphe de Saxe." *Tea at Trianon*, January 14, 2016.
11. Delors, Catherine. "Madame Elisabeth, Duchess of Parma, daughter of Louis XV." *Versailles and More*, November 13, 2008.
12. Campan, p. 22.
13. Cronin, p. 42.
14. Brière, Léon de la. *Madame Louise of France,* translated by Meta and Mary Brown. London: Kegan Paul, Trench, Trubner and Co., Limited, 1907, p. 4.
15. Campan, p. 21.
16. Ibid, p. 27.
17. Ibid, p. 22.
18. Delors, Catherine. "Madame Sophie, daughter of

Louis XV." *Versailles and More*, February 4, 2009.
19. Ibid. "'La Petite Reine' is not Marie-Antoinette" *Versailles and More*. October 5, 2008.
20. Brière, p. 4.
21. Ibid.
22. Ibid, p. 5.
23. Ibid.
24. Campan, p. 24.
25. Brière, p. 10.
26. Ibid, p. 185.
27. Ibid, pp. 25-26.
28. Ibid, p. 125.
29. Ibid, p. 196.
30. Cronin, p. 31.
31. Seward, Desmond. *Marie Antoinette*. New York: St Martin's Press, 1981, p. 127.
32. Cronin, p. 48. Delorme, p. 52.
33. Rudy, Lisa Jo. "What Are the Diagnostic Criteria for Asperger Syndrome?" *About.com*, March 19, 2015.
34. Petitfils, p. 74.
35. Morris, Gouveneur. *A Diary of the French Revolution*, edited by Beatrix Cary Davenport. Amazon Digital Services LLC: Morris Press, 2013, pp. 3658-3659. Entry of July 14, 1791.
36. Younghusband, pp. 478-479.
37. Petitfils, p. 241.
38. Younghusband, p.200.
39. Campan, p. 91.
40. Petitfils, p. 241.
41. Younghusband, p. 200-201.
42. Cronin, p. 36.
43. Petitfils, p. 30.
44. Ibid, p. 73.
45. Younghusband, p. 479.
46. Cronin, p.38.
47. Wormeley, Katherine Prescott. *The Ruin of a*

Princess. New York: The Lamb Publishing Company, 1912, p. 4.

Chapter 4: Scandal

1. Fraser, p. 94.
2. Ibid, p. 67.
3. Younghusband, p. 439.
4. Bernier, ed., p. 79.
5. Ibid, p. 77.
6. Delorme, p.83.
7. Bertière, Simone. *Marie-Antoinette l'insoumise*. Paris: Editions de Fallois, 2002, p. 219.
8. Rocheterie, Vol.1, p. 75.
9. Younghusband, p. 568.
10. C. Weber, p. 99.
11. Weber (French version), p. 27.

Chapter 5: The Temple of Love

1. Fraser, p. 157.
2. Cronin, p. 51.
3. Delorme, p. 93.
4. Cronin, p. 191.
5. Ibid, p. 51.
6. Ibid, p. 52.
7. Ibid.
8. Younghusband, p. 136.
9. Cronin, p. 52.
10. Lever, ed., p.115. Letter from Marie-Antoinette to Maria Theresa, July 17, 1772.
11. C. Weber, p. 86.
12. Delorme, p. 71.
13. Lever, ed., p. 142. Letter from Marie-Antoinette to Maria Theresa, April 18, 1773.
14. Ibid, p. 47. Letter from Comte de Mercy to Maria

Theresa, June 15, 1770.
15. Ibid, p. 139. Letter from Marie-Antoinette to Maria Theresa, March 15, 1773.
16. Ibid, p. 394. Letter from Marie-Antoinette to Maria Theresa, September 19, 1780.
17. Marie-Antoinette, Reine de France. *Lettres de Marie-Antoinette: recueil des lettres authentiques de la reine, Tome 1 et 2.* Paris: Alphonse Picard et Fils, 1895, I, p. 8. Letter from Marie-Antoinette to Maria Theresa, July 12, 1770.
18. Cronin, p. 191.
19. Webster, 1937, pp.116-117.
20. Bertière, p. 357.
21. Petitfils, p. 264- 265.
22. Webster, 1937, p. 113.
23. Petitfils, p. 74.
24. Lever, ed., p. 150. Letter from Marie-Antoinette to Maria Theresa, August 13, 1773.
25. Cronin, p. 65. Petitfils, p. 74.
26. Petitfils, p. 81.
27. Bertière, p. 364.
28. Webster, Paul. "Marriage myths." *The Guardian.* August 2, 2002.
29. Webster, 1937, p. 157.
30. Fraser, p.156.
31. Lever, ed., p. 291. Letter from Marie-Antoinette to Maria Theresa, August 30, 1777.
32. Ibid, p. 293. Letter from Comte de Mercy to Maria Theresa, September 12, 1777.
33. Seward, Desmond. *Marie Antoinette.* New York: St Martin's Press, 1981, p.81.
34. Bertière, pp. 374, 401.

Chapter 6: Death and Coronation

1. Marie-Antoinette, Reine de France, I, p. 41. Letter

from Marie-Antoinette to Maria Theresa, January 13, 1773.

2. Seward, p. 43.

3. Marie-Thérèse d'Autriche et al. *Correspondance secrète entre Marie-Thérèse et le comte de Mercy-Argenteau, avec les lettres de Marie-Thérèse et de Marie-Antoinette, 2 Volumes.* Paris: Firmin-Didot, 1874, I, pp. 63-64. Letter from Comte de Mercy to Maria Theresa, November 12, 1773.

4. Brière, p. 64.

5. Ibid, p. 67.

6. Fraser, p. 116.

7. Brière, p. 68.

8. Cronin, p. 74.

9. Ibid, p. 68.

10. Lever, ed., p.183.

11. Ibid.

12. Ibid.

13. Delorme, p. 96.

14. Cronin, p. 77.

15. Ibid.

16. Ibid.

17. Ibid, p. 79.

18. Fraser, p. 134.

19. Vidal, Elena Maria. "The Happy Day of France." *Tea at Trianon*, November 10, 2011.

20. Petitfils, p. 210.

21. Leo XIII. "Nobilissima Gallorum Gens: On the Religious Question in France His Holiness Pope Leo XIII, February 8, 1884." *New Advent*, 2007.

22. Kurth, Godefroid. "Clovis." *The Catholic Encyclopedia.* Vol. 4. New York: Robert Appleton Company, 1908.

23. Petitfils, pp. 209, 211.

24. Dawson, William Francis. *Christmas: Its Origin and Associations.* London: Elliot Stock, 1902, p. 9.

25. Goyau, Georges. "Hugh Capet." *The Catholic Encyclopedia.* Vol. 7. New York: Robert Appleton Company, 1910.
26. Kanehl, Steven R. "Jehanne la Pucelle: A mini-biography, February 1431." *The Joan of Arc Center.*
27. Bertière, p. 248.
28. Lever, ed., p. 215. Letter from Marie-Antoinette to Maria Theresa, June 22, 1775.
29. Bertière p. 249.
30. Lever, ed., p. 215. Letter from Marie-Antoinette to Maria Theresa, June 22, 1775.
31. Smythe, Lillian C. *The Guardian of Marie Antoinette: Letters from the Comte de Mercy-Argenteau, Austrian Ambassador to the Court of Versailles, to Marie Thérêse, Empress of Austria, 1770-1780,* 2 Volumes. London: Hutchinson and Company, 1902, I, p. 419.
32. *Gazette de France,* no. 49 (19 June 1775), 221.
33.Doyle, William. "The Execution of Louis XVI and the End of the French Monarchy." *History Today,* Issue 36, March 2000.

Chapter 7: Their Most Christian Majesties

1. Campan, p. 93.
2. Lever, ed., p. 225. Letter from Marie-Antoinette to Count von Rosenburg, July 13, 1775.
3. Ibid, p. 226. Letter from Maria Theresa to Comte de Mercy, August 13, 1775.
4. Webster, 1937, p. 52.
5. Campan, p. 94.
6. Dégert, Antoine. "Gallicanism." *The Catholic Encyclopedia.* Vol. 6. New York: Robert Appleton Company, 1909.
7. Ibid.
8. Cronin, p. 349.

9. Shawn Tribe, "Bonniwell: The Solemn Mass in the Gallican Rite of the 7th-8th Century." *The New Liturgical Movement*, October 10, 2009.

10. Seward, p. 128.

11. Anderson, James Maxwell. *Daily Life During the French Revolution.* Westport, Connecticut: Greenwood Press, 2007, p. 61-62.

12. Miltoun, Francis. *Royal Palaces and Parks of France.* Boston: L. C. Page and Company, 1910, pp. 43-46.

13. Grubin, David. "Grand Park." *Marie-Antoinette and the French Revolution.* David Grubin Productions, September 13, 2006.

14. Thrale, Hester Lynch. "Thrales meet King Louis XVI and Queen Marie Antoinette." *Thrale.com,* 20 September 2009.

15. C. Weber, p. 93.

16. Campan, p. 46.

17. Yonge, pp. 62-63.

18. Schama, Simon. *Citizens: A Chronicle of the French Revolution.* New York: Vintage Books, 1989, pp. 419-420.

19. Sainte-Beuve, Charles Augustin. *Portraits of the eighteenth century: historic and literary, Volumes 1-2*, translated by Katharine Wormley. G.P. Putnam's Sons, 1905, I, p. 465.

20. Campan, p.165.

21. Bernier, ed., pp. 211-212. Letter from Marie-Antoinette to Marie Theresa, February 17, 1777.

22. Fraser, p. 160.

23. Yonge, p. 94.

24. Campan, p. 167.

25. Rocheterie, Vol. I, p. 119.

26. Saint-Amand, Imbert de. *Marie Antoinette and the End of the Old Régime*, trans. Thomas Sergeant Perry. New York: Charles Scribner's Sons, 1914, pp. 4.

27. Webster, Nesta H. *Louis XVI and Marie Antoinette during the Revolution.* New York: Gordon Press, 1976, p. 175.
28. Webster, 1937, pp. 292-293.
29. Campan, pp. 71-72.
30. Petitfils, p. 299
31. Webster, 1976, pp. 41-42.
32. Webster, 1937, p. 206.
33. Ibid., p. 207.
34. Ibid.
35. Petitfils, p. 246.
36. McCullough, David. *John Adams.* New York: Simon and Schuster, 2002, p. 202.
37. Ibid.
38. Ibid., p. 213.
39. Ibid., p. 203.
40. Ibid., pp. 212-213.
41. Nagel, Susan. *Marie-Thérèse: Child of Terror.* New York: Bloomsbury USA, 2008, p. 49.
42. Delors, Catherine. "Lapérouse, explorer *extraordinaire*, at the Musée de la Marine." *Versailles and More.* May 20, 2008.

Chapter 8: Follies and Escapades

1. Fraser, pp 146-147.
2. Hamilton, Ross, "Playing with Chance: Rousseau's Illumination." *The Romanic Review*, May 2004, Vol. 95, No. 3.
3. Barnhart, Russell T. "Gambling in revolutionary Paris — The Palais Royal: 1789–1838." *Journal of Gambling Studies*, Summer 1992, Volume 8, Issue 2, pp. 151-166.
4. Bicknell, pp. 95-97.
5. Campan, p. 96.
6. Rocheterie, I, p. 147.

Chapter 9: Marie-Antoinette and the Arts

1. Rocheterie, I, pp. 46, 107.
2. Bernier, ed., p. 40. Letter of Marie-Antoinette to Maria Theresa, July 12, 1770.
3. Marie-Thérèse Charlotte de France et al. *Royal Memoirs on the French Revolution*, translated by John Wilson Croker. London: John Murray, 1823, p. 184.
4. Goodman, ed., pp. 54-55.
5. Vigée-Lebrun, Louise-Élisabeth. *Souvenirs of Madame Vigée Le Brun*, translated by Morris Franklin Tyler. New York: R. Worthington, 1879, p. 40.
6. Ibid. p.46.
7. Delors, Catherine. "Marie-Antoinette's best likeness." *Versailles and More*, July 28, 2008.
8. Ibid. "Marie Antoinette naked?" *Versailles and More*, November 8, 2012.
9. Lever, ed., p. 293. Letter from Comte de Mercy to Maria Theresa, September 12, 1777.
10. Goodman, ed., p. 65.
11. Cronin, p. 216.
12. Brown, Leah Marie. "Tuesday's Treasure: Marie Antoinette's Books." *Titillating Tidbits: The Life and Times of Marie-Antoinette*, January 10, 2012.
13. "Legacy Library: Marie Antoinette." *The Library Thing*.
http://www.librarything.com/profile/MarieAntoinette

Chapter 10: Marie-Antoinette and Music

1. Cronin, pp. 217-218.
2. Campan, p. 85.
3. Wygant, Amy. "Fire, Sacrifice, Iphigénie." *French Studies: A Quarterly Review*, 60.3. 2006, pp. 305-319.
4. Smythe, II, p. 403.
5. Saint-Amand, Imbert de. *The Duchess of Angoulême*

and the Two Restorations. New York: Scribner's, 1901, p. 33.
6. Elliot, Grace Dalyrmple. *Journal of my life during the French Revolution.* London: R. Bentley, 1859, pp. 65–66.

Chapter 11: Marie-Antoinette and Fashion

1. Holland, Rupert Sargent. *The Story of Marie Antoinette* (ebook). New York: A.J. Cornell Publications, 1910, pp. 95-96.
2. Fraser, pp. 148-149.
3. Webster, 1937, pp. 60-61.
4. Ibid, p. 31.
5. C. Weber, p. 109.
6. Delors, Catherine. "18th century court costume and Marie-Antoinette." *Versailles and More*, September 8, 2009.
7. Fraser, p. 175.
8. Rocheterie, p. 183.
9. Hosford, Desmond. "The Queen's Hair: Marie-Antoinette, Politics and DNA." *Eighteenth-Century Studies, Vol. 38,* no. 1, 2004, pp. 183-200.
10. Delpierre, Madeleine. *Dress in France in the Eighteenth Century.* New Haven: Yale University Press, 1997, p110.

Chapter 12: Marie-Antoinette and Her Journey of Faith

1. Brière, p. 125.
2. Ibid, pp. 186-196.
3. Fraser, p. 40.
4. Ibid.
5. Lenôtre, George. *The Last Days of Marie Antoinette*, translated by Mrs. Rodolph Stawell. Philadelphia: J.B.

Lippincott Company, 1907, p. 219.
6. Petitfils, p. 246.
7. Rocheterie, Vol. 1, p. 324.
8. Ibid, Vol. 2, p. 69.
9. Tour du Pin, Madame de la. *Memoirs: Laughing and Dancing Our Way to the Precipice*. London: The Harvill Press, 1999, p. 74.
10. Rocheterie, Vol. 2, p. 69.
11. Louis XVI, Roi de France. *Testament de Louis XVI*. Dijon: Noëllat, 1816, p. 26.
12. Ibid, p. 28.
13. Marie Antoinette, Reine de France. *Lettres de Marie-Antoinette, recueil des lettres authentiques de le Reine, Tome II*. Paris: Alphonse Picard et Fils, 1896, pp. 441-444.

Chapter 13: Holidays at Versailles

1. Rocheterie, Vol 1, p. 324.
2. Yonge, p.183.
3. Campan, p. 209. Montjoie, p. 140. Yonge, p. 239. Here is a translation:

"Lovely and good, to tender pity true,
Queen of a virtuous King, this trophy view,
Cold, ice and snow sustain its fragile form
But every grateful heart to thee is warm.
Oh, may this tribute in your hearts excite.
Illustrious pair, more pure and real delight.
While this your virtues are sincerely praised,
Than pompous domes to servile flattery raised."

4. Duindam, Jeroen Frans Jozef. *Vienna and Versailles: The Courts of Europe's Dynastic Rivals, 1550-1780*. Cambridge: Cambridge University Press, 2003, p. 136.
5. Delors, Catherine. "La Fête des Rois, Feast of the

Kings." *Versailles and More*, January 6, 2011.
6. Bernier, ed., p. 102. Letter of Marie-Antoinette to Maria Theresa, February 15, 1773.
7. Webster, 1937, p. 21.
8. Bernier, ed., p. 104. Letter of Maria Theresa to Marie-Antoinette, March 3, 1773.
9. Ibid, p. 159. Letter of Maria Theresa to Marie-Antoinette, March 5, 1775.
10. Ibid, p. 160. Letter of Marie-Antoinette to Maria Theresa, March 17, 1775.
11. Campan, p. 26.
12. Ibid, p.94.
13. Smythe, II, p. 672.
14. Jordan, David P. *The King's Trial*. Los Angeles: University of California Press, 1979, p. 87.
15. Élisabeth of France, Madame. *The Life and Letters of Madame Élisabeth de France, Sister of Louis XVI*. New York: Versailles Historical Society, 1899, p. 279.
16. Chalon, p. 235.
17. Rocheterie, I, p. 329.
18. Spawforth, Tony. *Versailles: A Biography of a Palace*. New York: St. Martin's Press, 2008, p. 84.

Chapter 14: The Children of Louis XVI and Marie-Antoinette

1. Nagel, p. 48.
2. Ibid.
3. McCloy, Shelby T. *The Negro in France*. Lexington, Kentucky: University of Kentucky Press, 1961, p. 30.
4. Ibid, p. 101.
5. Fraser, p.168.
6. Ibid, p. 170.
7. Campan, p. 139.
8. Smythe, II, p. 614.
9. Delorme, pp. 170-171.

10. Nagel, p. 48.
11. Campan, p. 144.
12. Rocheterie, I, pp. 243-245.
13. Romer, Isabella Frances. *Filia dolorosa, memoirs of Marie Thérèse Charlotte, duchess of Angoulême, the Last of the Dauphines, Vol.1.* London: Richard Bentley, 1852, p. 13.
14. Yonge, p. 226. Webster, 1976, p. 81.
15. Cronin, p. 270.
16. Chalon, p. 456. Fraser, p. 431.
17. Rocheterie, I, p. 324.
18. Ibid, II, pp. 65-66.
19. Fraser, p. 424.
20. Lever, Evelyn. *Marie-Antoinette: The Last Queen of France.* New York: Macmillan, 2001, p. 303.

Chapter 15: Marie-Antoinette and Friendship

1. Yonge, p. 458.
2. Petitfils, p. 280.
3. Goodman, ed., pp. 199-238.
4. Marie-Antoinette, Reine de France. "Portrait charmant, portrait de mon amie." *The LiederNet Archive.* http://www.lieder.net/lieder/get_text.html?TextId=58693
5. Translated by Professor Maryse Demasy.
6. Bernier, ed., p. 193.
7. Webster, 1976, p. 108.
8. Yonge, pp. 458-459.
9. Duindam, p. 94.
10. Marie Antoinette, Reine de France, II, 1896, p. 205. Letter of Marie-Antoinette to the Duchesse de Fitz-James, December, 1790.
11. Tour du Pin, p.14.
12. Campan, p. 97.
13. Hanet-Cléry, Jean-Baptiste C. *Journal of What Took Place at the Tower of the Temple During the Captivity of*

Louis XVI, translated by J. Bennett. London: Longman, 1828, pp. 23-24.
14. Duindam, p. 94.
15. Webster, 1937, p. 147.
16. Smythe, II, pp. 588-589.
17. Lever, ed., p. 256. Letter of Marie-Antoinette to Maria Theresa, September 14, 1776.
18. Ibid, p. 294. Letter of Comte de Mercy to Maria Theresa, September 12, 1777.
19. Ibid, p. 384. Letter of Comte de Mercy to Maria Theresa, July 18, 1780.
20. Feuillet de Conches, F., editor. *Louis XVI, Marie-Antoinette et Madame Élisabeth: lettres et documents inédites, Tome Premier*. Paris: Henri Plon, 1864, p. 246. Letter of Louis XVI to the Duchesse de Polignac, July 29, 1789.
21. Nagel, p. 29.
22. Campan, pp. 162-163.
23. Vidal, Elena Maria. "Madame de Polignac and the Politics of Calumny." *Tea at Trianon*. December 6, 2007.
24. Gontaut, Duchesse de. *Memoirs of the Duchesse de Gontaut*, trans. by Mrs. J. W. Davis. 2 Volumes. New York: Dodd, Mead, and Company, 1894, I, p. 104.
25. Ibid, p.105.
26. Ibid.
27. Ibid, p. 107.
28. Ibid, p.108.
29. Ibid, p. 110.
30. Ibid, p. 113.
31. Ibid, p. 114.
32. Ibid, p. 118.
33. Ibid, pp. 121-122.
34. Webster, 1976, p. 64.
35. Nagel, p. 66.
36. Campan, pp. 107, 109-110.

37. Ibid, p. 113.

38. Rocheterie 2, p. 364.

39. Marie-Antoinette, Reine de France. *Lettres inédites de Marie-Antoinette et de Marie-Clotilde de France (sœur de Louis XVI), reine de Sardaigne*. Paris: Firmin-Didot, 1877, p. 87. Letter of Marie-Antoinette to Charlotte of Hesse-Darmstadt, Duchess of Mecklenburg-Strelitz, June 1785.

40. Lever, ed., p. 219. Letter of Marie-Antoinette to Maria Theresa, July 14, 1775.

41. Brière, p. 109.

42. Élisabeth of France, Madame. *The Life and Letters of Madame Élisabeth de France, Sister of Louis XVI*. New York: Versailles Historical Society, 1899, p. 37. Letter of Élisabeth of France to the Marquise de Bombelles, June 25, 1787.

Chapter 16: Gentlemen Friends

1. Bernier, ed., p. 161. Letter of Comte de Mercy to Maria Theresa, March 18, 1775.

2. Ibid, p. 163. Letter Maria Theresa to Marie-Antoinette, June 2, 1775.

3. Smythe, p. 562.

4. Ibid, pp. 560-564.

5. Goyau, Georges. "Marie Antoinette." *The Catholic Encyclopedia*. Vol. 9. New York: Robert Appleton Company, 1910.

6. Ligne, Charles-Joseph (prince de). *The Prince de Ligne: His Memoirs, Letters, and Miscellaneous Papers, 2 Volumes*, selected and translated by Katharine Prescott Wormeley. Boston: Hardy, Pratt and Company, 1902, I, pp. 197-201.

7. Ibid, pp. 201-202.

8. Yonge, p. 69. Marie-Antoinette, Reine de France, I, p. 37. Letter of Marie-Antoinette to Maria Theresa,

December 15, 1772.
9. Campan, p. 105.
10. Fraser, p. 128.
11. Campan, pp. 128-129.
12. Ibid, p. 117.
13. Tytler, Sarah. *Marie Antoinette: The Woman and the Queen.* London: Marcus Ward, 1883, pp. 95-98.

Chapter 17: The Fersen Legend

1. Ligne, I, p. 197.
2. Hézècques, Félix. *Recollections of a Page at the Court of Louis XVI*, translated by Charlotte M. Yonge. London: Hurst and Blackett, 1873, pp. 26-27.
3. Tour du Pin, p. 14.
4. Chalon, p. 187.
5. Petitfils, p. 284.
6. Ibid, p. 287.
7. Lever, ed., p. 360. Letter of Monsieur de Creutz to Gustavus III, April 10, 1779.
8. Webster, 1937, p. 281.
9. Chalon, p. 188.
10. Webster, 1937, pp. 281-282.
11. Chalon, p. 235. Seward, p. 128.
12. Seward, p. 168.
13. Webster, 1937, p. 282.
14. Ibid, 1976, p. 105.
15. Fraser, p. 203.
16. Ibid, p. 217.
17. Bertière, pp. 388-390.
18. Ibid, pp. 388-389.
19. Campan, pp. 162-163.
20. Bertière, p. 541.
21. Foreman, Amanda. *Georgiana, Duchess of Devonshire.* New York: The Modern Library, 1998, p.177.

22. Ibid, p. 308.
23. O'Meara, Barry Edward. *Napoleon in Exile: Or, A Voice from St. Helena: the Opinions and Reflections of Napoleon on the Most Important Events of His Life and Government in His Own Words, Volume 2*. Philadelphia: W. Simpkin and R. Marshall, 1822, p.110.
24. Croker, John Wilson. "An Answer to O'Meara's Napoleon in Exile," *The Quarterly Review*, Vol. 28. New York: T. & J. Swords, 1823, pp. 60-61.
25. Webster, 1976, p. 108.
26. Ibid, p. 111.
27. Ibid, p. 112.
28. Ibid, 1937, p. 289.
29. Ibid, 1976, p. 125.
30. Ibid, p. 115.
31. Ibid, p. 167.
32. Ibid.
33. Ibid.
34. Ibid, p. 218.
35. Campan, pp. 322-323.
36. Tourzel, Louise-Élisabeth de Croÿ de. *Memoirs of the Duchess de Tourzel: Governess to the Children of France during the Years 1789, 1790, 1791, 1792, 1793 and 1795, Volume 1 and Volume 2*. London: Remington & Company, 1886, I, p. 47.
37. Webster, 1976, pp. 360-361.
38. Ibid, pp. 361-362.
39. Yonge, p. 458.
40. Ibid.
41. Ibid.

Chapter 18: Palaces, Châteaux, and Gardens

1. Oberkirch, I, p. 326.
2. Rocheterie, I, p. 175.
3. Campan, p. 237.

4. Oberkirch, I, pp. 238-305.
5. Ibid, p. 238.
6. Rocheterie, I, p. 261.
7. Oberkirch, I, p. 244.
8. Rocheterie, I, p. 259.
9. Campan, p. 159.
10. Grant, Mrs. Colquhoun. *A Mother of Czars: A Sketch of the Life of Marie Feodorowna, Wife of Paul I, Mother of Alexander I and Nicholas I*. London: John Murray, 1903, p. 103.
11. Ibid, p. 101.
12. Ibid, pp. 90-91.
13. Seward, p. 97.
14. Campan, pp. 160-161.
15. Webster, 1937, p. 227.
16. Nolhac, Pierre de. *Marie Antoinette*. London: Arthur L. Humphreys, 1905, p. 235.
17. Hézecques, pp. 27-31.
18. Bertière, p. 401.
19. Vidal, Elena Maria. "Drawing of a Tavern in Austria." *Tea at Trianon*, January 8, 2016.
20. Nolhac, pp. 226-227.
21. Campan, pp. 147-148.
22. Saint-Amand, Baron Imbert de. *Marie Antoinette and the End of the Old Régime*, translated by Thomas Sergeant Perry. New York: Charles Scribner's Sons, 1914, pp. 139-141.
23. Hanet-Cléry, p. 99.
24. Hézecques, pp. 79-82.
25. Cronin, p. 342.
26. Richards, J.H. "Favorites of Louis XVIII." *The Nation, Vol.69*. New York: The Evening Post Publishing Company, 1899, p. 371.
27. Croker, John Wilson. *Essays on the Early Period of the French Revolution*. London: John Murray, 1857, p. 155.

28. Croker, John Wilson, ed. Royal Memoirs on the French Revolution. London: John Murray, 1823, p. 104.

Chapter 19: The Diamond Necklace

1. Dickinson, Joan Y. *The Book of Diamonds: Their History and Romance from Ancient India to Modern Times.* Mineola, New York: Dover Publications, 2001, p. 97.
2. Lever, ed., p. 153. Letter of Maria Theresa to Marie-Antoinette, August 29, 1773.
3. Rocheterie, I, p. 318.
4. Campan, pp. 196-197, 199-200.
5. Mossiker, p. 547.
6. Beckman, Jonathan. *How to Ruin a Queen: Marie Antoinette and the Diamond Necklace Affair.* Philadelphia: De Capo Press, 2014, p 302

Chapter 20: The Revolution

1. Webster, 1976, p. 6.
2. Ibid, p. 9.
3. Ibid, p.64.
4. Ibid, p.175.
5. Ibid, pp. 274-274.
6. Adolphus, John. *Biographical Memoirs of the French Revolution, Volumes 1 and 2.* London: Cadell and Davis, 1799, II p. 183. Toussaint-Samat, Maguelonne. *A History of Food*, translated by Anthea Bell. Oxford: John Wiley & Sons, 2009, p.136.
7. Cronin, p. 266.
8. Adolphus, I, p. 28.
9. Thomas, p. 13.
10. Ibid, p. 64.
11. Blanc, Louis. *Histoire de la révolution française, Volume 2.* Paris: Chez Langlois et Leclercq, 1847, pp.

71, 110-111.
12. Webster, 1937, p. 237-238.
13. "Louise-Marie-Thérèse-Bathilde d'Orléans, duchesse de Bourbon (1750-1822)." *Louis-Claude de Saint-Martin: Amis et Disciples.* http://www.philosophe-inconnu.com/Amis_disciples/duchesse_bourbon1.htm.
14. Ségur, Louis-Gaston de. *Le Sacré Coeur de Jésus: mois du Sacré Coeur.* Paris: Haton, 1873, pp. 86-190.
15. Marie-Antoinette, II, p. 192. Letter of Marie-Antoinette to Leopold II, August 17, 1790.
16. Webster, 1976, p. 178.
17. Marie-Antoinette, II, pp. 312-316. Letter of Marie-Antoinette to Comte de Mercy, September 28, 1791.
18. Ibid, pp. 321-331. Letter of Marie-Antoinette to Comte de Fersen, October 31, 1791.
19. Campan, pp. 209-210.
20. Seward, p. 132.
21. Webster, 1976, p. 18.
22. Cronin, p. 292.
23. Campan, p. 226.
24. Lemaire, Henri. *Histoire de la Révolution Française, 2 Vols.* Paris: Le Dentu: 1816, I, p. 365.
25. Yonge, pp. 970-971.
26. Webster, 1976, pp. 49-50.
27. Huë, François. *The Last Years of the Reign and Life of Louis XVI.* London: Cadell and Davies, 1806, p. 129.
28. Rocheterie, II, p. 49.
29. Saint-Amand, 1914, pp. 258-267.
30. Tourzel, I, p. 34.
31. Rocheterie, II, p. 51.
32. Huë, p. 127.
33. Cadbury, Deborah. *The Lost King of France.* New York: St. Martin's Griffin, 2002, p. 46.
34. Rocheterie, II, p. 53.

Chapter 20: At the Tuileries

1. Rocheterie, II, pp. 265-267.
2. Ibid, pp. 267.
3. Saint-Amand, Baron Imbert de. *Marie Antoinette at the Tuileries, 1789-1791*, translated by Elizabeth Gilbert Martin. New York: C. Scribner's sons, 1893, 223-224.
4. Ibid, pp. 225-226.
5. Ibid, pp. 226-227.
6. Rocheterie, II, p. 70.
7. Ibid.
8. Ségur, pp. 186-190. The English translation is mine. Here is the original French:

Consécration de la France au Sacré-Coeur de Jésus

Vous voyez, ô mon Dieu ! toutes les plaies qui déchirent mon coeur, et la profondeur de l'abîme dans lequel je suis tombé. Des maux sans nombre m'environnent de toutes parts. A mes malheurs personnels et à ceux de ma famille, qui sont affreux, se joignent pour accabler mon âme, ceux qui couvrent la face du royaume. Les cris de tous les infortunés, les gémissements de la religion opprimée retentissent à mes oreilles, et une voix intérieure m'avertit encore que peut-être votre justice me reproche toutes ces calamités, parce que, dans les jours de ma puissance, je n'ai pas réprimé la licence du peuple et l'irréligion, qui en sont les principales sources ; parce que j'ai fourni moi-même des armes à l'hérésie qui triomphe, en la favorisant par des lois qui ont doublé ses forces et lui ont donné l'audace de tout oser.

Je n'aurai pas la témérité, ô mon Dieu ! de me justifier devant vous ; mais vous savez que mon coeur a toujours été soumis à la foi et aux règles des moeurs ; mes fautes sont le fruit de ma faiblesse et semblent dignes de votre grande miséricorde. Vous avez pardonné au roi David, qui avait été cause que vos ennemis avaient blasphémé contre vous ; au roi Manassès, qui avait entraîné son peuple dans l'idolâtrie. Désarmé par leur pénitence, vous les avez rétabli l'un et l'autre sur le trône de Juda ; vous les avez fait régner avec paix et gloire. Seriez-vous inexorable aujourd'hui pour un fils de saint Louis, qui prend ces rois pénitents pour modèles, et qui, à leur exemple, désire réparer ses fautes et devenir un Roi selon votre coeur ?

O Jésus-Christ ! divin Rédempteur de toutes nos iniquités, c'est dans votre Coeur adorable que je veux déposer les effusions de mon âme affligée. J'appelle à mon secours le tendre Coeur de Marie, mon auguste protectrice et ma mère, et l'assistance de saint Louis, mon patron et le plus illustre de mes aïeux.

Ouvrez-vous, Coeur adorable, et par les mains si pures de mes puissants intercesseurs, recevez avec bonté les voeux satisfactoires que la confiance m'inspire et que je vous offre comme l'expression naïve de mes sentiments.

Si, par un effet de la bonté infinie de Dieu, je recouvre ma liberté, ma couronne et ma puissance royale, je promets solennellement :

1 De révoquer le plus tôt possible toutes les lois qui me seront indiquées, soit par le Pape, soit par un Concile, soit par quatre Evêques choisis parmi les plus éclairés et les plus vertueux de mon royaume, comme contraires à la pureté et à l'intégrité de la foi, à la discipline et à la juridiction spirituelle de la sainte Eglise catholique, apostolique, romaine, et notamment la Constitution civile du clergé;

2 De prendre, dans l'intervalle d'une année, tant auprès du Pape qu'auprès des Evêques de mon royaume, toutes les mesures nécessaires pour établir, suivant les formes canoniques, une fête solennelle en l'honneur du Sacré-Coeur de Jésus, laquelle sera célébrée à perpétuité dans toute la France, le premier vendredi après l'octave du Saint-Sacrement, et toujours suivie d'une procession générale, en réparation des outrages et des profanations commises dans le temps des troubles, par les schismatiques, les hérétiques et les mauvais chrétiens.

3 D'aller moi-même en personne, sous trois mois, à compter du jour de ma délivrance, dans l'église Notre-Dame de Paris, ou dans toute autre église principale du lieu où je me trouverai, et de prononcer, un jour de dimanche ou de fête, au pied du maître-autel, après l'offertoire de la messe, et entre les mains du célébrant, un acte solennel de consécration de ma personne, de ma famille et de mon royaume au Sacré-Coeur de Jésus, avec promesse de donner à tous mes sujets, l'exemple du culte et de la dévotion qui sont dus à ce Coeur adorable.

4 D'ériger et de décorer à mes frais, dans l'église que je choisirai pour cela, dans le cours d'une année à compter du jour de ma délivrance, une chapelle ou un autel qui sera dédié au Sacré-Coeur de Jésus, et qui servira de monument éternel de ma reconnaissance et de ma confiance sans bornes dans les mérites infinis et dans les trésors inépuisables de grâce qui sont renfermés dans ce Coeur Sacré.

5 Enfin de renouveler tous les ans, au lieu où je me trouverai, le jour qu'on célébrera la fête du Sacré-Coeur, l'acte de consécration exprimé dans l'article troisième, et d'assister à la procession générale qui suivra la messe de ce jour.

Je ne puis aujourd'hui prononcer qu'en secret cet engagement, mais je le signerais de mon sang s'il le fallait ; et le plus beau jour de ma vie sera celui où je pourrai le publier à haute voix dans le temple.

O Coeur adorable de mon Sauveur ! Que j'oublie ma main droite et que je m'oublie moi-même, si jamais j'oublie vos bienfaits et mes promesses, si je cesse de vous aimer et de mettre en vous ma confiance et toute ma consolation. Ainsi soit-il.

9. Mason, Laura and Rizzo, Tracey, eds. *The French Revolution: A Document Collection*. New York: Houghton Mifflin, 1999, pp. 152-155.
10. Webster, 1976, p. 149.
11. Ward, Charles A. *Oracles of Nostradamus*. New York: C. Scribner, 1891. Kindle edition by Evinity Publishing Company, 2009, p. 153.
12. Bertière, p. 692.
13. Campan, p. 303.
14. Webster, 1976, p. 231.
15. Tomokiyo, S. "Ciphers of Marie-Antoinette and Axel von Fersen (1791-1792)."
http://cryptiana.web.fc2.com/code/fersen.htm
16. Chalon, p. 347.
17. Ibid, p. 352.
18. Heidenstam, O.G., ed. *The Letters of Marie Antoinette, Fersen and Barnave,* translated by Mrs. Winifred Stephens and Mrs. Wilfrid Jackson. London: Read Books, Ltd. 2013, p. 51.
19. Feuillet de Conches, II, p. 54. Letter of Marie-Antoinette to Comte de Mercy, May 14, 1791.
20. Patarin, Jacques and Nachef, Valérie. "I shall love you up to the death" (Marie-Antoinette to Axel von Fersen), 2009. http://eprint.iacr.org/2009/166.pdf
21. Tomokiyo, http://cryptiana.web.fc2.com/code/fersen.htm.
22. Patarin and Nachef, http://eprint.iacr.org/2009/166.pdf.
23. Maury, Lucien. *Revue littéraire et critique - Revue Bleue, Numéro 17*, 5ème série, Tome VII, Paris: Bureaux de la Revue Bleue, 1907, pp. 536-538.
24. Patarin and Nachef, http://eprint.iacr.org/2009/166.pdf.
25. Chalon, p. 349.
26. Patarin and Nachef, http://eprint.iacr.org/2009/166.pdf.

27. Tomokiyo, http://cryptiana.web.fc2.com/code/fersen.htm.
28. Marie-Antoinette, II, p. 158. Letter of Marie-Antoinette to Madame de Polignac, December 29, 1789.
29. Gibson, Anna. "'Don't They Ever Get Tired of These Ridiculous Stories?' A Critical Look at Recent Claims about Marie Antoinette and Axel Fersen (Part 2)." *Treasure for Your Pleasure*, January 16, 2016.
30. Ibid.
31. Zaleski, Erin. "Revealed: Marie Antoinette's Scandalous Secret Letters to Her Lover." *The Daily Beast*, January 17, 2016.
32. Élisabeth of France, p. 234.
33. Marie-Thérèse Charlotte de France, pp.183-185.

Chapter 21: Les Adieux

1. Hanet-Cléry, p. 44.
2. Nagel, p. 131.
3. Huë, p. 375.
4. Nagel, p. 130.
5. Hanet-Cléry, pp. 104-196.
6. Johnson, Alison. *Louis XVI and the French Revolution.* London: McFarland and Company, 2013, pp.185-187.
7. Louis XVI, Roi de France. *Testament de Louis XVI.* Dijon: Noëllat, 1816.
8. Jordan, David. The King's Trial. Los Angeles: University of California Press, 1979, p. 109.
9. Ibid, p. 128.
10. Ibid, p. 135.
11. Marie-Thérèse Charlotte de France, pp. 199-203.
12. Edgeworth de Firmont, Henry Essex. *Memoirs of the Abbé Edgeworth: Containing His Narrative of the Last Hours of Louis XVI,* edited by C. S. Edgeworth. London: Rowland Hunter, 1815, p. 177.

13. Hanet-Cléry, p. 171.
14. Edgeworth, p. 179.
15. Ibid, pp. 179-180.
16. Ibid, p. 183.
17. Ibid, p. 184.
18. Ibid, p. 185.

Chapter 22: The Agony

1. Marie-Thérèse Charlotte de France, p. 206.
2. Lenôtre, George. *The Dauphin or the Riddle of the Temple.* New York: Doubleday, Page, 1921, p. 127.
3. Yonge, p. 451.
4. Marie-Thérèse Charlotte de France, pp. 223-225.
5. Ibid, p. 230.
6. Rocheterie, II, p. 342.
7. Pernoud, Georges and Flaissier, Sabine. *The French Revolution*, translated by Richard Graves. New York: Capricorn Books, 1970, pp. 203–205.
8. Chapman and Company, editors. *Authentic Trial at Large of Marie Antoinette, Late Queen of France.* London: Chapman and Company, 1793. (Entire account of the trial.)
9. Marie-Antoinette, Reine de France, II, pp. 441-444. Letter of Marie-Antoinette to Madame Élisabeth of France. Here is the letter in the original French:

Ce 16 octobre, à quatre heures et demie du matin.

C'est à vous, ma soeur, que j'écris pour la dernière fois. Je viens d'être condamnée, non pas à une mort honteuse – elle ne l'est que pour les criminels, mais à aller rejoindre votre frère. Comme lui innocente j'espère montrer la même fermeté que lui dans ses derniers moments. Je suis calme comme on l'est quand la conscience ne reproche rien. J'ai un profond regret d'abandonner mes pauvres enfants. Vous savez que je n'existais que pour eux et vous, ma bonne et tendre soeur, vous qui avez par votre amitié tout sacrifié pour être avec nous, dans quelle position je vous laisse ! J'ai appris par le plaidoyer même du procès que ma fille était séparée de vous. Hélas ! la pauvre enfant, je n'ose pas lui écrire, elle ne recevrait pas ma lettre, je ne sais pas même si celle-ci vous parviendra. Recevez pour eux deux ici ma bénédiction ; j'espère qu'un jour, lorsqu'ils seront plus grands, ils pourront se réunir avec vous et jouir en entier de vos tendres soins. Qu'ils pensent tous deux à ce que je n'ai cessé de leur inspirer : que les principes et l'exécution exacte de ses devoirs sont la première base de la vie, que leur amitié et leur confiance mutuelle en fera le bonheur. Que ma fille sente qu'à l'âge qu'elle a, elle doit toujours aider son frère par les conseils que l'expérience qu'elle aura de plus que lui et son amitié pourront lui inspirer ; que mon fils, à son tour, rende à sa soeur tous les soins, les services que l'amitié peuvent inspirer ; qu'ils sentent enfin tous deux que dans quelque position où ils pourront se trouver ils ne seront vraiment heureux que par leur union ; qu'ils prennent exemple de nous. Combien, dans nos malheurs, notre amitié nous a donné de consolation ! Et dans le bonheur on jouit doublement quand on peut le partager avec un ami, et où en trouver de plus tendre, de plus uni que dans sa propre famille? Que mon fils n'oublie jamais les derniers mots de son père que je lui répète expressément : qu'il ne cherche jamais à venger notre mort.

J'ai à vous parler d'une chose bien pénible à mon coeur. Je sais combien cet enfant doit vous avoir fait de la peine. Pardonnez-lui, ma chère soeur, pensez à l'âge qu'il a et combien il est facile de faire dire à un enfant ce qu'on veut et même ce qu'il ne comprend pas. Un jour viendra, j'espère, où il ne sentira que mieux le prix de vos bontés et de votre tendresse pour tous deux. Il me reste à vous confier encore mes dernières pensées. J'aurais voulu les écrire dès le commencement du procès, mais, outre qu'on ne me laissait pas écrire, la marche a été si rapide que je n'en aurais réellement pas eu le temps.

Je meurs dans la religion catholique, apostolique et romaine, dans celle de mes pères, dans celle où j'ai été élevée et que j'ai toujours professée, n'ayant aucune consolation spirituelle à attendre, ne sachant pas s'il existe encore ici des prêtres de cette religion, et même le lieu où je suis les exposerait trop s'ils y entraient une fois. Je demande sincèrement pardon à Dieu de toutes les fautes que j'ai pu commettre depuis que j'existe ; j'espère que, dans sa bonté, il voudra bien recevoir mes derniers voeux, ainsi que ceux que je fais depuis longtemps pour qu'il veuille bien recevoir mon âme dans sa miséricorde et sa bonté. Je demande pardon à tous ceux que je connais et à vous, ma soeur, en particulier, de toutes les peines que, sans le vouloir, j'aurais pu leur causer. Je pardonne à tous mes ennemis le mal qu'ils m'ont fait. Je dis ici adieu à mes tantes et à tous mes frères et soeurs. J'avais des amis, l'idée d'en être séparée pour jamais et leurs peines sont un des plus grands regrets que j'emporte en mourant ; qu'ils sachent du moins que, jusqu'à mon dernier moment, j'ai pensé à eux.

Adieu, ma bonne et tendre soeur ; puisse cette lettre vous arriver. Pensez toujours à moi ; je vous embrasse de tout mon coeur ainsi que ces pauvres et chers enfants. Mon Dieu, qu'il est déchirant de les quitter pour toujours ! Adieu, adieu ! je ne vais plus m'occuper que de mes devoirs spirituels. Comme je ne suis pas libre dans mes actions, on m'amènera peut-être un prêtre ; mais je proteste ici que je ne lui dirai pas un mot et que je le traiterai comme un être absolument étranger.

10. Yonge pp. 458-459.
11. Rocheterie, II, p. 370.
12. Ibid, p. 372.

Chapter 23: The Orphans

1. Lenôtre, 1921, p. 211.
2. Yonge, p. 446.
3. Marie-Thérèse Charlotte de France, pp. 235-237.
4. Yonge, p. 268.
5. Webster, 1976, p. 340.
6. Ibid, p. 323.
7. Marie-Thérèse Charlotte de France, pp. 259-260, 264
8. Cadbury, p. 138.
9. Nagel, p. 152.
10. Cadbury, pp. 270-272.
11. Pimodan, Claude Emmanuel Henri Marie, comte de. *Les Fiançailles de Madame Royale*. Paris: Plon-Nourrit, 1912, pp. 9-15.
12. Ibid, pp. 45, 53.
13. Ibid, p. 70.
14. Ibid, p. 102.
15. Daudet, Ernest. *Madame Royale, Daughter of Louis XVI and Marie Antoinette: Her Youth and Marriage*, translated by Mrs. Rodolph Stawell. New York: George H. Doran, 1913, pp. 246-247.
16. Nagel, pp. 230-231.
17. Ibid, p. 247.
18. Ibid, pp. 291-292.

Chapter 25: Legacy

1. Delors, Catherine. "Marie-Antoinette at Saint-Denis." *Versailles and More,* February 2, 2009.
2. Marie-Thérèse Charlotte de France, p. 104.
3. Marie-Antoinette, Reine de France, I, p. 91. Letter

from Marie-Antoinette to Maria Theresa, July 2, 1775.

4. Wollstonecraft, Mary. *An Historical and Moral View of the Origin and Progress of the French Revolution; and the Effect it Has Produced in Europe, Volume the First.* The Second Edition. London: Printed from J. Johnson, in St. Paul's Church-Yard. 1795. Preface.

5. Burke, Edmund. *Reflections on the Revolution in France.* London: Parfons, 1790. Amazon Digital Services LLC: Chios Classics, 2015, pp. 83-84.

6. Tour du Pin, pp. 89-90

7. Vigée-Lebrun, p. 44.

8. Rocheterie, II, p. 69.

9. Charles-Roux, J.M. "Marie-Antoinette: The Martyred Queen of Christian Europe." *Royal Stuart Review*, Vol. 6, Number 3, 1987 and Number 4, 1988, pp. 55-62, 72-85.

10. Petitfils, p. 973.

11. Ibid.

12. Ibid.

13. Ibid, p. 974.

14. Ibid, p. 975.

BIBLIOGRAPHY

Primary Sources

Adolphus, John. *Biographical Memoirs of the French Revolution, Volumes 1 and 2*. London: Cadell and Davis, 1799.

Angoulême, Duchess of. *Private Memoirs of Madame Royale*, translated by John Wilson Croker. London: John Murray, Albemarle Street, 1823.

Barruel, A. *Memoirs Illustrating the History of Jacobinism*. Fraser, Michigan: Real-View-Books, 1995.

Beaulieu, Claude-François. *Essais historiques sur les causes et les effets de la Révolution de France, avec des notes sur quelques évènemens et quelques institutions*. Paris: Chez Maradan, 1801.

Boigne, Adéle de. *Memoirs of the Comtesse de Boigne, 1781-1814, Vol I*, edited by M. Charles Nicoullaud. New York: Charles Scribner's Sons, 1908.

Burke, Edmund. *Reflections on the Revolution in France*. London: Parfons, 1790. Amazon Digital Services LLC: Chios Classics, 2015.

Campan, Madame. *Memoirs of Marie-Antoinette*. New York: Collier and Son, 1910.

Chapman and Company, editors. *Authentic Trial at Large of Marie Antoinette, Late Queen of France*. London: Chapman and Company, 1793

Chateaubriand, Vicomte de. *Memoirs d'Outre-Tombe, 2 Vol.* Paris: Flammarion, 1949.

Croker, John Wislon, ed. *Royal Memoirs on the French Revolution*. London: John Murray, 1823.

Edgeworth de Firmont, Henry Essex. *Memoirs of the*

Abbé Edgeworth: Containing His Narrative of the Last Hours of Louis XVI, edited by C. S. Edgeworth. London: Rowland Hunter, 1815.

Élisabeth of France, Madame. *The Life and Letters of Madame Élisabeth de France, Sister of Louis XVI*. New York: Versailles Historical Society, 1899.

Elliot, Grace Dalyrmple. *Journal of my life during the French Revolution*. London: R. Bentley, 1859.

Feuillet de Conches, F., editor. *Louis XVI, Marie-Antoinette et Madame Élisabeth: lettres et documents inedites, Tome Premier*. Paris: Henri Plon, 1864.

Gontaut, Duchesse de. *Memoirs of the Duchesse de Gontaut*, trans. by Mrs. J. W. Davis. 2 Volumes. New York: Dodd, Mead, and Company, 1894.

Hanet-Cléry, Jean-Baptiste C. *Journal of What Took Place at the Tower of the Temple During the Captivity of Louis XVI*, translated by J. Bennett. London: Longman, 1828.

Heidenstam, O.G., ed. *The Letters of Marie Antoinette, Fersen and Barnave*, translated by Mrs. Winifred Stephens and Mrs. Wilfrid Jackson. London: Read Books, Ltd. 2013.

Hézècques, Félix. *Recollections of a Page at the Court of Louis XVI*, translated by Charlotte M. Yonge. London: Hurst and Blackett, 1873.

—*Souvenirs d'un page de la cour de Louis XVI*. Paris: Perrins et Cie, 1895.

Huë, François. *The Last Years of the Reign and Life of Louis XVI*. London: Cadell and Davies, 1806.

Hyde, Catherine, editor (Marquise Gouvion Broglie-Scolari). *Secret Memoirs of Princess de Lamballe*. London: Walter Dunne, 1901.

Lafont d'Aussonne, L. *Mémoires secrets et universels des malheurs et de la mort de la reine de France*. Paris: Petit, 1825.

Lemaire, Henri. *Histoire de la Révolution Française, 2*

Vols. Paris: Le Dentu: 1816.

Lever, Evelyn, ed. *Correspondance de Marie-Antoinette (1770-1793)*. Paris: Tallandier, 2005

Ligne, Charles-Joseph (prince de). *The Prince de Ligne: His Memoirs, Letters, and Miscellaneous Papers, 2 Volumes*, selected and translated by Katharine Prescott Wormeley.Boston: Hardy, Pratt and Company, 1902.

Louis XVI, Roi de France. *Testament de Louis XVI*. Dijon: Noëllat, 1816.

Louis XVIII. *Memoirs of Louis the eighteenth, written by himself, Vol I*, translated by E.L. de La Mothe-Langon. London: Saunders and Otley, 1832.

Louis-Philippe. *Memoirs 1773-1793*, translated by John Hardman. New York: Harcourt, Brace, Jovanovich, 1977.

Marie-Antoinette, Reine de France. *Lettres inédites de Marie-Antoinette et de Marie-Clotilde de France (sœur de Louis XVI), reine de Sardaigne*. Paris: Firmin-Didot, 1877.

—*Lettres de Marie-Antoinette: recueil des lettres authentiques de la reine, Tome I*. Paris: Alphonse Picard et Fils, 1895.

—*Lettres de Marie-Antoinette, recueil des lettres authentiques de le Reine, Tome II*. Paris: Alphonse Picard et Fils, 1896.

Marie-Thérèse d'Autriche et al. *Correspondance secrète entre Marie-Thérèse et le comte de Mercy-Argenteau, avec les lettres de Marie-Thérèse et de Marie-Antoinette, Tomes 1-3*. Paris: Firmin-Didot, 1874.

Marie-Thérèse Charlotte de France et al. *Royal Memoirs on the French Revolution*, translated by John Wilson Croker. London: John Murray,1823.

Montjoie, Félix-Louis Galart de. *Histoire de Marie-Antoinette-Josephe-Jeanne de Lorraine, archiduchesse d'Autriche, reine de France*. Paris: H.L. Perronneau, 1797.

Morris, Gouveneur. *A Diary of the French Revolution*, edited by Beatrix Cary Davenport. Amazon Digital Services LLC: Morris Press, 2013.

Oberkirch, Henriette Louise. *Memoirs of the baroness d'Oberkirch, countess de Montbrison*, ed. by her grandson, the count de Montbrison, Vol.1. London: Colburn and Company, 1852.

O'Meara, Barry Edward. *Napoleon in Exile: Or, A Voice from St. Helena: the Opinions and Reflections of Napoleon on the Most Important Events of His Life and Government in His Own Words, Volume 2*. Philadelphia: W. Simpkin and R. Marshall, 1822.

Tour du Pin, Madame de la. *Memoirs: Laughing and Dancing Our Way to the Precipice*. London: The Harvill Press, 1999.

Tourzel, Louise-Élisabeth de Croÿ de. *Memoirs of the Duchess de Tourzel: Governess to the Children of France during the Years 1789, 1790, 1791, 1792, 1793 and 1795, Volume 1 and Volume 2*. London: Remington & Company, 1886.

Vigée-Lebrun, Louise- Élisabeth. *Souvenirs of Madame Vigée Le Brun*, translated by Morris Franklin Tyler. New York: R. Worthington, 1879.

Weber, Joseph and Barrière, Jean-François. *Mémoires de Weber, frère de lait de Marie-Antoinette, reine de France*. Paris: Firmin-Didot, 1860.

Weber, Joseph. *Memoirs of Maria-Antoinetta, Queen of France and Navarre*, translated by R.C. Dallas. London: Rickaby, 1805.

Wollstonecraft, Mary. *An Historical and Moral View of the Origin and Progress of the French Revolution; and the Effect it Has Produced in Europe, Volume the First*. The Second Edition. London: J. Johnson, in St. Paul's Church-Yard. 1795.

Articles

Barnhart, Russell T. "Gambling in revolutionary Paris — The Palais Royal: 1789–1838." *Journal of Gambling Studies*, Summer 1992, Volume 8, Issue 2, pp. 151-166.

Brown, Leah Marie. "Tuesday's Treasure: Marie Antoinette's Books." *Titillating Tidbits: The Life and Times of Marie-Antoinette*, January 10, 2012.

Charles-Roux, J.M. "Marie-Antoinette: The Martyred Queen of Christian Europe." *Royal Stuart Review*, Number 3, 1987 and Number 4, 1988.

Creighton, Mandell et al. "Short Notices." *The English Historical Review*, Vol. XXIII. London: Longmans, Green, and Company, 1908.

Croker, John Wilson. "An Answer to O'Meara's Napoleon in Exile," *The Quarterly Review*, Vol. 28. New York: T. & J. Swords, 1823.

Dégert, Antoine. "Gallicanism." *The Catholic Encyclopedia*. Vol. 6. New York: Robert Appleton Company, 1909.

Delors, Catherine. "Lapérouse, explorer extraordinaire, at the Musée de la Marine." *Versailles and More*. May 20, 2008.

—"Marie-Antoinette's best likeness." *Versailles and More*. July 28, 2008.

—"'La Petite Reine' is not Marie-Antoinette." *Versailles and More*. October 5, 2008.

—"Madame Elisabeth, Duchess of Parma, daughter of Louis XV." *Versailles and More*, November 13, 2008.

—"Marie-Antoinette at Saint-Denis." *Versailles and More*, February 2, 2009.

—"Madame Sophie, daughter of Louis XV." *Versailles and More*, February 4, 2009.

—"18th century court costume and Marie-Antoinette." *Versailles and More*, September 8, 2009.

—"La Fête des Rois, Feast of the Kings." *Versailles and More*, January 6, 2011.

—"Marie-Antoinette naked?" *Versailles and More*, November 8, 2012.

Doyle, William. "The Execution of Louis XVI and the End of the French Monarchy." *History Today*, Issue 36, March 2000.

Ederer, Rupert J. "The false goddess: Liberty." *Fidelity*. Vol. 8, Number 8, July, 1989.

Faulkner, Liam. "Johann Joseph Gassner – Exorcist Healer." *History in an Hour*, March 11, 2013.

Gibson, Anna. "Letters: Maria Theresa to Marie Antoinette, 21 April 1770." *Treasure for Your Pleasure*, March 23, 2010.

—"'Don't They Ever Get Tired of These Ridiculous Stories?' A Critical Look at Recent Claims about Marie Antoinette and Axel Fersen (Part 2)" *Treasure for Your Pleasure*, January 16, 2016.

Gazette de France, no. 49 (19 June 1775), 221.

Goyau, Georges. "Hugh Capet." *The Catholic Encyclopedia*. Vol. 7. New York: Robert Appleton Company, 1910.

—"Marie Antoinette." *The Catholic Encyclopedia*. Vol. 9. New York: Robert Appleton Company, 1910.

Grubin, David. "Grand Park." *Marie-Antoinette and the French Revolution*. David Grubin Productions, September 13, 2006.

Hamilton, Ross, "Playing with Chance: Rousseau's Illumination." *The Romanic Review*, May 2004, Vol. 95, No. 3.

Hosford, Desmond. "The Queen's Hair: Marie-Antoinette, Politics and DNA." *Eighteenth-Century Studies*, Vol. 38, no.1, 2004.

Kanehl, Steven R. "Jehanne la Pucelle: A mini-biography, February 1431." *The Joan of Arc Center*.

Kuehnelt, Leddihn, Erik von. "Operation Parricide: Sade, Robespierre, and the French Revolution." *Fidelity*, Vol. 8, Number 8, July 1989.

Kurth, Godefroid. "Clovis." *The Catholic Encyclopedia.* Vol. 4. New York: Robert Appleton Company, 1908.

"Legacy Library: Marie Antoinette." *The Library Thing.* http://www.librarything.com/profile/MarieAntoinette

Leo XIII. "*Nobilissima Gallorum Gens:* On the Religious Question in France His Holiness Pope Leo XIII, February 8, 1884." *New Advent*, 2007.

Löffler, Klemens. "Maria Theresa." *The Catholic Encyclopedia*. Vol. 9. New York: Robert Appleton Company, 1910.

"Louise-Marie-Thérèse-Bathilde d'Orléans, duchesse de Bourbon (1750-1822)." *Louis-Claude de Saint-Martin: Amis et Disciples*. http://www.philosophe-inconnu.com/Amis_disciples/duchesse_bourbon1.htm

Marie-Antoinette, Reine de France. "Portrait charmant, portrait de mon amie." *The LiederNet Archive*. http://www.lieder.net/lieder/get_text.html?TextId=58693

Maury, Lucien. *Revue littéraire et critique - Revue Bleue*, Numéro 17, 5ème série, Tome VII, Paris: Bureaux de la Revue Bleue, 1907, pp. 536-538.

Patarin, Jacques and Nachef, Valérie. "I shall love you up to the death" (Marie-Antoinette to Axel von Fersen), 2009. http://eprint.iacr.org/2009/166.pdf

Peppiatt, Michael. "The Hamlet of Marie Antoinette." *Architectural Digest*, October, 1998.

Richards, J.H. "Favorites of Louis XVIII." *The Nation*, Vol.69. New York: The Evening Post Publishing Company, 1899.

Rudy, Lisa Jo. "What Are the Diagnostic Criteria for Asperger Syndrome?" *About.com*, March 19, 2015.

Schmidt, Louise Boisen. "The King's Birdcage." *This Is Versailles,* May 7, 2013.

The American Catholic Quarterly Review, Vol. 32, Jan-Oct, Philadelphia, 1907.

The Court and Lady's Magazine, Vol. IV. "Memoir of Isabella, Queen of Spain, Consort of Philip the Fourth."

London: Dobbs and Company, 1839.
Thrale, Hester Lynch. "Thrales meet King Louis XVI and Queen Marie Antoinette." *Thrale.com*, 20 September 2009.
Tomokiyo, S. "Ciphers of Marie-Antoinette and Axel von Fersen (1791-1792)."
http://cryptiana.web.fc2.com/code/fersen.htm
Tribe, Shawn. "Bonniwell: The Solemn Mass in the Gallican Rite of the 7th-8th Century." *The New Liturgical Movement,* October 10, 2009.
Vidal, Elena Maria. 23. Vidal, Elena Maria. "Madame de Polignac and the Politics of Calumny." *Tea at Trianon.* December 6, 2007.
—"The Happy Day of France." *Tea at Trianon,* November 10, 2011.
—"St. John the Baptist and the Durieux Sisters." *Tea at Trianon*, January 7, 2016.
—"Drawing of a Tavern in Austria." *Tea at Trianon*, January 8, 2016.
—"Marie-Josèphe de Saxe." *Tea at Trianon*, January 14, 2016.
Webster, Paul. "Marriage myths." *The Guardian.* August 2, 2002.
Wygant, Amy. "Fire, Sacrifice, Iphigénie." *French Studies: A Quarterly Review*, 60.3. 2006, pp. 305-319.

Books

Abert, Hermann. *W.A. Mozart*, translated by Stewart Spencer. New Haven: Yale University Press, 2007.
Anderson, James Maxwell. *Daily Life During the French Revolution*. Westport, Connecticut: Greenwood Press, 2007
Anthony, Katherine. *Marie Antoinette*. New York: Alfred A. Knopf, 1933.
Barbey, Frédéric. *A Friend of Marie-Antoinette (Lady*

Atkyns) translated by V. Sardou. London: Chapman & Hall, Limited, 1906.

Beckman, Jonathan. *How to Ruin a Queen: Marie Antoinette and the Diamond Necklace Affair.* Philadelphia: De Capo Press, 2014.

Belloc, Hilaire. *Marie Antoinette.* New York: Doubleday. Page, and Company, 1909.

Bernard, J. F. *Talleyrand.* New York: G. P. Putnam's Sons, 1973.

Bernier, Olivier, editor. *Secrets of Marie Antoinette: A Collection of Letters.* New York: Fromm International, 1986.

Bertier de Sauvigny, Guillaume de. *The Bourbon Restoration,* trans. by Lynn M. Case. Philadelphia: The University of Philadelphia Press, 1966.

Bertière, Simone. *Marie-Antoinette l'insoumise.* Paris: Editions de Fallois, 2002.

Blanc, Louis. *Histoire de la révolution française, Volume 2.* Paris: Chez Langlois et Leclercq, 1847.

Bicknell, Anna L. *The Story of Marie-Antoinette.* New York: The Century Company, 1897.

Bireley, Robert. *Ferdinand II, Counter-Reformation Emperor, 1578-1637.* New York: Cambridge University Press, 2014.

Bluche, Françoise. *La Vie quotidienne au temps de Louis XVI.* Paris: Hachette, 1980.

Boyer, Marie-France. *The Private Realm of Marie-Antoinette.* New York: Thames and Hudson, 1995.

Brière, Léon de la. *Madame Louise de France,* translated by Meta and Mary Brown. London: Kegan, Paul,Trench, Trubner and Company, 1907.

Buloz, François and Buloz, Charles et al, editors. *Revue des deux mondes,* Volume 59. Paris: Au bureau de la Revue des deux mondes, 1865.

Bush, William. *To Quell the Terror.* Washington, DC: ICS Publications, 1999.

Cadbury, Deborah. *The Lost King of France*. New York: St. Martin's Griffin, 2002.
Carlyle, Thomas. *The French Revolution, Volume One*. London: J.M. Dent and Sons, 1837.
Castelot, André. *Queen of France*, trans. by Denise Folliot. New York: Harper and Brothers, 1957.
Chalon, Jean. *Chère Marie-Antoinette*. Paris: Perrin, 1997.
Charles-Roux, Jean. *Louis XVII: La Mère et l'Enfant martyrs*. Paris: Collection Cerf Histoire, 2007..
Clegg, Melanie. *Marie-Antoinette: An Intimate History*. Amazon Digital Services LLC: Madame Guillotine, 2015.
Clouard, Henri and Leggewie, Robert. *Anthologie de la litteréature française, Tome 1*. New York: Oxford University Press, 1975.
Crankshaw, Edward. *Maria Theresa*. New York: Viking Press, 1969.
Croker, John Wilson. *Essays on the Early Period of the French Revolution.* London: John Murray, 1857.
Cronin, Vincent. *Louis and Antoinette*. London: Harvill Press, 1996.
Crowdy, Terry. *The Enemy Within: A History of Spies, Spymasters and Espionage*. Oxford: Osprey Publishing, 2008.
Daudet, Ernest. *Madame Royale, Daughter of Louis XVI and Marie Antoinette: Her Youth and Marriage*, translated by Mrs. Rodolph Stawell. New York: George H. Doran, 1913.
Dawson, William Francis. *Christmas: Its Origin and Associations.* London: Elliot Stock, 1902.
Delorme, Philippe. *Marie-Antoinette: Épouse de Louis XVI, mère de Louis XVII*. Paris: Pygmalion/Gérard Watelet, 1999.
Delpierre, Madeleine. *Dress in France in the Eighteenth Century.* New Haven: Yale University Press, 1997.

Desmond, Alice Curtis. *Marie Antoinette's Daughter*. New York: Dodd, Mead, and Company, 1967.

Dickinson, Joan Y. *The Book of Diamonds: Their History and Romance from Ancient India to Modern Times*. Mineola, New York: Dover Publications, 2001.

Duindam, Jeroen. *Vienna and Versailles: The Courts of Europe's Dynastic Rivals, 1550-1780*. Cambridge: Cambridge University Press, 2003.

Guéranger, Dom Proper, OSB. *The Liturgical Year, Volumes I-XV*, translated by Dom Laurence Shepherd, OSB. Powers Lake, North Dakota: Marian House, 1983

Faÿ, Bernard. *Louis XVI ou la fin d'un monde*. Paris: La Table Ronde, 1981.

Foreman, Amanda. *Georgiana, Duchess of Devonshire*. New York: The Modern Library, 1998.

Fraser, Antonia. *Marie-Antoinette: The Journey*. New York: Anchor Books, 2002.

Gaulot, Paul. *A Friend of the Queen*, trans. by Mrs. Cashel Hoey. New York: D. Appleton and Co., 1893.

Goodman, Dena, ed. *Marie-Antoinette: Writings on the Body of a Queen*. New York: Routledge, 2003.

Grant, Mrs. Colquhoun. *A Mother of Czars: A Sketch of the Life of Marie Feodorowna, Wife of Paul I , Mother of Alexander I and Nicholas I*. London: John Murray, 1903.

Greenlaw, Robert W., editor. *The Social Origins of the French Revolution*. Lexington, MA.: D.C. Heath and Company, 1975.

Guérin, E.-L. *La Princesse Lamballe et Madame de Polignac, chroniques des Tuileries, Volume I*. Paris: Recoules, 1845.

Hérissay, Jacques. *Les Aumôniers de la Guillotine*. Paris: Librairie Arthème Fayard, 1935.

Herold, J. Christopher. *Mistress to an Age: A life of Madame de Staël*. New York: Charter Books, 1962.

Hobsbawm, E.J. *The Age of Revolution, 1789-1848*.

New York: New American Library, 1962.
Holland, Rupert Sargent. *The Story of Marie Antoinette.* New York: A.J. Cornell Publications, 1910.
Hibbert, Christopher. *Versailles.* New York: Newsweek, 1972.
Hilton, Lisa. *Athénais: The Life of Louis XIV's Mistress, the Real Queen of France.* New York: Back Bay Books, 2004.
Huisman, Philippe and Jallut, Marguerite. *Marie Antoinette.* New York: The Viking Press, 1971.
Hunt, Lynn. *Politics, Culture, and Class in the French Revolution.* Berkeley: University of California Press, 1984.
Hyde, Melissa Lee and Milam, Jennifer Dawn. *Women, Art and the Politics of Identity in Eighteenth-century Europe.* Burlington, Vermont: Ashgate, 2003
Jahn, Otto. *Life of Mozart, Volume 1*, translated by Pauline Townsend. London: Novello, Ewer & Company, 1882.
Jardin, André and Tudesq, André-Jean. *Restoration and Reaction, 1815-1848,* translated by Elbog Forster. Cambridge, Cambridge University Press, 1983.
Johnson, Alison. *Louis XVI and the French Revolution.* London: McFarland and Company, 2013.
Jordan, David. *The King's Trial.* Los Angeles: University of California Press, 1979.
Knapton, Ernest John. *The Empress Josephine.* Cambridge, MA.: Howard University Press, 1982.
Kohler, Sheila. *Bluebird, or the Invention of Happiness.* New York: Berkley Books, 2008.
Latour, Thérèse Louise. *Princesses, Ladies and Republicaines of the Terror.* New York: Alfred A. Knopf, 1930.
La Vergne, Yvonne de. *Madame Elisabeth of France.* St Louis: D. Herder Book Company, 1947.
Lenôtre, George. *The Flight of Marie-Antoinette,*

translated by Mrs. Rodolph Stawell. Philadelphia: J.B. Lippincott Company, 1906.

—*The Last Days of Marie Antoinette*, translated by Mrs. Rodolph Stawell. Philadelphia: J.B. Lippincott Company, 1907.

—*The Dauphin or the Riddle of the Temple*. New York: Doubleday, Page, 1921.

Lever, Evelyn and Temerson, Catherine. *Madame de Pompadour: A Life*. New York: St. Martin's Griffin, 2003.

Lever, Evelyn, *Marie-Antoinette: The Last Queen of France*. New York: Macmillan, 2001.

Loomis, Stanley. *The Fatal Friendship: Marie Antoinette, Count Fersen and the Flight to Varennes*. New York: Doubleday, 1972.

Macfall, Haldane. *Vigée Le Brun*. New York: Frederick A. Stokes, 1922.

Macleod, Margaret Anne. *There were Three of Us in the Relationship: The Secret Letters of Marie Antoinette, Vol I*. Irvine, Scotland: Isaac MacDonald, 2008.

Mahan, Alexander J. *Maria Theresa of Austria*. London: Read Books Ltd, 2013.

Manceron, Claude. *Their Gracious Pleasure, 1782-1785*, trans. by Nancy Amphoux. New York: Alfred A. Knopf, 1980.

Mason, Laura and Rizzo, Tracey, editors. *The French Revolution: A Document Collection*. New York: Houghton Mifflin, 1999, pp. 152-155.

Matheson, Lister M. *Icons of the Middle Ages: Rulers, Writers, Rebels, and Saints, Volume 2*. Oxford: Greenwood, 2011.

Maurois, André. *Chateaubriand: Poet, Statesman, Lover*, trans. by Vera Fraser. New York: Harper and Brothers, 1930.

McCloy, Shelby T. *The Negro in France*. Lexington, Kentucky: University of Kentucky Press, 1961.

McCullough, David. *John Adams*. New York: Simon and Schuster, 2002.

Miltoun, Francis. *Royal Palaces and Parks of France*. Boston: L. C. Page and Company, 1910

Minnergerode, Meade. *The Son of Marie Antoinette*. New York: Farrar and Rinehart, 1934

Mitford, Nancy. *Madame de Pompadour*. London: Hamish Hamilton, 1954.

— *The Sun King*. New York: New York Review Books 1967.

Morris, M. C. O'Connor. *The Prisoners of the Temple; Or Discrowned and Crowned*. London: Burns and Oates, 1874.

Mossiker, Frances. *The Queen's Necklace*. London: Phoenix, 1961.

Nagel, Susan. *Marie-Thérèse: Child of Terror*. New York: Bloomsbury USA, 2008.

Nezelhof, Pierre. *La Vie Joyeuse et Tragique de Marie-Antoinette*. Paris: Frédérique Patat, 1933.

Nolhac, Pierre de. *Marie Antoinette*. London: Arthur L. Humphreys, 1905.

Pernoud, Georges and Flaissier, Sabine, *The French Revolution*, translated by Richard Graves. New York: Capricorn Books, 1970.

Petitfils, Jean-Christian. *Louis XVI*. Paris: Perrin, 2005

Pick, Robert. *Empress Maria Theresa: The Earlier Years, 1717-1757*. New York: Harper and Row, 1966.

Pimodan, Claude Emmanuel Henri Marie, comte de. Les *Fiançailles de Madame Royale*. Paris: Plon-Nourrit, 1912.

Pinkney, David H. *The French Revolution of 1830*. Princeton: Princeton University Press, 1972.

Price, Munro. *The Road from Versailles: Louis XVI, Marie Antoinette, and the Fall of the French Monarchy*. New York: St. Martin's Press, 2002.

Raspail, Jean. *Sire*. Paris: Editions Fallois, 1991.

Reynolds-Ball, E. A. *Paris, Volume II*. Boston: Dana Estes and Company, 1900.

Rocheterie, Maxime de la. *The Life of Marie Antoinette, Volume 1 and 2*, translated by Cora Hamilton Bell. New York: Dodd, Mead and Company, 1906.

Romer, Isabella Frances. *Filia dolorosa, memoirs of Marie Thérèse Charlotte, duchess of Angoulême, the Last of the Dauphines, Vol.1*. London: Richard Bentley, 1852.

Saint-Amand, Baron Imbert de. Les femmes de Versailles: *Les beaux jours de Marie-Antoinette*. Paris: E. Dentu,1882.

—*Marie-Antoinette and the Downfall of Royalty*, translated by Elizabeth Gilbert Martin. New York: Charles Scribner's Sons, 1891.

—*Marie Antoinette at the Tuileries, 1789-1791*, translated by Elizabeth Gilbert Martin. New York: C. Scribner's sons, 1893

—*The Youth of the Duchess of Angoulême*. New York: Scribner's, 1901.

—*The Duchess of Angoulême and the Two Restorations*. New York: Scribner's, 1901.

—*Marie Antoinette and the End of the Old Régime*, translated by Thomas Sergeant Perry. New York: Charles Scribner's Sons, 1914.

Sainte-Beuve, Charles Augustin. *Portraits of the eighteenth century: historic and literary, Volumes 1-2*, translated by Katharine Wormley. G.P. Putnam's Sons, 1905.

Schama, Simon. *Citizens: A Chronicle of the French Revolution.* New York: Vintage Books, 1989.

Schoenfeld, Hermann. *Women of the Teutonic Nations.* Philadelphia: Rittenhouse Press, 1908.

Scurr, Ruth. *Fatal Purity: Robespierre and the French Revolution*. New York: Metropolitan Books, 2007

Ségur, Louis-Gaston de. *Le Sacré Coeur de Jésus: mois*

du Sacré Coeur. Paris: Haton:1873.

Seward, Desmond. *Marie Antoinette*. New York: St Martin's Press, 1981.

Shriner, Charles Anthony. *Wit, Wisdom and Foibles of the Great: Together with Numerous Anecdotes*. New York: Funk and Wagnalls, 1920.

Smythe, Lillian C. *The Guardian of Marie Antoinette: Letters from the Comte de Mercy-Argenteau, Austrian Ambassador to the Court of Versailles, to Marie Thérêse, Empress of Austria, 1770-1780, 2 Volumes*. London: Hutchinson and Company, 1902.

Spawforth, Tony. *Versailles: A Biography of a Palace*. New York: St. Martin's Press, 2008.

Stevens, A. de Grasse. *The Lost Dauphin*. London: George Allen, 1887.

Stryienski, Casimir. *The Daughters of Louis XV*, translated by Cranstoun Metcalfe. New York: Brentano's, 1912.

Thomas, Chantal. *The Exchange of Princesses*. Translated by John Cullen. New York: Other Press, 2014.

—*The Wicked Queen: The Origins of the Myth of Marie-Antoinette*, translated by Julie Rose. New York: Zone Books, 2001.

Toqueville, Alexis de. *The Old Regime and the French Revolution*. New York: Doubleday, 1955.

Turquan, Joseph. *The King Who Never Reigned*. London: E. Nash, 1980.

—*Madame Royale: The Last Dauphine*. New York: Brentano's, 1910.

Toussaint-Samat, Maguelonne. *A History of Food*, translated by Anthea Bell. Oxford: John Wiley & Sons, 2009.

Tytler, Sarah. *Marie Antoinette: The Woman and the Queen*. London: Marcus Ward, 1883.

Van der Kemp, Gerald and Meyer, Daniel. *Versailles*.

Paris: Editions d'Art lys, 1981.

Vovk, Justin C. *In Destiny's Hands: Five Tragic Rulers, Children of Maria Theresa.* Raleigh, North Carolina: Lulu.com, 2009.

Ward, Charles A. *Oracles of Nostradamus.* New York: C. Scribner, 1891. Kindle edition by Evinity Publishing Company, 2009.

Weber, Caroline. *Queen of Fashion: What Marie Antoinette Wore to the French Revolution.* New York: Henry Holt and Company, 2006.

Webster, Nesta H. *Louis XVI and Marie Antoinette before the Revolution.* London: Constable, 1937.

—*Louis XVI and Marie Antoinette during the Revolution.* New York: Gordon Press, 1976.

Whaley, Joachim. *Germany and the Holy Roman Empire: Volume II: The Peace of Westphalia to the Dissolution of the Reich, 1648-1806.* Oxford: Oxford University Press, 2012.

Wharton, Grace and Philip. *The Queens of Society.* New York: Harper and Brothers, 1861.

Wight, William W. *Louis XVII: A Bibliography.* Boston: T. R. Marvin and Sons Printers, 1915.

Woodgate, M.V. *The Abbé Edgeworth.* New York: Longmans, 1946.

Wormeley, Katherine Prescott. *The Ruin of a Princess.* New York: The Lamb Publishing Company, 1912.

Yonge, Charles Duke. *The Life of Marie Antoinette, Queen of France.* New York: Harper and Brothers, 1876.

Younghusband, Helen A. *Marie-Antoinette, Her Early Youth (1770-1774).* New York: Macmillan, 1912.

INDEX

A
Adams, John, 149-150
Adélaïde of France, 45, 71-74, 84, 91-92, 109, 114, 116, 250, 332-334, 380, 471
Albert of Saxony, Duke of Teschen, 27
America, 128, 148-150, 312
Amilcar, Jean, 220
Anne-Henriette of France, 70-71
Antoinette (see Marie-Antoinette, Queen of France)
Armand (François Michel Gagné), 218-219
Atkyns, Charlotte, 458-459
Artois, Charles-Philippe, Comte d' (Charles X), 51, 60, 86, 115, 124, 125, 155, 158, 162, 173, 209-210, 222, 224, 259-265, 267, 273, 276-279, 284, 286, 287, 302, 334-335, 361, 363, 395, 471, 472, 475, 484
Auguié, Adélaïde, 270-271

B
Balbi, Comtesse de, 336-338
Barnave, 144, 350, 360, 403
Barry, Madame du, 28, 44, 45, 51, 64, 73, 91-96, 113, 116, 187-188, 199, 234, 248, 256, 291, 341, 445
Bastille Day, 86, 136, 364
Bertin, Rose, 187, 190, 222
Besenval, Baron de, 284, 286-288, 292
Bonaparte, Napoleon, 128, 196, 268, 271, 272, 279, 280,

292, 301, 338, 459, 470-471
Boulogne, Joseph (Chevalier de Saint-Georges), 183
Bourbon, Duc de, 124, 278
Bourbon, Duchesse de, 277-278, 358
Bourbons, 8, 23, 59-61, 79, 180, 268, 287, 474
Bourgogne, Louis-Joseph, Duc de, 67, 79-80, 351
Brienne, Lomenie de, Archbishop of Toulouse, 353-354
Brionne, Madame de, 54-56

C

Calonne, 353
Campan, Madame, 4, 8, 13, 52-52, 75, 79, 126, 134, 142, 145, 158, 170-171, 212, 237, 243, 267-271, 286-287, 289, 299, 301, 306-307, 313, 319, 340, 343-345, 363, 373, 477
Capuchin crypt, 22, 26, 33
Charles Joseph, Archduke, 28
Charles VI, 23, 68
Chartres, Duc de (see Égalité, Philippe)
Chimay, Princesse de, 224, 233, 238-239
Choiseul, Duc de, 45, 54-55, 60, 140, 285, 288
Clothilde of France, Queen of Sardinia, 51, 60, 86-87, 120, 125, 471, 483
Coigny, Duc de, 246, 479, 284, 292
Condé, Prince de, 124, 263, 278
Conciergerie, 167, 434-437, 453, 458-459

D

Dauphin Louis-Auguste (see Louis XVI)
Dauphin Louis-Ferdinand, 66-69, 72, 103
Dauphin Louis-Joseph, 146, 170, 224-226, 254, 297, 299, 316, 327, 351, 362, 363, 478
Dauphin Louis-Charles, 69, 170, 173, 182, 184, 201, 219, 225-228, 231, 266-267, 309, 364-370, 373-377, 391, 407-409, 411-414, 429-434, 436, 442, 445, 457-466, 467-469

Diamond Necklace, 42, 90, 139, 158, 216, 252, 254, 268, 272, 297, 299, 340-348
Dillon, Thérèse-Lucy, 233, 241, 246, 294
Dumont, 173-174

E

Edgeworth, Abbé, 420-426
Égalité, Philippe (Chartres/Orléans), 124, 158, 278, 289, 291, 302, 335, 338-339, 350, 352-354, 356, 361, 365, 395, 420, 437
Élisabeth of France, 51, 60, 88-89, 120, 125, 144, 173, 182, 184, 200, 214, 222, 224, 237, 244-246, 251, 266, 273-274, 308, 309, 311, 318, 329-332, 333, 350, 363, 365, 367, 387, 389-391, 399, 405, 407-409, 411, 437, 438, 442, 447-450, 464-467, 472-473, 483-484
Élisabeth of France, Duchess of Parma, 25, 69-71
Ernestine (Marie-Philippine Lambriquet), 219-220
Estates-General, 254, 349, 360-363
Esterhazy, Count Valentin, 284-286, 304-305

F

Ferdinand, Archduke, 30-31
Ferdinand II, 15
Ferdinand III, 14
Fersen, Count Axel von 4-8, 90, 97, 143, 192, 201, 210, 276, 284, 291-310, 350, 386, 390, 392-405
Fitz-James, Duchesse de, 233, 239-240
Francis Maximilian, Archduke, 33-34
Francis II, 29, 34, 470-471
Francis Stephen of Lorraine, Holy Roman Emperor, 15, 21-24, 103, 199
Franklin, Benjamin, 149
Freemasonry, 165, 242, 244, 250, 339, 356-358
Freud, Sigmund, 104, 297

G

Gluck, 18, 178-180
Gontaut, Madame de, 258-261, 264
Grand Trianon, 312
Great Britain, 128, 150, 254, 280, 312
Guéménée, Princesse de, 222, 224, 244-247, 251, 273-274, 289, 329
Guînes, Duc de, 280
Gustavus III, 7, 293, 295-296, 304, 319-321, 391-392

H
Habsburgs, 11, 33, 123, 172, 280
Hanet-Cléry, 411
Henri IV, 23, 60, 95, 101, 180
Hesse and by Rhine, Grand Duchess (of), 272
Hüe, 411

I
Isabella of Parma, 25-26, 70, 252

J
Jarjayes, 144
Jeanne d'Arc (see Saint Joan of Arc)
Jefferson, Thomas, 149
Joseph I, 68
Joseph II, 14, 25-28, 95, 97, 148, 160, 273, 280, 294, 317

K
Kucharski, 173

L
Labille-Guiard, Adélaïde, 167-168
Lafayette, 148, 150
Lamballe, Princesse de, 158, 217, 224, 236, 242-245, 254, 271, 283, 357, 362, 398, 410, 412-413
La Pérouse, 151-152

Lauzun, Duc de, 158, 288-289
Leopold I, 11
Leopold II, 29-30, 34, 97, 358, 398, 403
Ligne, Prince de, 280-285, 292
Lisbon earthquake, 13
Louise of France (Thérèse de Saint-Augustin of Saint Denis), 65, 75-79, 198, 273-274
Louis XIII, 47, 60, 216
Louis XIV, 47-48, 61-62, 86, 101, 146, 208, 214-216, 243, 327-329
Louis XV, 14-15, 28, 29, 34, 36, 44, 46-48, 55, 59-60, 61-65, 69-78, 84, 86, 91-94, 96, 113-114, 116-117, 141, 187, 208, 215, 227, 248, 250, 328, 332, 341
Louis XVI
almsgiving, 54, 202-204, 207, 349, 352
children, 170, 220-229, 279, 351, 363, 411, 416
coronation 119-125
death, 204-205, 420-426, 484
education, 72, 84, 126-127
faith, 65, 85, 99, 114, 116, 120, 129-132, 208, 214-215, 300, 358, 361, 363, 380-386, 412, 414-418, 484-485
health, 67, 76, 80, 107-108, 115, 128, 132, 300, 327, 349-351, 390-391
hobbies, 81-83
hunting, 82, 132-135, 136
marriage, 7, 36, 38, 43, 46, 57-58, 73, 83, 97-109, 116, 146, 153, 164, 173, 174, 220-222, 269, 294, 299-300, 323-324, 350, 416, 417, 478-479
reforms, 116-119, 147-148, 192, 349
trial, 419-420
Louis XVII (see Dauphin Louis-Charles)

M
Mackau, Madame de, 88-89, 222, 254, 273, 330, 381, 470
Madame Royale (Marie-Thérèse-Charlotte of France) 6,

137-138, 170, 173, 180, 184, 195, 200, 202, 214, 220-223, 228, 246, 258, 266-267, 268-271, 279, 301, 316, 327, 339, 365, 367-368, 380, 388, 407-409, 411-412, 420, 428-434, 456-466, 468-476, 477-478, 484
Maison Philanthropique, 6
Malesherbes, 353, 426
Maria Carolina, Queen of Naples, 30-32, 109, 221, 236, 252, 398, 470
Maria Christina (Mimi), Archduchess, 25-28, 357
Maria Elisabeth, Archduchess, 28, 471
Maria Johanna, Archduchess, 30
Maria Josepha, Archduchess, 30, 37
Maria Josepha of Bavaria, 26, 30
Mariana Victoria, Queen of Portugal, 13-14, 62
Maria Theresa, Holy Roman Empress, 12-34, 38-41, 68, 90-91, 102-103, 105-109, 116, 123, 127, 138, 140, 145, 157, 167, 193, 199, 209-211, 213, 220-221, 250, 251, 277, 280, 284, 285, 294, 295, 341, 398
Maria Amalia, Archduchess, 28-29, 398
Maria Anna, Archduchess, 14, 24-25, 41
Marie-Adélaïde de Savoy, 61
Marie-Antoinette, Queen of France
 almsgiving 5-6, 19, 54, 110-111, 112, 116, 134-135, 200, 202-204, 207, 223, 481-482
 arts, 76, 119, 163-175, 269, 322-323, 325, 478-479, 482
 baptism, 13-14
 betrothal, 36
 birth, 12, 13
 books, 175-176
 clothes and hair, 51, 58, 90, 95, 134, 171-172, 187-195, 211, 256, 451-452
 death, 169, 196, 205, 310, 453-455, 484
 education, 18-19
 etiquette, 17, 33, 136, 146
 faith, 18, 20, 99, 114, 116, 123, 131, 159-160, 195,

197-205, 215, 297, 310, 321, 361, 363, 412, 437, 449, 453-454, 484
  gambling, 12-13, 19, 104, 155-158, 217, 334-335
  health, 18, 214, 221, 298, 299-300, 429, 451
  last letter, 447-450
  marriage, 7-8, 32-33, 46, 83, 95, 97-109, 116, 127, 136, 153, 164, 173, 174, 221-222, 269, 293-294, 299-300, 323-324, 350, 417, 478-479
  motherhood, 105, 170, 190, 211, 218-229, 282, 296, 297, 299, 300, 310, 362-363, 373-378, 411, 416, 443, 445, 448-450
  myths of affairs, 6-8, 81, 90, 96, 154, 284, 291-310, 294, 299, 310, 399-405
  opera, 119, 177-185, 297, 317
  prophecies, 19-20
  remise, 41-42
  reputation, 4-6, 284, 291-292, 294-295, 299-300, 484
  trial, 427, 438-447
  wedding, 51-55, 58
Marie-Josèphe de Saxe, 51, 66-69, 227, 287
Marie Leszczyńska, Queen of France, 14, 34, 46, 62, 64-65, 87, 145, 189, 238, 240, 283, 312
Martyrs of Compiègne, 46, 199, 468
Maurepas, Comte de, 115-116, 250-251
Mecklenburg-Strelitz, Duchess (of), 272
Mercy-Argenteau, Comte de, 7-8, 45, 54, 98, 100-101, 108, 111, 116, 124, 157, 159-160, 190, 210, 213, 247, 248, 250, 251, 277-278, 280, 289, 294-296, 298, 392, 398
Mestastio, 12
Mirabeau, 144, 350, 365, 390
Morris, Gouverneur, 82-83
Motte, Madame de la, 254, 288, 342, 344-348, 445
Mozart, Wolfgang Amadeus, 34, 280

N

Necker, 353, 362, 365, 453
Noailles, Vicomtesse de, 56-57, 154, 237
Nords, 314-319, 472

O

Oberkirch, Baroness de, 42, 312, 314, 316
Orléans, Philippe Duc d' (see Égalité, Philippe)
Ossun, Comtesse d', 192, 224, 256-257

P

Petit Trianon, 6, 97, 109, 116, 166, 171, 193, 200, 203, 222, 226, 250, 252, 270, 273, 277, 279-282, 285, 297, 298, 311-326, 330, 333, 343, 400, 444-445
Polastron, Louise, Vicomtesse de, 258-265, 335
Polignac, Gabrielle, Duchesse de, 103, 109, 219, 223, 232-234, 236, 240, 242, 244, 248-256, 258-263, 266, 279, 283, 296, 309, 341, 358, 376, 400, 402
Pompadour, Jeanne Antoinette, Marquise de, 6, 34, 44-45, 59, 70-72, 91, 116, 166, 188, 234, 250, 291, 332
Provence, Louis-Stanislas-Xavier, Comte de (Louis XVIII), 51, 80, 83, 85-86, 115, 124-125, 126, 209-210, 221, 277-279, 302, 336-338, 356, 361, 392, 395, 453, 470, 472-473, 475, 479

R

Robespierre, 240, 440-441
Rohan, Prince-Cardinal Louis de, 42-43, 139, 158, 225, 340-348

S

Saint Cyr, 5, 74
Saint Joan of Arc, 14, 44-45, 46, 96, 110, 122-123, 429, 482-485
Saint Teresa of Avila, 15
Sophie of France, 71, 75-76, 113, 332
Sophie of France (infant), 170, 214, 227, 274, 297, 299,

327, 351
Swiss Guards, 124, 286, 288, 289

T
Tarente, Princesse de, 257-258
Temple, 6, 245, 267, 270, 308, 331-332, 408-409, 411-423, 429-434, 453, 458-459, 469-470
Thérèse of France, 71, 74, 77
Trianon (see Petit Trianon)
Toulan, 350, 459
Tour du Pin, Madame de la, 203, 241-242, 294
Tourzel, Madame de, 167, 184, 228, 265-267, 307, 308, 369, 373, 378, 381, 387, 470
Tuileries, 266-268, 270, 298, 306, 358, 369, 373-407, 473, 477
Turgot, Anne Robert de, 118-119, 353

V
Vallayer-Coster, Anne, 168-169
Varennes, 144, 294, 307, 308, 379, 388
Vauguyon, Duc de la, 46, 80, 84, 98, 127
Vendée, 429-430, 463-464, 469, 480
Ventadour, Madame de, 61-62
Vermond, Abbé, 18, 45, 101-102, 222, 289
Versailles, 6, 33-34, 47-50, 54, 99, 100, 113, 131, 142, 146, 151, 158, 165-166, 191, 198, 203, 211, 214-216, 225, 237, 241, 273, 282, 298, 327-328, 352, 361, 370
Victoire of France, 71, 73-75, 113, 212, 332-333, 380, 471
Vigée-Lebrun, Élisabeth, 167-172, 194, 269

W
Weber, Joseph, 16-17
Wertmüller, 170-171

Z

Zoé (Jeanne Louise Victoire), 219-220

ABOUT THE AUTHOR

Elena Maria Vidal was born in Florence Oregon in 1962 but grew up in Frederick County, Maryland. She received her BA in Psychology from Hood College and her MA in Modern European History from SUNY Albany. Elena enjoys traveling and working with the elderly. She lives on Maryland's Eastern Shore with her family. Elena's *Tea at Trianon* blog (http://teaattrianon.blogspot.com) deals with social, religious and political issues as well as history. *Marie-Antoinette, Daughter of the Caesars* is her fifth book.

Marie-Antoinette, Daughter of the Caesars

Printed in Great Britain
by Amazon